D0648024

Quality Control Systems

Quality Control Systems

Procedures for Planning Quality Programs

James Robert Taylor
Professional Engineer

McGraw-Hill Book Company

New York   St. Louis   San Francisco   Auckland
Bogotá   Hamburg   London   Madrid   Mexico
Milan   Montreal   New Delhi   Panama
Paris   São Paulo   Singapore
Sydney   Tokyo   Toronto

Library of Congress Cataloging-in-Publication Data

Taylor, James Robert.
  Quality control systems.

  Includes index.
  1. Quality control—Planning. 2. Production
planning—Quality control. I. Title.
TS156.T38   1989   658.5′62   88-9164
ISBN 0-07-063160-3

1234567890   DOC/DOC   89321098

ISBN 0-07-063160-3

*The editors for this book were Betty Sun and Galen H. Fleck, the
designer was Naomi Auerbach, and the production supervisor was
Suzanne W. Babeuf. This book was set in Century Schoolbook. It
was composed by the McGraw-Hill Book Company Professional &
Reference Division composition unit.*

Printed and bound by R. R. Donnelley & Sons Company.

*For more information about other McGraw-Hill materials,
call 1-800-2-MCGRAW in the United States. In
other countries, call your nearest McGraw-Hill office.*

To
B.J., R.L., and D.M.
and to the memory of
J.M.

Contents

Section VI   Employee Participation Programs, Quality Costs, and Just-in-Time

Section VII   Glossary of Terms Used in Quality and Reliability

Preface

Quality systems are composed of the totality of organization, work, and materials by and from which products, services, and systems are brought into being. Within industrial and business activities it is necessary to arrange and structure quality systems into orderly programs. That is promoted, in modern industrial nations, by preparing documentation in three hierarchical categories. All three tiers of these documents are of equal importance, and each lower tier should be derived from and meet all pertinent requirements of the next higher tier. We call these three documentation tiers *standards* at the national level, *general procedures* at the top of the company level, and *detailed procedures* at the workface.

The first of the three tiers is established when a national or professional society committee prepares a standard for each area of activity. This standard then becomes the national document which is called up in contracts by customers. Companies doing business under a contract which stipulates such a national standard must prepare and implement general procedures that will ensure that their activities comply with the standard.

General procedures, the second tier, must ensure that all requirements in the national standard will be met. This book contains comprehensive sets of general procedures for quality systems in each of the mass manufacturing, services, and the project (construction) industries. The procedures for the mass manufacturing industry meet the requirements of American National Standard ANSI/ASQC Z-1.15-1979.

General procedures are broad statements in documented form of *what* should be done in a company or business activity. They correspond to the policy level of management instructions, and they remain relatively unchanged from product to product. Companies doing business with a variety of domestic and international customers must ensure that their general procedures are sufficiently broad to cover each of the several national standards which may be imposed by contract. The general procedures given here have been prepared to satisfy that requirement.

Detailed procedures describe *how* to do the required work; they are specifically concerned with the products, services, or systems produced or provided by each company or business. They must be different for each type of product or service, and they can be prepared for most effective use only by the planners within an individual company. Whereas general procedures remain unchanged for long periods and will satisfy the needs of many companies, detailed procedures are unique to each company and what it produces or provides. They must frequently be altered to cope with the continuing variety of products, services, and operating situations, as well as the evolution of each.

When a general procedure organizes work in sufficient depth and covers all the things that must be done, it will be found to meet the requirements of most customers. The general procedures of this book provide quality systems that have been proved to meet the requirements of government, industry, and private customers. They will meet the requirements of MIL-Q-9858, MIL-I-45208, ANSI/ASQC quality standards, British standard BS-5750, Australian standards AS-1821/2 & 3, Canadian standards Z-299.1,2,3,4, and 5, and other international standards such as the Japanese JUSE standards. They go further, however, and cover new advances in the quality field. Procedures included here prescribe quality system requirements for services quality systems, project quality systems, just-in-time quality and productivity programs, employee participation programs, product recall programs, and others.

The quality system procedures presented here can be implemented and applied by managers and staff in any company with minimal effort and at minimal cost. Professional quality staff will be required for their correct interpretation, implementation, and application. It is only necessary to characterize them with specific company requirements and then implement and apply them.

Since general quality system procedures define the total scope of activities organized, this book contains the procedures most needed to organize all work carried out by any company or business for the achievement of total quality control. The procedures extend all the way from organizing design and development work through the production and delivery or commissioning of the completed product, service, or project. They have the unique ability to satisfy the needs of all types of business activities and the companies that engage in them.

In addition to their direct application by a company, the procedures can be used for training programs in industry, and the book will be found useful as a reference for college courses in management and quality control. Communications are invited from users of the book on anything which might improve the procedures presented in it.

The author is indebted to many organizations and individuals for assistance in preparing this book. Thanks are due the Standards Association of Australia (SAA) and the Canadian Standards Association (CSA) for their cooperation. Particular thanks are due the American Society of Quality Control (ASQC) for its review of and comments on the manuscript and for its publications, from which the author has benefitted for many years as a senior member and certified quality engineer. Thanks are due the Standards Association of Australia (SAA), on whose committees the author has served and which have been a proving ground for ideas.

The author is also indebted to the Australian Telecommunications Commission (Telecom Australia), where national quality systems currently in use were prepared while the author represented that organization on the Australian National Standards Committees, and to the many companies, both national and multinational, that have sought the author's assistance in designing and establishing their quality systems. Individual thanks are due Mr. R. M. Burt, Fellow-ASQC, for many useful discussions and to Dr. H. Blanks, University of New South Wales, who reviewed the author's material on quality costs from which Section VI, Chapter 2 was developed.

James Robert Taylor

Introduction

1

Introduction to Industry

1 Introduction to Human Industry

Human industry has evolved through many phases, each time retaining certain aspects of each phase as it moved onward. Today examples of each of the various categories and kinds of industry in which people have engaged can be found. From anthropological and archaeological evidence we know that primitive peoples move first from a gathering stage to herding and other land uses such as farming and a limited form of mining. Then comes the development of cottage-type industries in which things are made by hand in people's residences. From these came the tentmaker, the boatwright, the wheelwright, the millwright, the farrier, and many other skilled and semiskilled tradesmen.

Skilled tradesmen formed close associations called guilds, the forerunners of modern-day unions. During the thirteenth century, charters for companies were first issued in England and groups of tradesmen were employed to work for the company owners. It was in one of these that we find our first example of quality control by inspection. One tradesman was selected to inspect and standardize the grade of workmanship produced by each of several stables of leather workers.

Modern industry has come a long way, and today the physical tools with which mankind first began experimenting some half million years in the past have replaced or enhanced virtually all of mankind's physical exertions. The abac, or sand tablet used by the Phoenicians some 3500 years ago, the abacus of the Chinese, then the mechanical calculating machine of Europe, and now the sophisticated computer replaced or enhanced the processes of the human mind. Today there is no area of human industry that has not been invaded by the tool creations of human minds.

We divide human industry into five general hierarchical levels:

Category	Examples
Primary industry	Agriculture and mining
Secondary industry	Manufacturing
Tertiary industry	Retail sales
Quaternary industry	Banking and finance
Quinquenary industry	Government and teaching

We find this manner of categorizing industry useful in only a general way. In order to derive a more usable understanding of human industries, let us examine what the purposes of each are and what their output is.

2   The Kinds of Industrial Output

As our mental processes have become more refined, we have come to deal with two kinds of things. One of them is physical; it can be handled and seen, and it is what we call tangible. We call this kind of output from industry by the names "materials," "products," or "goods." The second kind of thing is more ethereal; we say it is intangible. We call intangible things by the name "services." Services are things done by people for other people, sometimes with the use of materials, i.e., products.

Most people in industry readily recognize products and services as the output of industrial effort. There is a third kind of output, however, of which many of us are less aware, simply because we have not given it much thought. Yet it is a kind of output essential to society and one which must be appropriately categorized and defined if we are to apply quality control (QC) principles to all industry. This third kind of output is what we call project works and management systems. *Projects* are the project industry counterpart of products in the manufacturing industry; management systems are the project industry's counterpart of services. Increasingly we see management in large companies using the project form of organization with which to bring into being new temporary or permanent management systems. Some of these also carry out project works to their completion.

3   The Three Principal Divisions of Industry

From the above we categorize companies into one or the other of three principal divisions of industry. The first of these, and the best known, is the manufacturing industry, which produces products as its major form of output. The second is the services industry, which provides services as its major form of output. And the third is the project industry, which uses both tangible and intangible things to construct projects, as well as management systems.

Into what industrial category may we fit a particular company, and how do we determine it? Division into product-producing companies or service-providing companies is not always easy, because all companies use some mix of both. We can, at present, reach this decision only on the basis of some standard such as percentage of kinds of items produced. If, for example, a company provides most of its output in the form of intangible things, then it falls in the services industry. If it principally produces some form of products, then it is in the manufacturing industry. If it takes a range of products and uses a range of services, and from them brings into being a complex work, such as an airport, harbor, high-rise building, or retirement village, then it falls in the project industry group.

What we have discovered is that a quality control standard, or general procedure, prepared for one of these three divisions of industry will *not* work when applied to one of the other divisions. That is, it will not work to control the quality of output from an industry in one of the other categories. It is of little or no use to try to apply MIL-Q-9858 to the training of soldiers, the operating of a chain of beauty shops, or any other of a whole range of services-providing activities. Although there are some controls in the manufacturing industry standard that are applicable, other controls in the manufacturing standard are so different or totally lacking as not to provide an adequate degree of quality control in the services or project industry.

For example, where is the quality control in MIL-Q-9858 that provides for the quality of well-being of the customers while they are in the control of the services supplier? Many other of the services controls, such as control of action time and queueing time, are missing. Also, the control of customer-supplied materials in the manufacturing industry is quite different from that needed in a repair (services) business.

We find the same situation to hold for the project industry. Neither a manufacturing industry standard or procedure nor one prepared for use in the services industry is entirely suitable for project work. It is a matter not only of missing or unsuitable controls, but also of where the source of control must be in project work. In project work, such as nuclear power generating plant construction, the jurisdictional authority plays a much more dominant role than in most service companies, and jurisdictional authorities are almost never involved in the supplier-customer interaction found in the manufacturing industry.

We conclude, therefore, that there must be three quite different sets of standards and general procedures for use in the three divisions of industry. Yet there will be found similarities between the different standards and procedures. The fundamental theories of quality control and quality assurance are found to hold in all human industry. The preparation of standards and operating procedures becomes a matter of preparing and applying documents that, in scope and detail, cover appropriately each of the three areas of industry.

4   Quality Control and the Kinds of Work

We find that each phase of the sequence of activities involved in bringing into being a product, service, or project contributes in some degree to the finished product used by the customer. Increasingly we are realizing that products and services, as well as projects, can be designed for quality, as well as constructed or produced for quality. It is therefore desirable to have general procedures for the control of quality in each phase of these activities. Let us examine the usual sequence of activities to generate products and see what their similarities, from the viewpoint of quality control's general procedures, are.

4.1 Basic research. At present, basic research is not generally covered by quality control methods and procedures. There are, however, many things, such as calibration of measuring instruments, certification of reference materials, and statistical design of research experiments, which are standard quality control principles that can be and are used.

4.2 Design and development (applied research done by engineers). The 1980s saw a major effort in the United States and other industrialized nations to extend the principles of quality control into the design and development phases of manufacturing industry. This type of activity has a great similarity to the work done in a *job shop,* in which only a limited number of each product is to be produced and the design is subject to change at any stage.

Manufacturing of the one-off item is equivalent to the development phase in a design and development activity. Design and development has a counterpart in the project industry. In most project work, the designers remain active and may be called upon to modify the design at various stages of bringing the end works system into existence. A typical example is the construction of a new type of naval vessel in small quantities.

From the above we may expect to find, and do find, that the same quality control general procedure that applies to design work for manufactured products will apply to the design of a project. Similarly, the use of the QC general procedure for mass production will *not* work well in a job shop, where there is no opportunity for feedback and corrective action to work, and designers may alter the design during manufacture.

5 Vertical Communications in Industry

We find that management teams in all kinds of industry need to use appropriate organization and systems of communication to achieve effective interaction among their employees. Organizations differ greatly from one company to another and also from one kind of industry to another. As far as vertical communications needs are concerned, however, there is great similarity among companies. Here we can set forth the vertical sequence of hierarchical authority of such communications. It has been called the six P's of vertical communication.

Vertical Control Communications in Industry

Written	Philosophy (from CEO's office) Policy (general procedures) Procedure (detailed procedures)
Oral	Practice (what is usually done) Precedent (what has been done) Problem (needs solution now)

The horizontal line indicates the workface level above which all formalized communications are documented. If they are not documented, a company experiences wider variation in what is done from time to time, and this reflects in poor quality of output. Oral forms of communication are used within the work area only to overcome immediate problems urgently needing solutions. Otherwise, the solution of a problem should await a detailed procedure which is derived from the applicable general procedure (policy). In turn, the general procedure must derive from the CEO's philosophy of the direction in which the corporate ship must sail. Typically, the CEO will require that policies be in accord with customer-stipulated standards; hence, the general procedure must comply with the national or other stipulated customer standard.

6 The General Procedures of This Book

When faced with the task of preparing general procedures, the author must decide among a number of alternatives. For example, when a system of standards is to be produced, the original system designer must decide between two possible avenues concerning what goes into each standard or procedure:

1. Minimize duplication of contents in standards and procedures by referencing other standards or procedures in which the needed material is located. This results in:
   a. Less voluminous standards or procedures.
   b. Lower cost of producing individual standards and procedures.
   c. Greater difficulty in using individual standards or procedures, as all other such referenced documents must be obtained before the desired document may be used. (*Note:* In many cases this aspect will more than cancel the lower-cost aspect. In one extreme case, the author found that he needed 17 standards of one nation in order to use the one he first required.)
2. Maximize the independence of individual standards and procedures by including, so far as is practicable, all requirements in the one standard. This results in:
   a. Greater volume of information in each standard or procedure.
   b. Higher cost for purchase of an individual standard or procedure.
   c. More redundancy between standards or procedures.
   d. Ability to use each standard or procedure by itself, without reference to several other documents.

In preparing the procedures of this book the author chose the second avenue. He has found that it is desirable to have quality control general procedures which can be used to:

1. Minimize the complexity and voluminous nature of referenced documentation in contract negotiations.
2. Minimize the total amount of superfluous documentation that results and confuses individuals who must reach decisions, as at the work station.
3. Make it easier to formulate more accurate descriptions of the matters covered in the documents that apply to significantly different situations.

As a result, the user of these procedures will find that matters such as planning and organizing are covered in each individual procedure. That makes it possible to send one procedure to a vendor, for example, and know it will be unnecessary for the vendor to obtain many additional documents before the document supplied can be used. It also means that the supervisor on the production floor has, in most cases, only one place to look for his or her guidance. This book is divided into seven sections as follows:

Section I contains an introduction to QC principles and to each of the more modern developments in the QC field.

Section II contains the QC general procedures needed to extend quality control throughout the design and development activity of a company. Chapter 4 of Sec. II contains introductory guidance to the hardware designer on the inclusion of reliability in his or her designs.

Section III contains the general procedures needed to control the quality of all types of activities involved in bringing products, services, and projects into being in the three major divisions of industry. It will be found that procedures are given for both large and small companies, which enables the small companies that do not have the capability to introduce and use statistical process controls to control their quality by inspection. Control of quality by inspection of completed products is also covered in Chap. 6 of Sec. III.

Section IV contains the general procedures most used in purchasing activities. Although the procedures are independent, it would be necessary to specify in purchase documents applicable procedures from the other sections of this book to adequately control quality of purchased materials.

Section V contains the product recall procedure. This procedure applies almost solely to those companies producing some form of product, but it can impact on any services or project company.

Section VI contains three essential procedures. The procedure in Chap. 1 is one of the more modern approaches to total quality control through employee participation programs (EPP). Quality circles will be found to be a part of the EPP activity, and just-in-time (JIT) methods are found to be more easily introduced and applied within the framework of an operating EPP activity. Chapter 2 describes an effective program of quality cost control. It has the additional aspect of providing guidance in the adjustment of quality costs to both optimize and minimize those costs in operating situations. Chapter 3 contains a procedure prescribing methods for the introduction of a JIT quality and productivity improvement program.

Section VII contains a quality and reliability glossary of more than 1000 definitions. The glossary will be found to meet the most modern interpretations of such documents as ISO-8402, "Quality Assurance—Vocabulary," and ANSI/ASQC A1, A2, and A3 covering acceptance sampling and quality systems. It is also compatible with the EOQC 14 language glossary of quality terms and their definitions.

It is recognized that standards of various nations are continually under review for change and updating, and some of the terms in this document will be altered accordingly. Also, there are some terms that vary from company to company and nation to nation. In the United States, for example, companies have different names for the item of product that is chosen from early production for examination against design specifications. Many companies use the term "first piece"; Western Electric Company has for years used the term "tool-made sample"; and other companies (mostly overseas) use the term "first off." Only the term "first-piece production sample" is used herein.

7   Selecting and Applying QC General Procedures

Most of the QC general procedures in this book have titles which are self-explanatory. A professional quality engineer should have no difficulty in choosing the correct procedure or combination of procedures to apply in each situation. There is, however, the greater scope of QC activity now needed as a result of our understanding the three different kinds of industrial activity.

Recognition of the differences found in activities of organizations whose primary output consists of either products or services introduces a new and more effective approach to total quality control (TQC). This recognition and the general procedures contained in this book permit TQC to be more fully implemented according to the meaning of Dr. A. V. Fiegenbaum. In his book, *Total Quality Control,** Fiegenbaum defines total quality control as follows:

> Total Quality Control is an effective system for integrating the quality-development, quality-maintenance, and quality-improvement efforts of the various groups in an organization so as to enable production and service at the most economical levels which allow for full customer satisfaction.

The general practice in manufacturing industry in the past has been to consider that organizations and their activities are divided into two categories according to whether the organization's contribution to bringing the product into being is direct or indirect. Each organization that contributes directly to the product in some way must be incorporated under the umbrella of the quality control procedures and must carry out all of its activities in accord with QC principles. Organizations such as finance, accounting, and purchasing are not provided with QC procedures. Clearly, such a company is not practicing TQC. If an accounting function tries to comply with MIL-Q-9858, it quickly finds that the standard does not apply to most of its work.

Now, with the advent of QC general procedures which apply to all

---

*McGraw-Hill, New York, 1961.

kinds of work, services-providing organizations within the overall company or plant activity, such as accounting, can embrace quality control in their work. When it is necessary for the company to construct a new manufacturing plant, it will have available a procedure that can be stipulated for the project work in the contract. We find, then, that a large company or division of a corporation will have need of all three types of QC general procedures (and QC standards when they are available). The general procedures are found in this book in Sec. III, Chap. 2, for mass manufacturing, Chap. 3, for services, and Chap. 4, for project works. Supporting or ancillary procedures are to be found in the other chapters of the book. See Sec. I, Chap. 3 for more information on applying the QC procedures included in this book.

The conclusion we reach is that our view of the work performed in industry has now changed. In the past our view was largely limited to that of mass-manufacturing industry. Now procedures covering all types of work in industry are available and we can implement total quality control in the full meaning of Fiegenbaum's definition.

The reader's attention is called to the fact that all general procedures included in this book are concise and definitive and contain mandatory clauses. As such, they cannot be as comprehensive as textbooks written entirely about the one subject of a given procedure. Each procedure, however, contains the essential controls required to cover that particular area of work in industry.

Human industry, like humanity itself, is continually evolving. Though the general procedures contained in this book may at this time be representative of the most modern thought available, they must be viewed as open to the changes brought about by new methods and by new ideas. They are therefore offered in forms made convenient for adaptation to the specific needs of individual companies, as well as possessing the facility for further development as needed.

Chapter

2

Quality Control:
Its Origin and Modern
Development

1 Beginning and Growth of Quality Control

Quality is a universal need. Though we may first think of quality in terms of items of product or service, we seek quality in all that we do. This means that, in a company, there is quality of management, quality of accounting, quality of purchasing, quality of production, quality of serving, and indeed quality of quality assurance and control.

History shows us that mankind has for many centuries expected to receive value in exchange for the things that were bartered, and later, for the money paid. One such record is to be found in the case laws of King Hammurabi of the Babylonians, who ruled the first dynasty of Babylon in the eighteenth century B.C. Among Hammurabi's 282 laws were those on trade and commerce, under which subjects giving poor service or unequal value in trade had to satisfy their customers by correcting the deficiencies in the services they provided or commodities they traded.

In the fourteenth century A.D., the British company of Cordwainers and Curriers, leather merchants, assigned a skilled leather worker the task of moving from stall to stall among the tradesmen for the purpose of examining the products being made and ensuring that all the products were up to a minimum standard. We might call this one of the first instances of formal inspection in human industry.

Neither of the above examples represented actual control of quality. Each consisted of examination of finished commodities by either the customer or an inspector for the purpose of ensuring the quality of the material or service.

True quality control began in the United States. Two developments were needed before the concepts of modern quality control could be applied in manufacturing industry:

1. An understanding of variability and how statistical mathematics can be stochastically used to explain, predict, and control variability had to exist. It did not come with the growth of statistical mathematics in the nineteenth century; it had to wait for the introduction of such mathematics into production activities of industry in the first half of the twentieth century.

2. True quality control as it is practiced today had to wait for the sequential production line type of manufacturing activities made possible by Frederick Taylor's introduction of early planning and Henry Ford's introduction of the production line method of manufacturing. The latter came in the 1913 to 1917 era.

A third, and perhaps most significant event, was also needed before the true beginning of quality control can be recognized. This was the documentation of the principles by which statistical mathematics and sequential production line operations could be used together to achieve control of the variability which occurs in manufacturing. This third step came in the United States when Dr. Walter A. Shewhart of the Bell Laboratories studied the control of manufacture in Western Electric Company production lines. Shewhart's first papers on the subject of QC methods began appearing in 1924, and in 1931 his book *Economic Control of Quality of Manufactured Product* was published by D. Van Nostrand Co.

The introduction of QC principles throughout industry was slow in coming, even in the progressive U.S. industrial companies. Though Western Electric Company was using the methods from the 1930s, records indicate their next significant use took place at Picatinny Arsenal during the early days of World War II (1940 to 1945) when they were used to control the quality of artillery shells. By the late 1940s, larger U.S. companies, such as General Electric, Westinghouse, and U.S. Steel, were beginning to apply QC principles.

It was the early 1950s that saw QC principles transferred to Europe,

Asia, and other parts of the industrialized world. Britain, France, and Germany then began to adopt the new principles. In the mid-1950s two men (Ron Stewart, of Amalgamated Wireless Australasia Ltd., and John Marchant, of Plessey Australia Pty. Ltd.) were sent to the United States from Australia for several months to study and carry back to Australia the new methods of economic manufacturing management. It was through the auspices of the U.S.-financed Japan Productivity Center headquartered in Washington, D.C., and by way of the thousands of Japanese businessmen the center brought to the United States to study manufacturing and management methods, that the principles of quality control were transferred to Japan. By 1960 the principles of quality control were in use throughout the industrialized world.

During its early decades, the new management science of quality control was applied first to the sequential manufacture of products in mass-manufacturing operations. When the principles were applied to job shops, or small-lot production, they did not seem to work so well. At first there was no thought of applying them to the provision of services, and it has been recognized only in the late 1980s that there is another kind of industry, the project industry, that might benefit from the methods. Design also is in 1988 an activity which, in most companies, though greatly influencing the ability of the company to produce quality output, has not benefited fully from the application of QC principles.

2   Some Theories of Quality and Organization

Quality control is an accepted and essential decision-making discipline of scientific management. Like many other areas of scientific management, it began as a practical way of improving manufacturing. Today QC techniques are used by all management levels in both manufacturing and nonmanufacturing departments. This evolved scientific discipline therefore influences the widest possible variety of business decisions. For total quality control, *all* managers must apply the disciplines of quality control to their areas of work.

It is the variability of all events and all work that gives the science of quality its mathematical base in statistics. No matter how precisely we attempt to control some equipment or area of work, there will be variability in the output. It is the techniques of quality control that permit the degrees of variability entering into the work that is done to be controlled by management. The mathematical disciplines of statistics permit us to stochastically predict the outcomes before we do the work, once sufficient knowledge about the process has been gained.

The purpose of a QC program was, for many years, to reduce variability to an economic minimum and maintain it there consistent with management objectives. The concept was that, though zero variability was not necessarily beyond our ability to comprehend, part of the variability of processes would always be beyond our ability to control it at an acceptable economic level. This resulted in acceptable quality levels (AQLs) being set at some level agreed to by supplier and customer on the basis of the economics (product price) involved. Much of industry was, in the 1960s and 1970s, imbued with the older thinking associated with the two forms of finance in business. They involved partitioning finances into two categories: opportunity expenditures and cost reduction expenditures. Opportunity economics involves expenditure for the purpose of increasing a company's market volume or segment; cost reduction economics involves the company in reducing its internal expenditures in satisfying an existing market segment. The economics of quality control, being practiced only within the climate of mass production, coincided with cost reduction expenditures. *It has only recently been recognized that expenditure on quality control has a greater component of opportunity economics than of cost reduction economics.*

The older management philosophy of containing quality control economics within some most achievable level of product variability and setting AQLs and hence product defect levels at the highest level a customer would agree to (or the level the manufacturing system would produce) is no longer acceptable. It is now the purpose of quality control, through a continuing program of opportunity expenditure, to conduct continuing quality improvement programs aimed at eliminating all—yes, that is correct, 100 percent of—defects and nonconformities.

In this new view, it is essential to recognize that product reliability is a characteristic within the overall quality domain requiring the attention necessary to satisfy customer expectations. It is also necessary to recognize the influence which design and development activities have on the quality of products produced and to extend quality control principles throughout design and development organizations.

One of the greatest needs of modern industry stems from the influence exerted by accounting methods on the ability to control and improve the quality of any company's output. It will be necessary for a major study of the structure of accounting curriculums in universities and institutes of technology to be undertaken if we are to realize a maximum benefit from zero nonconformity quality control. These courses should turn out graduates in accounting who have at their fingertips the techniques needed to provide business management with opportunity quality cost accounting. This would be a major step, since current courses in accounting seldom touch on older methods of quality cost control accounting now in use and the new view is still largely an unknown.

The task of organizing businesses into efficient and effective smoothly functioning programs capable of providing products and services free of nonconformities and defects confronts business managers in all countries. That American industry will prove equal to the task is not in doubt, but the time available for this advance is limited by the competitiveness of international trade. Major leaps forward are needed. To help make them, we will now seek to better understand this abstract thing we call quality and then examine some of the more successful modern concepts and methods.

3 Some Quality Terms Interpreted

We define quality as the totality of characteristics and features of a product, service, or system that bear on the items' ability to satisfy the customers' perceived desires. The items may comprise the output of a company to its marketplace, or they may consist of the output from one company department to another.

Let us examine two key phrases from the above definition. First, "characteristics and features." Any item of product or service can be viewed from the system concept, i.e., each thing can be broken down into its constituent parts. Since the achievement and measurement of quality require the classification of things that must be controlled, and those things must be specified by designers, we must break each object or item down into measurable aspects. It is here that we frequently fail in the classification process.

Features or functions cannot be measured in quantitative terms. For example, a handset is a feature of a telephone. Although the handset as a feature cannot be measured, its characteristics can be. They involve such characteristics as physical dimensions, color, finish, and sensitivity. In order to control quality, each item of product will have features and functions, none of which can be measured, whose characteristics must be classified by the designer. It is the values of the characteristics of the features and functions of an item of product that must be presented to the quality technician or inspector for measurement.

Next let us consider the phrase "customer's perceived desires." All too often, customers place the blame for dissatisfaction with a product on aspects of the product that have nothing to do with what we have traditionally called the item's quality. For example, when the OPEC oil price increases caused Americans to frantically search for cars with greater mileage per gallon capabilities, they found the small Japanese cars ready and waiting. To a very large extent this meant that the Japanese cars had better quality than cars from Detroit; the smaller Japanese vehicles satisfied one of the customer's most important perceived desires.

The lesson we learn from this is that the term "quality," at least in the eyes of the consumer, embraces all aspects of the product, whether those aspects came from the market research activity, the design and development activity, the production or providing activity, or some other activity in the sequence used to make the item available in the marketplace. It was a further bonus to the Japanese producers that their cars had traditional quality as well.

Another of the consumer's "perceived desires" of long standing, and one that will not diminish, is the desire to get durability or reliability in the things he or she buys. In order to achieve more fundamental study of the reliability aspects of products, the United States has made reliability a profession additional to the field of quality. To that end the American Society for Quality Control has divided the original certified quality engineer (CQE) field and created two fields: the CQE and the certified reliability engineer (CRE). To some, this has meant that there are actually two separate fields of activity. In most other countries reliability is seen as one of the more important quality attributes of good-quality products and only one science therefore exists. In the natural evolutionary experience of mankind, there are at play forces that will, once a division has been established, seek to strengthen that division and make each of the two "separate" parts more separate and somehow more different. In this way each justifies its existence, growth, and longer life.

The fields of quality and reliability now exist in the United States side by side as close, but separate, allies. From the above it can be argued that an effort is needed in the United States to bring these two essential fields of activity in manufacturing industry closer together and allow them to be seen and practiced as constituent parts of the one whole. Any benefits deriving from such effort will also be needed in the quality activities now entering the service and project industries.

Let us next consider the relation between the terms "quality control" and "quality assurance." For practical purposes, we may consider these terms from the viewpoint of work done and why. Quality *control* work consists of all the work elements carried out by a manager or by those in his or her organization which contribute to the quality of the output of the organization. Quality *assurance* work consists of all the work elements carried out by a manager or by those in his or her organization which contribute to the quality of the output of some other organization.

From the above definitions it can readily be seen why the title of the management person in an American company who has the responsibility for the quality organization has evolved from the earlier term "quality control manager" to the current most frequent term "quality assurance manager." It is actually the production managers, purchasing managers, accounting managers, etc. who must control the quality of the product or service work done within their organizations. The quality assurance manager's staff must assist them in achieving quality in the items supplied to the marketplace.

4 The Evolution of Quality Control

The control of quality is an evolving management science now being taught on bachelor, master, and doctoral levels in universities in America and overseas. In many countries, however, it is still being treated as a one-semester course required of industrial engineering or manufacturing engineering graduates. This caused an evolutionary difficulty to exist in many companies during the 1960s when a place was being sought for the new organization, quality control. Many companies saw QC as a responsibility of their production engineering departments. At least one large U.S. company tried placing quality control under its value analysis department. When the QC function was first given a separate organization of its own, production engineers, trained in some QC disciplines, saw the new organization as doing their work. Probably no new arrival on an existing scene encountered more difficulties in finding its proper niche. Today the search goes on as the concepts of quality embrace all activities of the entire company.

We now recognize that the chief executive officer of each company is that company's most senior quality control person. We also recognize that it is the duty of all employees of an organization to control the quality of what they do. Quality assurance is itself a service provided to the rest of each company organization by the staff of the QA organization. Many new methods and techniques by which quality of the things we use and the lives we live can be improved have been discovered. We shall next examine some of them.

5 Modern Developments in Quality Methods

5.1 Three different kinds of industry. One of the newest discoveries in the field of quality has been the recognition that quality standards and general procedures prepared for the mass-manufacturing industry cannot be used for effective control of quality of services and project works. When we have applied MIL-Q-9858, or its derivative standards, to services-providing or to project-type work, many of the requirements of control areas in the two kinds of industry have not been met. Further examination of total human endeavor in the light of quality standards and general procedures reveals that there are only *three* kinds: mass manufacturing, services, and the project (construction) industries.

Standards prepared by national and international standards bodies and by professional societies for the mass-manufacturing industry have been found unsuitable by professional quality engineers working in the services and project (construction) industries. As a result, individual segments of the latter two kinds of industry have had to undertake self-regulation and prepare regulatory standards for themselves, sometimes, as in the case of the nuclear power industry (a project industry), with the assistance of the jurisdictional authority concerned.

A further examination of the kinds of work carried out in the manufacturing industry reveals that each and every large company, at one time or another, needs *all* the different kinds of quality standards. Companies need the new standards and procedures in order to apply total quality control in the complete meaning of Fiegenbaum's definition. For example, the departments within a company that provide only services to another department need a services standard with which they can comply and a services general procedure to which they can work. Similarly, when the company management decides to construct a new manufacturing plant, there is need for a project quality standard to use in contracting for the work and the successful bidder will need a project QC general procedure under which to carry out the construction work.

During 1985, the Standards Association of Australia's Quality Committee was in the final stages of revision of the national Standard on Quality Control Systems for manufacturing industry. The committee was approached by both the electric power industry, which uses project-type management of its construction works, and the pressure vessel industry, likewise a project industry. Neither organization had been able to successfully use the earlier manufacturing industry standards, nor did either find the revised versions to be satisfactory. Both project industries found it necessary to use a Canadian Standard, CSA Z299.1, which had been prepared by the CSA committee during a period when much of its membership was involved with Canada's major expansion of its electrical generating capacity.

During the early 1980s, ISO's TC-176 Quality Committee was preparing the new 9000 series of international quality standards. ISO committee members saw the Z299 CSA standards as less suitable for manufacturing industry than the ANSI/ASQC and European standards (such as BS-5750). The new ISO 9000 series of standards have therefore been issued as mass-manufacturing standards. In 1987 the need still existed for both U.S. and ISO standards to cover the services and the project-type industries.

There are regulatory-type standards in a number of areas of both the service and the construction industries in the United States. The bodies responsible for the more important areas of work have heretofore produced their own. In the medical field, detailed procedures exist for both the control of sanitation and the technical operation of medical organizations. Dr. Dennis O'Leary, M.D. works with the Joint Commission on Accreditation of Hospitals (JCAH) throughout the United States to hold doctors and hospitals responsible for whether or not their patients get well.* JCAH accredits some 7500 health care organizations in the United States. Another example is the U.S. Nuclear Regulatory Commission, which also has adopted excellent procedures that include project construction controls essential to that most important activity.

The United States can be said to be on a par with or ahead of other nations in documenting the needs of the services and project industries. In Australia and Ireland attention is now being given to the preparation of standards for the services industry, and in Australia, as in Canada, a project industry standard is already in use.

5.2 The importance of interfaces of all kinds. There have been many developments in the field of quality control in an attempt to overcome what is, according to any measure, the most prevalent quality problem: the interface. The multitude of interfaces in our human organizations, our working systems, and the products and services we deliver cause us more difficulty than all the regions within individual organizations and groups of material. When we look at the manner in which evolution works, we see why. Nature divides all things into groups or populations of things. The key word here is "divides," for there are interfaces (divisions) between both the separate and the mixed groups of things.

Now, there is a natural attempt by all things to bring about harmonious and efficient functioning within groups. There is, correspondingly, a natural attempt to create and perpetuate differences at the interfaces that will prohibit two interacting groups from "joining" one another. It is these differences that we discover to be the causes of almost all of our quality problems, and hence our problems have a very great tendency to occur at interfaces.

Within a company, there are people-to-people, manager-to-employee, union-to-management, manager-to-manager, supplier-to-customer, and organization-to-organization interfaces. Each manager can quite effectively, if he or she is a good manager, mold the members of his or her organization into a cohesive motivated group whose con-

---

*See Michael L. Millenson, "Making Health Care Measure Up," *Quality Progress*, May 1987.

certed energies are directed toward common goals. It is when the organization interacts with other company organizations that difficulties arise.

To overcome much of the interface difficulty, a whole new range of quality programs were undertaken in the 1980s. They included such programs as quality circles which bridge a number of organizations and employee participation programs that unify the entire workforce—managers and employees. In Australia, for example, there was a drive to reduce that nation's some 246 unions to a few dozen larger unions in the interest of lessening jurisdictional disputes, lack of cooperation, and a host of difficulties that inherently occur more frequently when there are many interfaces.

We find that the same situation exists with inanimate materials as with organizations and people. Designers of system components go to great lengths to eliminate difficulties within their individual components or materials. It is when the materials are combined into more complex systems that we find the interface problem has not been solved adequately.

Clearly, an area of considerable potential gain is in concentrating on bridging or eliminating interfaces between contentious or uncooperative groups. Similarly, greater design attention is needed on our more complex systems directed toward understanding and harmonizing interactions at the interfaces between components and subassemblies throughout product lifetime.

5.3   Percent defective or zero defects.   As we shall see in Art. 5.7, the term "defect" becomes "nonconformity" in most of our future work. That has been so in the United States for some time, but it is only with the advent of ISO's TC-176 committee standard, ISO 8402-1985, that many other nations will encounter the new terminology. For our purposes, however, we find that there was, during the mid-1980s, a major revolution in the degree to which perfection in products was sought. It was the phenomenal success of the Japanese manufacturing system in the international marketplace that has brought the revolution about.

Traditionally, manufacturing industry in western nations has used the acceptable quality level (AQL) expressed as a percent defective to reach an economical level of quality control acceptable to cooperating customers and suppliers. Until the early 1980s, the general public, as consumers, found the practice of controlled lifetimes and a service and maintenance contract satisfactory. That is still the case, except that customers now expect items purchased in the marketplace to have much longer lifetimes of total fault freedom. Whereas 1 percent of incoming supplies, for example, was an acceptable quality level and 0.5

percent of faulty outgoing products was acceptable in many commercial operations, manufacturing companies are now expecting, and receiving, 0.1 percent fault levels of incoming supplies, and many are approaching zero functional failures in final products. Great strides are also being made in eliminating the "nuisance" types of failures; small characteristics of a cosmetic nature are now receiving more attention.

With the recognition that quality is an opportunity aspect of products, manufacturing industry is prepared to spend money to initiate and propagate a whole range of programs to improve quality. The older poor qualities associated with high levels of percent defectives in outgoing products is no longer acceptable. Quality professionals must devise programs that will enable defects and nonconformities to approach true zero without the infinite cost barrier previously seen as the impossible hurdle. This is achieved through ongoing quality improvement programs that are designed to identify and remove all manner of poor-quality sources.

5.4 Quality improvement programs. "Quality improvement program" became the buzzword of quality professionals in the 1980s. It is essential that all companies, and divisions of companies, have such a program if they expect to survive in today's competitive environment. Without such a program it will be virtually impossible for the required levels of quality needed in the international marketplace to be achieved. Just what is a quality improvement program?

Across the United States, quality improvement in companies takes as many forms as there are management and quality teams. Each consultant offers his or her own brand of program designed to raise the quality levels and quality of life of workers in industry. The more successful programs are being exported to other countries; and in the more progressive nations, homegrown programs have developed. Many of those programs contain new information useful for the United States.

A typical quality improvement program labeled just-in-time (JIT) is also designed to improve productivity. A procedure for implementing it is given in Sec. VI, Chap. 3. Just-in-time is a new name given to a much older group of quality control techniques that have evolved over many years. They are techniques such as establishing management teams, analyzing product failures, tracing failures to their basic or root causes, eliminating the root causes of failure, and continuing the program in an ongoing manner.

There are many other programs, such as the employee participation program (Sec. VI, Chap. 1), which will make major contributions toward quality improvement. One is the quality circle program now well introduced to American companies. The drive for better quality will continue to be a major effort, and it may be expected to grow in intensity as international competition increases.

5.5   Just-in-time quality control and productivity.   Quality improvement programs are becoming a way of life in modern industry. It has been recognized that the traditional levels of quality designed to meet a rather artificially set range of acceptable quality levels (AQLs) was not good enough. Some companies produced products that were free of nonconformities at the 0.1 to 1 percent level while competitors (including the Japanese) were producing the same products totally free of fault characteristics. It was not possible to make the sudden transition from a 1 percent fault level to a zero fault level. Hence there have come into being national and international programs of quality improvement.

Perhaps the most effective program of quality improvement for an existing production line is what has been called just-in-time (JIT). The JIT quality improvement program makes use of activities already existing in most companies by combining the activities in a more effective way. Defect or nonconformity analysis is, in some countries, called failure mode and effect analysis (FMEA). In a JIT program, analysis of failed products is coupled with the tracing of failures to their basic causes, so that, when the causes are removed, the future product no longer fails by that mode.

When these activities are carried out within a planned management program that provides for finance and the integration of the activity with production and the JIT activities are made a part of the total company effort, we have a very effective ongoing program of quality improvement. It is then only necessary to aim the quality improvement program at the achievement of products that are 100 percent good. Over time, these programs can steadily build the quality of a product to a level that will be competitive with other producers of the same type items.

"Just-In-Time Quality Control System," Sec. VI, Chap. 3 of *Quality Control Systems,* presents a procedure by which a company can implement an effective JIT quality and productivity improvement program.

5.6   Employee participation programs.   Early examples of employee participation programs had their origin in the United States; in the late 1940s, both the Bell Laboratories at Murray Hill and the General Electric Company started using examples of employee participation to solve problems. The Bell Laboratories called their program cross pollination; it consisted of scientists and engineers making presentations of their immediate work activities to audiences of their peers within the laboratories. As a part of this program, the peer group would critique an activity being presented and offer ideas and concepts for solutions of problems or expansion of the effort.

At the General Electric Company, the early program was called brainstorming. In this program a group of individuals from a wide cross section of skills and professions assemble with a program facilitator who presents the problem needing solution. The participants are given a limited time in which to provide solutions. Typically a tape recorder is used to record the fast-flowing stream of ideas, and anyone voicing a negative view on an idea is asked to leave the room. A time interval of 30 to 45 minutes is allowed; at the end of it all further discussion is cut off and the session is terminated. With this synergistic magnification of the ideation process it is not unusual for 200 to 300 solutions to a problem to be recorded in one half hour. Of course, only a very few ideas are found to be entirely practical. However, there are usually some new ones that prove to advance the work and effect highly satisfactory solutions.

Japanese businessmen visited the United States by the thousand during the early 1950s under the auspices of the Japan Productivity Center, Washington, D.C. There is little doubt that these Japanese were introduced to the early methods of employing a "circle" of employees in the solution of problems encountered in a company's work. But it was clearly a Japanese innovation to extend the idea to the improvement of quality control in products, and now the Japanese quality circle approach is famous worldwide.

United States companies have adopted a whole range of employee participation programs that vary widely in how they work and what they are called as each of the larger corporations seeks to improve its quality position in the marketplace. Frederick W. Taylor, in the latter half of the nineteenth century, introduced the concepts of productivity and methods of planning that made modern productivity improvements possible. Though the methods of modern scientific production management introduced by Taylor have received much criticism for their contribution to repetitiveness in the workplace, it is precisely the repetitiveness that is responsible for the quality found in products. What we are trying to do today is find ways to improve the quality of life of employees and tap the vast employee reservoir of knowledge about the quality problems needing solutions, without losing employee contribution to the quality of production. In that way job security of both management and employees can be enhanced. Today's enlightened managements recognize that their employees are not only their most valuable assets but the greatest untapped pool of knowledge about quality problems and how to solve them.

5.7   New definitions for "defect" and "nonconformity."   Quality professionals have for decades recognized the difference between what designers perceive to be the set of characteristics needed by a product and the range of needs perceived by the product user. Out of this division have come the two forms of specification. On the one hand, we have the product design specification, which defines what the product is to be and do. On the other hand we have the customer's user specification, which defines what the user needs are. In most cases there is some difference between the two; in extreme cases the two are widely different.

When products are to be produced in one nation for customers in another nation, there will be many delays and rejections because of the differences in what is specified. During 1984, some 60 percent of U.S. exports to Japan were forced to lie for up to 5 months on the docks awaiting further testing and/or modification before they could be released by Japanese customs. In the opposite direction, less than 5 percent of Japanese shipments were similarly delayed. Governments of other nations were experiencing similar difficulties in their trade with one another.

In an effort to provide a partial solution to the problem of differences between supplier and customer definitions of a product, the International Standards Organization's TC-176 Committee on Quality issued Standard ISO 8402-1985, "Quality Assurance—Vocabulary." In this standard the terms "defect" and "nonconformity" are redefined for international trade. During 1987, ASQC revised Standards A1, A2, and A3. These are compatible with the ISO Standard. "Defect" and "nonconformity" are defined as in ISO 8402-1985:

> 3.20 Nonconformity: The nonfulfillment of specified requirements.
> Notes: 1. This definition covers the departure or absence of one or more quality characteristics from specified requirements. It also covers the departure or absence of an element of a quality system.
> 3.21 Defect: The nonfulfillment of intended usage requirements.
> Notes: 1. This definition covers the departure or absence of one or more quality characteristics from intended usage requirements.

It can be seen that, in the producer's acceptance inspection and quality assurance work, we will no longer have any "defectives" when characteristics of products or services are compared with product specification requirements. "Defects" will not occur in such activities, and hence other terms need redefinition: "percent defective" now becomes "percent nonconforming" and "defect" becomes "nonconformity." All these terms are covered in the glossary in Sec. VII, Chap. 1.

5.8   Liability and statistical process control.   A not so new, yet still modern, development is product liability. The newness comes from what is taking place in this area. It has been estimated that, in the United States, corporations are spending at the rate of more than $5 billion a year for insurance premiums which are intended to protect them from product liability claims.* Protecting themselves through insurance is not the only thing corporations are doing, however. It is now recognized that supplying products and services in all areas carries with it a liability to the end user for any harm that may arise from that use.

In addition to the vast increase of litigation in the product liability area, which has provided a further major impetus to the expansion of the legal sector in the United States, the legislators have been active. There is a considerable body of state law on liability, largely based on the Uniform Product Liability Act (UPLA), which was reported out of committee and published in October 1979. There is also an evolving body of federal law. When wearing his product liability hat, the director or manager of quality assurance carries an increasing burden. Corporate reaction to liability litigation has provided major support for quality control in the process control area as well as the design area.

It has been found that, in the great preponderance of liability cases which have been lost by corporate defendants, the defendants were unable to prove, to the satisfaction of juries, that they had kept all characteristics of the items concerned within the specification limits by statistical process control methods during manufacture. That and the increasing demand of military and space customers for improved quality and reliability have given major emphasis to improving statistical process control in the manufacturing industry in both the United States and the rest of the western world.

---

*F. A. Birmingham, "Product Liability Prevention: A Teamwork Approach," *AQC Transactions,* 1985.

3

Procedures by
Type of Industry

1 Introduction

We saw in Chap. 1 of this section that different kinds of work are undertaken in human industry and that there are different influences and controls on that work. We further saw that we can divide the different kinds of work into three major categories: mass manufacturing, services, and project work. For the purpose of generating procedures, e.g., policy-type general procedures, for use in organizing the work of industry, it is necessary that the procedures be correctly tailored to the type of work. No single procedure of usable length and clarity is able to control all work.

We have repeatedly found that standards and procedures designed for the mass-manufacturing industry do not work for either the service industry or the project industry. In the United States, several regulatory bodies such as the nuclear power industry (a project industry) and the medical field (a service industry) have had to prepare their own standards and procedures. These are not of a general nature, however, and they apply to very limited parts of the total project and service industries. It has therefore been necessary, in this book, to cover the two additional kinds of industry.

It is appropriate to comment on two specialized industrial activities that require unique treatment. The first of these is the manufacture in a job shop type of operation of one or a few of a single type of product for which the design is usually not frozen and which is to be made in such small numbers as to preclude the working of feedback and corrective action methods of mass production. In this type of work neither the methods nor the procedures of earlier standards are adequate.

The control of the job shop type of work requires either of two methods. The work may be planned in such meticulous detail all the way through that the design can be frozen and the product manufactured in exact accordance with plans. Alternatively, the one-piece product may be made subject to design oversight all the way through, with design changes being made as required at any point up to final acceptance. The latter approach requires that documentation of all actions and changes be made, but during and following production of the item, rather than before. One-piece production work is similar to design and development work, and the two can be controlled by the same general procedures.

The second special kind of work requires that project-type organization and controls be established within the overall and ongoing activities of a major production or services company. This "internal" project activity may be initiated at any time and cease its work when some new management system is designed and documented, or it may take the project to some more complete stage at which products are being produced or services are being provided before the work is turned back to the company organizations normally responsible. The quality of work done in this environment and project organization requires the use of project general procedure control methods. That is true despite the fact that the overall company or division may be using a "core" general procedure that is different for its product or services output.

It is the responsibility of individual companies, or divisions of companies, to prepare, issue, and establish the general procedures and detailed procedures that tell, respectively, *what* work is to be done and *how* the work is to be carried out. General procedures are those that pertain to divisional or interdivisional methods of operation and that, normally, remain constant within the company or business activity for a given range of products, services, or project work. General procedures normally draw their authority and structural content from the national and international standards covering the type of industry concerned. The quality systems in this book are of the general procedure type; and because of their unchanging nature, they are sometimes referred to as systems standards.

Detailed procedures used in industry are those which are created for and pertain to a specific product, service, or type of project work. Written detailed procedures are concerned with the production techniques, test devices, special packaging or presentation activities, and all other work concerned with bringing into being the product, service, or project work. The detailed procedures consist of work instructions which describe in detail *how* to do the work that is done and who will do it, and when it will be done, as well as prescribing the supplies, materials, and services to be used and the criteria to be satisfied.

Detailed procedures are normally prepared by a company or business management as part of planning to produce some product, provide some service, or construct some project. Detailed procedures should receive their organizational relationships from the general procedures of the company or business activity. When detailed procedures are prepared without the guidance of what is to be done by the directive natures of general procedures, it has been found that there is considerable duplication of effort. Also, necessary actions are missed because of the usual urgency of preparing detailed procedures. In general, each requirement from a general procedure of this book which is found to be applicable to a particular business should be implemented by preparing detailed procedures that explain how to carry out the work on the particular product or service.

2   The Structure of This Book

This book has been prepared to have the same sequence of general procedures as the flow of work in industry. Basic research leads to the discovery and documentation of fields of knowledge composed of large numbers of individual physical facts about nature. Design and development work then selects certain of those facts and assembles them into some useful product or service for mankind. The end results of such design and development work are documentation and models of the product or service that are then used to reproduce the product or service any desirable number of times.

This book is divided into seven sections each containing a number of chapters. Since individual general procedures are normally used by themselves in industry, an attempt has been made to make each procedure as independent of other procedures as practicable. For that reason it will appear to the casual reader that there is a considerable amount of redundancy. When a procedure is taken on its own, as it normally is, the redundancy disappears.

Section I introduces the subject matter, presents the more recent important developments in the management of quality, and describes how the procedures are used for the three kinds of industry. Sections II through VI contain the 21 procedures presented in the book. Section VII contains a glossary of more than 1000 terms used in the quality field.

For any one user in a single nation there will be terms that are not commonly used or that do not appear to be defined with the same wording as the definitions with which that person may be familiar. The reason is that the glossary has been so prepared that it will be usable by people from all developed nations. If terms from any one nation's terminology standard alone had been used, the glossary would have contained only some 200 to 300 terms. Members of ASQC, EOQC, AOQC, CQC, etc. will find the terms and definitions with which they are familiar. The new 1985 ISO definitions for "defect and "nonconformity" have been used, and the effect of those definitions on other terms throughout the glossary will be seen.

3   The Design and Development Program

3.1   Product design and development.   The quality control system procedures applicable to product design and development work are to be found in Sec. II, Chaps. 1 and 4 and also Chap. 2 when software is to be designed.

3.2   Services design and development.   The design and development of services involves many unique areas of control which are either totally absent from or are greatly changed in the case of product design and development work. The quality control system general procedures for control of this type of design work are found in Sec. II, Chap. 3.

3.3   Project design.   Project design work can at times involve all four of the general procedures given in Sec. II. The design of systems, which is the output of project design work, is essentially similar to the design of complex products, and it will involve in addition the use of services to assemble the products into systems.

Construction work requiring project control is production-type work, and it uses the core general procedure of Sec. III, Chap. 4.

4   Fitting the General Procedure to the Work

4.1   Mass manufacturing industry

4.1.1   Products design work.   See Sec. II, Chaps. 1, 2, and 4.

4.1.2   Mass production

1. Core general procedure. See Sec. III, Chap. 2 (and also Chaps. 5 and 6 as dictated by economics or special circumstances).
2. Essential ancillary general procedures. See Sec. III, Chaps. 3 and 7 to 10; Sec. IV, Chap. 1; Sec. VI, Chaps. 2 and 3; and Sec. VII, Chap. 1.

3. Recommended ancillary general procedures. See Sec. II, Chap. 2; Sec. III, Chap. 4; Sec. IV, Chap. 2; Sec. V, Chap. 1; and Sec. VI, Chap. 1.

4.2 Services industry

4.2.1 Services design work. See Sec. II, Chap. 3.

4.2.2 Services-providing industry

1. Core general procedure. See Sec. III, Chap. 3.
2. Essential ancillary general procedures. See Sec. III, Chaps. 6 to 10; Sec. IV, Chap. 1; Sec. VI, Chap. 2; and Sec. VII, Chap. 1.
3. Recommended ancillary general procedures. See Sec. III, Chaps. 2 to 5; and Sec. VI, Chaps. 1 and 3.

4.3 Project industry

4.3.1 Project design work. See Sec. II, Chaps. 1 to 4.

4.3.2 Project construction

1. Core general procedure. See Sec. III, Chap. 4.
2. Essential ancillary general procedures. See Sec. III, Chaps. 2, 3, and 5 to 10; Sec. IV, Chap. 1; Sec. VI, Chaps. 2 and 3; and Sec. VII, Chap. 1.
3. Recommended ancillary general procedures. See Sec. IV, Chap. 2; and Sec. VI, Chap. 1.

Notes

1. Some auxiliary general procedures will be required for use by suppliers from whom products and/or services are purchased.
2. Not all recommended auxiliary general procedures will be used in all instances, but they should be used when need for them arises.

Quality Systems
for Design
and Development

1

Product Design and Development Procedure

PART A. REVIEW AND GUIDANCE

1 Review

This procedure provides guidance both to those who must establish design and development activities and carry them out while doing design and development work and to those who work in quality assurance for customers and have the need to undertake assessments of suppliers and prospective suppliers' capabilities.

In this procedure the use of the word "shall" is to be taken to mean that the system characteristic, or work activity, is considered to be obligatory for the successful outcome of design and development work. When desirable but nonessential matters are discussed, they will be indicated as such by the use of words that leave the requirement optional. Typically the word "should" implies that the user of this procedure may choose to do or not do the work indicated but is advised to comply.

Design and development work will ordinarily be in-house designs, or it will be done under contract for a customer. When contract requirements differ from similar requirements of this procedure, the contract requirements will override the stated or implied requirements of this procedure. The contents of the procedure are suitable for use in the great majority of industries, and they will be found applicable in most design situations and contracts.

Because of the freedoms which must exist in a creative environment and the complexities which are encountered, it is essential that the managers or assessors of such organizational activities remain flexible in their approach and viewpoint. All design and development work involves a succession of compromises between alternative, and often conflicting, requirements and capabilities. Design of more complex products with more demanding operational requirements will require more sophisticated design organizations with varied backup and support facilities. Less complex products can be designed with less than the entire system as characterized by this procedure. It will be the responsibility of the manager or assessor concerned to recognize the needs of the product range represented by design work to be carried out and to subtract from or add to the capabilities expressed here.

The customer may, through design reviews, monitor the progress of the design. Each stage of the development may require trials and tests to be carried out. If so, the stage is complete only when they have been done and the results have been analyzed. Following the successful testing and proving of reliability in the final design model, it will be possible to estimate the costs of production, including test and production equipment and staff involved.

This procedure provides for the design house to carry out in-house formal design reviews at strategic stages of the design work. In that way, ongoing awareness and quantitative knowledge of progress and success or failure of the design can be acquired. It is considered essential to carry out some design reviews, even on the more simple product designs and modifications, and this shall be done.

There may be no clear cutoff line between design and development work on the one hand and ongoing production on the other. Though there will be a need for a point to be reached in the ongoing activity when it can be said the design and development is complete and the start of production can begin, design refinements of a minor nature may continue on through pilot-line production to reach the final production model. In these mass-production situations, it is normal for the design to become progressively *frozen* as the longer-term procurement production tools and skills are sought and acquired. Following the *design freeze* stage, no further changes to the design can be made and the designers are free to take on other work. This mass production situation is different from job shop or project-type work, in which the construction of only one or a few of the design results in the designers remaining active throughout the construction phase.

2   Guidance

When modification to an existing design is required, the contract may invoke only a part of this procedure. In other situations, the content of this procedure may need slight additions to cover very specialized work. It is, however, quite adequate to cover the great majority of situations in industry in which products of a hardware nature are to be brought into being in the first instance or new designs must be developed from existing designs. Each manager, confronted with the need to implement controls over design and development work which will ensure the successful outcome of such work, will find that in almost all cases it is sufficient to specify and implement this entire procedure.

When viewed as a quality assurance procedure that is to be applied as a requirement document in a contract, the requirements clauses of this procedure are an effective communication to prospective suppliers of what the customer considers necessary in the way of design and development controls. It will communicate, for example, that the customer intends to participate in formal design review meetings toward the end of the design phase as a means of gaining confidence that the operational requirements of the product are being met. Also, the customer can use this procedure to communicate the range of things which will be assessed by a quality assurance representative prior to or concurrent with the assigning of a contract.

The requirements of this procedure prescribe *what* is required without implying the specific dimensions, scope, or kind, and even the *what* is modified by the fact that some design activities do not need specific capabilities which may be essential in the design of other products. It is the duty of the manager of a design and development activity to acquire and apply the staff and facilities, as well as tools, which are adequate to the work that is to be undertaken. It is the work of the assessor to check that the staff, tools, and facilities available to the supplier are adequate for the work the supplier claims he can or will do in the event of being assigned the contract.

This procedure takes the approach that some product is to be designed and developed from first principles, i.e., that there is not now a product in existence or manufactured by the supplier which is closely similar to that being designed. It recognizes that the design is sometimes carried out by one company and then is produced by quite another. In the latter case the product of the contract will be the design, plus any one or more of the design models built by the supplier.

It is assumed that the supplier will use this procedure to help in planning, organizing, and establishing an effective design and development effort. There is no attempt herein to cover basic or pure research, which are allied but different programs. Research activities, both the basic and the pure variety, are far more varied and less well organized than are straightforward design and development efforts. There is, in all new designs, a certain amount of highly original work representing first-time creation. In most designs, however, a very large proportion of the work consists of routine application of good design practices and existing design standards. It is this latter fact which makes it possible to specify in reasonable completeness what is to be done in arriving at some new product containing a new way to assemble, or a new dimension of assembling, the necessary physical principles.

2.1 Assessment of design capabilities. It will be the purpose of the assessors, for there are often more than one, to check that the supplier has the staff, tools, and facilities adequate to the design work that is to be done. In order to do this, it is necessary for the assessment team to contain at least one experienced designer. The team must review the contractual requirements if they have been set down in a quotation or tender schedule containing the requirements of the customer.

The assessment team must make itself familiar with the current status of any manufacturing of products which are similar to the product to be designed and which may be underway. It is from this area that a considerable amount of confidence can be gained, because the supplier has previously designed and developed some product of a similar kind.

Before visiting the supplier's premises, the assessment team should take care to thoroughly familiarize itself with all possible aspects of the work to be done, as well as the nature and status of communications between customer and prospective supplier. Then arrangements with the supplier concerning the dates of arrival and the time period which the assessment is anticipated to cover should be made. It is seldom necessary for an assessment in respect to a single moderately complex product to take more than a week. When it does require more than a week, it is sometimes best to break the assessment into two or more stages or phases. Visits to the supplier's premises should be made, insofar as possible, at times that are convenient to the prospective supplier.

During an assessment of a supplier's design and development capabilities, the assessors converse with supplier managers and staff, read company documents, observe the design work that is going on, examine design support facilities and design tools for their adequacy and currency as to such things as calibration and operational condition. Assessors must routinely seek to verify all oral claims made by the supplier's staff. When there are questionable areas, it is essential that the assessor dig deeply to find the correct answer.

It is essential that assessors report only facts, not opinions. When something appears to be discrepant or questionable, it is to be discussed with the supplier's managers and, after being noted and agreed to, recorded in the assessment record. The assessment shall be thorough.

PART B.   PROCEDURE

Product Design and Development

1   General

1.1 Scope.   This procedure defines the requirements of the company for non-software-type product design and development work done under contract for the company, or by the company for its own purposes.

1.2 Application.   This procedure shall apply in the following cases:

1. When this procedure is called up in a contract.
2. When hardware products are to be designed and developed by the company.
3. When new equipment is to be designed and no alternative quality system is specified.

1.2.1.   When the terms of the contract and the terms of this procedure conflict, the terms of the contract shall prevail.

1.3 Definitions. Definitions of terms used in this procedure shall be those as defined in Sec. VII, Chap. 1 of *Quality Control Systems** unless otherwise stated.

1.4 Referenced documents. The following documents from *Quality Control Systems* are considered to be essential parts of this procedure either when called up in a contract or when the equipment being designed uses the principles of this document.

1. "Software Design and Development," Sec. II, Chap. 2.
2. "Reliability Control," Sec. II, Chap. 4.
3. "Services Design and Development," Sec. II, Chap. 3.

2 Requirements

2.1 Review of operation requirements

2.1.1. The first task to be accomplished when it is recognized that some new product design is required is the preparation of an operational requirements (OR) specification. It is this document, or these documents, that set forth what the new product is to do and the environment in which it is to be done. In many cases the OR specification will also set forth *how* the new product will accomplish its purpose. It is the duty of the customer, or the marketing department of the company, to carry out the research and to prepare the OR specification. In contractual situations, while the customer must prepare the OR document, it is the supplier who must interpret it, and there is always the possibility of error in this activity. Consequently, there is a critical need for both customer and supplier to ensure that the OR stipulations have been effectively communicated and interpreted. In order to accomplish this, there may be a number of stages of this transfer when complex products are involved.

2.1.2. When the customer is a government department, in particular, the military, or a prime contractor to the government, the customer will often feel a need to participate directly with the supplier in the design and development program. This is necessary to ensure effective transfer of information and progress in carrying out the work. As a result, the customer shall define a number of phases of the project, these phases being indexed with some overall and ongoing development program for the larger system in which the product will fit. Such

---

*James R. Taylor, *Quality Control Systems: Procedures for Planning Quality Programs,* McGraw-Hill, New York, 1989.

a system may include aircraft, power stations, harbors, airports, and buildings. In such overall projects which must work together there may be many individual design and development projects. When working in this environment, the design organization must be prepared to accept a succession of project definition inputs, each of which may require a new planning review effort.

2.1.3. In project-type work, the need for changes in the operational requirements of the finished product will sometimes arise. The need may arise at any time during the design and development phase on the part of the supplier. Upon being made aware of necessary changes, the supplier shall conduct a new review and determine the best way to introduce the change to the existing design activity. All such design changes shall be approved by the customer or by the marketing department if for in-house use. Such changes will normally require alteration to both the fiscal and time aspects of the contract. It is essential, however, that they do not alter the product configuration requirements.

2.1.4. The most important aspect of the operational requirements definition and transfer is to ensure that *all* relevant factors have been considered and allowed for in the requirements documentation provided to the supplier. This important aspect can be greatly aided by extensive discussion and review meetings between customer and supplier. The more staff from each organization involved in these communication interchanges the less likely that necessary factors will remain unconsidered.

2.1.5. There are many factors which must be considered and included in the OR documentation; some of them are reliability, availability, maintainability, and testability. Each such OR shall be communicated in sufficient depth to make it fully effective. The supplier shall be made aware of such matters as the numbers of staff and their skills who will be provided by the customer to carry out maintenance, any economic order quantity plans that will affect spares stocking plans or other matters affecting the contract. The customer shall ensure that the supplier is made aware of all necessary information on such policy matters as spares stocking levels, repair turnaround times, operational readiness times, etc.

2.2   Design and development planning

2.2.1. A documented review of design and development needs as they relate to the work to be done shall be made as early as is practicable. When the work is to be done under contract, the planning review shall be carried out with direct relevance to the specific stipulations and clauses of the contract and any referenced documentation or other source information. The review shall be followed by detailed planning on ways and means to satisfy the needs as expressed by the customer or potential customer.

2.2.2. Supplementary reviews for planning refinement purposes shall be held as the needs become clearer and the availability of ways and means for satisfying the needs are known. Included in these plans shall be the supplier's system for quality control of design and development. When the design contract calls for product development as the final contract phase and the item developed is the item to be delivered, along with the design, each necessary activity and control required for bringing the product into being shall be the subject of a part of the planning review. All activities which are considered necessary shall be reviewed at the planning stage to identify needs and to assure that the needs are satisfied.

2.2.3. One of the main objectives of planning is to identify new or special requirements which must be satisfied in order to assure a successful design and development effort. These may involve the acquisition of advanced facilities, new academic disciplines, unique measuring instrumentation, or more powerful computing equipment. Almost always it will be necessary to identify unique points of measurement and review. The need to record design and development events and actions as the work progresses must be a consideration during the planning activity.

2.2.4. The planning committee shall, as a particular requirement, review the various parts of this procedure and anticipate the needs which will be required in order to comply with the various demands and requirements set forth there. This review must cover the communications from the customer or by the marketing department when the requirement develops in-house. It may be that the customer or marketing department has inadequately, ambiguously, or too stringently specified requirements. It is during the planning exercise that the supplier's design staff must study the stated requirements to ensure that such specification deficiencies are resolved before the work of design is begun. Plans shall provide for detection and removal of errors in data regardless of where the errors originate.

2.3 Design organization

2.3.1. The carrying out of design and development work requires the availability of a unique assembly of people, facilities, and organization within which the assembly can operate to produce the best-quality design. The mix of staff skills and experience, the range of support facilities, and the harmonious working environment with an adequate reward matrix are important factors in making the design organization effective. Formation of the above factors into a harmoniously interacting efficient organization is the task of the supplier's design management.

2.3.2.   Once the requirements of the product to be designed are known, management may review the existing organization to identify its strengths and weaknesses in respect to the needs expressed in the operational requirements documentation. It becomes the task of design management to augment the existing capabilities of the organization as necessary to ensure successful outcome of the design and development effort. The planning review discussed in an earlier section shall identify needs when they exist. It shall also identify areas where there may exist resources which will not be needed for this new task, and those resources can be assigned to other work.

2.3.3.   Design work is normally composed of a major percentage of what we may call routine work, there being a lesser amount of creative capacity required in most design work. The job of designing most new products that are similar to earlier models becomes one of routinely reviewing individual aspects of the new product and, by use of design guides, design standards, and standard components lists, carrying out the necessary calculations, locating and specifying the appropriate components and methods of assembling them and testing and recording results. It is when the range of first-time requirements must be extended to give the product capabilities that are greater than or different from those of the competition that the need for fresh new skills or innovative use of existing skills is required. It is the task of design management to ascertain the mix of such skills and creative abilities that is required and to provide it. Then appropriate delegations of work must be made to ensure continuing harmony of relationships, along with appropriate rewards for work well done.

2.3.4.   The quality of design work will be directly proportional to the effectiveness of the organization, among other factors. The nature, scope, content, and objectives of the design work shall be organized to meet prescribed design goals. The nature of design staff required to meet the goals demands flexibility in the organization to accommodate a variety of intellects and personalities. These factors shall be a feature of the design organization.

2.3.5. Design work is not solely conceptual and laboratory-oriented, supported by calculations and logic; there is need for data generation and documentation as well. The design disclosure requirements of the customer shall be provided for in the organization of the work involved. This will require keeping records throughout the design work as it progresses toward completion. The usual output from a design organization, prior to product development, comprises drawings, parts lists, software programs, and specifications which document and communicate the design. The supplier management shall allow for these in organizing for design.

2.4   Design management and control

2.4.1. The production of designs having quality acceptable in the high-technology environment of modern business requires management to satisfy three basic requirements:

1. The acquisition and assignment of competent, highly trained, and skilled staff possessing the appropriate mix of academic training and skills gained through experience.
2. The provision and allocation of appropriate support facilities having the ranges, accuracies, and technical capabilities needed for the type of design work to be done.
3. The creation of an effective organization within which the staff may work and make most effective use of the support facilities in carrying out their design and development work.

2.4.2. The supplier can have in his or her organization what appears on paper to be an excellently qualified design organization, but qualifications on paper, though important, are not sufficient in themselves. The best possible way to ascertain whether a company has a good design team is to examine past performance. When a team has turned out some comparably complex products of the same category that have performed well, it is difficult to find more suitable evidence. If such evidence exists, it shall be made available, when appropriate, to the representative of the customer.

2.4.3. As was mentioned above, design work is of two general types. The first type requires a creative insight to the particular need which often goes beyond logic and is capable of producing concepts that reach to the core of the problem. The second type of design work is pragmatic, methodical, and detailed, and it covers all relevant factors and eliminates all uncertainties from the design. The two types of work, when applied in suitable proportions, will most often produce designs which will prove successful and manufacturable. Often the individual with the creative insight needs someone with the methodical detailed approach to provide logical justification for the new idea and turn it into a practical working design. It is important that the design teams have both types of people.

2.4.4. The supplier shall have a design organization with supporting facilities consistent with the type of design work involved. Design of single items of a simplistic nature or narrow range can be accomplished with a small team of people. When, however, the need is for highly complex and sophisticated designs of products or the range of design criteria is considerable and/or the product types to be designed are numerous, there is need for a large organization indeed, one with skills and experience duplicated over and over. The supplier shall take cognizance of these requirements and satisfy them as appropriate.

2.4.5. The ability of people to work together toward common goals in a concerted manner as a team is essential in design and development work. This requirement shall be an objective of the managers of this work. Given goodwill and intelligent harmonious cooperation between the members of a design team, almost any such team can produce good designs. Without such goodwill and harmony between members, no amount of organization rearrangement and adjustment of work is likely to overcome the difficulties. The position of the design manager and his staff in the overall corporate organization and the delegated responsibilities, authorities, and opportunities must be of appropriate magnitude and scope to engender the output of good design and development work.

2.4.6. It shall be a recognized duty of each and every member of the design and development organization to constantly recognize his or her responsibility for quality and to seek to achieve quality in all design and development work. The most senior person, organizationally, in the design team shall be directly responsible for all design work and its output. In large organizations, the chief designer on subteams shall take responsibility for the quality of output from his or her component of the overall organization. The head of the design and development team shall be responsible for quality control of the total work involved. The quality assurance manager of the corporation shall provide the quality systems and associated documentation needed by the design and development team. The two organizational managers, the quality assurance manager and the design and development manager, shall report in parallel to the senior management or chief executive officer (CEO) of the company, who shall carry the ultimate responsibility for quality of work done.

2.4.7. Delegation of organizational responsibilities, and the levels and scope of managerial work, shall be within the recognized capacities and in accordance with the accepted principles of industrial organization. To that end, the design managers shall have no more than seven (7) subordinates reporting to the head of each design unit. The quality assurance manager shall, in respect to the design effort, provide such specialized services as are uniquely available from the quality assurance team. They include operational quality–related procedures, which may comprise statistical analyses, reliability testing and analysis, specialized performance testing, calibration services, testability design guidance, environmental testing, and special training in quality control techniques. The quality assurance organization, being a company-wide activity, shall provide coordination for the design activity with the remainder of the company on quality matters. Such functions as standardization, reliability, testability, maintainability, safety and quality control, as well as liability, shall be coordinated with each other and with the design effort to ensure achievement of the required performance.

  To that end the quality assurance organization shall provide a quality manual for the company which shall extend to and include the related activities of the design organization on quality. A quality plan shall be prepared by the quality assurance organization for each contract or major work effort. It shall include the quality control activities considered essential from the design and development organization. At the direction of the CEO, the design manager shall monitor the quality control efforts of his or her organization and the quality assurance manager shall provide a quality audit of the essential quality and reliability activities of the design and development work.

2.4.8. Support facilities for design and development work are essential to the successful outcome of this effort. They include such diverse things as site and surroundings of buildings, pleasant working conditions within the buildings, adequate access to resources such as materials, materials science and research, components, academic facilities, and testing and conditioning facilities to evaluate the products of the design effort at the various stages where concepts and trials are most suitably assessed. Modern computing facilities with appropriate graphic capabilities for computer-aided design are essential to efficient use of technical skills in design work. When an adequate range of supporting facilities is available, the manner in which the facilities are controlled and made available to the staff can have a marked effect on the quality of life and hence quality of work of the design staff. It shall therefore be a requirement of the design and development work that the management of both the human and material support resources shall be made a prime consideration of all corporate managers from the CEO down.

The design and development work must not, however, be permitted to develop into a country club type of activity. Such techniques as networking and critical path analysis shall be used to ensure that an ongoing and productive atmosphere is engendered at all times. Where, as in small companies, these capabilities do not exist, periodic reviews of progress, and other appropriate management techniques, shall be used to ensure that time objectives will be met.

2.5   Design documentation and disclosure

2.5.1.   In addition to the supporting documentation from several areas, which include standards, design guides, quality plans, software support programs, reference books, and tables, the design and development team will produce a considerable amount of information and data from its efforts.

There are a number of compelling reasons why information and data generated during the course of bringing some new product design into being shall be preserved, and when appropriate, made available to the customer as well as other staff in the designer's corporate organization. The principal reasons why design information needs to be recorded and preserved throughout the course of the design work are the following:

1. To provide objective evidence that the design meets the design objectives and operational requirements.
2. To provide adequate information with which to effectively advance the design into production with the required quality and reliability and then into use by the customer.
3. To provide design information with which to make any design changes which may become necessary during the course of production and allow for equipment modification and maintenance growth during use as necessary without altering the basic design principles.

2.5.2.   Disclosure of design information is the responsibility of the organization or company doing the design work, though the customer may, through contractual clauses, place an obligation on the design organization to reveal information for which he has paid. Income-expansion expenditures in the area of design and development are a most profitable form of expenditure for companies, and the ownership of original and creative work results is a matter for contractual agreement prior to beginning the work. Disclosure by a design employee carrying out design work must be complete to the employer, but disclosure to the customer shall be in accordance with agreements made in a contract. It may range from no disclosure at all to total disclosure.

Usually any original or new information deemed to be profitable will be patented or copyrighted to preserve ownership and control. Items of such information are called industrial properties, and they are subject to being sold or traded in the marketplace or preserved and developed and produced for sale in the marketplace. The design manager shall ascertain what type of data and information is appropriate to record and keep and the form in which it shall be preserved in order to meet normal accepted legal requirements in such matters. Design data and information shall be recorded in bound notebooks or other prescribed forms, and it shall be signed, witnessed, and dated in accordance with the legal requirements necessary to demonstrate origin, ownership, and date of creation.

2.5.3. Design data and information compiled and maintained shall include design assumptions, the results of brainstorming or ideation meetings, details of mathematical calculations, software program development records (including debugging copies), sketches, drawings, work instructions, test instrument adjustments, and readings for collection of data about the design as it progresses toward completion. Of particular importance, and comprising results to be kept, are the results obtained from tests and trials. Decisions made about the choice of alternatives, why decisions were made, and minutes from such meetings shall be kept as part of the design records. Documentation necessary to the understanding of other information in the design disclosure package shall also be kept as part of the design records. All information necessary for the preparation of maintenance and operators manuals shall be kept and made available for that purpose.

2.5.4. When the contract between supplier and customer is considered complete with the transfer of the results of the design effort plus any development models which may have been required, it is important to ensure that sufficient information to permit another company to manufacture the product is prepared, preserved, and transferred. The content of such a design transfer package shall include, among other things:

1. Essential aspects of the theory and analysis of the design

2. Test specifications and reports of any test results obtained

3. Detailed records of the design, including software programs, specifications, drawings, parts lists, and control drawings

4. Installation and maintenance information

5. Any specialized test procedures, alignment instructions, and diagnostic procedures necessary to the working and use of the product

6. Life cycle cost analyses depicting the relationship between design and production on the one hand and installation and maintenance throughout life on the other

2.5.5. Though the information called for in this article is not delivered until the completion of the design effort, it is included here to provide for better generation and preservation of all needed information and data. As part of the design retrievability requirement, the design and development organization shall establish and maintain a drawing number control system which is downward compatible. By this is meant that documents with higher revision states shall be traceable to the earlier changes and their reasons appearing on the lower revision states. The drawing projection angle shall be that which is in prevalent use in the nation where the design organization is located, unless stated otherwise in the contract.

2.6 Design quality requirements

2.6.1 Value and cost of quality. Each aspect, material, and component used to make up the finished product contributes some value of quality to the product at an identifiable cost of quality. It shall be an objective of the design and development organization to adjust the value of quality to the value corresponding to the cost which the customer is willing to pay. In order to realize the planned value of quality in the product when being produced, it is necessary that the designer plan for and ensure that the product will have the characteristics necessary for manufacturability. Since the relation between value of quality and cost of quality can be used to maximize profit for the producer, it shall be a direct responsibility of both the manager of the design organization and the assessor to ascertain that the value of quality designed into the product is consistent with the operational requirements specification.

2.6.2 Quality information. Since the quality of a product is the ability to satisfy the user at any time throughout the product's lifetime, we find quality information coming from all phases of design and development, production, installation, use, and maintenance. The quality information which is available from the design and development activity is of prime importance in ensuring that the product, when made in full conformance with the design, will possess maximum designed quality.

There are two views of quality in products. The most common in manufacturing industry is what is called quality of conformance, meaning the degree to which the product when finished, conforms to the design. The other, and the one which we are discussing here, is the broader term, meaning quality of product, or the capability of the product to satisfy the customer's need in all situations. Quality information has, or quality data have, three major aspects.

2.6.2.1 Design quality control data. These data are generated during the design phase. They comprise all the records of value of quality vs. cost of quality considered during the design action, as well as all quality data needed to provide objective evidence that the design work was under control and that it produced a design which had characteristics meeting the manufacturability and operational requirements.

2.6.2.2 Reliability and maintainability quality information. This information shall be recorded and provided to the customer when required. It shall comprise, as a minimum, the data from reliability determinations, including tests and calculations, as well as all maintainability data from design. The designers shall have access to and make use of reliability and maintainability data from earlier designs of similar products, especially when similarity comparisons are used to claim reliability for the product.

2.6.2.3 Defect reporting and analysis. Defect reporting and analysis shall be used to provide quality information to the designers about production of similar products, as well as defects which occur during use of those similar products by customers. Quality information on operational fitness for use concerning products which are similar to the product being designed shall be collected, analyzed, and made available to the designers. When such information is possessed by the customer, it shall be made available to the design organization for use in the design work.

2.6.3 Materials and components quality. Quality control of the design work shall include paying due attention to the selection of materials and components, as well as the methods used to join them into complete assemblies which will become part of the designed product. All raw materials chosen and all components specified for the product shall have known characteristics and behavior patterns under the operational requirements profiles of the final product. Methods chosen for processing the materials and components and joining them together shall meet the operational requirements specification and, when not specified, support the requirement for such operational capabilities.

2.6.4 Calibration of measuring instruments and devices. All measuring instruments and devices used in the course of the design work shall be used only within their specified calibration time intervals and shall produce results of known accuracy. Only certified reference materials from accredited laboratories and with known characteristics shall be used. Extrapolations of range or accuracy shall not be used in the design work, and all measuring instruments shall be used within their calibrated ranges and accuracies when determining product design characteristic values.

2.6.5 Quality of development. Development work and design changes made as a result of discoveries during development and testing shall be evaluated within the framework of the overall design objectives. It shall be a requirement of the design work that no change to the evolving design is authorized or made unless due consideration is given to both reliability and value of quality. Design changes made following early design reviews shall be examined for their effect in respect to those reviews. All such changes authorized and made shall be recorded in sufficient detail to communicate both the reason for the changes and the nature and degree of success achieved by the changes relative to operational requirements. All measurements made on a product to obtain data which will be used to specify the product and determine its reliability and operational capability during development shall meet the above requirements.

2.6.6 Standard practices. The design team shall, to the maximum extent practicable, have available and make use of standard design practices. Design guides that make use of the considerable body of knowledge which has been accumulated in all fields of materials and components shall be made available to the design team. These guides shall, to the maximum extent appropriate to the design concerned, be used by the design team to ensure:

1. Proper mounting and relative positions of components
2. Proper application of materials

3. Control of characteristic values within established ranges of operation

4. Positioning of characteristic values between known limits

5. Proper allowance for known material and component interaction parameters

6. Design of system characteristics to operate within transport and operational physical environmental exposure limits

7. Control of trade-off situations when it is necessary to give up desirable limit conditions in one area to obtain necessary operational performance in another

2.7   Design standards and guides

2.7.1   Physical standards.   Physical standards are used in design work in two principal ways: (1) for the identification of materials by comparison or for the determination of the purity of materials by analysis and (2) for calibration of unknown values and readings of instruments or devices by comparison. All too often, the instrumentation used in design work is not included within the metrological recall and calibration system of companies, making all measurements made on that instrumentation suspect. The result is that the product cannot be controlled during production, and it may not meet operational requirements.

2.7.2   Documented standards.   A wide range of documented standards is used in design work. The standards, typically prepared by the nation's standards-writing bodies, by standards-writing bodies in the industry concerned, or by one of the international standards-writing bodies, are used for many purposes. They shall be used as appropriate to specify the tests to be carried out on the things being designed. To the extent possible, the national standards, and other such documents available to customers and other sections of industry, will serve to increase the testability of the product. To the extent that they exist, standards derived by the designer's organization from earlier work in the field shall be used in the design work.

Prevention of the development of "variety" in respect to the product being designed is necessary to contain costs, assure greater maintainability and interchangeability, and provide for consistency of quality control in production and interpretation of quality information. Standardization shall be used to save time in the maximum number of areas associated with the designed product. Those areas include, but are not limited to, development, production, training, maintenance, logistics, and costing.

2.7.3 Certified reference materials. The tests of the designed and developed product specified to be conducted shall, when practicable, make use of certified reference materials which have been supplied by reliable national or other specified laboratories. Unknown reference materials shall not be used or specified for use in respect to the design. When reference materials are specified either they shall be independent of the method of test or the test method shall be specified.

2.7.4 Design guides. It is normal for experience, and prior test results as well as prior information from similar products, to be assembled into books which set forth both good and bad practices. These guides shall be used to assist in ensuring that only known good practices are used and incorporated into the design of the product.

2.8 Reliability requirements

2.8.1 Modeling. When available or, if not available, to the extent practicable under the contract or within the design project plans, the reliability of the product shall be modeled in mathematical form to ensure that all operational requirements in respect to reliability are given due consideration. Any mathematical calculations of reliability based on the mathematical model and drawing upon the reliability claims of component and material suppliers shall have their basis of calculation stated. Results of calculations of product reliability using data from the product finally developed shall be in agreement with the operational requirements for the product.

2.8.2 Testing. Reliability testing shall be in accordance with documented test specifications. Success-failure determinations shall be in accordance with the operational requirements stated in the product performance specifications. Results from reliability tests shall be evaluated in terms of the reliability definition: "the ability of an item to perform a required function under stated conditions for a stated period of time."

Since high reliability is normally expensive, the designer shall examine the operational requirements specifications for incompatible stresses of greater magnitude than can be justified in comparison with other operational considerations and shall call any that are found to the attention of the customer or marketing department. Compatible stressing conditions shall be used. Costs of reliability shall be minimized by matching known strengths of materials and components to known stresses in all areas.

The results of the reliability testing or calculations shall be provided in the form of expected reliability of the product. Such results shall contain a confidence level statement expressing the range or interval over which the statement is true. To aid in the interpretation of reliability statements, the designer shall state the manner and conditions under which the results were obtained.

Reliability, like other aspects of quality of which it is one subset, has its sources in three areas: operational concepts, design, and production. Each of these contributes to the ultimate degree to which the product is able to perform its required function under stated conditions for the stated period of time. Due consideration shall be given to the reliability requirements for the product when choosing configuration concepts and modes of operation. Reliability requirements shall be used in determining which materials and components to use. Workmanship and operational process capabilities shall be determined and controlled during production consistently with reliability requirements.

2.8.3 Availability. Availability is the combination of reliability and maintainability. When the product is not of the throwaway type, it shall be maintainable and the appropriate tools, test equipment, and instruction manuals shall be provided as part of the design and production effort. Availability considerations shall be of prime importance when the maintainability aspects to be designed into the product are being determined.

When, during design, maintainability is traded for reliability, due consideration shall be given to the costs to the user during product life; when those costs are unacceptable, the trade-offs shall not be made. The customer, or marketing department, shall contribute to the decision which determines the appropriate trade-offs in this area.

2.8.4 The failure pattern. Most products have failure patterns of the bathtub type: The failure rate begins high, drops rapidly to flatten out during a random failure period, and increases during what is called the wear-out period. The first two phases are called the wear-in or infant mortality period and the random failure period. Infant mortality is due to a lack of quality control during production of either the product or the materials or components of which the product is made.

The above statement assumes that the design is adequate and that product strengths are not exceeded by environmental stresses. The random failures occur because of the variability of strengths in properly produced items or the variability of stresses imposed by the varying environment. Such failures can occur when the statistical distributions of stress and strength overlap because of design errors or limitations. It shall be a prime aim of reliability testing to derive knowledge about the strengths of the product and the stresses of the environment and to ensure that the characteristics of the product failure pattern are consistent with the operational requirements specifications.

2.8.5 Reliability in design. Part of the quality plan for the design and development project shall be a reliability plan. It shall seek to concentrate the design effort on methods, materials, and practices known to be unreliable. Areas of known weakness shall be examined in detail, and the dimensions and characteristics chosen shall be compatible with what is known about the environmental stresses to which the product will be subjected. In value engineering, particular care shall be taken not to unacceptably reduce the product strengths.

2.8.6 The reliability program. Reliability modeling shall be used to identify the weaker areas where component or material change or redesign should take place. If appropriate, passive or active redundancy shall be used to meet reliability requirements. After introducing such changes, the model shall be adjusted and the effects of the changes to the product shall be evaluated.

At an early stage the relative reliability of components, subassemblies and modules shall be estimated, and the estimates shall be used to design the reliability test program. When practicable, the total reliability shall be so divided between the components and subassemblies as to eliminate any critically weak members of the system and distribute the strengths in accordance with the stresses anticipated in use.

A criticality analysis of the product system shall be made by using failure mode and effect information. A comparison of failure modes and the effects they will have on operational requirements for the product shall also be made. The reliability test program shall be concentrated on the areas of doubtful strength-stress relationship and on the failure modes which appear to be incompatible with the operational requirements.

When required, the reliability growth to be anticipated during maintenance life shall be predicted. If such calculations are made, the assumptions as to degree of part replacement vs. failure cause removal, and other interpretive aids, shall be stated. To the maximum practical extent, standard known parts shall be designed into the product. New and unknown materials and components shall be used only after extensive testing and evaluation have defined their reliabilities and strengths relative to stress under use.

The reliability of the product shall be expressed in terms that are required by the contract or are applicable to the operational requirements.

2.9   Designing for safety

2.9.1   Safety aspects in design.   There are two major aspects of safety with which the design and development activity is concerned:

1. The safety of the people who must work with the product when producing it and of the people who must use the product. The motivations for safety control are both moral and legal.
2. The safety of people whose skills and knowledge are important to the overall activity and whose well-being must be preserved for economic reasons, as well as moral and legal ones.

The design and development manager and staff are concerned with both reasons to maintain safety. Safety goes beyond protection of people; it includes damage or potential damage to property as well. Safety in respect to the designed product shall be considered the responsibility of the designer.

2.9.2   The safety plan.   The design and development manager shall prepare and implement a safety plan for the design and development program. The elements of the plan shall be coordinated with other work on the product during design and development. The plan shall clearly establish responsibilities and assign them to the various staff members, who shall be responsible for seeing that they are carried out.

2.9.3   The safety program.   The safety program consists of carrying out the safety plan, and it has three distinct stages: prediction, control, and verification. Normally there will already be safety procedures which apply to staff involved in design and development work. These procedures shall apply to their fullest extent, and procedures unique to the new product work shall be applied only when it has been determined that they are essential. Whenever possible, standard safety procedures drawn from existing safety manuals shall be used.

2.9.4   Work environment and product safety.   The staff involved in design and development work will be involved in two ongoing safety programs at the same time. Those programs involve the need to be aware of and obey the safety requirements for work of the kind underway in the area. They also involve the ongoing need to design into the evolving product all the characteristics and controls which will make it possible for the product to be used safely after being produced in a safe manner. Standard procedures and methods shall be applied in situations of both types to the maximum extent possible.

2.9.5 Reliability testing and safety. The reliability testing program shall be used to derive information on what safety factors are most important from a failure standpoint. Failure modes will identify the most likely reasons for injury, if any, if the product should fail in use. Special design and development measures shall be used to ensure that the product is made safe to use even under failure conditions.

2.9.6 Potential hazards. The following are some common hazards to those responsible for using or being around the product:

- Radiation (nuclear and electromagnetic)
- Weight (when heavy parts must be moved by hand)
- Noise (including supersonic and subsonic)
- Poison (when poisonous gases or materials are present or generated during use)
- Sharp points and edges
- Moving parts
- Human error in use or operation
- Fire, heat, and fumes
- Explosion and shock (e.g., shock from collision)
- Toxic and corrosive gases, fumes, or liquids (which may become suddenly exposed through container rupture)
- Biological hazards (viral, bacterial, fungal)

The designer shall routinely review the designs for possible existence or development of such hazards and include precautions and means by which the user can be protected from them. All hazards, when confirmed as existing, shall be categorized as to action needed or accepted as needing no action. When it is needed, the defined action shall be taken.

2.9.7 Protection, detection and warning, or acceptance. Once a hazard has been identified as existing and has been categorized, it shall be the subject of design action. This action shall provide protection for the user, provide warning so the hazard may be avoided, result in redesign to remove the hazard, or result in definition of the nonexistence of a hazard. In the latter event, acceptance of the product without correction shall follow.

2.9.8 Safety verification. The third phase of the safety program is verification that all hazards have been eradicated from the design or that warning devices and protective aspects are designed into the system to counteract the existence of the hazards. It shall be a function of the design organization to ensure that all hazards, including those uncovered during reliability testing, shall be eliminated by (1) redesign or (2) the use of detectors and alarms to warn users or shall be reduced by writing special procedures for using the product to avoid injury or property damage.

All hazards shall be eradicated or controlled prior to the final design review. It shall be a responsibility of design management to ensure that all safety precautions are carried forward through production and use of the product.

2.10   Configuration management

2.10.1.   All complex products, and many of the more simple ones, depend on product configuration being correct before the product or products will work or can be used by the customer. Configuration does not mean packaging; rather, it means the way the various parts of the system are assembled so that a functional system is achieved. The more complex systems will work properly only when their various subassemblies and subsystems are configurationally connected and interrelated so that appropriate dependencies and sequences of operation exist. It shall be the responsibility of the design managers to ensure that the proper configuration of the product is defined and documented in the paperwork design. The configuration will be derived from the overall performance requirements and will, in the first instance, derive from the operational requirements specification.

2.10.2.   The quality assurance manager shall ensure that the configuration requirements for the product are met. To that end he or she shall perform inspections and tests against the documented and stipulated requirements. The quality assurance manager shall share with the design manager responsibility for ensuring that the completed design and product have the configurations necessary to carry out the total functions of the product.

2.10.3.   Configuration management shall, when required, continue from the start of the design disclosure package assembly, through the development phase, and into production. To the extent required by the customer, the supplier may be responsible for maintaining configuration definition and control during the use of the product.

2.10.4.   It is an important requirement of configuration management that the supplier, during development of the product, model the paperwork or computer design. Models may take the form of physical mockups, computer simulations, or drawings. By trying the various subassemblies and subsystems in different places and in different interrelations on the mockup model, the supplier can develop the most effective configuration for the product. It is more easily visualized in the model form because the interfaces and component workings can be seen more readily.

To the extent that it is appropriate, modeling shall be used to define the configuration of the product being designed. The design manager shall see to it that configuration management takes place throughout all activities and stages following definition of the configuration.

2.10.5. The designer shall, by being involved in approval of all design changes, ensure that the product configuration is protected throughout production. The design manager shall use configuration management to ensure that all designers working on the design are fully aware of progress at all times so as not to defeat the efforts of colleagues. Configuration management shall be used in assembling the design disclosure package.

2.11 Design for maintenance

2.11.1 The meaning of maintenance. Maintenance means servicing, repairing, rebuilding, reclaiming, taking reliability growth actions, and carrying out any inspection, testing, and classification needed to assess the maintenance activities and place the equipment in a given state of readiness for use after failure. The designer shall be concerned with those activities, and in particular with maintainability.

The designer needs information on the numbers of maintenance staff, amount of downtime and time to repair, and expected life when the information is important to the customer. By using the information, the designer can match the product's reliability and maintainability to the requirements to satisfy the customer's needs. The customer, or the company marketing organization, will normally adopt a maintenance policy. This, too, should be provided to the designer to better ensure the product's compatibility with the requirements of this document.

2.11.2 Repair by replacement, or throwaway. Some products, by the nature of their use or construction, fall into the throwaway category. In particular, components or parts of products are more and more falling into the throwaway group of items. The decreasing availability of skilled maintenance staff, the increasing difficulty of maintenance of high-technology products, the relatively low cost of replacement parts vs. probability of compromising the operational requirements when parts are repaired, all these and more cause an increase in the number of items being thrown away and replaced by new parts or products.

Printed-board assemblies (PBAs) are sometimes more economically thrown away than repaired. Machinery components often wear so badly that, when they are replaced, it is not practical to repair them and new parts must be used. The designer shall take into consideration the repair or maintenance practice to be adopted by the user of the product. Design decisions shall be taken in accordance with this information for each part of the design.

2.11.3 Maintainability. Maintainability is defined as the ease with which maintenance of the product can be carried out within a specified time, under stated conditions, and by using specified procedures. It is normally expressed in either mean time to repair (MTTR), or as a probability. The customer or marketing department shall provide the maintenance policy in the operational requirement documents. The designer shall have as one of the design objectives that the product will meet the maintainability requirements.

2.11.4 Maintenance spares. The spares stocking policy of the user of products, or of the company which maintains the products, will have to be derived from the anticipated reliability of the product and the MTTR. The designer shall provide sufficient information to the customer or user to enable appropriate decisions about the level of spares stocking to be made.

2.11.5 Maintenance manuals. When so specified in the contract, the design organization shall, as a part of the design program or other requirements documentation, provide maintenance manuals that tell the maintenance technician the correct procedures by which to analyze faulty products and systems and the correct sequences to use in disassembling, repairing, and reassembling the equipment. Based on the reliability program, the designer shall provide information on the more likely failure modes and causes.

2.12 Value engineering requirements

2.12.1 Life cycle cost. Value engineering is an organized program by which operational requirements can be met while providing the lowest life cycle cost. It is one method by which the value of quality can be adjusted to be met at the lowest compatible cost of quality. Its principles are applied only when they can provide effective improvements in cost of quality without lowering the value of quality.

The cost of quality which is to be decreased by value engineering shall be the life cycle cost, i.e., the costs of design, development, production, installation, and maintenance and service throughout life.

2.12.2 Assessment by function. A product shall be value-engineered by reducing the cost of the product's functions rather than the cost of individual parts. The value engineering team shall concentrate on the functions of the product one at a time and seek to maintain the function while reducing the cost of achieving it at the same quality level. When the product has more than one function, its functions shall be grouped by the several things it is expected to do when in use. Each group of functions shall be treated individually for cost reduction in this way.

2.12.3 The value engineering plan. Value engineering shall not be carried out on a product during the design activity used to establish the reliability, and great care shall be used in introducing changes to a product that has had its reliability established. Some changes that appear to be necessary to reduce the cost of quality as a result of value engineering can alter the reliability of the product. The design organization shall assure that a product which has been value-engineered has not had its reliability reduced by any changes made. When considered necessary, additional reliability tests shall be made following the value engineering changes and prior to introducing the product to the production phase.

2.13 Design reviews

2.13.1 Design reviews: when held and who participates. In the course of progress toward the completed design, the design manager shall hold design reviews from time to time. These design reviews may have any degree of formality, but all conclusions upon which action will be taken shall be documented as part of the design disclosure package if the customer should so decide. A design review shall be conducted as a formal, documented, and systematic study of the design by designers, management, and users, including specialists who must provide for production, quality assurance, maintenance, and other essential activities not directly part of the design process.

Initially, while the design process is still underway, design reviews need only involve the members of the design team. As the design progresses toward completion, design reviews shall be held when contributions may be made by each organization which has a major part to play in later production, quality assurance, installation, or maintenance activities. The designers shall receive and act on inputs from other organization specialists participating in design reviews with a view to making any necessary design adjustments necessary to satisfy specific needs. All design reviews shall have been completed prior to freezing design and putting the product into production.

2.13.2 The purpose of design reviews.   The design review shall be held with a view to bringing out any conflicts of opinion or judgment which may bring into the open design aspects capable of adversely affecting subsequent activities, including use. The purpose of a design review is to undertake an objective evaluation of the design for preventive purposes. The designer shall, as a result of design reviews, seek to prevent the product from failing to satisfy any of the essential needs that become evident from later work on it.

Conflicts in the requirements of the diverse participants in a design review shall be resolved by the design manager, who remains in charge of the design until the product has entered production. During a design review, each participant shall be given an opportunity to review and discuss all aspects of the product which may affect that participant's area. Junior staff may attend design reviews as an appropriate part of their training.

2.13.3 Design review progress.   Preliminary design reviews shall be held to ascertain that all necessary activities have been planned for in the total design program. Other preliminary reviews of an ad hoc nature shall be held as appropriate to choose the best alternative from among those available.

Design reviews shall be held during the intermediate stages of the design and development work to ensure that the best possible product design characteristics are being chosen and to pass along to those in production information for long-time procurement actions.

One or more design reviews shall be held as the design nears or reaches completion. The final review shall confirm that the design meets the operational requirements specification. It shall be on the basis of a successful final design review that drawing freeze takes place, when production is to begin.

2.14 Change control management

2.14.1 The role of the designer in change control.   An efficient design disclosure system is an essential prerequisite for an effective change control program involving a new product design. As the design progresses toward completion, the design disclosure package of information about the product and its capabilities grows. It is essential to protect the configuration of the product from change. The design disclosure system will define the product configuration which must exist as the design proceeds toward completion. The design manager shall, through the designers, control the design configuration at each stage of design work.

2.14.2. The operational requirements specification for a product will be best satisfied by one specific product design configuration the materials and components of which are those the current manufacturing industry of the world is capable of producing with reliability. It is the task of the design team, under the control of the design manager, to find that particular product configuration, and to express it in documented form. The next step is to achieve the product in model form, i.e., a prototype, for mass production or the finished product when only a few units are to be built.

2.14.3. Designers find it necessary to be able to make frequent changes to the product as it is progressively brought into being. For that reason the optimal configuration cannot be limited to one structure and composition. We say, therefore, that the designers practice *configuration management*. When the product is released for manufacture, it becomes necessary to ensure that the product configuration does not change from that reached in design. Here we say the production manager (and quality assurance manager) must practice *configuration control*. The design team shall so express the product configuration in the design documentation that the product can be manufactured from available supplies and meet that configuration.

2.14.4. During the design phase, it is necessary to bring into being not only the product modules but also the interfaces that join the modules together into the finished system. The design team shall clearly define in the product specifications the various module interfaces and their workings. They shall be managed effectively for achievement of optimum configuration.

2.14.5. When the design effort involves more than one design office or the design team includes more than one design unit, a formal procedure for configuration management shall be prepared and promulgated to all designers. Designers shall rigorously follow the design configuration management procedure; and as a vehicle for such management, they shall maintain their design disclosure activity by routinely recording in prescribed documented form all calculations, material inspection and test data, component and subassembly criteria and dimensions, and any other decisions and results which are necessary to achieve fully documented design disclosure. Changes to previous decisions shall always be disclosed in documented form and noted as such, with reference to previous relevant data and conclusions.

2.15   Subcontractor control

2.15.1.   The supplier shall establish control over all subcontractors by extending through contracts all necessary design disclosure procedures, configuration management procedures, operational requirements, and any other such controls and objectives necessary to ensure successful completion of the design effort.

2.15.2.   The supplier shall, during the planning stage, have identified the areas of the design and development work that will require the use of subcontractors. In each case in which a subcontractor is used, the supplier shall prepare detailed statements of requirements and thereby integrate the efforts of each subcontractor into the total design and development effort. These planned actions applicable to each subcontractor shall be a part of any contract with that subcontractor.

2.15.3.   All subcontracted work shall be assessed by the supplier and shall be the responsibility of the supplier. Such work shall be compatible with and form part of the design disclosure and shall have its aspects of configuration managed within the overall configuration management program.

2.16   Trials and testing

2.16.1   The three categories of trial.   Most design projects involving design and development will require three general categories of trial and testing:

1. Feasibility testing carried out during the early stages of the design project to choose the best of several alternatives.
2. Design model and prototype testing of models constructed during the course of design and development to establish that performance, maintainability, and other stipulated requirements are being met.
3. Product evaluation testing shall be performed and is concerned with three aspects: performance, reliability, and environment.

Each of these three general categories of tests shall be conducted in a depth sufficient to assure that all relevant parts of the operational requirements are being met by the product design.

2.16.2   The designer's involvement in trials.   The designer shall be intimately involved with the quality assurance organization in the test program intended to assess or evaluate the part of the design with which each is concerned. He or she shall help design the tests and shall ensure that the stresses applied to the product are within the strength limits of the product. The designer shall be provided with the results of all tests carried out on the product which he or she has designed. The reliability test staff shall ensure that testing of products which are to be shipped to the customer do not "use" more than an agreed to or acceptable portion of the product's life during the time and stress of the tests.

2.17   Software control and integration

2.17.1.   When, in the product being designed, software or the logic-controlling form of software called firmware is essential to the successful performance of the end product, it shall be a fundamental responsibility of the supplier to establish and maintain control over such firmware and software whether purchased separately from the hardware or not and to maintain control during integration of software with hardware.

2.17.2.   Software shall be designed and developed in accordance with Sect. II, Chap. 2 of *Quality Control Systems:* "Software Design and Development."

2.17.3.   Many errors can enter the software, when it is designed and developed separately from hardware design and development, in bringing into being a total product. Much paperwork and magnetic memory device material requires reproduction and integration with the microprocessor-controlled systems of hardware. Errors entering through the production and integration phases can nullify much of the effectiveness obtained from the design and development of the software. It shall be a fundamental responsibility of the supplier to achieve and maintain control over the reproduction, embedding, integration, or other work needed to make the combining of software and hardware totally effective. The outcome shall meet the full stipulations of the operational requirements specifications.

2.17.4   Software and product design verification.   The product design model from the final prototype stage shall be tested, and the tests shall be carried out with the software program performing its intended control or other purpose. In such tests, the product shall satisfy the full operational requirements specification provided for the product. The quality assurance organization shall conduct the final product qualification tests, with the participation of the design organization. It shall be a fundamental responsibility of the supplier to ensure that the final qualification records demonstrate in an objective manner that the product meets all the operational requirements.

2

Software Design and Development Procedure

PART A. REVIEW AND GUIDANCE

1 Review

Bringing into being a new software program, in all its facets and system aspects, is applied research and development work, not production. Production, in respect to software, means the reproduction in quantity of the goods-type products of the output of a software design and development effort. For that reason, some nations, such as Australia, have legislation that defines software as a goods-type product rather than a service item.

It must be clearly understood that, if its preparation is put in the category of production-type work, a new software package or program will suffer serious deficiencies in the planning, visibility, management, and quality control areas. It will also be unsatisfactorily documented, because design documentation may not be seen to be part of the end product in a production situation.

The design and development of software are similar in many respects to the design and development of hardware. Consequently, it can be expected that there will be several areas of similar work, controls, and output.

Software quality, like hardware quality, can be viewed from two perspectives. The first, and all embracing, is expressed by the definition of software quality as the degree to which users perceive the software program to be entirely suitable for its purpose. This definition includes both the design and development work on the one hand and any production work on the other. The more restricted definition covers only the production component: the degree to which the software program and goods containment system conform to specified requirements. Here we are concerned with the broader perspective and embrace the preparation of the software program as a design and development project-type work that results in one usable system which can then be reproduced as many times as desired.

We can define the quality attributes of software programs in quite adequate terms to permit program identification, segregation, and measurement. Software programs possess all the traditional quality attributes such as reliability, maintainability, testability, usability, and expandability. All those attributes are attainable in software programs by placing the preparation of the programs on an engineering science basis rather than on the traditional art-of-programming basis. This requires software design and development to be placed on an industrialized basis with the application of traditional quality assurance methods.

Software quality assurance is a specific engineering discipline closely intertwined with software design and development engineering (sometimes called simply software engineering).

2   Guidance

In various countries, industrial management has experienced an unanticipated and unusually great amount of difficulty in achieving control of bringing software programs into being. Some of the problems encountered have derived from the need to introduce software quality assurance engineers, a specific engineering discipline not normally possessed by software programmers, into the traditionally sacrosanct domain of the designers. Other problems have derived from the historical nature of academia; for many years the great majority of software programmers have come from the faculties of arts and sciences rather than engineering. Then the math and science graduates were placed in the unfamiliar and foreign domains of engineering requiring greater regimen in their daily work.

The problem is one of management, and it is best resolved by the use of the team concept, whereby team-leader-type managers are assigned to integrate the efforts of the multidisciplinary teams of software design and development employees into a cohesive and productive team of creative individuals. Full use must be made of the necessarily independent software quality assurance engineers, who bring to the effort the necessary new discipline and degree of objective assessment and reporting so important for effective management. Integrating software quality assurance engineers and math and science people into a software engineering team and implementing a program of nonconformity prevention and/or removal, while treating the preparation of software programs as design and development work according to the requirements of this procedure, will provide a means of achieving success in software programming.

PART B.   PROCEDURE

Software Design and Development

1   General

1.1   Scope.   This procedure defines the requirements of the company for software design and development work done under contract or within the company. When the work is done within it, the company shall be considered the contractor and the intended user is the customer.

1.2   Application.   This procedure shall apply in the following cases:

1. When it is called up in a contract

2. When software programs are to be prepared by the company for control of hardware

3. When new software program(s) are to be prepared and no alternative standard is specified

1.2.1. When the terms of the contract and the terms of this procedure conflict, the terms of the contract shall prevail.

1.3 Definitions. Definitions of terms used in this procedure shall be those defined in Sec. VII, Chap. 1 of *Quality Control Systems** unless otherwise stated.

1.4 Referenced documents. R. Dunn and R. Ullman, *Quality Assurance for Computer Software,* McGraw-Hill, New York, 1982.

2 Requirements

2.1 Review of operational requirements. There shall be prepared an operational requirements (OR) specification. When the software program is to be prepared under contract by another body, the OR specification shall be prepared by the customer and provided to the contractor at the time of requesting bids or tenders. When the software program is to be prepared by the company, the preparation of the OR specification shall be carried out in the same way as for contract work, and the specification shall be forwarded to the software design and development organization for action.

The OR specification for software programs shall cover, as appropriate, each of the features discussed in the following subarticles.

2.1.1 Size. Software products vary greatly in size; they range from the more complex telecommunications control programs of 500,000 to 1,000,000 words, with a similar quantity for tools, testing, production, and maintenance, on the one hand to relatively insignificant sorting programs requiring no basic computer skills to write a few hundred words on the other. The OR specification shall detail the size of the software product to be delivered.

2.1.2 Scope. Software products are expandable. Additional modules can be added, and new routines and subroutines can greatly increase the size and range of functions. The OR specification shall clearly delineate the scope of software product to be produced under the contract or in the particular situation to which this procedure applies.

---

*James R. Taylor, *Quality Control Systems: Procedures for Planning Quality Programs,* McGraw-Hill, New York, 1989.

2.1.3 Multifunctionality. Software programs may need to satisfy several different functional requirements. For example, a software product for a modern fighter plane would need to control the plane's thermal, hydraulic, navigational, fire control, communications, flight control, and pilot care systems. Financial computer programs must be capable of performing several different financial calculations in discharging all the necessary work of a modern accountancy business. Yet, single-function computer programs are sometimes needed for relatively simple but possible highly important purposes such as security controls. The OR specification shall clearly delineate all the required functions the software program must achieve.

2.1.4 Operational functions. The OR specification shall individually treat each of the operational functions to be provided by the software program. It shall clearly outline each function in complete detail and identify the real-time relevance of any of the functional modes and actions. For example, the sequential nature of operational functions and the blanking, canceling, and enhancing, integration, dependence, and independence, and other mutually interactive natures of the various functions shall be clearly communicated in the OR specification.

2.1.5 Implementation aspects. The OR specification shall clearly and comprehensively delineate the various implementation functions needed to make the software program most useful when applied in the computer control system of the customer. The implementation aspects covered shall include database systems, operating system layers, input/output systems, access modes, etc. When possible, and to the extent applicable, the OR specification shall communicate the range of special disciplines known to be needed to bring the software program into being with greatest overall quality.

2.1.6 Modularity. When the software design and development project encompasses two or more projects or purposes, each requiring unique tailoring to specific user needs, the OR specification shall clearly identify them together with their sizes, scopes, functions, and implementation aspects. Sufficient modular information shall be provided to permit the designed and developed software program to provide for:

1. Improvements of and additions to the software system's functions during system lifetime
2. Different versions of functions to be created for different uses and customers
3. Replacements of or additions to new software packages in the operational system

4. The use of separate compilation techniques

5. Automatic production of software systems from standard methods based on new specifications

6. System development control

2.1.7 Tools, techniques, and methods. The OR specification shall define the use of any specific software development tools, techniques, or methods known to be necessary for carrying the work out successfully. In particular, any techniques or methods known to be unsuitable shall be identified and outlined. Particular tools which must be developed in parallel with software program development will require attention by the contractor, and any requirements in that respect must be clearly communicated in the OR specification.

The contractor, or the organization performing the software design and development, shall, in the absence of an OR specification or to the degree that the specification supplied is found to be unsatisfactory, complete the preparation of an OR specification. This specification shall be submitted to the customer and to any applicable jurisdictional authority for review and approval prior to beginning of software design and development work.

When the contractor or the organization performing the design and development work has an approved OR specification for the project, a thorough and detailed review of the specification shall be undertaken to determine the scope, quantity, quality, and cost of work to be undertaken and carried out in discharging the requirements of the contract. From this review the contractor shall prepare plans for the software design and development work to be performed.

2.2 Design and development planning

2.2.1. The contractor shall undertake, at the earliest practical time, a program to plan for the work, resources, personnel, tools, and other requirements needed to meet the requirements of the contract. The contractor shall plan for the development and implementation of a system of quality control and design and development which will ensure accomplishment of work and conformance with all software requirements of the contract.

2.2.2. Working from the review of the OR specification, the contractor shall prepare a quality control plan which will identify in detail the work breakdown structure that will develop a coherent division of the many work elements into small manageable tasks. The contractor shall then aggregate these elements into roughly contiguous groups of elements or phases.

work elements. Those work elements shall be grouped on the charts into phases or contiguous time intervals in proper sequence.

2.5.2. On the documented quality program each point at which the program routines and subroutines can be profitably tested and evaluated shall be identified and so indicated. Plans shall be made to ensure that the programmers will involve the quality assurance staff in any and all testing of the software work elements, as well as in all nonconformities (errors) detected.

2.5.3. All nonconformities in the program shall be documented. No nonconformities shall be corrected without due regard to any effects, if appropriate, on the software system configuration. In particular, the quality assurance organization shall be notified before any corrective action which can affect the configuration requirements for the system is taken.

2.5.4. The documented quality program for the software product shall identify the appropriate point for formal qualification testing of each module as well as the completed software system.

The quality assurance organization shall participate in, and shall record all nonconformities found in, module and/or system qualification testing. The quality assurance staff shall participate in all decisions concerning corrective action as a result of nonconformities found at qualification tests.

2.6   Management visibility and control

2.6.1. The contractor shall use methods, standards, tools, and training of programming personnel which are conducive to the achievement of quality in software. The contractor shall encourage an orderly development methodology on the part of each software developer, with specific assignment to work on plainly and clearly defined phases of the project.

2.6.2. By the use of quality plans documented to reveal the specific phases and work elements in which the tasks will be performed and with frequent element, phase, and module testing and analysis, the contractor shall maintain management visibility of the software program as progress is made through the entire contractual effort.

2.6.3. The quality assurance organization, in conjunction with software programmers, shall keep management aware of specific targets and goals as each is met and of quality problems encountered. In particular, in the course of contractual work, management shall be informed of any impediments to further work in any direction and of any qualification results obtained.

2.7   Design and development reviews

2.7.1. The contractor shall provide documented procedures by which reviews are to be defined and held to ensure that the software meets the contractual requirements. For a moderately complex software program the following minimum life cycle stages will be identified, and for each of them there shall be a scheduled review. They are:

1. Operational specification phase
2. Software design phase
3. Coding and component testing phase
4. Integration, formal qualification, and release phase

In addition to the above, there is sometimes a maintenance phase, during customer use, for which the contractor remains responsible. When that is the case, the contractor shall plan for and conduct a further review of the maintenance phase.

2.7.2. The software design shall be subject to review by the customer and also by any applicable jurisdictional authority.

2.7.3. Software designs shall be reviewed by the contractor prior to release for coding. The staff carrying out the reviews shall be independent of the software designer.

2.7.4. Documentation and plans for reviews shall cover:

1. A description of the review objectives
2. Identification of the functions of review personnel
3. A statement of the matters to be reviewed for each review held during design and development
4. Provision for recording analyses and recommendations from reviews
5. Methods of ensuring that timely action is taken as a result of recommendations coming from reviews

2.8 Documentation.   Software documentation consists of four princi-pal categories:

1. Operational requirements specification and its supporting docu-mentation detailing functional, environmental, language, and other requirements of the customer or user that are needed to plan and carry out the design, coding, and formal qualification testing
2. Planning and design documentation including flowcharts and de-tailed program requirements
3. The coded program debugged, configured, and qualified
4. Quality assurance documentation giving the result of audits, tests, evaluations, and qualification of the model and program

2.8.1.   The customer shall:

1. Prepare and provide to the contractor, or intending contractor, documentation covering operational requirements for the soft-ware program(s), plus any additional matters required for satis-factory discharge of the contract.
2. Prepare and provide known documentation concerning jurisdic-tional authorities, their areas of concern, and requirements con-cerning the legal or regulatory requirements for the software program.

2.8.2.   The contractor shall:

1. Working from the customer-supplied information, prepare a plan covering the scope of and detailing the work of preparing the software program(s).
2. Identify, and reference in the plan, the documentation standards, coding conventions, practices, and procedures to be used in pro-gressing and accomplishing the programming work.
3. Prepare and document procedures which will provide for break-ing the work down into manageable and testable cells and for management visibility through the quality assurance tests car-ried out as cell tests, module tests, and surveillance of the design and programming work.
4. Prepare and publish documentation which sets forth the work plans and tasks (or cells) which demonstrate the continuity

through contiguous relations within aggregates of work elements and tasks.

5. Provide for nonconformity prevention, in preference to nonconformity correction, during the coding phase of the work. Clearly document and provide the widest practical knowledge of configuration requirements, and maintain rigid controls to prevent departure from defined configuration goals.

6. Provide for documentation of nonconformities discovered, corrective actions taken, and test results obtained throughout the coding work.

7. Provide for delivery, embedding, qualification testing, and operational performance verification for the customer and, to the extent applicable, any jurisdictional authorities.

2.9 Support tools, techniques, and methods. The contractor shall make provision for the identification, documenting, and validation of applicable software support tools, techniques, and methods provided for use or used to support the development, maintenance, and expansion of the software.

When the contract calls for software maintenance throughout life, the contractor shall document the support tools and methods provided for software program maintenance. The documentation shall include a description of how support functions satisfy or support the software quality requirements.

The contractor shall provide for validation of support software prior to its use, including the testing and use from which knowledge about and confidence in the support software is derived. To the extent that they are used, but not excluding others, the following shall be included in and documented in respect to support tools, techniques and methods.

1. Examples of support software needs:

- Definition of programming standards for structured programming
- Design requirements for the support software
- Definition of documentation standards
- Manual techniques for documentation reviews
- Validation requirements for support software
- Support software visibility methods
- Compilers, assemblers, simulators, test programs, and analyzers of software

2.10 Nonconformity prevention and corrective action. The contractor shall use reviews and re-reviews of each stage of the software design and development effort for the purpose of eliminating design and coding nonconformities. Particular effort shall be made to eliminate design nonconformities and to prevent the correction of design nonconformities from altering the software configuration.

The contractor shall use methods as set forth in *Quality Assurance for Computer Software,** or some other suitable reference work, to identify means for minimizing errors and assisting in subsequent detection of any nonconformities which may be included. To this end the contractor shall:

1. Use verifiable requirements for program coding
2. Use verifiable processors
3. Use structured programming
4. Apply systematic design decomposition methods
5. Use graphic documentation free from ambiguity
6. Use programming languages with error-defeating redundancy

2.11 Configuration control. The contractor shall establish and maintain a discipline of configuration management for the software design and development work. In this respect the contractor, working from the operational performance specification and related information, shall prepare documents which delineate the functional, physical, and interrelational characteristics of the software design. This part of the design shall be considered the configuration, and special efforts shall be made to ensure that the configuration is not altered during further design and coding work, except by approved configuration change control methods.

During development, changes to the software program are an ongoing activity. Specifically, the contractor shall prepare and publish procedures containing methods for:

1. Identifying module or program
2. Keeping masters secure
3. Providing and maintaining validated copies
4. Obtaining approvals to implement a modification
5. Providing assurance that modifications are properly integrated

---

*Robert Dunn and Richard Ullman, *Quality Assurance for Computer Software,* McGraw-Hill, New York, 1982.

6. Ensuring that software media are properly marked, handled, and stored

7. Ensuring that identification inspection status is rigorously maintained

8. Ensuring that support software is controlled

9. Ensuring that nonconforming software is identified, segregated, and prevented from mixing with conforming software

10. Issuing versions of software modules and programs

The contractor shall ensure that the quality assurance staff closely monitors the software design, coding, and testing and that records of errors detected, corrections approved and applied, and all changes which affect software configuration are kept.

2.12 Subcontractor control.   The contractor shall:

1. Prepare procedures for control of software, tools, methods, and other items procured from subcontractors.

2. Ensure that all software procured from subcontractors conforms to the requirements of the prime contract.

3. Prepare procedures specifically delineating the quality control requirements for subcontracts.

4. Clearly define the prime contractor's responsibility for auditing, monitoring, and reviewing the subcontractors' quality control systems.

5. Ensure that subcontractors are assigned contracts only for clearly manageable segments of the total contract and that such segments shall be a part of the integrated whole of the final program.

6. Stipulate in subcontracts when the customer or jurisdictional authorities may audit, monitor, surveil, or in other ways participate in subcontractor activities.

Further in the assurance of subcontractor quality the contractor shall review the software test requirements and prepare procedures identifying when testing shall be carried out and the part which the quality assurance personnel shall take in this work. The contractor shall ensure that criteria for testing are identified, that test documents are prepared, and that the tests, evaluations, and formal qualification testing will be carried out.

Specifically, the contractor shall provide for:

1. The analysis of software requirements and design to ensure testability
2. Reviews of criteria, tests, and their feasibility and traceability
3. Reviews of test documentation
4. Verification that tests are properly conducted
5. Reviews and approval of test reports
6. Identification and verification of software tools, test date, records, and hardware used for software testing
7. Provision of specifications for software preparation, delivery, embedding, and integration

2.13 Customer-supplied items control. The contractor shall prepare, establish, and maintain procedures for the acceptance, storage, and maintenance of all items supplied by the customer for use on the contract.

Items supplied by the customer may consist of either goods or services, and shall, when they become part of the software product, meet all the requirements of the contract, and it shall be the responsibility of the contractor to see that these requirements are met.

2.14 Change control management. The contractor shall prepare, publish, implement, and maintain procedures for control of change. In particular, these procedures shall stipulate the approved methods of making changes to the software product and supporting tools. The quality assurance personnel shall be notified of any change, and they shall be given permission to verify or validate that the change does not unacceptably alter the software configuration.

Following the start of coding, the process of making design changes shall become increasingly difficult. The only changes that are approved shall be those that do not materially affect the configuration, and none which are not brought to the quality assurance personnel's attention shall be approved.

2.15 Testing and formal qualification. In support of the software contract, the contractor shall review the software test requirements and prepare procedures identifying when testing shall be carried out and the part which the quality assurance personnel shall take in this work. The contractor shall ensure that criteria for testing are identified, that test documents are prepared, and that the tests, evaluations, and formal qualification testing will be carried out.

Specifically, the contractor shall provide for:

1. The analysis of software requirements and design to ensure testability
2. Reviews of criteria, tests, and their feasibility and traceability
3. Reviews of test documentation
4. Reviews and approval of test reports
5. Identification and verification of software tools, test data, records, and hardware used for software testing
6. Provision of specifications for software preparation, delivery, embedding and integration

2.16 Preparation for software delivery. The contractor shall prepare, publish, implement, and maintain procedures for marking, handling, storing, preserving, packing, and shipping of software so as not to violate the software integrity of the products to be delivered.

The contractor shall ensure that shipped software can be confirmed as being in conformity with the requirements of the contract.

2.17 Software embedding and hardware integration. The contractor shall ensure that the hardware, firmware, and software can be fully integrated and are compatible. When it is possible and appropriate, the contractor's quality assurance organization shall carry out formal qualification testing following integration of software and hardware, to prove the operational performance specification requirements have been met.

The qualification testing of integrated and embedded software shall, when required in the contract, demonstrate the full conformance of the software program with requirements.

2.18 Access, accommodation, and assistance

2.18.1. The contractor shall, on his own behalf and on behalf of his subcontractors, ensure that the customer and any applicable jurisdictional authority shall be given access to appropriate parts of the premises during working hours.

2.18.2. When applicable, the contractor shall provide the customer and any responsible jurisdictional authority with accommodation for the purpose of verifying that requirements are met.

2.18.3. The contractor shall, when called upon to so do, provide testing facilities, staff, and other assistance as appropriate to the customer or applicable jurisdictional authorities for the purpose of demonstrating conformance and providing evidence that the requirements of the contract have been fully discharged.

3

Services Design and Development Procedure

PART A   REVIEW AND GUIDANCE

1   Review

The output of human industry consists of what we call commodities. Commodities are composed of three kinds of things: products, services, and systems. Products are goods, tangible kinds of things which are *produced* by human industry. Services are intangible kinds of things *provided* to others by human industry. Systems are brought into being by construction work in the project industry, and they consist of combining products and services into complex systems. It is important to remember that services are provided and products are produced.

Services are things which people do, sometimes with the aid of products, for other people. Because of the more recent evolution of the services industry, as compared with the products industry, we find that the degree of definition, documentation, orderliness of work, and recognition of the disciplines which carry out the services work are all at a lesser stage of development. The services industry is therefore in a position to benefit to a very great degree from improved definition and design of its work.

What we call human factors are a further major beneficiary of quality in the services industry. Human factors are the subject of human interactions and interrelations. It is necessary to develop our understanding and control of the human factor elements in service industries; those contribute greatly to the performance of employees in the service field. We can treat the matter of machine ergonomics to readily overcome some difficult problem of operator-machine interaction. Among other things, we must work on the people-to-people interface when improving quality of services.

2   Guidance

In order to establish quality of design in a service company it is necessary to go through much the same sequence of activities as are gone through in the product industry. There is the need to identify what services are needed by the consumer and to specify them in unambiguous terms. Then there is the need to identify the desirable characteristics of the services and which characteristics are undesirable. It is then possible to classify all characteristics, the good and the bad, into defect or nonconformity classes which can be assessed by auditors and assessors of the business.

In a way quite analogous to the operational requirements specification of the products industry, the services industry requires specification of the services to be provided. Quality of design in the services industry, like similar design effort concerning products, must be concerned with the sources of poor quality. We know that the same four general sources of poor quality that are to be found in the product industry occur in the services industry. They are:

1. Operator-caused variability

2. Machine-caused variability

3. Machine setup–caused variability

4. Management-caused variability

In the products manufacturing industry the relative proportions of the total product variability arising from each of the above four sources depends on a number of factors. With a high degree of automation, (3) and (4) become predominant. With high operator input, the people carrying out the various production operations contribute greatly to the variability. We can safely say that (1) and (4) are major causes of variability in most services provided to the general public. The products manufacturing industry has mastered the production of high-quality equipment to such a degree that the equipment seldom contributes to poor quality service. Failings of the equipment operators because of poor training and skills development, as well as poorly planned and designed management systems, are among the major sources of services quality variability.

The needs of the user must be specified clearly and unambiguously as requirements that can be satisfied by providing some service. Several aspects of the service come into the specification, however. It is necessary to satisfy the characteristic of volume or large numbers provided. Just as in the products industry, there are situations in which the need is satisfied by the providing of only one or a few of the same service. In most service companies, however, the same service must be provided over and over again. Success in the services industry is dependent on having a good-quality service or a good-quality product and service combined.

Starting a service business is much like starting a products-manufacturing business. It will have the same parameters, although to different degrees. The task of the services company manager is to carry out all the duties as set forth in this procedure and the services-providing procedure of Sec. III, Chap. 3 of *Quality Control Systems.**

PART B. PROCEDURE

Services Design and Development

1   General

1.1   Scope. This procedure defines the requirements of the company for services design and development work done under contract for the company or for such work done within the company.

---

*James R. Taylor, *Quality Control Systems: Procedures for Planning Quality Programs*, McGraw-Hill, New York, 1989.

1.2 Application. This procedure shall apply when:

1. Called for in a contract by the customer
2. A service-providing activity is to be undertaken by the company
3. Called up in any contractual situation

1.2.1. When requirements in this procedure conflict with similar requirements in a contract which requires the use of this procedure, the requirements of the contract shall prevail.

1.3 Definitions. The terms used in this procedure shall be interpreted in accordance with the definitions of terms in "Glossary of Quality and Reliability Terms," Sec. VII, Chap. 1 of *Quality Control Systems* unless required otherwise.

1.4 Referenced documents. The following documents from *Quality Control Systems* shall comprise part of this procedure:

1. "Quality Control System for Services," Sec. III, Chap. 3.
2. "Calibration Control System," Sec. III, Chap. 9.
3. "Product Recall System," Sec. V, Chap. 2.
4. "Glossary of Quality and Reliability Terms," Sec. VII, Chap. 1.

2 Requirements

2.1 Review of program requirements

2.1.1. In the case of services design and development, the review of program requirements takes the place of the operational requirements specification used in the products design and development situation. When a services business is begun, it is necessary to carry out certain market research and service design work to identify and satisfy a need of the prospective customers. The review of program requirements shall constitute a documented program of needs outlining what is to be provided and the general characteristics of what the limiting factors on such things as range of items sold and scope of the activity will be.

2.1.2. A study of the market potential, including customer surveys, market scope, service range, time constraints, products needed, and customer needs for well-being, as a minimum, shall be made. The results of the study shall be documented and analyzed to produce an outline, with stipulative details, of the service to be provided and any supporting products to be used and/or supplied to the customers. The comprehensive review of program requirements shall be provided to the designers, who shall use this information as a basis for service design.

2.2 Design and development planning

2.2.1. The design organization shall prepare plans in documented form for all aspects of the services, and any supporting products, to be provided to customers by the organization.

A clear distinction shall be made in the plans when it is intended that products are to become part of what is to be sold to customers, whether those products are to be given in support of the services or represent only equipment and other tangible goods used to make supply of the services to the customers more effective.

When products are to be used in support of the supply of services but not become the property of customers, the quality plans shall identify the quality and reliability requirements for such products. In addition, such things as employee-training needs and customer-training needs are to be specific requirements of the planning effort.

When the product is to become some part of the routinely sold service to customers, the product and service shall be considered together as a joint customer need and shall be integrated into one harmonious service-product addition to the customer's well-being.

2.2.2. The design and development planning shall be conducted at the earliest stage of any contract discharge and shall cover any jurisdictional authority requirements concerning the business. Customer requirements and jurisdictional requirements shall be considered together; and when more than one such authority is involved, all jurisdictional authorities shall be kept informed of plans and the progress affecting each particular authority.

2.2.3. The planning shall cover such matters as:

- Customer training required to use the service
- Technical assistance required by customers
- Simplicity requirements for the multiply-supplied services
- Providing a range of choice
- Control and preservation of customer's property
- Modularity requirements for the services system
- Backup assistance for made-to-order customer needs

- Auxiliary services to be provided with the products and/or services sold to customers

2.2.4. A specific requirement of design and development plans shall be an in-depth planning for all time aspects of providing customers with the products and/or services. Specifically, the plans shall cover customer well-being, queuing, action time, and access principles of the activity.

2.2.5. When the service constitutes some installation, repair, maintenance, cleaning, or similar service, the plans shall consider in detail the customer well-being factors of the business. When practicable, the plans shall give due consideration to continuity of service when that is a factor of the service provided to customers.

2.3   Design organization. The usual design work on services will be carried out within the company. When some product is concerned, a contract will usually be entered into by the company with a supplier to produce and supply the product.

Services, in themselves, constitute things which are designed within the company that is going to market them. This means that, in some head office or general administration area, there will be a group to which is delegated the responsibility for specifying, documenting, and distributing the requirements for the services and supporting products of the company.

The design organization shall be comprised of a senior manager and staff who are skilled in the kind of service to be provided. For example, in a restaurant business, the designers shall be at least partially comprised of senior experienced chefs and managers with extensive experience in running restaurants. This means they will be familiar with all aspects of such a business, including auxiliary things like customer parking, air conditioning, customer seating, and restaurant atmosphere.

In addition to the individuals who can bring extensive experience to the design task, there shall be a quality assurance function in the organization. Though this is not normally called quality assurance in the service business, auditors who go from site to site and audit the entire local activity, prepare formal reports, and keep the total company operations on an even operational keel are carrying out quality work. These auditors shall carry out an audit of any designs which are prepared by the company's designers.

2.4   Quality assurance and design

2.4.1. There shall be established within the company a quality assurance organization which shall plan, design, document, and promulgate quality systems and procedures for services activities. When a quality audit function already exists, it shall be integrated with and shall be part of the quality assurance organization, which shall continue to carry out the quality audits.

2.4.2. The quality assurance manager shall work with all design and development activities, including those of suppliers, to ensure that quality of design exists in the services provided by the company and that the services provided have known levels of quality.

2.4.3. Specifically, in design work, the quality assurance manager shall work with the design manager to ensure that services and support facilities and equipment are "measurable." This means the identification of characteristics of each and every service that are essential to the providing of quality in that service and the devising, developing, and providing of ways and means for measuring and monitoring the ongoing quality of service provided to customers.

2.4.4. The quality characteristics of services provided shall be classified by their seriousness, and the level of seriousness of a service failure shall be used by the company to determine the degree of corrective action to be taken. The classification and potential defect or nonconformity listing shall be a part of the services design documentation specified by the company and used by it or by suppliers.

2.4.5. When equipment and facilities are used in the conduct of business by the company, they shall be integrated into the quality specifications in such a way as to be totally compatible with the quality of services to be provided. Both equipment quality and reliability shall be of prime importance in providing for continuity of service, and they shall be clearly stipulated in measurable terms in contracts and purchase orders of the company.

2.5 Customer property control design

2.5.1. The customer entrusts his or her person, property, and well-being to the custody and protection of the service company. Here we shall consider the problem of designing for control of customer's property. The customer entrusts money to the bank and expects that it will grow. The telephone company, assigned the right-of-way across the farmer's property, is expected to rebuild any cut fences, refill trenches and holes, etc. The repair industry is entrusted, at one time or another, with most of the more complex items possessed by the customer when they fail in some way. These are only some of the examples of the service industry accepting custody of and responsibility for property belonging to the customer.

2.5.2.   It shall be a requirement during the design of services that any custody which the company may become involved in for property belonging to customers, during the course of providing a service, shall be adequately specified in the service design as to:

- Conditions of receipt and custody of the property
- Establishment of the condition of the property when received
- Specification, in detail, of any work to be carried out or modification in any way of the customer property during the time of custody
- Conditions and manner of returning custody of the property to the customer or to another customer after the company's custody is terminated
- Security measures to be taken during the custody period
- Measures to be taken to protect the company from claims by customers in respect to any custody of property owned by the customers

2.6   Customer well-being control design

2.6.1.   Customer well-being enters into almost all areas of the services industry's activities. It takes many forms, and it is essential to the profit of the service company. For the purpose of design of customer well-being into the services to be provided, we shall review the three principal categories of human well-being.

2.6.2.   There shall be recognized and used in the design activities three categories of customer well-being.

2.6.2.1 **Material well-being.** All people seek to increase both the amount of possessions they own and control and the condition of those possessions. Since the conditions of material goods will deteriorate with time and use, it is of great importance in the design of services that the employees of the company use all reasonable precautions to prevent deterioration of the property and possessions of customers from their original condition and appearance during the times of providing some service.

2.6.2.2 Prestige well-being. Customers like to feel important, be accepted, feel they are intelligent and knowledgeable, and be treated with respect. It is therefore necessary that the design of services take these characteristics of customers into consideration and provide in the design of the service and the training of staff who provide the service all features needed to add to the customers' prestige well-being.

2.6.2.3 Physiological well-being. Physiological well-being covers the well-being of both the body and the mind. Great care is needed in the design of services to prevent the customer from developing worry, fear, trepidation, or other mental anxiety conditions in respect to the service being offered. Similarly, it is of great importance to so design services that the physical well-being of customers will be protected, or enhanced. The design of services shall be directed toward protecting the customer's physical well-being at all times and, when possible, enhancing it. Services designs shall also seek to provide the customer with a feeling of mental joy and exhilaration at having received the service.

2.6.3. The design of services shall take into consideration all three of the above categories of customer well-being, and shall, to the extent that is practicable, ensure that each is comprehensively entered into and integrated with the providing of the service being designed.

2.7   Design of modular systems

2.7.1. When the service provided to the customer is determined in part by the influence of the customer on the system, e.g., the telephone customer determining the type of call to be made, the restaurant customer determining the kind of meal to be eaten, or the bank customer determining the kind of account to be opened, it is of major importance that the services designer devise and develop modularity in the system.

2.7.2. The designer shall clearly and thoroughly examine the interface of the services business from the customer's viewpoint and subdivide the service spectrum into clear and defined modules. Each service module shall have its unique characteristics, parameters, and limits beyond which the customer cannot go in making his or her choice. Each service module shall constitute a complete service or essential segment or part of a larger service. These service modules shall be defined and specified in documented form in the company's documentation system.

2.7.3. The designer shall follow up the identification and documentation of service modules with an in-depth design of each module into the total services-providing system of the company. Each module shall be measurable by the company in respect to which and to what degree the customer has availed himself or herself of that particular service module. The services designer shall design into the operations of the company the capability to control, extend, contract, create, or cancel service modules.

2.7.4. The services designer shall provide for communication to and from the customer by the company in respect to services offered in modular form. Such communications shall provide information to the customer on methods for availing himself or herself of the services being offered and the cost or obligation assumed by so doing. Communications provided for from the customer to the company shall be designed to provide the company with measures of adequacy, satisfaction, customer well-being, and other quality characteristics needed.

2.8   Designing for simplicity

2.8.1. Customers in large numbers, the typical situation for successful services businesses, represent a broad cross section of the population in each nation. As such they represent the entire range of education, ethnic beliefs and needs, and economic welfare found in the nation. A small number will be able to cope with and master the most complex and sophisticated service delivery system. The preponderant number, however, will expect the service being offered to be simple to access and receive. For that reason it shall be a primary responsibility of the designer to ensure that the modules of services designed are kept clearly defined, communicated, and simple to access and use.

2.8.2. People everywhere like a certain amount of variety in their lives, but the great need is for regularity and reliability upon which they can depend. The services designer shall provide both characteristics in the following way:

2.8.2.1. Variety shall be provided by designing a range of different modules offering different services or the same service in different ways and degrees. Each such module for a given type of service shall possess a routine sameness each time it is accessed so the customer can become confident in the service and rely upon accessing it successfully each time.

2.8.2.2. Service modules shall be retained in the business for such periods of time, unchanged in major degree, to permit customers to learn the methods of accessing and using them so as to become confident in their regularity and reliability. For this purpose, change of service modules shall be kept to a minimum once the module has become accepted by the broad range of customer clientele.

2.8.3. In general, the broader the range of customers using a service, the greater must be the simplicity and clarity of communication about the service. Many consumers prefer not to master complex rules, codes, and regimens requiring great taxing of the memory each time they try to access the service. To many customers, the time required to learn difficult access rules is itself prohibitive, and they will turn to some more simple service area to satisfy their needs. For reasons such as these, and in the interest of maximizing the numbers and range of customers using the service, it shall be a requirement that the service designer "keep it simple."

2.9 Designing for auxiliary services

2.9.1. A particular concern shall be for auxiliary services. Such services are often "free" to the customer, yet they may carry considerable cost for the company supplying them. As a result, close control shall be maintained in respect to the cost to the company vs. the benefit to the company. It shall be a particular aspect of service design that, for each module of service offered, a comprehensive cost-benefit study is made to determine the range of beneficial auxiliary services to be offered as a part of the primary module service. The auxiliary services found to be beneficial on a cost basis to offer to customers shall be considered characteristics of the module design and shall be designed and specified as part of each respective module.

2.9.2. Not all services can be kept so simple that the entire population can access them. Some services, by their nature and purpose, require the customers to possess a relatively high degree of education, sophistication, and knowledge gained through experience. When the designer is concerned with such service modules, it shall still be a primary responsibility that the module shall be kept as simple as possible. At no time shall service modules be intentionally made more complex than is essential for their successful accessing by the expected range of customers.

2.10   Designing for customer choice

2.10.1.   Choice by customers of the service they want requires knowledge of the individual and separate service modules offered. Sometimes competitors will describe their service in terms nearly identical to those of the company, though there may be great differences when the services are actually received. It shall be a specific responsibility of the services designer to so describe the different service modules offered that the customer can readily know when he or she is accessing one vs. the other.

2.10.2.   When it becomes necessary to provide a service module with content identical to that of others offered, except for certain additions or extensions, the services designer shall clearly provide for the customer to identify the sequence of such services as being a progressive extension of the most simple one.

2.10.3.   The services designer shall include, in the documented design and specifications, ways and means whereby changes to services being offered can be introduced and will be clearly communicated to customers.

2.11   Designing for service continuity

2.11.1.   The services designer shall examine each service with a view to identifying any need for providing continuity of service. In this sense, continuity is meant to be on a time basis, and continuity has to do with disruption of service accessibility for any reason.

2.11.2.   The services designer shall, once the need for continuity of service is confirmed, determine to what degree and in what manner the continuity of service will be offered. Having made such a determination, the designer shall include, in the service module design, specific requirements for providing customer access to the service for periods of time and in ways or by methods to be clearly prescribed. All these shall be parts of the service module specification.

2.12   Designing customer time controls

2.12.1   Customer access time.   The services designer shall analyze the full range of customer access problems, determine solutions to each problem, and clearly specify in the service module specification the methods and conditions for controlling customer access time. In this respect particular attention shall be given to making the access as simple, nontechnical, and pleasant as possible. Of principal importance shall be the amount of customer time used in gaining access to the service offered.

2.12.2 Customer queuing time. The services designer shall examine the customer access problem to determine if queuing is a factor. When it is, the designer shall provide methods and means for customer queuing that will:

- Minimize the waiting time
- Make the waiting time as pleasant as possible
- Prevent queue jumping by late arrivals
- Assure the customer that he or she is in the correct queue
- Provide prompt delivery of service to customers who have had to wait in a queue

2.12.3 Supplier action time. The services designer shall analyze the activities that must take place during the interval beginning when the customer's order is taken and ending when the service is provided. Specific attention shall be given to making this time as short as possible and yet providing the customer with the correct service module.

When designing the action time interval in providing service to customers, the designer shall take into consideration the various consequences of delays and supplying the wrong service module. When such situations arise, the customer may not only develop valid complaints but suffer payable damages. To achieve and maintain control over service access, queue and action times, the designer shall establish standards for the various components of service time and set up controls to enforce them. He or she shall provide ways by which times not meeting the standards established can be brought into line and ensure that the standards are extended into all future service module designs.

2.13 Designing for technical assistance

2.13.1. The services designer shall analyze the type of service to be supplied in terms of the customer's need for technical assistance. The technical assistance shall be divided into two major categories:

1. Technical assistance which can be satisfied by oral or written communications (including instruction books)
2. Technical assistance such that the supplier must provide techni-

cal staff to undertake and carry out on behalf of the services customer work of a technical nature

2.13.2. The services designer shall determine the extent to which
technical assistance shall be provided and specify the assistance to be
provided by the company in each case.

2.13.3. When the service is provided with the aid of equipment, particularly high-technology equipment, the company shall provide, in
accordance with the design specification for that service module,
equipment and facilities which will provide and maintain the quality
of service defined in the design specifications. It shall be a specific responsibility of the designer to ensure that the aspects for which quality is specified are themselves measurable in quantitative terms.

2.14 Design records control

2.14.1. The designer shall document services designs in the detail
needed to introduce them to new areas, to train people in their access
and use and how to provide them, and provide for auditing and maintaining the quality system of the business.

2.14.2. The service designs shall be described in documentation that is
clear, concise, free of ambiguities, and technically correct and that
provides for maintenance of the documentation system.

2.14.3. The documentation system, including the service module specifications, shall comprise a complete design disclosure of the analyses,
calculations, studies, including market studies, material formulations, processing records and procedures, and all other documentation
needed to arrive at and justify decisions taken in the course of the design work.

2.14.4. Design records shall be provided by the company, and shall be
retained in files or archives, for such times and in such retrievable
manner as may be prescribed by a jurisdictional authority or by the
anticipated needs of the company.

2.14.5. During the course of the design work, the designers shall keep
records in notebooks, correspondence, reports, studies, modeling, computer files, and documents and in such manner as is most suitable for
perpetuating the evidence of work and its outcome, as well as the progressive evolution of the overall service company plans and service
module structures.

2.14.6. When there are jurisdictional authority requirements in respect to justification of actions and use of secret recipes, formulas, formulations, etc., the company shall keep and maintain records which will satisfy all such authority requirements.

2.15 Designing human factors. A matter of great importance is associated with the interpersonal relationships characteristics of people engaged in the services industry. This aspect is of great importance in any situation in which people must interact in their daily affairs. It can be seen to affect the careers of people employed in the products-manufacturing industry, as well as the quality of products manufactured. This characteristic is a principal factor in making the quality circle work so well in Japanese culture.

The services industry requires that special attention be given to the personal characteristics of employees who must meet the general public, and customers of the company in particular. Employees are needed who will be pleasant, secure, confident, and who will convey to customers the feeling of pleasure and confidence in dealing with the company. To this end there shall be prepared for each defined position required to meet or deal with the customers an employee position specification which will define the qualities and personal characteristics needed by that particular person for optimal discharge of the duties of the position.

2.15.1. Services designers shall make use of psychologists, social scientists, and other specialists as necessary to prepare the tests, examinations, physical attributes descriptions, and other requirements for the employee position specifications. Such a specification shall be prepared for each and every position that requires the employee who fills it to work directly with customers.

2.15.2. Services designers shall, for employee training and assessment purposes, clearly specify the complete carrying out of a service interaction between an employee of the company and the customer. This specification shall cover the entire interaction, including all human factors essential to its success. This type of human factors specification shall be prepared for each different service module provided.

2.15.3. The services designer shall give due consideration to the customer's well-being needs in preparing the human factors specification for each services module. The methods used to provide services shall be clearly documented and so shall be the characteristics needed by the employee who is to provide the service. The requirements for the technical specialist who is to support the supply of services shall also be identified and documented.

2.16 Designing the services environment. An essential aspect of successfully providing services is the customer well-being gained from the environment in which the service is provided. The environment is also important in transmitting to the employees of the company the desirable outlook and personality for the maximum service quality when there is interaction between the employee and the customer.

The services environment consists of the building, or other location where the customer takes delivery of the service, the decorations, spaciousness, and plants or other atmosphere-generating characteristics of the environment. Some services require that the correct mood be established for the customer to gain the maximum benefit from the service. In this type of situation the designer shall pay particular attention to the environmental requirements for service quality and shall satisfy them in the specification for the respective service modules.

2.17 Designing for security and safety

2.17.1 Security. Security comes into the providing of services in three quite general ways: security for the customer's property, for the customer himself or herself, and for the company's employees and property while the customer is receiving service.

2.17.1.1. Security for customer property while in the custody of the supplier is of prime importance. The designer shall give due consideration to including in specifications and other documentation, when appropriate, the requirements for insurance coverage, property protection, methods of handling and segregation, methods of labeling, methods of accepting property, and methods of returning control of such property to the customer.

2.17.1.2. Security for the customer while the customer is receiving some service. The designer shall give due attention to methods for achieving and maintaining security for the customer at all times while the customer is involved with the company in any way. This shall include such matters as security of the customer's property on the premises but not in the control of the company during the time concerned. The design of the total site security shall cover all necessary aspects of customer security.

2.17.1.3. Security of the company's property and employees is also of great importance. Perpetuation of the company's good name and security of its property are matters of prime importance in the design of the site where the services will be provided. This is particularly true where valuables are traded, and in such businesses as banking. The site designer shall include in the design of the site all the necessary security aspects needed to provide optimum security for the company and its employees and property.

2.17.2 Safety. In many service businesses in which the customer is temporarily in the custody of the company while an entertainment or physical exercise or similar service is provided, it becomes of prime importance that the designer provide for safety of the customer as well as the safety of the supplier's personnel. The services designer shall, at all times, and particularly when designing sites and buildings in which services will be provided, include in the design all the factors required to guarantee safety of customers and others on the premises.

2.18 Design documentation and records control. At the start of the design program the design manager shall establish and document a design disclosure plan. This plan shall define what methods and system of documentation shall be used for the disclosure of the entire design, the manner of plan derivation and justification and the results of analyses, data gathering, mathematical calculations, drawings, specifications, procedures, policies, and all other such documents which comprise a part of the design output.

The design manager shall ensure that the requirements of any or all jurisdictional authorities are included in the design and development program. The plan shall provide for those requirements to be raised at the appropriate times and to be met in complete detail and for the clearances and authorizations of the jurisdictional authorities to become a part of the recorded output of the design effort.

Provision shall be made for the retention, storage, and retrieval of design records, including the design plan and complete design disclosure package. When stipulated in a contract, any patentable, copyrightable, or other form of industrial property generated in the course of the design work shall become the property of the company. The supplier shall provide sufficient documentation, properly recorded, dated, signed, and authorized, to permit the company to protect any property rights accrued thereby and to prosecute infringers.

4

Reliability System Procedure

PART A. REVIEW AND GUIDANCE

1   Review

This quality assurance procedure provides guidance and requirements for use by companies who must meet reliability requirements in the design and production of products. It also provides information to assist the quality assurance staffs of customers who are responsible for assessing the quality systems of suppliers and prospective suppliers. The procedure is intended to assist management by providing an understanding of the approach which the designer and production manager must take in order to obtain reliability in the output of the company, regardless of whether the product is for the consumer market or is being designed and produced under contract.

Rather than provide a formula by which a particular reliability of a product can be determined, this procedure is of a general-purpose nature; it shows all designers and managers in all types of industries certain of the methods used to achieve and assure the reliability of products. It will be found that the methods contained in this procedure are applicable in part or in whole to all kinds of products. The assessor who has to examine the design effort of a company in accordance with the procedure in Chap. 1 of this section will find this procedure helpful when assessing the efforts of the design organization to achieve a given reliability in its product. Only when this procedure is specified in a contract will the assessor be able to know that the design organization will use the principles and methods contained herein.

When this procedure is applied as a requirement in a contract, it must be viewed by the assessor as being of a general guidance nature intended to assist the supplier of the product. Only the techniques chosen from this procedure may be considered to be binding on the supplier. This procedure will also give less-experienced staff the insights necessary to choose an approach to obtaining a given reliability in a product.

2 Guidance

As a guidance document, this procedure contains a considerable amount of instructive material. It describes the sources of reliability and the kinds of things done in industry to carry out a theoretical determination of the reliability of a system, and it introduces the new person in the field to methods of modeling. Reliability predictions made by using models of the components, subsystems, and system are essential parts of the theoretical prediction of reliability. The methods contained in this procedure are quite general and can be applied to almost any kind of system, including materials in all their phases.

Methods of reliability prediction, although qualitative in their findings, are techniques useful to the designer as well as the customer of product designs. They aid the designer in making such choices as ratio of simplicity to complexity, ratio of new technology to proven technology, and ratio of new component designs to proven component designs that he or she may use to achieve a given range of reliability within a new product. Customers of complex designs, faced with the task of choosing from among a range of competing products, will find reliability prediction techniques useful in evaluating bids or tenders when time is short.

Methods of comparative prediction by using the known performance of similar equipment are described. The sources of data for such similarity comparisons are discussed, and the need for the organization using the comparative method of prediction to establish programs for collecting and analyzing such data is emphasized. Also discussed in some depth is the deficiency technique, which is particularly useful for the maintenance contribution to reliability through its ability to identify reliability weaknesses and thereby lead to their reliability enhancement during repair and part replacement.

Of particular importance to those who have not previously worked with reliability control is the guidance given in this procedure concerning definition of systems and the establishment of their reliability requirements. As is explained in detail in Sec. VI, Chap. 2, the economics of the total life cycle is the source of information needed to scientifically derive the appropriate quality level of a product, as well as the appropriate reliability for that product in order to yield a given life cycle cost. Ultimately, as in all other human endeavors, the technical nature of products must conform to economic requirements if the products are to perform well in the marketplace.

In addition to the guidance given in this standard for the derivation of systems reliability models, examples to assist the user in interpreting the contributions from various activities and areas of materials and components to the resultant product reliability are provided. Of particular importance is the discussion of the environmental factors which contribute most to the unreliable behavior of products of all types. It is those contributors to unreliability of which the designer must be aware. Each potential source of unreliability must be given thorough attention during product design.

PART B.   PROCEDURE

Reliability System

1   Introduction

1.1   Scope.   This procedure contains guidance for people who are responsible for designing products with predetermined reliability levels, as well as people who are responsible for assessing the reliability programs of supplier organizations for their adequacy under contractual situations. It sets forth an approach to determining the reliability of systems yet to be designed, as well as methods for adjusting the reliability of systems already installed and operating.

1.2 Application. This procedure is to be applied in all situations in which it is called up in a contract and in other situations in which it will assist in carrying out work that concerns the reliability of components and systems.

1.3 Referenced documents. This procedure draws from and makes reference to certain documents and source material which, to the extent they may apply to the reliability work undertaken in respect to this standard, shall be considered to apply. The documents and sources are:

1. United States Military Handbook, MIL-HDBK-217D, *Reliability Prediction of Electronic Equipment.*
2. Igor Bazovsky, *Reliability Theory and Practice,* Prentice-Hall, Englewood Cliffs, N.J., 1962.
3. United States Military Standard, MIL-STD-756, "Reliability Prediction."
4. United States Military Standard, MIL-STD-414, "Reliability Testing."

1.4 Terms and definitions. Unless otherwise stated, the terms used in this procedure shall be interpreted in accordance with the definitions in Sec. VII, Chap. 1 of *Quality Control Systems.**

2 Reliability Prediction

It is to be noted that the prediction of reliability is not a quantitative science. The methods described below are only qualitative, and they are to be used only as indicators of what may be anticipated. In no case are the methods of reliability prediction to be used to arrive at the reliability of equipment for sales, advertising, marketing, or technical description purposes. They are of some help, however, in assessing bids or tenders when time is limited and the prospective suppliers have presented sufficient information.

---

*James R. Taylor, *Quality Control Systems: Procedures for Planning Quality Programs,* McGraw-Hill, New York, 1989.

2.1   Reliability prediction methods.   Three of the methods by which it is possible to make reasonable qualitative predictions about the reliability of systems are:

1. The similar equipment technique
2. The deficiency technique
3. The parts count technique

2.1.1   The similar equipment prediction technique.   When two different equipments are constructed in a similar manner of similar parts and must carry out the same end purpose, it is possible that, given information about the operational performance of one of the two systems, the reliability of the second can be predicted. The argument is based on the similar equipment constructions and the use of parts having similar individual reliabilities.

Assuming that the system reliability has been both calculated and determined from experience for equipment number one, it is possible to ascertain the probable differences for equipment number two by considering any differences in system assembly, parts count, and parts reliability.

When the system assembly configuration in equipment number two has inherently higher reliability, then it can be predicted to have higher reliability than number one. In a similar way a smaller number of parts in equipment number two will impart greater reliability, and so will the use of some higher-reliability parts if used in equipment number two.

For equipments undergoing normal technological evolution, and especially improved models from one company, it is possible to arrive at good qualitative estimates of the relative reliabilities of later-generation systems from the known performance of the earlier-generation systems. Simple calculations that take into consideration only the areas of configurational difference, or part variation, will give quite accurate predictions of the reliability of equipment of later generations.

The similar equipment method of predicting reliability is capable of giving reasonable accuracy only when the two equipments are essentially identical, i.e., successive models of the same equipment for the same purpose. When the knowledge of reliability is important, the similar equipment method shall be used only when it will yield the estimated reliability within the stipulated confidence interval.

2.1.2   The deficiency technique of prediction.   The deficiency technique derives from a reliability program, and reliability growth is often used to influence the predicted reliability. In particular, the deficiency technique will provide information on the benefits to be gained from implementing a reliability growth program. In this technique all the things done throughout the design, development, production, and maintenance activities on the product which affect reliability are used to provide inputs to the prediction effort.

Outputs from design reviews, parts-derating policies, joining and assembly training, part selection and application procedures, part-screening programs, failure analysis to determine failure modes, criticality analyses, and maintenance programs are collected and analyzed to determine the contributions of each area to the overall system unreliability. (*Note:* The relations between deficiencies, failures and failure rate must be known in order to apply this technique.)

When this technique is used, it is necessary to adopt this definition: A deficiency is any departure from completeness, which means the part, subassembly, or system is lacking in some quality necessary for completeness. Deficiencies defined in that way are potential causes of failure. The deficiency may be failure of a part to meet its specification, or it may be a failure of the specification to adopt or adhere rigorously to the derating policy necessary for a given reliability. It may also be failure of the total manufacturing system to comply with some form of workmanship requirement or method of joining or assembly.

Deficiencies, active or passive, can exist in hardware and never cause failure simply because the part is never stressed environmentally to the limit of the specification. Since all failures are caused by deficiencies, more than one failure may be caused by a deficiency or several deficiencies may be needed to cause one failure.

Sometimes deficiencies cause failures that do not prevent the system from performing its function. Though some quality programs may not classify such failures as reliability failures, it is important to recognize that they are deficiencies. When the deficiency method of reliability predictions is used, it is important to recognize that "failure rate" means the rate at which deficiencies manifest themselves in failure, and not the rate at which the equipment fails to perform its intended function.

It can be seen that the approach to reliability growth requires the successive elimination of deficiencies in the system. When maintenance is performed on operating equipment, it is possible to introduce deficiencies which were not there before. We see, therefore, that there are initial deficiencies and introduced deficiencies and the deficiencies in the system will be equal to the sum of initial and introduced deficiencies minus the number of eliminated deficiencies. Hence,

$$d_T = d_i + d_n - d_e \tag{4.1}$$

where d_T is the total number of deficiencies and d_i, d_n, and d_e are respectively the number of initial, introduced, and eliminated deficiencies. The predicted failure rate is calculated as follows:

$$\lambda = Kd_t \tag{4.2}$$

where λ is the failure rate and K is an empirical factor which relates failure rate and total number of deficiencies in similar equipment previously produced.

It will be instructive to consider some sources of initial deficiencies and introduced deficiencies. Initial deficiencies occur in:

- Design
- Fabrication
- Installation
- Maintenance
- Operation
- Publication

Design deficiencies include such things as ambiguities, improper derating of parts, misleading information included in specifications, limits or other necessary information not included in specifications, and misjudgments made in the configuration design. Fabrication deficiencies include all the deficiencies related to translation of the design into finished product. They occur in purchasing, fabrication, assembly, testing, quality control, packaging, and shipping. The natures of the other deficiencies are implicit in the names. Sources of introduced deficiencies are:

- New environment requirements
- Design schedule variation (tighter or looser)
- Higher technological nature
- Use of untried parts
- Changes in personnel
- Introduction of new part requirements

Introduced deficiencies are usually viewed in relation to the design and supply of similar but previous equipment.

The estimated reliability, or failure rate, shall be determined in the following way:

1. From records of activities relating to similar but previous equipment, determine the number of equipment deficiencies for which

effective corrective action has not been implemented in the new design.

2. Estimate the number of introduced deficiencies in the new design. Experience with previous designs shall be used here, with account being taken of the relative complexities of the new and the earlier design from which information is taken. When no earlier design of a similar equipment exists, the customer may supply such information from other sources. The introduced deficiencies are estimated by

$$d_n = d_{n_0} \times C_n/C_0 \qquad (4.3)$$

where d_n is the number of introduced deficiencies in the new design, d_{n0} is the number of introduced deficiencies in the earlier design, and C_n/C_0 is the ratio of complexities of the two equipments, i.e., the ratio of total number of parts.

Equation (4.1) shall now be used to estimate the total number of deficiencies which will remain in the new design when it is frozen and the equipment is produced and is in use in the field. Equation (4.2) shall be used to estimate the reliability or failure rate of the new equipment.

2.1.3 The parts count technique of prediction.
The parts count technique of predicting reliability requires relatively little information, and that information is generally available early in a program involving new equipment. It is, therefore, useful in connection with bidding or tendering for new business. It is applicable early in the design phase and during proposal formulation. The information required for reliability estimation based on parts count is generally that concerning quantities of different part types, different environment of use, and different quality levels of parts.

Increasingly, new contracts require a bidder or tenderer to provide a statement of reliability as well as agree to a level of quality for the equipment to be supplied. The matter of quoting on quality level has, of necessity, become more or less routine for most companies. Generally, larger companies that have been involved with defense contracts are familiar with reliability prediction; the smaller companies, which are most often placed in the subcontractor category, are unfamiliar with reliability prediction. The methods in this standard are presented for the purpose of closing that gap.

The information needed to apply the parts count method of failure rate prediction includes:

- Knowledge of the generic part types

- Part quality levels against known tests
- The environment in which the equipment will operate when in use by the customer

In order to know the above information, it is only necessary to know the generic part types intended for use in the new equipment and to purchase those types within a rigorously controlled purchasing program once the equipment is designed and the parts are called for. There are several sources from which information on failure rates of individual part types can be obtained. One of them is US-MIL-STD-217D. U.S. NPRD-1, AD-A059901 gives information on nonelectronic parts.

To know the part quality levels, it is necessary to make an early decision as to what grade of part will be purchased. That means deciding on what test specifications the parts will be required to have met before they can be used in the new designed equipment. Once again there are a number of sources, including the parts manufacturers, as well as US-MIL-STD-217D, from which this information can be obtained. It is then necessary to ensure that, during the parts purchasing program, the quality levels used in the reliability prediction are the quality levels of parts obtained from the parts manufacturers.

It is the customer's responsibility to characterize the operational environment(s) in which the equipment will operate, and that information shall be provided in the operational requirements specification contained in the request for bids. This information provides the prospective supplier who is preparing the bid with data required to determine the derating policy which shall be adopted while the design, development, and production of the new equipment is carried out.

The method is particularly applicable to electronic equipment, but it can also be applied to mechanical, physical, and all other types of systems by using appropriate information of the above three categories. For example, for mechanical parts, information on the material and its characteristics available from raw material suppliers will serve the same purpose as that of information from MIL-STD-217 for the electronics equipment producer.

The general expression for equipment failure rate using the parts count method is

$$\lambda_{\text{equip}} = \Sigma_{i\,=\,1}^{i\,=\,n} N_i(\lambda_G\lambda_Q)_i \tag{4.4}$$

where λ_{equip} = total equipment failures in 10 hours
$\quad\quad\quad \lambda_G$ = generic failure rate for the ith generic part (failures per 10 hours)
$\quad\quad\quad \lambda_Q$ = quality factor for the ith generic part
$\quad\quad\quad N_i$ = quantity of ith generic part
$\quad\quad\quad n$ = number of different generic part categories

The expression in Eq. (4.4) applies only to the case in which the entire equipment is to operate in one fixed environment. When there are a number of environments and different parts of the system must operate in different ways, it is necessary to apply Eq. (4.4) to each subsystem part for the environment in which the equipment must operate until the entire system has been analyzed. The individual failure rates from the different environments are then added to obtain the system failure rate for the bid.

Similarly to the case above, when several environments are given in the operational requirements specification, it is necessary to repeat the calculation of Eq. (4.4) for the total system operating in each of the environments and for each different failure rate to be quoted with its environment.

Table 4.1 shows a sample calculation method for a parts count reliability prediction for a relatively complex telephone switching exchange using modern electronic parts. In the example given here it is assumed that the operational requirements specification requires an hourly reliability of not less than 97 percent. A fixed environment typical of a switching exchange building is assumed. When there are no nonenclosed electromechanical relay contacts and similar switching devices, the environment does not need the clinical cleanness of the earlier exchanges, but the temperature and humidity must be controlled within specified limits. In the example shown, the failure rate is 0.039 failure per hour.

The failure rate for the exchange can be calculated as follows:

$$R_{1h} = e^{-(0.039)(1)} = e^{-0.039} = 96.2\% \text{ reliability per hour}$$

By carrying out the derating exercise during design of the various exchange subassemblies when the components are designed into the system to work at lower stresses, it can be seen that the reliability is improved to 96.5 percent, a gain of 0.3 percent. It is clear that there will have to be additional design work, preferably in the area of the least reliable components. Additional reliability can be gained by using fewer RAMs with a larger bit count per RAM, replacing the non-hermetically sealed RAMs with hermetically sealed ones, replacing

TABLE 4.1 Sample Calculation Method for a Parts Count Reliability Prediction

Total number generic parts	Failure rate per component per 10^6 hours	Failure rate per group per 10^6 hours	Derated failure rate per component per 10^6 hours	Derated failure rate per group per 10^6 hours
1292 microelectronic random logic—hermetic	0.044	156.85	0.034	43.93
496 microelectronic ROMs—hermetic seal	0.06	29.76	0.05	24.80
248 microelectronic ROMs—nonhermetic	0.10	24.80	0.08	19.84
3620 microelectronic RAMs—hermetic seal	0.44	1592.80	0.33	1194.60
905 microelectronic RAMs—nonhermetic	1.20	1086.00	0.90	814.50
809 microelectronic linear dev.—hermetic	0.084	67.96	0.072	58.25
816 discrete semiconductors, hermetic	0.024	19.58	0.020	16.32
4201 resistors RL type	0.016	67.21	0.015	63.02
2756 capacitors CZR type	0.012	33.07	0.011	30.32
1027 printed board assembly, dbl-sided	0.0029	2.98	0.0028	2.88
422 printed-board assembly, multilayer	0.36	151.92	0.34	143.48
2500 reed relays	0.27	675.00	0.26	650.00
1449 connectors print-bd assembly	0.24	34.78	0.022	31.88
1342 connections, flow solder	0.00029	38.94	0.00029	38.94
2200 connections, wire wrap	0.000005	0.011	0.000005	0.01
Total failure rate	Original	3901.661	Derated	3632.77

the reed relays with solid-state switching, and working in production to improve the reliability of multilayer boards.

Most part count reliability predictions will not be so complex as the above example, but they shall be carried out in the same manner.

3 Defining Systems

3.1 Abstract systems concepts. A prerequisite for developing system reliability models and communicating them and their characteristics to others is understanding the definition of the system concerned. Equipment and other types of systems have a wide range of complexities. Even the most simple and seemingly elementary part of a system can become extremely complex and demanding when considered in sufficiently fine detail. What one person calls a part, another will think of as a system.

The differences between people in understanding concepts go further than just parts, subsystems, and systems as seen by one person. They have to do with the fact that what one company considers to be the system it is designing and producing a customer of that company will fit with a number of equally complex systems into an operating system that is even more complex overall. An example is a fire control radar system designed and constructed by one company put to use with a gunnery system from another, a hydraulic control system from another, an airframe from yet another, and so on until all the highly complex systems are put together by the final or prime contractor, who tests the total product being delivered to the final customer in the complex supplier-customer sequence.

3.2 Communicating about the system. Since, as was explained above, the concept of a system can be misunderstood by various people in the overall program, it is essential that the interfaces at which particular systems stop and others begin must be clearly defined in documented form. It becomes the task of the prime contractor to so define those interfaces and the harmonious way each of the systems delivered by subcontractors must work across them that an effective total mission performance will be achieved.

It is equally important to each of the subcontractors to fully understand the extent of the system they are to design and produce, whether it be parts for a bulldozer, an artificial heart, an airplane, or a ballpoint pen. Since reliabilities of systems are most often expressed in terms of the probability of success, which can be translated into failure rate, it is of prime importance to the customer that the prime contractor and each subcontractor have a clear and compatible understanding of what each is responsible for.

In system definition, emphasis is placed on properly specifying reliability within the context of all the other capabilities and constraints that comprise a balanced functioning system. A complete definition of the system for the contractor and subcontractors covers the use, performance, restraints, and failure definitions. The following aspects shall therefore be defined:

- The intended purpose or use of the system
- The reliability requirements for the system
- The performance parameters of the system

- The boundaries of the system
- The conditions which constitute system failure

Each of the above shall be properly defined to provide meaningful requirements and goals for the design, development, production, and application activities associated with the system. The above aspects or definition parameters shall be used to determine when the system is operating within its intended environments, when it is performing as specified, and when it has failed.

For each system the reliability shall be defined as the probability that the system will perform each specified function for the specified time under the specified conditions. From that definition, a reliability requirement for functional or operational success shall include:

1. A definition of system performance that clearly identifies each condition as success or failure. That will require a thorough understanding of system modes of operation.

2. A definition of environmental conditions that clearly specifies equipment duty cycles and stress conditions prevailing in relation to the various environmental extremes on a real-time basis.

3. A definition of operational time and subintervals of time during which the various subsystem's operational modes of the overall system are to be carrying out their intended functions. The environmental variations and stress conditions must be related to the operational time and subintervals of time so that the system performance is totally comprehended.

3.3 Developing the system definition.   There are five principal steps to defining the system, each of which shall be thoroughly carried out.

3.3.1   Step 1: Define in clear unambiguous terms the intended purposes or uses of the system and its subsystems.   This step includes the following:

3.3.1.1   Defining the system and subsystem functions and modes of operation.   More sophisticated systems are expected to carry out more than one operational function. Each of the subsystems can be expected to carry out specific functions such that the overall system delivers many different total functions, often of different kinds. Mobile systems can be expected to carry out different functions under different environmental conditions or the same function under different environments. There are many possible iterations, and each iteration expected of the system shall be defined.

A given system may have more than one mode of operation, one being the functional mode and the others alternative modes. A function is a task to be performed by a system or subsystem. When it is performing this function, the system is in its functional mode. The system may also carry out some function that is not an intended function; in that case it is operating in an alternative mode. The intended system and subsystem functional modes of operation shall be clearly and thoroughly understood.

3.3.1.2 Defining the environmental profile encountered during the system's functional mode of operation.   The environmental profile is a presentation of the environmental conditions anticipated during the system's operational time. Such a profile may include the environmental conditions during each of the various modes of actual performance by the system, but conditions during storage and transportation which can degrade reliability are not to be included. It is, however, essential for overall operational success to consider causes of failure both in the system's design and in the environments to be encountered.

Systems can be expected to operate in more than one environment, or at least at the extremes of an environmental range. Operational success also may consist of several phases of both the environmental times and the operational modes during those times. For reliability purposes, a phase of operation shall be a period of time during which a specified environment prevails.

In system reliability models, environmental considerations are handled as detailed below:

1. For systems which have more than one end use with one associated environment, the system reliability model shall be the same for all environments except that the failure rates for the various subsystems and components may be different for the various environments.

2. For systems having several phases of operation, a separate reliability model shall be generated for each phase of operation, and the models shall then be combined into one overall system model.

3.3.1.3 Defining periods of operation, or duty cycles, for the system.   The defining of system operation shall be accomplished by subdividing the system into subsystems or components and preparing a plot of the intended use through time for each subsystem or component. The duty cycle is the ratio of on time to total time, and the variations in part stresses between on and off times which have been taken into consideration in part failure rate data shall not be reconsidered here. Calculations on duty cycles are carried out as follows:

1. When components and subsystems have negligible failure rates during off times, modify the failure rate by the duty cycle factor.

2. When components and subsystems which have nonnegligible failure rates during off times are encountered, use the following equation:

$$P_S = e^{-f_1 t_d + f_2 t(1-d)} \qquad (4.5)$$

where
P_S = probability of success
f_1 = failure rate during the ON time
f_2 = failure rate during the OFF time
t_d = duty cycle time
t_{1-d} = duty cycle time subtracted from one cycle time

3.3.2 Step 2: Establish the reliability requirement. Normally, the customer will have specified the reliability requirement in the terms best suited to the system's intended use. There are two possible approaches. When the system already exists and the purpose is to find the reliability of the system being offered, for example, on bid or tender, the requirement shall be treated as the task of calculating the reliability as offered. When the system is still to be designed and produced, it is necessary to establish a reliability that is considered suitable for performance of the intended function at an acceptable life cycle cost.

Reliability may be expressed in a number of ways. The one most often used is probability of success; the others are in terms of system availability: mean time between failures (MTBF) and, for throwaway items, mean time to failure (MTTF).

It is seldom adequate to state a single reliability figure for a complex multimoded system. Different subsystems carrying out different functions in different environments and for different time intervals will often require quite different degrees of reliability. The reliability expressions for the system and its subsystems shall be stated in the terms required in the operational requirements specification, if any; otherwise, they shall be stated in the terms and to the accuracy most applicable under the known operating conditions.

3.3.3 Step 3: Establish and specify the system and subsystem operational parameters and limits. Construct a chart listing the operational parameters that completely define the entire system under consideration. If necessary, construct several charts each of which shows the operational parameters of the more complex subsystems. Develop and show the upper and lower limits allowed for each parameter. The charts shall be comprehensive and shall include all essential parameters of the system.

3.3.4   Step 4:   Determine and fix the physical and functional boundaries of the system

3.3.4.1. For functional boundaries, define the interfaces between the various subsystems of the system and also those between the system and any other systems with which it must work in carrying out its intended operation.

3.3.4.2. When determining the physical boundaries, fix *all* necessary boundaries of the system. Some examples of boundaries are:

- Size dimensions
- Weight dimensions
- Ergonomic constraints
- Material strengths
- Safety requirements
- Software dimensions

3.3.5   Step 5:   Determine and specify the conditions which constitute system and subsystem failure.   A failure shall be taken as an incapability of the system or one of its subsystems to perform one of the intended functions because one or more of the system's or subsystem's performance parameters are outside specified limits.

It is always important to remember that both the strengths of the various parts and the stresses placed on the parts by the environments in which they operate will consist of a distribution of values. All too often the MTBF, for example, is taken as a single figure without realizing that it represents the median of a distribution of failures having a possible variance of considerable spread.

Each operating function of the system and its subsystems shall be included in the list of failure conditions. Each operating function shall be treated in each of the various ways it can fail to be carried out during system performance.

4   System Analysis and Synthesis

4.1   Top-down, bottom-up analysis. At this stage in the reliability determination, the system has been examined in some depth and defined in terms of its operational modes and environmental constraints. The next stage is to build the reliability model of the system, beginning with a top-down, bottom-up analysis.

Examination of the system from an analytical viewpoint is called a top-down view. In this stage the designer selects the configuration for the system, selects the subsystems and reaches decisions on how they will be joined, and selects the parts and raw materials of which the subsystems will be constructed. Each of these activities and decisions contributes to or detracts from the ultimate system reliability. In arriving at the system functions, subsystem structures, environmental and operational characteristics, and all the other detailed aspects of the system set forth in preceding articles, designers are involved with a top-down view. We now turn our attention to the bottom-up or synthesis view from which the reliability models will be constructed.

Synthesizing the system begins at the raw material and component level. Choice of raw materials to meet a specific reliability goal is of major importance in system design. Starting at the bottom and building the system from its many materials and parts results in an examination of each material and part, with the result that all essential parts and materials are considered from the standpoint of their contributions to the system reliability and function. This approach also causes the designer to give due consideration to the many methods of joining and packaging the various materials and parts together into the subsystems and ultimately the system.

5   Constructing Reliability Models

5.1   Introduction. At this stage the system definition will have reached the point at which the intended principal purpose of the system is known, the phases of operation of the system are defined, and the functions and alternate modes of operation (if any) of the system in performing those functions have been decided. It is now appropriate to begin constructing the reliability model in order to ascertain the probability of success. There are seven discrete steps in constructing a reliability model:

1. Define operational success requirements.
2. Translate operational success requirements into a success diagram.
3. Write an equation for the system probability of survival.
4. Calculate probability of survival P_X for each subsystem in the system.

5. Insert each P_X for each subsystem into the equation for the probability of success of the system.

6. Calculate P_S, the system probability of survival, for several successive times, and plot survival curves.

7. Make system changes, recalculate system survival P_S for each change, and optimize system-subsystem survival lifetime to that required (e.g., to a stipulated MTBF).

As stated earlier, it is necessary to define the specific operation or function the equipment must perform, the phases of operation, and the subfunctions and alternate modes of operation needed to perform the system functions.

At this stage the system definition will have reached the point at which the intended principal purpose of the system is known, the phases of operation of the system are defined, and the functions and alternate modes of operation have been decided. It is now appropriate to begin building models to determine the degree of operational success that may be expected from the system.

Defining the operational success of a system consists of writing a word statement which describes what equipment or combination of equipment is required to be in an operational state during the time concerned in order for the system to perform the intended functions. For an example of this see Fig. 4.1.

5.2 Constructing models and success statements. In writing word statements it will be necessary to make certain that all system blocks have been included and all system interconnects have been allowed for. For the reliability block diagram of Fig. 4.1, the word statement would be: "Equipments A, B, and C, or D and E, and equipment F must work for successful function performance."

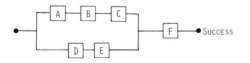

Figure 4.1 A six-component series-parallel-connected system.

The probability of success P_S equation for Fig. 4.1 is

$$P_S = P_A P_B P_C P_F + P_D P_E P_F - P_A P_B P_C P_D P_E P_F \qquad (4.6)$$

where P_n is the probability of success of equipment represented by block n.

Systems can be single-functioned or multifunctioned. For purposes of analysis, the two will be considered separately. Conceptually, the blocks in the following introduction to reliability model building can be taken to represent a component part of a system, a subsystem constructed of many components, or a system constructed in turn of many subsystems. Regardless of what hierarchical level the block is taken to represent, it is necessary at some earlier stage, for complex blocks, to have computed the probability of the operational success of each of the lesser parts within the block.

When there is only one equipment in the system and it is required for the system to carry out its required operational performance in providing the function, the success diagram is as shown in Fig. 4.2.

Figure 4.2   A single-component system.

For the equipment diagramed the word statement would be: "Equipment A shall perform its function." The success equation is then

$$P_S = P_A \tag{4.7}$$

The probability of failing is $P_F = 1 - P_A$.

When two equipments are in series, the diagram is as shown in Fig. 4.3.

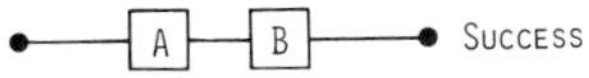

Figure 4.3   A two-component series-connected system.

The success equation is

$$P_S = P_A P_B + (0)(1 - P_A)$$
$$P_S = P_A P_B \tag{4.8}$$

For three equipments joined in series, the operational performance success diagram is as shown in Fig. 4.4.

The success equation is found as follows:

Figure 4.4   A three-component series-connected system.

$$P_S = (P_B P_C)P_A + (0)(1 - P_A)$$

$$P_S = P_A P_B P_C \qquad (4.9)$$

Two parallel equipments have an operational performance success diagram as shown in Fig. 4.5.

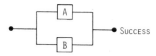

Figure 4.5   A two-component parallel-connected system.

The success equation is found as follows:

$$P_S = P_A + P_B(1 - P_A)$$

$$P_S = P_A + P_B - P_A P_B \qquad (4.10)$$

Three parallel equipments have an operational performance success diagram as shown in Fig. 4.6.

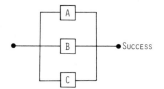

Figure 4.6   A three-component parallel-connected system.

The success equation is as follows:

$$P_S = P_A + P_B + P_C - P_A P_B - P_A P_C - P_B P_C + P_A P_B P_C \qquad (4.11)$$

Now let us consider some slightly more complex equipment assemblies such as that shown in Fig. 4.7. Here we see a number of series and parallel paths through the system.

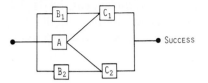

Figure 4.7 A five-component system connected with redundancy.

The operational statement for the system shown in Fig. 4.7 is as follows: "The system requirement is that equipment A and either C_1 or C_2 must work, or that equipments B_1 and C_1 must work, or that B_2 and C_2 must work, in order for success to be achieved." The equation for system success (assuming $B_1 = B_2$ and $C_1 = C_2$) is

$$P_S = (2P_C - P^2{}_C)P_A + [2P_BP_C - (P_BP_C)^2] (1 - P_A) \qquad (4.12)$$

Often several subsystems are assembled into one larger, more complex system. Such an assembly is shown in Fig. 4.8, where subsystems already treated in earlier examples are connected together.

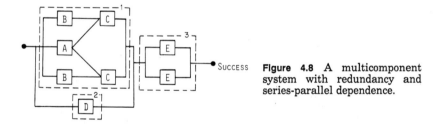

Figure 4.8 A multicomponent system with redundancy and series-parallel dependence.

The diagram for this model yields operational performance success equations as follows:

$$P_{S_1} = (2P_C - P^2{}_C)P_A + [2P_BP_C - (P_BP_C)^2] (1 - P_A)$$
$$P_{S_2} = P_D$$
$$P_{S_3} = 2P_E - P^2{}_E$$

By combining the above for the total model, we get:

$$P_S = ((2P_C - P^2{}_C)P_A + [2P_BP_C - (P_BP_C)^2] (1 - P_A)$$
$$+ P_D - P_D\{(2P_C - P^2{}_C)P_A + [2P_BP_C - (P_BP_C)^2](1 - P_A)\})$$
$$\times (2P_E - P^2{}_E) \qquad\qquad (4.13)$$

Equation (4.13), which can be expanded and reduced, can be used to generate equations for series-parallel configurations in systems. Figure 4.9 shows such a system, which can be represented mathemati-

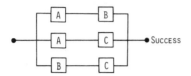

Figure 4.9 A six-component system connected with series-parallel redundancy.

cally by combining Eqs. (4.8) and (4.10). By using Eqs. 4.8 and 4.10, the success formula for the system represented in Fig. 4.9 can be written directly as

$$P_S = P_A P_B + P_A P_C + P_B P_C - P_A P_B P_A P_C - P_A P_C P_B P_C$$
$$- P_A P_B P_B P_C + P_A P_B P_A P_C P_B P_C \quad (4.14)$$

When success figures are calculated for situations in which equipments appear more than once in a diagram, probabilities must not be inserted into equations until the equations have been expanded into individual terms and terms of higher order have been reduced to single-order terms.

Sometimes more complex equipment assemblies such as the one shown in Fig. 4.10 are encountered. Here it is necessary to make iter-

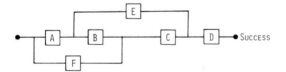

Figure 4.10 A multicomponent system connected with subsystem interdependence.

ative use of the formula

$$P_S = P_{\text{performance success with B working}} P_B +$$
$$P_{\text{performance success with B failed}} (1 - P_B)$$

When subsystem B works, the system diagram of Fig. 4.10 reduces to that shown in Fig. 4.11a.

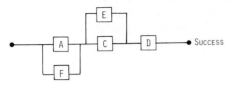

Figure 4.11a A first-stage reduction of the system of Fig. 4.10.

When B has failed, the performance success diagram for Fig. 4.10 becomes as shown in Fig. 4.11*b*.

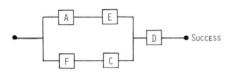

Figure 4.11b Reduction system of Fig. 4.10 with component B failed.

The statement leading to the success equation for Fig. 4.11*a* is as follows: "A plus E plus D, or A plus C plus D, or F plus E plus D, or F plus C plus D must work for performance success." The success equation for Fig. 4.11*b* follows directly from Eq. (4.6) for Fig. 4.1.

5.3 Design analysis example. A simple design analysis example will be presented here by using the system configuration of Fig. 4.7. (For more complex and detailed examples see Bazovski, *Reliability Theory and Practice,* Prentice-Hall, Englewood Cliffs, N.J., 1962, pp. 186–193.)

The equation for Fig. 4.7 is

$$P_S = (2P_C - P^2{}_C)P_A + [2P_B P_C - (P_B P_C)^2] (1 - P_A) \qquad (4.15)$$

We shall assume that $P_A = 0.7$, $P_{B1} = P_{B2} = 0.9$, and $P_{C1} = P_{C2} = 0.8$. Therefore, $(1 - P_A) = 0.3$, $(1 - P_B) = 0.9$, and $(1 - P_C) = 0.2$. By substitution in Eq. (4.15),

$$P_S = (1.6 - 0.64)0.7 + 2 \times 0.9 \times 0.8 - 0.9 \times 0.8 \times (1 - 0.7)$$
$$= 0.672 + (1.44 - 0.5184)0.3$$
$$= 0.948$$

As a first approximation to the reliability solution, the above success figure can be compared with the requirement to determine the need for additional work. Under this procedure, the above method of successive adjustments and recalculations as necessary shall be used until the required reliability in the completed equipment has been achieved.

6   Sources of Unreliability

6.1 The principal sources of unreliability.   The principal sources of unreliability occur during three phases:

1. Design and development
2. Production (i.e., manufacture)
3. Use and maintenance

In this procedure each of those sources will be considered in some depth with a view to providing guidance on the elimination of a maximum number of the problems which may be encountered in equipment the reliability of which has been determined in accordance with this procedure. It will help to review the primary environmental effects which come into all of the three phases. They are:

- Thermal considerations
- Shock and vibration considerations
- Time durability considerations
- Chemical considerations
- Application considerations
- User considerations

By far the most important environmental aspect affecting systems and their reliability is the thermal one. Every material, in whatever form, must carry out its intended purpose while subjected to some form of thermal stress. The temperature of the material changes or reaches a level that applies a high stress to the material. Any one of a number of effects, many of which are adverse, will derive from the thermal ones.

Shock and vibration, or motion-type considerations, have major influences on equipment reliability. These aspects shall be treated in depth adequate to ensure that the equipment will have the ability to perform in accordance with the operational performance specifications.

The time-durability contributions made by the designer to the reliability of equipment are major whenever there is any form of wear or change over time in equipment characteristics. Chemical reactions, often over extended periods of time, will determine whether many types of equipment will have the reliability required. These include such chemical actions as corrosion, chemical change of liquids such as lubricants, and deterioration of adhesive materials. The manner of applying equipment to its intended purpose can be a major factor in the reliability of equipment. When the equipment is wrongly applied or is applied under the wrong conditions, it may not be capable of performing its intended function. A closely related aspect is a user consideration; for misapplication of a product by the user may defeat any safety precautions taken by the designer and producer.

6.2 Design and development unreliability sources. Some of the areas in which the designer can and often does carry out design actions that contribute to the end limitation of reliability to an undesirably low level are the following:

- Choice of wrong material
- Choice of wrong material characteristics
- Choice of inappropriate limit range or values
- Failure to meet the operational temperature extremes for operation
- Failure to derate the material or part suitably for the extremes of thermal or other environmental factors
- Failure to consider the total production and test environment through which the product must go prior to use
- Inadequate contributions from disciplines outside the engineering discipline to chemical, thermal, or other life-related problems

In particular, the designer shall give attention to such matters as the following, in addition to the above and others as necessary.

- Maximum component "hot spot" temperature buildup time
- Maximum component temperature overshoot
- Maximum set-point control temperature
- Time period during component temperature overshoot
- Settling or recovery times for components

6.3 Production sources of unreliability. One of the major sources of unreliability during the production phase is failure or inability to consider pertinent reliability factors when it is necessary to substitute a component, material, or production method for the one specified in the design. It is quite common to consider only the functional capability of the replacement part and give little or no thought to reliability over full operating ranges. In all such cases the original design practices shall apply.

It is inevitable that the variance of component and material characteristics encountered in production will exceed that of the parts used during product development.

Typically, 200 resistors of some given value will be purchased for use during development of a product. Those resistors may well have had the complete supplier tests and carry the total warranty. They cannot, however, represent the entire variance of the 80,000 resistors which will be used in production of that value and type. Consequently, the design limits, unless rationalized with production after production starts, will be exceeded and the reliability ratings on the equipment may be no longer valid. This same variability situation applies to all the materials and components going into the product, each of which must be given appropriate consideration during the design and development phase as well as during the production phase.

A further source of unreliability is to be found in the production materials, techniques, and production equipment, as well as test facilities, which were not encountered during design and development. They can and will produce different characteristics in the product than those specified in the design. Two factors that arise from this situation must be covered. The first is the need to ensure that, each time a deviation occurs, the degree of deviation and its inference for the reliability of the equipment must be known and acceptable. The second is the need to undertake, with the cooperation of the designers and manufacturing engineers, a complete design-production drawing rationalization after the start-up of production. Care must be taken to ensure that equipment reliability integrity is maintained following the rationalization stage.

Inevitably during production, products which do not conform with the design requirements will be made. It is common practice to require this equipment to undergo evaluation for disposition purposes by a material review board. Sometimes there is no design representative on the board. At such times it is not always possible to ensure that all the reliability factors have been considered when the *use* decision is agreed to among the board's members.

It is a requirement of this procedure that *all* materials, parts, and methods used to produce equipment to the operational requirements specification shall have their reliability-determining factors controlled at all times.

6.4 Use and maintenance sources of unreliability. Commonly, equipment unreliability factors during the use and maintenance phase are under the control of the customer. Principal sources of unreliability include the faithful observance of the environmental limits set by the operational requirements specification given to the designer in the first instance and against which the product was designed. Most customers, having purchased a product and placed it in use, will not strictly observe the environmental constraints necessary to give the equipment the reliability expected. They will use the equipment in temperatures beyond the extremes of the performance specification or under stress conditions which are greater than those for which it was designed.

Yet another customer-induced source of unreliability is to be found in the maintenance activity established to keep the equipment operating. It is common in industry to find that the advancing technological nature of products will cause increasingly rapid obsolescence. A result is the cessation of production of spare parts for older models of the equipment in production, making it necessary for the customer to find substitutes. Seldom will the substitutes give the product as great a reliability as the original part did. Care shall be taken to ensure that this factor is not a reason for early failure of the equipment.

Use of untrained personnel on maintenance activities can be a major contribution to unreliability. It shall be the responsibility of the design and development organization to ensure that maintenance manuals, parts lists, and other documentation supplied with the equipment are complete and lucid and provide the maximum possible opportunity for the customer to get the planned reliability from the product.

7 Adjusting Reliability during Life

7.1 Designing for maintainability. All systems which are recoverable (i.e., not throwaway) and which are used for continuous or intermittent service are subject to maintenance. Off-schedule maintenance takes place when the system fails during operation or use; schedule maintenance embraces the things done to keep the system in a condition consistent with its built-in levels of performance, reliability, and safety.

We often refer to off-schedule maintenance as corrective maintenance and to schedule maintenance as preventive maintenance. Corrective maintenance is for the purpose of getting the system operable again after breakdown or failure.

System utilization is determined by the maximum system operating time; hence, system maintenance time, or equipment downtime, is subtracted from the total time to get the available operating time. It is the designer who can best vary the maintenance time by setting the reliability level appropriately and by reducing the time it takes to effect repairs. The designer's choice of system structure, assembly, assembly methods, and replacement parts philosophy, knowledge of the parts supply industry, and many other factors determine how long it will take to find faults and repair them once they occur. We see, then, that testability of the system is a further important consideration when the designer sets the maximum repair time.

The designer, when faced with reducing the equipment downtime, shall examine the parts and subsystem with the lowest MTBFs. By working on them, the greatest contribution can be made toward reducing the number of repairs that will be necessary. Further derating the components in use, further limiting the environmental stresses, if possible, and similar design actions will serve to improve the maintenance requirements for the system.

Sometimes when it is not possible to obtain sufficiently high system operating times, it is possible to design redundancy into the system. That will permit the system to continue operating while the inactive redundant member is being repaired. This method shall be used only when necessary, and only after other means of reducing the downtime have been tried, since redundancy requires more parts and increases cost.

A further technique that the designer can include in the system to reduce the maintenance downtime relates to the components with greatest failure rates, or lowest MTBFs. By assembling the system during packaging so that the lower-reliability parts can be more readily reached and removed for replacement, the downtime is decreased. Not only shall the lowest-reliability components and subsystems be more readily found and removed but the replacement part shall be more easily installed. Similarly, testing to identify faults that are due to the more fault-prone components and subassemblies shall be specifically made more direct and easily carried out as a design aspect of the equipment.

7.2 Failure rate variation during life. Component failure rate as a function of age follows a curve that is concave upward, as shown in Fig. 4.12. During the early failure period, components which have been damaged during production or testing, or which have inherently greater failure rates or have had inadequate screening during selection, can be expected to fail. The rate of failure during this period decreases exponentially to become asymptotic to the more or less con-

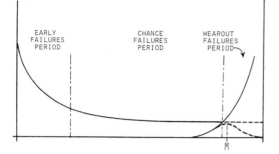

Figure 4.12 Bathtub compound curve showing failure periods.

stant failure rate period of useful life for the system. This period of the curve is called variously the early failure, infant mortality, or burn-in period. It is more or less identical with the warranty period during which the supplier of a product is expected by the customer to make repairs free of cost to the customer.

The decreasing but greater failure rate early in life of the system is due to one or more of several potential causes. The causes include inadequate testing or screening of components during selection or acceptance, damage to components during production, assembly, or testing, and choice of components which have too great a failure variability. It shall be a specific goal of the supplier to ensure that the early failure period is rigorously controlled and covered by a suitable warranty.

As can be seen from Fig. 4.12, the early failure period becomes asymptotic to the more or less horizontal useful life constant failure period. When the failure rate during this period is found to be greater than desired by the customer, there is a program whereby the failure rate can be consistently reduced. It consists of establishing a program of reliability growth. In this program, components that are found to cause unacceptably high failure rates are successively replaced, in a planned way, by similar components having a lower failure rate, or higher MTBF. Not only does a program of this type serve to decrease the system failure rate; it will also often extend the useful life part of the curve, and hence of the equipment.

The third and last part of the life curve in Fig. 4.12 is called the wear-out period. During this period, the increasing number of failures of components reaching the ends of their respective lives add to the useful life failure rate and eventually cause repair of the system to become uneconomic. At the same point M we reach the mean life of all the components in the system. This is different from the mean time between failures occurring during the useful life period. Repair and maintenance of the system may become uneconomic before point M is reached.

In most systems the mean time between failures for the components greatly exceeds the mean life of the system. The mean life of a component will usually be less than the mean time between failures by a considerable amount. If, for example, components have a 36.8 percent chance of surviving to their MTBF time, they may well have a mean life of only 10 percent of the MTBF life.

The MTBF figure shall be used in design and development of product reliability in accordance with this procedure to tell how reliable the components will be within their mean lives. Short-mean-life components shall be easily replaceable to ensure maximum availability.

Production, Provision, and Construction for Quality Control Systems

Quality Control in Industry

1 Introduction

All nations are dependent for their economic welfare on the entrepreneurial and business management capabilities of their people. It is principally the primary industry area (embodying mining and agriculture), the secondary industry area (embodying design, development, and manufacturing), and the tertiary industry area (embodying banking and corporate control) that determine a nation's standing in the currently industrialized world.

Nations at an earlier stage of their industrial development are more heavily dependent on the outputs from their agricultural and/or mining endeavors for their income. The more advanced and developed nations are, today, able to depend to a major degree on the manufacturing capabilities of their industrial enterprises. Two good examples of these are Australia, a relatively young nation, on the one hand, and the United States, a much larger industrial nation on the other.

In Australia, a country with a population of some 16.5 million (1987) and a land area of about 3 million square miles (not including its Antarctica territory), the export industry reflects the relative stage of development of the nation. Mining and agricultural products comprise some 80 percent of annual exports. In 1988, there were in the manufacturing and business community approximately 850,000 individual businesses ranging from the larger companies employing

10,000 to 20,000 persons down to the great majority of businesses run by a husband and wife or with at most 1 to 10 employees. The manufacturing and project industries account for the remaining 20 percent of Australian exports. There is a major drive by the Australian government to increase the proportion of manufacturing industry output.

In the United States, by comparison, there are some 242 million people and several million businesses, and some of the larger companies employ a workforce almost equal to one-tenth of the total workforce in Australia. The United States also with a land area of about 3 million square miles but a much larger area of arable land, has an export market composed of some 40 percent mining and agricultural products and 60 percent manufactured products. In the United States the proportion of small family-type shops and businesses is much smaller than in Australia.

The banking and finance activities, especially those involved with corporate control, have in the last few decades entered the arena of international wealth of nations as dominant factors. The proportion of world wealth flowing into a nation's coffers is increasingly dependent on the source of control of the investment money used to operate in the primary and secondary industry areas.

2 Categories of Industry

The businesses with which we are concerned herein produce or provide some items for sale to customers. Those items are what we call products, services, or systems. Products are tangible things, which must be designed, developed, and produced. We sometimes call these items goods. Services are things we do for other people, almost always with the use or transfer of products. These must be designed, developed, and provided. Most businesses sell both products and services in some ratio, usually in support of one another. Systems are projects brought into being in the project industry, and they are composed of both products and services.

Companies which make products as the major parts of their output are called manufacturing companies; companies which provide the major part of their output in the form of services are called service companies. Some service companies, such as fast food outlets, may provide a relatively greater part of their output in food value than in service value. A unique example is a company that supplies food through dispensing machines. In the third category of companies are those that provide projects as the output of their efforts. These are project (usually construction) companies, and their projects comprise a complex admixture of products and services resulting in some useful system in human society.

Projects comprise design work, followed by development and construction work, with some design refinement continuing throughout the construction activity. Work of this type is similar to the design and manufacture of a one-piece product by a manufacturing company. Accordingly, it can be expected that the quality controls used in a job shop producing 1 to 10 of many different items will be similar to those used in a design and development activity. Indeed, the two should use the same general-purpose quality system procedures. Alternatively, however, if there is to be designed and constructed only one of a kind of some complex item such as a ship or aircraft, it may be found more satisfactory to use the quality control procedure for projects of Sec. III, Chap. 4.

Typical forms of output from project work are buildings, airports, dams, electric-power-generating stations, major one-time services, and any item of product which is going to be supplied in quantities of one or a small number on a one-time basis. These would be designed in accordance with Sec. II, Chap. 1 and constructed in accordance with Sec. III, Chap. 4. Many large corporations also employ the project type of management system to bring into being new operating systems within their companies.

It is about the control of quality and hence the control of the work of people and machines and the management systems involved in bringing products, services, and systems into being that this book is concerned. Control of work requires the application of disciplines and a trained workforce within the framework of documented systems. It is most important that the documented procedures that establish the framework within which educated and trained employees must carry out their duties are ideally expressed in terms of *all* the work that must be done. For that reason the quality system general procedures in this book are structured to fit the actual work that must be done in each type of company in each industry.

3 Section II vs. Section III

Whereas Sec. II of this book contains general procedures for controlling the quality of design and development work, Sec. III contains the general procedures needed to control the quality of work done in bringing the products, services, and systems into being in the desired quantity. Achieving quality is interpreted here to be the correct carrying out of all duties and activities needed to produce each item of product or service with all characteristics being within specified limits the first time each time, the end item being what the customer wants. Since the control of such work is the responsibility of managers, these are management procedures. In each mass manufacturing company's activities, for example, several of the procedures from this book would be required to meet the requirements of a standard such as ANSI/ASQC Z-1.15-1979; see Sec. I, Chap. 3.

From the viewpoint of control it is the manner of conducting business by which all activities needed to produce a product, provide a service, or construct a project are carried out that must be covered by the management procedures. The several procedures needed will cover all the activities involved and will relate them to each other and to other procedures. When an action is mandatory, the procedure will use the verb "shall," and when some alternative action may do as well, the procedure will use the verb "should."

There are core procedures for each industry to use, and supporting them are auxiliary procedures that are just as necessary and should also be placed on vendors as requirements. An auxiliary procedure in one industry may be a core procedure in another. For example, Chap. 2 of this section, "Quality Control System for Products," is the core general procedure for a mass manufacturing company which wishes to use total quality control or to control its production plant by feedback and process controls. This procedure would be essential as a purchasing document in contracts placed by a project manager wishing to receive high-quality manufactured items for use on the construction work. So also would the general procedures of Chaps. 7 to 10.

Companies engaged in construction work as their principal effort should use the general procedure in Chap. 4 as their core procedure and then require the use of the other general procedures of this section and other sections when they are found to be useful. Companies engaged in the providing of services to the public as their principal output should use the core general procedure of Chap. 3, once again calling for auxiliary control procedures from this and other sections as necessary.

A company engaged principally in the supply of software designs is similar to one that supplies only designs of products or projects. Each company is what we call a design and development company doing applied research and development. Such companies should use as their core general procedure the procedure of Sec. II, Chap. 2. The software company should use the procedure in Sec. III, Chap. 2 as its core procedure when manufacturing the software media in large quantities.

It is appropriate here to comment on the very large number of companies today that engage almost solely in the supply of some type of service. In the United States, there is a gradual but significant increase in the proportion of companies that supply services of some type in the newly developing areas of human endeavor. As international divisions of companies move their hardware production activities offshore to the lower-labor-cost areas of the world, it becomes necessary for the services industry of the United States to expand its scope of activities.

Control of the quality of services design and development is set forth in Sec. II, Chap. 3, and the control of activities used when providing those services should be achieved by using the general procedure of Sec. III, Chap. 3.

Quality Control System for Products

PART A. REVIEW AND GUIDANCE

1 Review

Each of the world's industrialized nations has adopted standards that prescribe the systems of quality to be used in their mass manufacturing industry. In the United States, where quality control principles first developed, two quality system standards are in most common use. One is the ANSI/ASQC Z-1.15-1979, "Generic Guidelines for Quality Systems." This American National Standard is primarily oriented toward the mass manufacturing industry. The other U.S. quality control (QC) standard for manufacturing is the Department of Defense document MIL-Q-9858. The Japanese Union of Scientists and Engineers (JUSE) has produced a number of specific standards applying uniquely to different activities. In Australia, the manufacturing QC standard is AS-1821 or 1822; in Britain, BS-5750, supported by other standards, applies. In Canada it is CSA's Z-299.2 and 3 standards that cover mass manufacturing. In addition to satisfying the above national standards, this general procedure provides a quality system that will comply with the International Standards Organization (ISO) Standard ISO-9000.

The procedure set forth in this chapter, when supported by other referenced general procedures, will provide a quality system that meets the requirements of each of the above standards as well as most other national standards applying to the mass manufacturing industry.

In the mass manufacturing industry, each type of product is produced repeatedly in production line environments without design changes, or with only minimal and closely controlled changes in design. This category of industry encompasses the great majority of companies that produce products in volume. One exception is the high-volume job shop type of company that produces one or a few of many different kinds of products and product designs. It is necessary to control the quality of production in job shops by use of the project industry quality system procedure of Sec. III, Chap. 4 of *Quality Control Systems.**

2   Guidance

This procedure for control of quality in the mass manufacturing industry has been implemented and used successfully by numerous large and small companies. In the smallest manufacturing companies, however, the cost of implementing a total quality control (TQC) system is prohibitively high. To bear the cost of implementing a TQC system, a company should have an annual product sales volume adequate to meet the costs of the measurement and control systems required.

When a company has been growing gradually over 5 to 10 years, accumulating accurate measuring instruments and high-precision production tooling on a regular basis, it will be found that the extra effort, cost, and time incurred in moving to TQC can be quite low. If, however, a company seeks to move into a new plant and start producing some new product under a TQC system, doing so can cost several hundred thousand dollars more than an inspection system, and that cost will be transferred to customers. Usually 1 to 3 years of experience will be needed before total control of quality can be achieved in a new activity.

Implementing this procedure will require a strong commitment to quality by the chief executive officer (CEO). Team management is essential because managers must work closely together to achieve harmonious and effective cooperation between their respective organizations. The quality assurance manager and his or her staff will require both experience and education in quality. They must also possess the required technical knowledge of the products to be produced.

2.1   "Shall" vs. "should."   In this document the use of the word *"shall"* is intended to convey that the relevant requirement is obligatory and must be carried out in the quality system. The word "should" corresponds to the use of the word "may" in the ANSI/ASQC Z-1.15 Standard; it indicates a provision that, if used, will enhance the value of

---

*James R. Taylor, *Quality Control Systems: Procedures for Planning Quality Programs,* McGraw-Hill, New York, 1989.

the procedure to the user but is not considered vital to the success of the program.

Disciplines such as reliability, quality costing, employee participation programs, and just-in-time quality improvement programs are covered in other procedures of *Quality Control Systems*.

PART B.   PROCEDURE

Quality Control System for Products

1 Scope

This procedure defines the requirements of the company for a quality system to control the quality of mass manufactured products.

2 Application

The requirements of this procedure shall apply as follows:

1. When the procedure is called up in a contract or is referred to in other documents which are themselves called up in a contract.

2. To the operations carried on by this company when products are produced by it.

3. When a quality system standard is specified by a customer of the company to be used in mass manufacturing work of the company.

4. When an intending vendor or subcontractor seeks to have the respective quality control system for production of goods assessed and approved.

5. When conflict arises between the requirements of this procedure and other quality system requirements in a contract, the contract requirements prevail.

3 Definitions

For the purposes of this procedure, the following definitions shall apply:

1. Terms used in quality work as defined in Sec. VII, Chap. 1 of *Quality Control Systems*.
2. Terms as used in an alternate standard when called for in a contract.

4 Referenced Documents

4.1. The following documents from *Quality Control Systems* form part of this procedure:

1. "Product Design and Development," Sec. II, Chap. 1.
2. "Software Design and Development," Sec. II, Chap. 2.
3. "Reliability Control," Sec. II, Chap. 4.
4. "Nonconforming Material Control System," Sec. III, Chap. 7.
5. "Quality Control of Change System," Sec. III, Chap. 8.
6. "Calibration Control System," Sec. III, Chap. 9.
7. "Product Recall System," Sec. V, Chap. 1.
8. "Manufacturing Quality Cost System," Sec. VI, Chap. 2.
9. "Glossary of Terms Used in Quality and Reliability," Sec. VII, Chap. 1.

4.2. All documents referred to in a contract or work order shall apply, and they shall take precedence over any conflicting documents in 4.1.

4.3. The latest issue of each referenced standard or document as of the date of the contract or work order shall apply unless stated otherwise.

5 Quality System Requirements

5.1 Management

5.1.1 Organizing management for control

5.1.1.1. The company's system of controls which determine the quality of the items supplied shall have its inception with and gain its strength and coordination from the controlled division's functional management team. Each such operating division of the company that contributes to the quality of supplies shall be managed by a management team with specific functional responsibility for the quality of such products.

5.1.1.2. In a smaller company, or one operating a single plant, the controlled division's management team may be synonymous with the company management. In a larger or multisite company there may be several definable management-controlled divisions. The company shall maintain control through the respective management divisions and their management teams.

5.1.2 The control of work. Effective control of all work affecting the quality of the product shall be accomplished as follows:

1. The management-controlled division shall have a clearly defined and stable management structure.
2. Each of the necessary areas of control as set forth in this procedure that are within the division shall be clearly assigned or delegated as the responsibility of the respective functional manager. All control areas outside the division shall be clearly assigned to responsible managers who shall be held accountable.
3. Each functional manager shall know every other functional manager in the division and understand his or her working relationships with each of them.
4. Each functional manager shall establish and maintain effective control in his or her assigned area(s).

5.1.3 Management of quality assurance. Effective management of quality shall be clearly prescribed and documented in the company's policies and procedures.

5.1.3.1. The company shall have promulgated to all employees an effective quality policy approved by the chief executive officer.

5.1.3.2. The company shall appoint an appropriately educated and trained member of the management team who shall be delegated responsibility for ensuring that quality of products is obtained and maintained. He or she shall be called the quality manager, or a title covering the respective duties (hereinafter called the quality manager).

5.1.3.3. The quality manager shall report at a level commensurate with the authority needed to obtain coordination of quality effort and to ensure the resolution of quality problems throughout the activities covered in this procedure.

5.1.3.4. The quality manager shall be sufficiently free from conflicting duties and production or shipment pressures to permit the making of objective quality decisions.

5.1.3.5 The quality manager shall be provided the opportunity and have the authority to withhold from shipment any nonconforming supplies.

5.1.3.6. The quality manager shall cause to be assembled and issued a quality manual setting forth the quality system established to ensure that work is carried out in accordance with this quality control system procedure. The quality manual shall contain all the procedures and methods used to control the quality of products produced within the area of control of the management control division.

5.1.4 Quality policy. A documented quality policy that describes explicitly the chief executive officer's specific intentions with respect to quality shall be prepared, approved, and promulgated. This document shall specify an organized approach for carrying out those intentions and shall place the achievement of quality and customer satisfaction at the forefront of company objectives. The corporate quality policy document or, when they exist, individual middle-management quality policies, shall address major quality parameters including employee and user safety, product liability, adherence to legal requirements, and product fitness for use.

5.1.5 Quality planning. The company shall maintain two planning activities, one of which shall direct its energies toward ensuring that each new product will meet its quality objectives and the other of which shall direct its energies at an ongoing program of quality improvement for all products being manufactured.

5.1.5.1. To the end of securing quality improvement of all its products, the company shall conduct at the earliest stage of contract or work order performance a review of contract or work order requirements and carry out planning in sufficient detail, scope, and depth to ensure, during all phases of manufacture:

1. The adequate and documented control of manufacturing activities

2. The timely identification, acquisition, and qualification of personnel, tools, and measuring equipment, with particular emphasis on long-term procurement items

3. The updating of measuring methods, including the development or procurement of new measuring instruments or skills when they are appropriate

4. The updating of process controls and production methods, including the development or procurement of process equipment or personnel skills when they are appropriate

5. The preparation of documentation required for control of activities needed to achieve the required quality and reliability of products

6. The rationalization and achievement of compatibility among manufacturing methods and processes, measurement methods and accuracies, and applicable documentation

7. The rationalization and achievement of compatibility between design documentation and production documentation

5.1.5.2. The company shall carry out an ongoing planning activity having as its objective and methods the continuing improvement of documentation, training, skills, equipment, and awareness of customer needs and desires for the purpose of conducting a continuing quality improvement program. When it is appropriate, the company shall integrate the results of this ongoing planning activity with the activities of its employee participation program.

5.1.6 Product safety and/or liability planning. Explicit steps shall be prescribed for the identification and control of product safety and/or liability characteristics. Methods shall be devised for their definition and for their identification in products during design reviews, in-process inspection, finished product inspection, customer or user feedback analysis, and any other source for such control. All products shall be examined on a 100 percent basis for any identified safety or liability characteristic.

5.1.7 Quality manual. The quality manager shall assemble the documentation that defines the company's quality system in use. This documentation shall consist of:

1. The quality policy signed by the chief executive officer (CEO). When the quality system covers a division of the company, the

quality policy shall be countersigned by the division general manager.

2. An organization chart showing the management structure of the company or its manufacturing division. The chart (or charts) shall show the management structure for the division (or company) extending from the CEO or division general manager to the workface supervisors.

3. A description of the quality system, including a comprehensive set of the company's procedures, set either at the policy or the detailed procedure level. When detailed procedures are used to assemble the quality manual, evidence of policy documents to support them shall be provided. When policy documents are used, there shall be in existence detailed procedures implementing those policies in all areas required by this procedure.

4. A general description of quality planning requirements with specific details for each product category when there is more than one product.

5.2 Design quality assurance

5.2.1 Market research and user requirements. Prior to the start of a design and development program the company shall undertake and carry out the necessary market research to determine the broad and specific user requirements for the new product. When practicable, a user requirements specification shall be obtained for use in determining the new product's characteristics. When no user requirements document is available, the market research findings shall be used to prepare a product profile and set of performance specifications to be used in the design and development work.

Designing products for specific purposes requires accurate information concerning the product's intended use as well as user expectations. This information shall be used in deriving the product specification, as well as the reliability, safety, and other quality characteristics of the product. When practicable, sales models of the new product shall be used in field trials to ascertain from customers that their expectations have been met.

5.2.2 The design content. The design process shall generate drawings, specifications, computer programs, and other expressions of the design that provide a clear, cost-effective, and unambiguous definition of the design incorporating all applicable requirements.

The design process shall specify all measurement parameters in terms of measurable characteristics that permit establishment of a measurement capability appropriate to the product to be produced. To that end all design testing and measurements used in setting the product design characteristic values shall be performed on calibrated measuring equipment or with certified referenced materials of known accuracy and content.

5.2.3   Design reviews.   Timely, independent, and recorded reviews of drawings, specifications, computer programs, and other technical documents related to product development, safety, and use shall be held. Each organization and function concerned with the production and storage of the product shall participate in design reviews. The design reviews shall assure that all necessary design aspects have been covered and that design information and characteristics are clearly included and specified.

As part of the design work, the design function shall provide a comprehensive classification of the characteristics and performance requirements of the product for use by the in-line inspectors and quality assurance staff.

5.2.4   Design validation.   There shall exist a program which will ensure that one or more of the first pieces of any new product produced, or of an existing product that has had its design changed, will be examined against the design specifications for conformance to those specifications. Successful design validation shall be a prerequisite for entering into or continuing production of the product concerned.

5.2.5   Qualification of designs and redesigns.   Environmental, performance, and life tests shall be performed as necessary to assure the acceptable quality of the product design. These tests shall be carried out on new design products and repeated at intervals as necessary to ensure that the design integrity of the product continues to be met throughout the manufacturing program.

5.2.6   Design baseline.   The completed design shall provide an effective design baseline in the form of drawings, specifications, software, and other forms of expression that have been rationalized with the results of design reviews, qualification tests, life tests, and first-piece inspections.

5.2.7   Design change control.   All forms of expression of the design that define the design baseline shall be released, changed, or used only within the terms of an effective system of control. This system of controls shall ensure that all necessary communications concerning changes, their approvals, and their incorporation in the production activity, removal of obsolete drawings, specifications, and other forms of expression from work areas, and all other controls needed to protect the integrity of the product design and configuration are carried out.

5.3 Purchased material control. The company shall ensure that all material used meets the requirements of contracts, work orders, and customer needs. This shall include both material purchased from suppliers and that drawn from existing store stocks. For this purpose the company shall exercise effective control over purchases from and communications with suppliers.

5.3.1 Supplier selection. The company shall prepare and establish a program of supplier selection that will ensure that supplies are of the quality required to meet the needs of contracts, work orders, and customers. The program shall include supplier surveys, supplier qualification, approved supplier listing, and purchasing limitations concerning use of nonapproved suppliers.

5.3.2 Requirements for supplier quality systems. The company shall work closely with suppliers to ensure that they are aware of all requirements of the company in respect to quality aspects of the items they supply. In purchase orders and contracts, suppliers shall be assigned responsibility for meeting clearly defined and specified quality goals and objectives in the items they supply. To that end, the quality systems and the elements of which those systems are composed shall be subject to the approval of the company.

When a supplier's quality system is approved, that supplier shall be delegated full responsibility for the quality of items delivered and evidence of such quality, consistent with any audits, surveys, or surveillance that may be carried out by the company.

For each supplier the company shall identify and document the basis on which items delivered will be accepted. These shall include one of the following:

1. Full qualification and approval of the supplier's quality system
2. Evidence of quality of supplies provided with each delivery by the supplier
3. Inspection by the company at the source
4. Inspection of supplies upon their receipt by the company
5. A combination of the above

5.3.3 Selecting and qualifying suppliers. A part of the selection of all suppliers by the company shall consist of an assessment to the degree required of each supplier's ability to produce and/or provide items of a quality suitable to the company's needs. These assessments shall take the form of one of the following:

1. A full and comprehensive assessment of the supplier's quality system
2. A review of the supplier's quality history from items previously supplied to the company or other customers
3. An evaluation and inspection of items supplied by the supplier
4. A combination of the above actions

5.3.4 Purchased material quality assessment. As a result of the assessment program in 5.3.3, the company shall, for each supplier, place its reliance on the quality of supplies by defining the additional work of an inspection and test nature the company will do, if any, beyond that carried out by the supplier in order to gain confidence in the quality of supplies.

The company shall maintain strict control of nonconforming supplies. Information about failed supplies in sufficient detail to permit effective corrective action by suppliers shall be provided to each supplier.

When needed, and when it is appropriate to the company's activities, assistance shall be provided to suppliers to assist them in the achievement of the levels of quality sought by the company. A working relationship shall be sought with each supplier that will engender confidence and a two-way flow of information on a basis of mutual respect.

5.3.5 Source quality control. The company shall provide for and carry out sufficient quality checks and/or surveillance at a supplier's facilities to ensure that the quality of supplies is achieved and maintained. The decision to carry out source checks or surveillance shall be based on the benefits that will derive from each situation. The contribution to the finished product quality and the cost-effectiveness of the activity shall be factors that are used to make the decision.

When source surveillance is carried out, negotiations with the supplier shall provide for such facilities and for additional test and inspection capacity as are needed to support the necessary surveillance of the company's resident or visiting staff.

5.3.6 Incoming material control and measurement

5.3.6.1 Incoming material control. While material is entering, leaving, or being temporarily held in the receiving area or incoming inspection area, the company shall ensure that:

1. Quality characteristics are protected and preserved

2. Quantities received are determined and recorded

3. Proper identification of all material is maintained at all times

5.3.6.2 Incoming material measurement. The company shall provide for control of the quality of all material received from suppliers. When it is appropriate to the overall quality plans, such incoming material shall be subject to and shall be inspected for quality characteristics needed in the manufactured product. When incoming inspection is performed by the company on materials from suppliers, the company shall:

1. Maintain retrievable records of inspection history so that past supplier performance is available.

2. Provide adequate methods for identifying purchased material. Identification shall include the inspection and test status of the materials as needed for traceability.

3. Provide identification and verification of source-inspected items to validate documentation of inspections and testing performed on the items and the condition of items after shipment.

4. Provide adequate facilities and procedures for storage, handling, protection, and controlled release of purchased materials. All materials withheld or rejected shall be separated from material that is found to be satisfactory.

Each batch or lot of material received shall be given an individual batch or lot number, and this identity shall be maintained until the material has passed all necessary receiving tests or has been cleared by the appropriate authority for use in production, whichever occurs later in time.

5.4 Subcontracted work control. The company shall establish and maintain such controls over all subcontracted work as are necessary to ensure that materials used and items produced, as well as workmanship performed, conform to the requirements of the contract. The responsibility for quality of subcontracted work and materials shall be assigned to the subcontractor, with the company remaining responsible to the customer for such quality.

5.5 Material stock control

5.5.1. All material placed and held in stock shall be positively identified as to type, storage position, and date it was received in the stockroom. When source is an important quality indicator, it also shall be included in identification of the material. The identification shall be on a batch-by-batch basis, and each complete or partial batch will show its batch number and date of arrival in the plant or store.

5.5.2. Unless otherwise specifically authorized by the company, all raw material, compounds, components, piece parts, and subsystems shall be issued from stock on a first-in, first-out (FIFO) basis, consistent with the need to maintain production.

5.5.3. Material in stock having quality features which will deteriorate with time shall be identified and reviewed periodically in accordance with a documented program to assure that the required quality characteristics are maintained.

5.5.4. Material shall not be placed in stock in positions where its interaction with other material can cause deterioration of either material's quality characteristics.

5.6   Quality control of production

5.6.1   Planning production quality control. The capability of the product design to meet user requirements and the capability of the production quality system shall be evaluated by the company as a part of the planning of production. Plans shall be prepared and implemented for control of material during production that will:

1. Provide identity continuity of material at any or all stages of processing by using such means as tagging, marking, travel tickets, or other suitable means to the extent that all persons having the need to know can establish the type or kind of material without the use of measuring equipment.
2. Provide processing status continuity for all material such that the most recent processing step or measurement performed on that material can be readily determined.
3. Provide product flow continuity so that delays or breaks in the continuity of material flow will be readily observed and thereby prevent deterioration of quality characteristics. Faulty material shall not be processed further after its discovery without due allowance for the correction of, or concession for, the faults.

5.6.1.1. In respect to materials handling and in-line storage procedures, the company shall:

1. Plan the handling methods and in-line storage practices to be used.

2. Establish such handling and storage areas and procedures as are necessary and document and promulgate any special conditions or requirements.

3. See that all material in temporary storage areas is properly identified and that faulty material is adequately segregated from good material to prevent mixing or accidental use or further processing of faulty material.

4. Use particular attention during production, and by audits, to ensure that material is not damaged by the way it is stored, stacked, or otherwise held.

5.6.2 Control of production processes. The production process, including manufacturing tooling and any associated measuring instrumentation, shall be verified as being capable of producing the product as intended. Verification shall be by identifying each significant product characteristic and taking the necessary steps to assure that the inherent variability of the processes are within the variability allowed by product requirements. This step shall be taken prior to the start of production on each processing station.

When it is appropriate, process control charts or other automatic monitoring methods shall be installed for each controlled process. Special processes, and especially those that do not lend themselves to process control methods, shall be provided with detailed and precise work instructions. Special processes shall, unless otherwise approved by the quality organization, be performed only by qualified personnel.

5.6.3 Control of production operations. Production operations shall be documented to the greatest practical extent by detailed work procedures. It shall be the responsibility of the supervisors and managers of the company who are responsible for work to assure that all required production operations are performed in accordance with approved instructions when they exist. Use of skilled workers who do not use work instructions shall be limited to special production processes.

The detailed work procedures shall describe the criteria for determining satisfactory workmanship and work completion, as well as the requirements for compliance with quality standards.

5.6.4 In-process product inspection. In accordance with quality plans, inspection stations shall be located throughout the production processes at points where characteristics are brought into being and before they are masked by later operations. The type of in-process inspection used shall be chosen to suit the production operations concerned. For example,

1. When automated production processes are used, setup and first-piece inspection shall be used, followed by patrol inspection to sample the work underway.

2. Automated inspection using gauges or automated test equipment shall be used when productivity improvement or accuracy will justify the expenditure.

3. Fixed inspection stations at appropriate selected points throughout the manufacturing processes shall be used when they are appropriate.

4. Control charts shall be used and maintained with either of the above in-process inspection categories when they will provide the required warning signals of variance increase or data for proof of process controls.

5.6.5 Statistical methods in quality control. Statistical methods shall be used by the company whenever they will permit or enhance the degree of control over and knowledge from the manufacturing activities. Typical examples of when statistical methods shall be used are:

1. In the design of experiments, e.g., those associated with design work, reliability trials, and field trials

2. In the determination and maintenance of process capabilities

3. In the maintenance and adjustment of quality costs

4. In the design and use of sampling inspection plans

5. In the use and analysis of process control charts

6. In the analysis of data from suppliers and subcontractors and from the company's operations

7. In the analysis of data from users of the products of the company

Reinspection of material after it has been rejected and reworked requires that the history of the material be known to the inspector. It is therefore necessary that, for the statistical sampling methods used to be correct, the history of such material shall be provided to the inspector at the time the material is resubmitted for inspection.

5.6.6 Control of special processes. Special processes are those having parameters that affect product characteristics but cannot be economically controlled or economically measured by in-process inspection or test techniques or which affect the product only after it is placed in use.

In order to control special processes, the company shall:

1. Assure the stability of the processing and measuring equipment involved in the processes by periodically verifying the accuracy and control of variability of the equipment.

2. Assure the continuing capability of operators by using only qualified operators verified to have the necessary knowledge and skills for the process.

3. Assure that all parameters affecting the special processes, such as environment, times, and temperatures, are periodically verified and maintained within specified limits.

5.6.7 Control of production equipment.   Records of tool use and wear rates shall be established and maintained and be used to:

1. Maintain control of processes.

2. Budget for and replace tools no longer capable of being controlled to produce consistently conforming products.

Periodic assessment of tools shall be used to gather knowledge of tool use and wear or damage. No operator in the company shall knowingly use any tool that is unsuitable to produce the product characteristics for which it is intended. When tools constitute part or all of a manufacturing operation that is operating within a controlled process, they shall be monitored by the process controls as well as any existing periodic assessment program.

5.6.8 Control of measuring equipment.   The company shall plan, design, staff, and implement an effective program of measuring equipment procurement, calibration, and use that will ensure that the accuracy of characteristics produced are within the limits specified in design specifications and user information.

The company shall establish a measuring equipment calibration capability, or purchase and use the services of such a facility, as may be needed to ascertain and maintain the variability of product characteristics within specified and user limits. The calibration program shall comply with the requirements of the general procedure in Sec. III, Chap. 9 of *Quality Control Systems.*

Measuring equipment shall include all devices such as gauges, test equipment, tooling masters, production patterns, production tooling, jigs, fixtures, and templates used to control the manufacture of product characteristics or as a medium of inspection. The equipment shall be proved accurate prior to its use and shall be verified with sufficient frequency to assure only conforming characteristics are produced and accepted.

Certified reference materials used for measurement by the company shall be verified by the U.S. Bureau of Standards, or other national standards laboratory, to have the purity, chemical content, or other quality characteristic(s) required for their use. They shall be stored, used, and otherwise have their quality characteristics preserved appropriately to their intended use.

5.6.9   Control of nonconforming material.   Production material found by the company to be nonconforming shall be treated in accordance with the general procedure of Sec. III, Chap. 7, "Nonconforming Material Control System" of *Quality Control Systems.*

5.6.10   Document and document change control.   All documents used in the course of producing the products shall come under the control of the company's quality system. Detailed procedures, work instructions, drawings, specifications, data compilations, and the results of analyses used to make decisions shall all be regarded as part of the manufacturing documentation. These shall be maintained and retained in accordance with legal and contractual requirements in a retrievable and secure manner.

All documents used in manufacturing the product that comprise the manufacturing and measurement system shall be changed only in accordance with "Quality Control of Change System Procedure," of Sec. III, Chap. 8, of *Quality Control Systems.*

5.6.11   Stock control.   The term "stock" as used in this article shall refer to the material in process of being manufactured or temporarily being held in some intermediate or completed state of manufacture. The company shall provide designated storage areas equipped with air conditioning, marked or walled boundaries, and other environmental factors as necessary to protect the quality characteristics of the stock from deterioration or damage. Stock shall be so held during and following manufacture that items are prevented from becoming mixed, with particular attention being given to the segregation of faulty stock from that which has the required quality characteristics. The integrity of traceability and stock identity shall be maintained during all stages of manufacture.

5.6.12   Inspection of completed items.   The company shall plan for and carry out inspection of completed items of product by using either sampling inspection methods or 100 percent inspection, depending on the requirements. When safety or liability characteristics are involved, they shall be inspected on a 100 percent basis. All other product characteristics shall be inspected with a severity that will verify the quality of product at the required levels.

No completed items of product shall be shipped by the company without at least an audit of quality characteristics having been carried out on the items.

5.6.13 Records control. The company shall gather and retain quality information commensurate with the degree of control needed or stipulated in contracts and legal statutes. These records have two time periods of significance: during production and after products are shipped.

5.6.13.1 Quality records during production. These records shall include:

1. Materials source information, including suppliers, supplier approval information, materials identity, and quality data supplied or obtained at incoming inspection.

2. Inspection and quality procedures, standards, inspection and test instructions, certified reference materials records, and other working instructions of the quality system.

3. Production and stores procedures, methods and practices that are documented, and identity records that provide traceability of materials and items of product.

4. Product identification records that show what has been made, what operations were performed, which materials and production equipment were used, and by what operator(s) and on what date(s).

5. Inspection records that demonstrate what tests and inspections have been performed, the number of items accepted, the number of items rejected, and the disposition of rejected items.

6. Scrap and spoilage reports, and the sources and causes of scrap and spoilage.

7. Quality cost reports showing any optimization or minimization of quality costs through changes in the production or quality activities.

8. Quality reports to management in summary or other form showing quality performance.

5.6.13.2 Quality records following shipment. Several categories of records needed in the manufacture of products have varying degrees of importance to the company after the completed items are shipped. Records which shall be retained and stored in a secure, protected, and retrievable manner for prescribed periods of time are those which demonstrate that:

1. Specified materials were used in the manufacture of products.
2. Specified configurations were achieved and maintained in products.
3. Specified process controls were achieved and maintained during the manufacture of the product concerned.
4. Products shipped were inspected or tested with the stipulated or adequate severity and did indeed meet the quality requirements. These records shall include definite identification of the items inspected, the nature and number of observations made, the number and type of nonconforming characteristics found, the number of items accepted or rejected, and the nature of corrective action taken when appropriate.

For the purposes of this procedure, acceptance records for completed items of products shall be retained for all products shipped for a time period as specified in the contract or for the duration of the warranty, whichever is longer. All records required to be retained by legal statutes shall be retained and held as stipulated in those statutes.

5.6.14 Marking and packing control. The company shall assure that identity and other required information concerning completed items of product is maintained throughout the stages of packing, storage, shipment, installation, and use. Particular attention shall be given to the legibility of marking, the position in which marking is placed, and the permanence of such marking.

Completed items of product shall, as a minimum, be labeled with identity information, typically with part numbers that relate to drawings and specifications, and with a manufacturing date code that identifies the date from which the warranty period begins. When it is appropriate, completed items of product shall be labeled in a permanent manner with an individual serial number unique to each item of product.

The company shall establish and maintain a system that will ensure the protection and preservation of the quality of completed items and their security while they are in transit from final acceptance inspection to their points of use. Cartons, boxes, or other packing media shall be labeled and marked adequately to comply with shipping needs and with regulatory and safety requirements.

5.6.15 Handling, storage, and shipping controls. The company shall plan, establish, and maintain a system for the handling, storage, and shipment of completed items of product that will protect and preserve the quality characteristics of products from deterioration, degradation, damage, or other loss. The system shall also preserve information, such as serial numbers, manufacturing date codes, or other essential identity information necessary for the warranty of the items.

The system shall provide for control of shipping methods that assure that transit requirements are met and that appropriate shipping documentation is used and delivered with the items.

5.6.16 Product quality audits

5.6.16.1. The company shall conduct regular audits of outgoing product quality. These audits shall provide an effective indication of the conformance or nonconformance of outgoing product to specification and contractual requirements.

5.6.16.2. Records of the product quality audits and their results shall be kept for the duration of the relevant contract or for such other times as the items are covered by warranty.

5.6.16.3. The results of product quality audits shall be used as an integral part of the quality improvement programs.

5.6.16.4. Product audits shall cover items held in stock as well as items being processed or items that have been completed.

5.6.17 Quality system audits

5.6.17.1. The company shall establish and maintain a documented audit of the quality system, including the quality manual.

5.6.17.2. The company shall conduct a periodic audit of control areas included in this procedure which are applicable to the discharge of current or impending contracts or work orders.

5.6.17.3. The quality system audit shall assess the adequacy of the control areas of the system for capacity to contribute to the successful discharge of contracts or work orders. Each control area shall be rated in terms of its effectiveness of control in its area.

5.6.17.4. Records of the findings of the audit program shall be kept for the duration of any contract and for such longer times as the company shall find such records useful.

5.7 Product user or consumer quality control. The company's quality control program shall extend to encompass the sales, delivery, installation, and use of its products. Products shall be designed for specific purposes, and design specifications shall contain user or consumer requirements information against which the products shall be assessed. To that end, the company shall establish direct and indirect contacts with its customers for the purpose of communicating and collecting data and other information needed to develop its specifications and to provide total satisfaction to its customers.

5.7.1 Product literature for users or consumers. The company shall prepare, have published, and distribute to its customers literature in the form of owner's manuals, service manuals, assembly instructions, handling instructions, warning tags and labels, installation instructions, and warranty cards. All essential technical information needed by users or consumers to make the most effective and beneficial use of the company's products shall be distributed with the products.

The company shall have a program the purpose of which is to revise and keep up to date user or consumer literature in accordance with feedback from customers and changes in models and styles of products by the company.

5.7.2 Advertising and promotion. Advertising and promotion literature shall be a part of the company's quality system. This literature shall be reviewed to assure that it correctly reflects design and market research information. In particular, advertising literature shall be regularly reviewed for relevance to product performance, reliability, safety, quality, maintainability, and aesthetics to assure that it is accurate, clear, unambiguous, and complete.

5.7.3 Sales, installation, service, and use. The quality system shall provide for fast and accurate feedback of information on user product acceptance, field failures, and, in particular, any evidence that may indicate a need for a recall or field repair program.

The quality system shall incorporate measures to assure that the safety, quality, reliability, and performance characteristics of the product are not degraded during installation or service. In particular, precautions shall be taken to guard against improper installation or maintenance and against misuse.

5.7.4 User or consumer feedback. The quality system shall provide a well-planned and continuing program of feedback from users or consumers that will keep the managers of the company informed of real or potential problems in the field. All user or consumer complaints shall be given individual treatment in direct relation to their seriousness.

The user or consumer feedback program data shall be summarized on a regular basis, and the results shall be integrated into both the ongoing production program to improve quality and the design activities to strengthen the designs in relation to any faults or weaknesses found. The feedback program shall provide a direct input to the quality cost program on the cost of field servicing and field failures.

The particular feedback channels that shall be used will depend on the product involved; but as a general rule, the company shall use:

1. Analysis of all product returns and, in particular, of all failed products to determine the mode and basic cause.

2. A product failure early warning system, which shall function particularly in relation to newly released products.

3. A customer complaints program by which all complaints are dealt with on a timely basis, the objectives being to turn dissatisfied customers into satisfied customers and to provide information for quality improvement.

4. Product acceptance surveys among users or consumers.

5. Field trials which shall be statistically designed and the data from which shall be used to avert early failures.

6. All feedback information on safety as a part of its total product safety program.

5.7.5 Complaint servicing and corrective action. The company shall establish, as a part of its quality system, a capability for servicing complaints from users and consumers. This program shall be integrated into the company's total system of quality control, and, in particular, it shall make use of the company's change control and approval procedures.

Users and consumers shall be kept informed of findings derived from their complaints and of corrective action taken and being taken in respect to them. The company's quality system shall provide for analysis of each failure, and in particular repetitive failures, and classification of findings into categories and failure analysis for use in identifying failure modes and assigning basic causes for corrective action. A system for assigning priorities shall be developed and used to effect corrective action, and the effectiveness of corrective actions taken shall be verified.

5.7.6 Product return and failure analysis. The company shall provide a program for servicing customer-returned products and regaining customer confidence. Each occurrence shall be given timely attention in direct proportion to the seriousness of the matter. The program shall have as its objective the gaining and retention of customer satisfaction with the company's products.

5.8 Problem identification and corrective action. The company shall develop its ability to identify potential problems before they occur and to plan for problem prevention. It shall establish the ability to identify and define problems that are occurring in its manufacturing program and apply corrective action.

Corrective action creates a change in some element of the manufacturing activity. Any such change shall be permitted to occur only in an orderly and controlled way. The quality system shall provide for recording and classifying all instances of unsatisfactory quality, with particular attention being given to repetitive occurrences. They shall be correlated according to such common factors as product type, failure mode, and material supplier. Product failures shall be ranked according to cost, and corrective action shall be taken accordingly. Procedures used for corrective action shall ensure that needed changes are promptly incorporated in operating procedures.

5.8.1 Problem detection and documentation. Anyone seeing the need for corrective action shall report the problem in accordance with the quality system procedures. The quality system shall provide procedures that are designed to bring to the attention of the quality manager and other members of management the existence of each quality problem.

Quality problems, once identified and proved to exist, shall be documented, and copies of the documentation shall be forwarded to the quality organization of the company. Documentation shall include the first indication of the problem and information on its development. The quality manager shall assign both responsibility for collecting additional data as appropriate and responsibility for the problem.

5.8.2 Failure mode and effect analysis. Quality problems shall be investigated to the extent necessary to assign responsibility for their occurrence. When product materials are involved, their failure shall be the study of laboratory or other action as necessary to ascertain the failure mode and to assess and understand the effects. These shall be the subject of documentation of the quality problem.

5.8.3 Assigning problem responsibility. It shall be the duty of the quality manager to assign responsibility for quality problems. Responsibility for corrective action shall be specifically assigned to the function or functions within the company having direct responsibility for activities such that corrective action can remove the basic cause(s) of the quality problem.

Organizations that are responsible for actions that led to the quality problem (i.e., failed product or system) shall assist in determining what corrective action will be taken and then taking that action. Reports on such actions shall be prepared and forwarded to those having the need to know. When the company uses an employee participation program (EPP), the EPP working committee and the steering committee, as well as the quality manager, shall be provided with copies of the report. When corrective action is taken, it shall be implemented in accordance with the company's documented change control program.

5.8.4 Recurrence file. The quality manager shall establish a record system by which reports of quality problems and actions taken are filed for future use for preventing quality problems and comparing them with future quality problems to ascertain their recurrence or adequacy of solution.

5.8.5 Change and change control. The company shall implement and use a change control procedure which shall, in the absence of other requirements, be the procedure in Sec. III, Chap. 8 of *Quality Control Systems*.

5.8.6 Control of quality costs. The company shall implement and use a system for determining, recording, reporting, adjusting, and in general using quality costing for the purpose of containing and optimizing or minimizing the costs of product produced. The system used shall, in the absence of other requirements, be that in Sec. VI, Chap. 2 of *Quality Control Systems*.

5.8.7 Product recall quality program. The company shall prepare and implement a program for use in the event a product has to be recalled for any reason. The system used shall, in the absence of other requirements, be that in Sec. V, Chap. 1 of *Quality Control Systems*.

5.9   Employee selection, training, and motivation

5.9.1   Employee selection. The company shall establish a program to be used when establishing the need for employees. This program shall result in the examination of the work to be done, the education, experience, and skills needed to carry out the work, and other factors affecting the position(s) to be filled. The program shall result in the preparation of a specification of the position, including a statement of the duties and work elements to be carried out.

Employees shall be chosen for their efficiency and effectiveness in the position(s) and their abilities to satisfy the other position requirements not directly involved in the work to be done. The latter may include such factors as are not precluded by legislation, i.e., education, experience, and skills.

5.9.2   Employee training. The company shall plan, establish, and operate a program of employee training and further education that will assist employees in attaining their goals consistent with the best interests of the company and that will assure the successful carrying out of the work of the company.

5.9.2.1. The company shall assure that all measuring equipment operators are competent for carrying out their work. No completed items shall be accepted for shipment if conformance to their requirements has not been fully assured by fully trained and approved inspection and test personnel.

5.9.2.2. The company shall assure that all production personnel are competent for carrying out their duties. The training and approval procedures used shall assure that work done by an employee prior to the employee's having received full training and approval has appropriate inspection on a 100 percent basis to ensure its conformance with requirements.

5.9.2.3. Employees involved in highly complex work requiring higher-education degrees and training shall be encouraged to routinely update their knowledge by taking refresher courses and/or by pursuing advanced degrees.

5.9.3   Employee motivation. Employee motivation programs used by the company shall be based on leadership by management and shall, when it is appropriate, include employee participation programs that permit employees to:

1. Know they are making beneficial contributions to the security of their positions through their work in the company.

2. Receive recognition for work well done.

3. Be aware of corporate or company plans and failings that will affect them.

4. Feel that they, as much as managers, are essential parts of present and future company activities.

5. Feel secure in their employment.

6. Make contributions commensurate with their abilities to the progress and welfare of the company.

7. Be aware of the consequences of poor quality work and receive individual and group recognition for work that produces satisfactory or higher quality.

Managers shall permit employees to participate in the development of processes and in the development of measurements. Managers shall demonstrate to employees that they are the most important asset of the company.

3

Quality Control System for Services

PART A.   REVIEW AND GUIDANCE

1   Review

At the time this procedure was prepared, Ireland appeared to be further ahead in its preparation of a national standard for use throughout its services industry than other nations. The United States had several individual regulatory standards for application in specialized areas providing services, notably the medical field, in which cleanliness and equipment safety are paramount. Australia was establishing a committee within its Standards Association for the preparation of a services industry standard. The International Standards Organization Committee TC-176 was considering the preparation of a standard for services.

Services, unlike products, are intangible things which must be delivered directly to the customer. The business providing services must therefore be directly accessible by the customers it serves. Whereas the producers of products can locate their businesses thousands of miles from their customers and depend on service companies to deliver their products, service companies themselves or their divisions must have their outlets near or inside the customer's homes or wherever else the service is provided.

Banks, hotels, motels, restaurants, stock brokers, supermarkets, gasoline (petrol) stations, garages, telephone companies, golf courses, tennis clubs—the list is almost endless as the variety of service organizations grows. All of those organizations must be within an easy distance from the customer's residence or readily accessible by the customer.

2 Guidance

When major corporations have many divisions that provide services, it is normal for the head office to be many miles away. Control in such situations is somewhat akin to that for widely distributed divisions of a large multinational corporation. Local managers must be delegated enough autonomy to permit them to operate as independent companies within the usual corporate constraints from the head office.

This procedure presents the quality control requirements for a multidivision corporation. Smaller companies with only one service outlet each should see themselves as comprising the entire business activity. In those situations, the head office and service outlet are one and the same. All the requirements of this procedure that apply to *both* the head office and the service outlet will be found to apply to the small services company also.

2.1 Local and head office relationships.
We can list most of the things which should be controlled from the head office vs. those which must be controlled by the local manager of the operation.

2.1.1 Head office controls.
Controls which should be established and maintained by the head office include:

1. Overall corporate policy
2. The company name and image (on a national and international scale) and corporate level finance
3. Procedures which are identical for each of the various service outlets
4. The market research and product mix and range, plus goods production and distribution
5. The corporate training program for all functions of manager or for high-level technical or training qualifications
6. The ownership of the total company and its locations
7. The employee and service qualifications

2.1.2 Local office controls.
Controls which should be delegated to the local manager include:

1. All local employment matters
2. Local training of all hourly employees

3. All local company matters dealing with local officials, laws, and regulations
4. The resolution of all local problems, including quality
5. All day-to-day activities of the company
6. The local goodwill of the company
7. All policies, procedures, and financial matters of a local nature

Corporate control emanates from the head office of the company, and all divisions, operations, suborganizations, etc., owned in whole or at a majority level shall answer to the head office. Legal, fiscal, and corporate support must be provided to each division or suborganization controlled by the company. The company shall maintain rigorous control of communications and fiscal matters along prescribed lines for each division.

2.2 Quality control of services. Philosophically, the control of the quality of service output of a company, or of a department within a company, uses general principles similar to those developed for products. Services must be "fit for their intended purposes." They must be uniquely tailored to fit the needs of each individual customer, within the cost-effective levels found tolerable for company operations.

Services are controlled by clearly and unambiguously defining what is required by the customers, designing the best possible services to satisfy customer requirements, specifying and purchasing the best-quality products found most suitable for support of the services production and sales, and rigorous training and discipline of the employees who deliver the services to the customers. In other words, the right service, delivered in the right way, on time, and to the full satisfaction of the customer so that he or she is entirely happy with the company.

This general-purpose quality procedure has been prepared to show what to control in order to accomplish the above and deliver the best-quality services to customers.

PART B. PROCEDURE

Quality Control System for Services

1 Scope

This procedure defines the requirements of the company in respect to services provided by the company or purchased under contract from a company.

2 Application

The requirements of this procedure shall apply:

1. When the procedure is called up in a contract or is referred to in other documents which are themselves called up in contracts

2. To the operations carried on within the company in respect to providing services

3. When an intending contractor seeks to have the respective quality control system for the provision of services assessed and approved

2.1. If conflict between the requirements of this procedure and other quality system requirements in a contract arises, the requirements of the contract shall prevail.

3 Definitions

For the purposes of this procedure, the following definitions shall apply:

1. Terms used in quality and reliability as defined in Sec. VII, Chap. 1 of *Quality Control Systems.*[*]

2. Terms as used in an alternate standard when called for in a contract.

4 Referenced Documents

1. "Glossary of Terms Used in Quality and Reliability," Sec. VII, Chap. 1 of *Quality Control Systems.*

2. "Calibration Control System," Sec. III, Chap. 9 of *Quality Control Systems.*

5 Quality System Requirements

5.1 Management

5.1.1 The management-controlled organization

5.1.1.1. In the service industry the choice of management personnel is uniquely important. Each different location from which the services are provided to the customers requires a fully competent business manager capable of managing all aspects of the local division of the corporation. For a bank, motel, restaurant, or other service organization with 200 outlets, this means a requirement for at least 200 managers each capable of overall management in his or her area.

---

*James R. Taylor, *Quality Control Systems: Procedures for Planning Quality Programs,* McGraw-Hill, New York, 1989.

The company shall provide, for each service outlet, a team of completely trained and experienced management and technical service personnel capable of generating and delivering the full range of services offered by the company for that location.

5.1.1.2. The local manager shall be responsible for making all decisions in matters of a day-to-day nature and shall ensure that the quality of all services is rigidly controlled to specified levels.

5.1.1.3. The head office management shall:

1. Define, publish, and promulgate corporate policies on quality of services.

2. Choose a company name, register it in each state and county in which business is to be conducted, create, develop, and advertise a corporate image to which the quality of services may be ascribed.

3. Establish systems of business accounting, accountability, and communication throughout the company's locations of doing business, and manage the finances of the corporation.

4. Prepare, publish, and promulgate for all company operations procedures that are unique to the business and corporate image as well as common to the locations carrying out the same kinds of service provision and sales.

5. Carry out market research; define the mix and range of services to be sold; and arrange for the purchase, distribution, installation, and maintenance of equipment plus a supply of goods used.

6. Be responsible for providing trained local managers and all specialized personnel necessary to provide and maintain the corporate image and quality of services.

7. Determine location of, purchase sites for, erect buildings for, equip and furnish buildings, and in general provide all the many real estate and chattel property necessary to carry out the business at local sites.

8. Prepare, publish, and promulgate procedures for work carried out at all local sites where such procedures are necessary to provide the standard of services coordinated between the several service outlets.

5.1.1.4. The local office management shall:

1. Provide and ensure the use of uniforms, dress, or other appearance factors necessary to enhance and build the corporate image.
2. Provide training needed to support academic qualifications for locally hired staff for day-to-day activities.
3. Represent the company in all local matters affecting the company, including social, legal, political, community, and customer-related situations and matters.
4. Manage all aspects of the local division of the company on a day-to-day basis.
5. Define, promulgate, and enforce all local policies, procedures, and conditions necessary for the running of the local division.

5.1.2 The management of work

5.1.2.1. The local management of a division of the company shall provide for all work carried out by the services-providing outlet in accordance with procedures published by the head office and added thereto as necessary to adapt them to local conditions while maintaining the singleness of purpose and image of the company.

5.1.2.2. All training, all work, and all instructions given to employees shall be oriented toward the production of services having a quality commensurate with the aims and goals of the company.

5.1.2.3. Since work done for customers constitutes the outputs provided by the company in the form of services, all effort by the head office and by the local management staff shall be directed toward the maintenance and improvement of the quality of services.

5.1.3 Services quality management

5.1.3.1. The quality of services begins with design, so it shall be the direct responsibility of all company managers to ensure that all services are designed to meet the standards required to achieve and maintain a growth position in the marketplace.

5.1.3.2. In the design and management of services, due attention shall be given to the appearance of the employees who provide the services for customers, to the quality of the equipment and goods-type items delivered to customers as part of the service, and in particular to the quality and reliability of equipment on which the services are produced. (*Note:* Services are sometimes produced with the aid of equipment; at other times they are provided by employees after all equipment use has been completed.)

5.1.3.3. Human factors, including courtesy and customer responsiveness, shall be managed with great care to foster the highest degree of quality achievement in the services delivered.

5.2   Planning control

5.2.1   Project, program, and task planning

5.2.1.1   Project planning. Expansion planning for the company's national and international operations will involve the marketing studies, location of sites, construction of buildings and installation of facilities, and the establishment of fully operational (often turnkey) divisions. These activities, beyond the marketing study and decision as to site, will most effectively be managed on a project basis. The quality control of such projects shall be accomplished by applying the requirements of "Quality Control System for Projects," Sec. III, Chap. 4 of *Quality Control Systems.*

5.2.1.2   Program planning. Programs, as compared with projects, are long-term ongoing efforts of a company. Whereas projects can be, and usually are, begun and completed in a few months or at most a couple of years, programs go on uninterrupted for indefinite periods. Programs, however, do possess a fiscal year character. Quality control of the service company's programs will involve *all* the quality system procedures found in the quality systems manual. The core procedure used in a services-providing company shall be this procedure.

5.2.1.3   Task planning. Task, or work, planning is extremely important in all categories of industry, but it is most important in the services industry because a service output is delivered direct to the customer by employees of the company. The company shall prepare detailed task procedures by which the work of each employee is carried out. Particular attention shall be given to the areas of human factors as well as to the corporate image projected by employee dress, manners, and total behavior patterns. This area, together with all other areas planned for the company, shall project confidence in the company and satisfaction with the services delivered.

Work procedures prepared for carrying out tasks shall be specifically keyed to the unique characteristics of the various types of equipment and goods with which the employees must work in developing and delivering to the customer the many types of services concerned. One of the greatest areas of difficulty in service companies arises from the confusion and improperly produced and delivered services that occur when the employee's instructions are not clear and he or she must improvise with unfamiliar equipment, forms, or other goods in producing the services. This area shall be given attention when the work procedures for each of the several company divisions are prepared.

5.2.2 Planning the customer interface

5.2.2.1. Total customer interface planning covers the entire area of customer interaction with the company. It ranges from what is done before the customer is on the scene in anticipation of the customer's needs to the entire interaction during the customer's presence, and it includes the activities and considerations which continue after the customer's departure from the site. It is from this part of the company's total service performance that the most productive and profit-earning activities are carried out. Though all other areas, such as site selection and procedure preparation, are of great importance, if the company fails to deliver the services the customer wants during this critical interfacial visit to or contact with the premises of the company, the business will fail. For this reason the company shall give adequate attention to planning in detail all the activities and supporting resources to ensure the quality of services delivered will meet the customer's wishes.

5.2.2.2. In planning the customer interface, the company shall review the remainder of this procedure in complete detail and shall plan thoroughly all the areas and activities covered throughout the remainder of this procedure. These plans shall be documented and shall be delegated for action, with purposeful follow-up in each case, to employees of the company for their individual accomplishment.

Particular attention shall be paid to the tangible and intangible areas contributing to or detracting from the successful sale of services to the customer.

5.2.3 Planning quality measurement

5.2.3.1. Each different area of the service industry has its unique quality indicators, as well as those which are common to other areas. It shall be a specific task for the company to identify all the quality indicators which are required to measure the quality of services being supplied to the customers of the company. These indicators shall be ranked according to their importance in terms of good and bad influence on the customer. A seriousness scale of zero to 100 shall be used, and the different quality indicators and the nonconformities they highlight shall be given a demerit rating which shall be the inverse of the acceptable quality level (AQL) for that rating. For example, a demerit rating of 2 corresponds to an AQL of 0.5 percent nonconforming for all of that type of serious faults in the batch sampled.

Note: For services that have a given characteristic repeated in each of many thousands of such services, it may be necessary to use a demerit base of 1000 to 10,000, with AQLs of 0.001 or 0.0001 percent nonconformities for the most serious of them.

5.2.3.2. The measurement of quality is concerned with several forms of data collection. Some of the collection can be carried out at the site by staff on the payroll of the local manager, but measurement of the manager's performance, the performance of the technical staff and professionals such as chefs and pilots and their contribution to the quality of services provided to the public must be assessed by qualified individuals operating from outside the local area, and usually from the head office.

The company shall formulate and document plans for the collection, analysis, and reporting of the quality data which will reflect the ongoing degree of success in producing and delivering services of a quality suitable for their purposes.

5.3   In-line control areas—services

5.3.1   Control of customer property

5.3.1.1. Various services require the company to carry out some form of work on items of property belonging to the customer. An example is repair of small electrical appliances. At other times the customer will provide to the company some form of goods to be used as part of the goods production or services provision to be later carried out by the company. Without regard to the nature of the customer's property placed under the control of the company in respect to rendering to the customer some service, the company shall prepare plans, document procedures, train staff, and in general, carry out all the actions necessary to ensure that the service will be provided and delivered to the customer at the quality level agreed upon between company and customer or stipulated in the company's procedures.

5.3.1.2. Only fully qualified members of the company's staff shall be assigned to work on customer-owned property in rendering some service to the customer. Such work shall, when possible, be in accordance with procedures prepared for the purpose.

5.3.2 Customer well-being control. A major parameter of importance when planning and designing to satisfy the full range of customer needs in respect to some category of service involves the customer's well-being. The customer shall be served in an atmosphere appropriate to the service and with consideration for all aspects of the supplier-customer interaction and involvement. An atmosphere commensurate to the type of service being rendered shall be established by the company providing the service.

5.3.2.1. The company shall ensure that the customer is well informed of what to expect, and positive steps shall be taken to inform customers. The company shall take great care to ensure that no form of unpleasantness or dissatisfaction or cause for them is permitted to exist or occur when services for the customer are produced. In matters of quality the customer's desires are paramount, consistent with his or her willingness to pay.

5.3.2.2. The employees of the company shall be thoroughly trained in the constant use of all the human characteristics and mannerisms needed to give the customer a feeling of being wanted, happiness at being able to serve him or her, gratitude for his or her coming to the company for the service, and all other such human factors needed to convey to the customer the maximum degree of well-being.

5.3.3 Continuity of service control. When the type of service demands that the customer receive uninterrupted availability of the service, the company shall ensure that at no time during any night or day of the week, month, or year is the service not available to the customer.

When the service is the supply of some form of utility, such as electric power, telephone, or natural gas, any necessary interruption of service to customers shall be only after formal notification (preferably in writing) of the customers as to time, date, and area of such interruption. At times necessary for repairing, maintaining, or otherwise servicing the network of pipes, cables, etc. by which the service is delivered, the customer shall also be notified how long the service will be unavailable.

When the service involves the requirement for availability of access, such as to a doctor, lawyer, dentist, or hospital and even to banks or restaurants, the company providing the service shall take steps to establish, and make readily available to customers, phone numbers, 24-hour, 7-day offices, or other such access points through which the customer may make contact with the company and procure the needed service.

5.3.4   Time control

5.3.4.1 Access time control. Access time is defined as the length of time beginning when the customer first attempts to make contact with the company and ending when the service attention of the company has been gained. The company shall identify a quality measure for access time and shall implement controls to ensure that this requirement is met. The access time applies to customer-supplier interfaces.

5.3.4.2 Queuing time control. Queuing time is defined as the length of time beginning when the customer first enters the queue and terminating when the customer begins to receive the service for which the queue was entered. Many service companies require that customers, at times of peak demand, enter queues and wait their turn for service. During such times, the well-being of the customer shall be a major consideration of the company.

The company shall use queuing theory and, from past history and probability considerations, establish service outlets, service times, and customer movement rates such as to provide for queuing times that are acceptable to customers and economical to the company consistent with maximization of customer service rates.

The company shall establish controls to ensure the integrity of the queue. Some formula for providing service to customers in the queues which will be acceptable to the customers and understood by them before entering the queues shall be adopted. This formula shall be on a first come, first served basis unless valid considerations dictate otherwise.

5.3.4.3 Action time control. Action time is defined as the time beginning when the customer's order is first received by the company and ending when the requested service is supplied.

It is important that the customer's order placement time be taken to be the time of the first contact and not the time from which employees first fully understood and started work on the order. If there is any misunderstanding, the company must assume at least part of the responsibility and often the whole responsibility, because it is the company's duty to make all necessary matters about company services clear to customers. In designing the company's action time, the customer's viewpoint shall be a prime consideration in respect to elapsed time from request to satisfaction. Though the company will know all the reasons why supply of some particular service was difficult and time-consuming, the customer will frequently have no good appreciation of such matters. The customer can interpret the delays as deliberate or as indicating lack of responsiveness to the customer by the company.

5.3.5   Range control.   Very often the range of services provided by a particular company will not be clearly understood by the customer. As a result, the customer may demand the supply of services which the company is not organized, staffed, or equipped to deliver. Communications in this area can be simplified if the company clearly defines the range of services to be offered.

5.3.5.1   Services range control.   The company shall carefully control advertising and other communications with customers so that the range of services being offered is quite clear and unambiguous. When designing services, and planning to carry out their preparation and delivery to customers, the company shall cover in detail the services to be provided and shall recognize and acknowledge the exceptional circumstances which will arise from time to time when dealing with the general public. The company shall plan for the exceptional as well as the normal situations.

To the extent that customer idiosyncracy is to be catered to, the company shall prepare work procedures and provide staff at local sites with sufficient leeway to make decisions. In exceptional circumstances, it shall be the duty of the local manager to be constantly aware of deviations from the normal service range and to so control the staff that the deviations do not jeopardize the profit position of the company. Reports of all exceptional situations shall be collected and made to the head office so that they can be taken into consideration in future planning and procedures.

5.3.5.2   Products range control.   The goods used to support the preparation and sales of services by the company constitute essential resources. The company shall plan for, provision or purchase, and supply to the local sites the forms of goods necessary to an effective, efficient, and total quality discharge of the services responsibilities of the company. To that end, all paperwork, forms, procedures covering product use, and equipment used in preparation of services and all other forms of goods shall be identified, planned for, and integrated totally into the company's operations.

The local manager shall exercise management controls to ensure that unapproved forms of goods are not used in the conduct of the company's business. Alternatively, the local manager shall survey the goods needed to support the business of the company and shall ensure that adequate supplies of such goods are available at all times. It shall be the responsibility of the head office, or central administration, to define the range of goods needed in support of the preparation and delivery of services to customers.

5.3.6 Services measurement control

5.3.6.1. In the conduct of a service business, it is necessary to keep records of the number of transactions taking place, the frequency with which the transactions are completed satisfactorily, and the number of times things go wrong. It shall be a responsibility of the local manager to ensure that all necessary aspects of transactions between company and customer are recorded in a time-efficient manner and in the detail prescribed by the head office.

5.3.6.2. The staff of the head office or central administration of the company shall define the details to be collected by the company staff at the point where the service is delivered to the customer. These details shall include the quality characteristics to be monitored, such as time and customer opinions and concerns.

5.3.6.3. The conformance of services to their design is the most important quality parameter to be measured. For each service, the indicators of quality, and hence conformance to design, shall be built into the data collection paperwork.

Conformance of services have both internal and external aspects. Those internal to the company's operation are more readily measured because employees can be required to record, analyze, and report. The internal aspects present the problem of being subjective when they are measured and recorded by the person delivering the service. Those aspects of internal quality conformance measurement and reporting shall be taken into consideration in the design of the system, as well as in the use of the data.

Conformance of services is also measurable by certain external indicators, usually collected from the customer. Although they are almost always subjective, they carry a considerable amount of importance because they usually reflect the beliefs of the customer about the services being provided by the company. The company shall design, distribute, collect, and analyze forms on which customers report information on the quality of services provided.

5.3.7 Measurement calibration control. The field of measurement in the services industry is not as well developed as it is in the goods industry. There is a growing field of measurement involving the human senses of taste, smell, and feel, all of which provide quality information that is to

some degree subjective. Considerable progress is being made in quantifying the results of measurements made in the food, perfume, clothing, comfort, medical, and a host of other service categories.

5.3.7.1. Measurements made on the goods used in the services industries and the activities of service companies shall be made with instruments and gauges calibrated in accordance with "Calibration Control System," Sec. III, Chap. 9 of *Quality Control Systems*. All such measurement accuracies shall be traceable to the national standards in the country where the measurements are made.

5.3.7.2. Measurements made in certain of the service industry areas in which goods are sold for such purposes as medical, beauty, comfort, and food in support of service provision depend on certified reference materials (CRMs) for their validity. When CRMs are used in calibration work or in the performance of measurements, they shall be traceable to the national measurements laboratory of the nation in which the calibration is carried out. When there is no national CRM, the instrumentation on which the reference material is measured shall have its calibration traceable to the nation's highest calibration laboratory.

5.3.8   Quality system documentation control

5.3.8.1. Documentation used by the company shall be prepared by qualified staff. It shall be reviewed by management staff that must use and approve it. It shall be numbered and recorded and carry issue numbers, dates of issue, and approvals of the qualified members of the organization under whose authority they are issued.

5.3.8.2. Documents issued by the head office or central administration of the company for use by local area divisions of company operations shall not be changed by the members of a local organization without the express consent of the issuing organization.

5.3.8.3. The company shall prepare and issue documentation covering all essential activities needed to provide services to customers. These documents shall contain detailed information on all operations needed at each site location to prepare products, interact with customers, ensure customer well-being, and monitor quality characteristics and indicators for each of the services provided.

5.3.8.4. When local laws or regulations forbid the use of specific materials, procedures, or activities, the manager of the local site of the company organization shall consistently obey the local laws and regulations and shall take immediate steps to notify the head office or central administration of the company when conflicts arise. Such deviations, along with their effects, if any, on the quality of services, shall be recorded.

5.3.9   Technical assistance control

5.3.9.1   Training and education control.   The head office of the company shall provide all the training and education necessary to qualify the technical officers of the company's services-providing activities. That requirement may be fulfilled by setting standards for employees in each position to be met at the time of hiring. The training requirement shall concentrate on the quality of services and ensure that only the staff qualified to provide work of suitable quality will be assigned to carry out such work.

5.3.9.2   Material and equipment control

5.3.9.2.1.   The quality of services provided to customers depends on the quality of incoming supplies. The company shall therefore take steps to control incoming goods quality. In particular, the procedure "Quality Control by Completed Product Inspection," Sec. III, Chap. 6 of *Quality Control Systems,* shall be applied to all incoming supplies and equipment.

5.3.9.2.2.   The preparation of material, like the inspection of incoming material, shall be under the control of a fully qualified, experienced staff, which shall apply the recognized scientific methods of control set forth in this procedure. For example, in the restaurant business, the inspection of incoming supplies, as well as the preparation of the food in the kitchens, shall be under the direct control of a fully qualified chef at all times. In the hotel business, control shall be maintained by a trained, experienced hotel manager, and similarly in banking and other service businesses.

5.3.9.2.3.   All new equipment, uniforms, vehicles, machinery, measuring instruments and devices, furniture, computers, automatic controls, tools, and implements used in producing and supplying services to customers shall be inspected, before acceptance, by the methods set forth in "Quality Control by Completed Product Inspection," Sec. III, Chap. 6 of *Quality Control Systems*. Only items meeting the specified requirements shall be accepted.

5.3.9.2.4. Records that, as a minimum, show the quantity and types of items inspected, the number found to be faulty and the faults found, the company of origin, and any actions taken with the company of origin by the local manager shall be kept. These records shall be forwarded to the head office of the company at prescribed periods.

5.3.10   Records control

5.3.10.1. The head office of the company shall prescribe, for each subdivision and company site, what records shall be kept as a minimum. These records shall cover the financial, quality, operational, disciplinary, and legal and/or regulatory matters of the day-to-day running of the company's divisions. Quality records shall reflect the reliability being obtained from the operating equipment and facilities provided for the local site to conduct its business. As such, the records shall show the control problems encountered, what was done to correct them, and the frequency of equipment breakdowns and repairs required to correct the failures.

5.3.10.2. Each site manager shall be provided with adequate office space suitable to the running of the business, records preparation and storage facilities, means for communicating the results of record analysis and findings to the head office. Office capacity for additional non-management staff as necessary to keep the day-to-day records for the site shall be provided.

5.3.10.3. Records of the day-to-day quality aspects of incoming materials, inspected against standards to assure acceptable quality levels, shall be kept. They shall reflect the quantity of materials inspected, the quantities found faulty, and the disposition of faulty materials.

5.3.11   Services control

5.3.11.1. Control of the quality of services shall come from the very highest echelons of the company organization. The chief executive officer (CEO) shall delegate to one or more members of senior management the responsibility for periodic auditing of the control functions delegated throughout the company. These audits shall be carried out by fully qualified members of the organization, who shall report to sufficiently high levels to be able to obtain resolution of the most serious deficiencies, quality problems, and crises.

5.3.11.2. Audits carried out shall be recorded in a prescribed manner on forms prepared for the purpose. The auditors shall use bases chosen for the particular service business against which to report the results of their audits and in terms of which to evaluate the effectiveness of control at the particular site audited. When several sites carry out similar operations, the audits shall be capable of comparing the sites in respect to quality control and efficiency.

5.3.11.3. Individual site control of the quality of services shall be the direct responsibility of the site manager, who shall be answerable to the head office of the company. Such aspects of service quality as customer well-being and comfort, employee enthusiasm and helpfulness, employee training, rigorous control of customer access, queuing, and action times, and follow-up of customers shall be secured by using forms and communications methods devised at the head office.

5.3.11.4. The local site manager shall maintain rigorous control over the equipment, buildings, driveways, parking lots, swimming pools, furnishings, and access to the conveniences of other local companies providing transport, etc. and thereby ensure that the quality of services provided to customers is always at or above the standard set for the business.

5.3.12   Control of services follow-up

5.3.12.1. Advertising programs shall be devised for use by both local and national or international organizations to communicate to the clientele of the company the characteristics and conditions of service necessary to prepare customers for maximum benefit of company operations. Advertising shall highlight the quality-of-service aspect of the company and shall communicate both the range and types of services and products offered for sale in order to prepare customers for what to expect.

5.3.12.2. Questionnaires for determining the quality of services offered and provided by the company shall be prepared both for processing at the premises of the company and for mailing to customers' homes. Particular attention shall be paid to collecting the impressions, likes, and dislikes of the service before the customer has left the premises of the company. Customer response forms shall be designed with a view to obtaining a measure of the quality of services provided.

5.4   Ancillary control areas—services-providing

5.4.1   The quality system audit control

5.4.1.1. The company shall establish an audit of the quality system whereby control over the provision of services is achieved and maintained. The audit shall be conducted by a senior officer of the company who answers to the highest levels. The quality system audit shall be conducted periodically without prior knowledge of the local staff, including the local manager, of either the time or what will be examined.

5.4.1.2. The results of the quality system audit shall be compared with the controls specified in this procedure to determine if they meet requirements in each instance. The audit results shall be used constructively to improve the performance of the employees of the company and correct anomalies which may appear from time to time.

5.4.1.3. The quality system audit report shall be circulated to the various sites as well as the head office in order to give each site manager comparison figures against which to measure his or her performance.

5.4.2   The services quality audit control.   In addition to the audit of the quality system, the company shall design and implement an audit of the services being provided to customers. The services audit shall consist of an internal audit and an external audit.

5.4.2.1. The internal services quality audit shall be carried out by a qualified company representative from outside the area served by the site being audited. Preferably, the auditor shall be a higher-level person who is experienced in the work being audited and reports to the head office management.

5.4.2.2. The external services quality audit shall consist of forms specially designed to elicit from customers comments and replies to questions about the quality of services being provided by the company. These forms shall be either passed out at the site where the services are dispensed or sent by mail or other suitable means. Inducements shall be offered for answers. The answers obtained by this form of canvassing shall be analyzed and the results shall be used in adjusting the characteristics of services offered to customers.

5.4.3 Documentation change control

5.4.3.1. The company shall prepare, publish, and implement a system for control of documents used within the company. This system shall forbid the alteration of any procedure, maintenance routine, work instruction, product formulation, service description, or other such document used by the company in the conduct of the business without going through the prescribed procedure.

5.4.3.2. Before a formally issued document is changed, it shall be reviewed by a qualified team of management staff, who shall determine the need for the change, the degree of change, and the path of approval to be obtained before the changed document can be reissued. All changed documents shall pass through this routine before being reissued.

5.4.3.3. Documentation in use may be marked or changed in any way only by authorized members of the company organization. All changes shall be made in ink or other suitable indelible medium and shall be signed and dated by the person authorizing the change.

5.4.3.4. Upon the reissue of any document, all copies of the earlier issue of the document shall be replaced at points of use throughout the organization.

5.4.4 Customer feedback and corrective action control

5.4.4.1. The company shall provide a means for customer complaints, provide ready access by the customer to such means, and give assurance that the appropriate corrective action will be taken in response to valid complaints.

5.4.4.2. The manager of each division or site of the company's overall organization shall ensure that complaints which affect documentation, procedures, equipment, or services under the control of other parts of the company's organization are forwarded to the proper point for action.

5.4.4.3. The sensitivity of the company's staff to customer complaints shall be maintained at a level which will provide effective control of the area and prevent any growth in the dissatisfaction which accompanies poor services or poor-quality goods accompanying services.

5.4.5 Employee-training control

5.4.5.1. The company shall provide for effective training of all staff throughout the organization. This shall be divided into training that is run from the head office and that which is carried out under the direct supervision of the manager of the site where the work is done.

5.4.5.2. Training of the technical and professional members of the staff, as well as future managers who will be assigned to the various sites, shall be planned and carried out by the head office based on academic and other education and prior experience.

5.4.5.3. Training of workers who are paid at an hourly rate shall be carried out under the control of the manager of the site at which the employees will work.

5.4.5.4. All training which involves staff destined to work with the public shall receive human factors training.

5.4.5.5. Only staff members who have been thoroughly trained in the performance of their jobs shall be given the task of serving the public. Specialized training programs shall be devised and run to ensure that trained staff will always be available when needed.

5.4.6 Services environment control. The working environment in which employees of the company provide services to customers is a major factor in the well-being of the customer and the satisfaction received from the service. It is also of great importance to company employees in maintaining the enthusiasm, neatness of dress, and alertness needed to provide services of the high quality expected of the company. To this end the company shall research, document, design, construct, establish, and maintain a work environment which is compatible with the production and delivery of the highest levels of quality.

5.4.7 Services cost control

5.4.7.1.   It is not possible to apply the same quality cost analysis methods to the provision of services as to the production of goods or products. There are, however, certain cost control methods which greatly influence the quality-of-service area. In any service area in which products are a part of the service being provided, the quality of service can be improved by using the "Manufacturing Quality Cost System," Sec. VI, Chap. 2 of *Quality Control Systems.*

In broadest terms, customer complaints about the quality of service from a service company are of three kinds:

1. Dissatisfaction with the quality of goods supplied
2. Dissatisfaction with some time aspect of the service
3. Dissatisfaction with the way the service was provided by one or more of the company's employees

It is category 1 that can be improved by using the quality cost methods identified above.

5.4.7.2.   The company shall give due consideration at the corporate level to the percentage of the gross annual expenditure which will be devoted to quality. This expenditure shall be budgeted in the same general way as other company costs are. The expenditure of quality cost monies shall be planned and carried out as an integral part of the overall company expenditure.

5.4.7.3.   Quality costs incurred in running the company's quality control program shall be viewed as necessary operating costs. They shall include the costs of preparing quality documentation, running quality audits, purchasing quality equipment, instruments, and products for sale, and analyzing and taking action on quality data collected.

5.4.8 Security and safety control

5.4.8.1 Security control.   The company shall plan for, document, contract for, and implement security programs which will, as a minimum:

1. Safeguard, preserve, and protect site premises, including facilities, equipment, employees, and customers
2. Provide for the security of supplies needed to ensure the continuity of service to customers
3. Safeguard the resources, including the income from the services sold through the company's outlets

5.4.8.2 Safety control. The company shall adopt a policy that no work is too important or urgent to be done in an unsafe manner. A program of safety shall be compiled, documented, implemented, and carried out. This program shall include a periodic survey of the company's entire premises, with particular attention to a review of past hazards and the identification and rectification of any new hazards which may have been created since the last survey.

Safe working conditions are measurable by lost-time accidents. It shall be a goal of the company at each and all sites, as well as at the head office, to aim for and achieve a *zero level* of lost-time accidents. Particular attention shall be given to safety during training programs, and staff shall be strongly motivated toward working in safe ways.

Accidents resulting in either injury to staff or damage to equipment shall be investigated, recorded, and reported to the CEO of the company on a basis of urgency. Immediate appropriate remedial action shall be taken to remove the hazardous condition, and the injured person(s), if any, shall receive immediate medical attention.

4

Quality Control System
for Projects[*]

PART A: REVIEW AND GUIDANCE

1   Review

The methods developed for control of work in industry are uniquely correlated with the types of work and products involved. As compared with the control of the production of products in the mass-production industry, when some hundreds to many tens of thousands of a product item are to be manufactured, there is need to control work when only one item is to be constructed. When only one or a few items of a given type are to be designed and constructed, there is need for a uniquely different assembly of control methods. This procedure contains the methods found to be most effective in controlling project work.

There are three different situations in which project-type management control of work is found to be most applicable. The more complex of these situations arise in the construction industry when major capital works, such as harbors, airports, military bases, capital ships, power-generating stations, and high-rise buildings, must be designed, constructed, and commissioned. The second situation arises in the manufacturing industry when one or a small number of a product is to be produced. Typical examples occur in job shops, which most often design and produce 1 to 10 of some item and no more items of that particular design are then produced, or at least

*Acknowledgement and appreciation are extended to the Canadian Standards Association for permission to follow the general sequence and format of standard CSA Z299.1-1978 in providing guidance in the preparation of a procedure by which to control the quality of project work. This standard was chosen as the best such general-purpose national standard available in 1987.

not for a very long time. Project management of work is then found to be most suitable. In that situation, mass-production learning involving feedback and corrective action does not have the opportunity to function; therefore, reliance must be placed on planning by the project management team involving the designer, the developer, the producer, and the quality assurance organization.

The third situation in industry in which the methods of project management are found most suitable for controlling the quality of output arises when some major effort of usually short time duration (6 months to 2 years typically) is found to be needed and staff from several different organizational components of the company are pulled together to work as a team. In this situation, higher management appoints a project manager, who must then put together a team suited to the particular project work concerned. In this type of project management control, only a selected few of the controls of this procedure are needed. To summarize, capital works, the job shop, and the special project management team comprise the major uses of project control management methods.

2 Guidance

The choice of a control method is usually left up to the person in charge of work to be done. In project work the control of the project must be strongly administered from the individual or organization designated as the project manager. In capital works and building construction, that is the prime contractor; in manufacturing industry, control must emanate from the senior manager to whom the designer, developer, producer, and quality assurance people report, with the designer providing technical guidance throughout. When a project team is put together for some short-term project, the control must come from the project manager.

In each of the above cases it is the duty of the quality activity to provide the quality systems by which the project work can be successfully completed. This includes an oversight responsibility for the configuration control aspects of the project work. This procedure sets forth the areas of control needed in project-type work.

PART B. PROCEDURE

Quality Control System for Projects

1 Scope

This procedure defines the quality control requirements of the company in respect to construction work or other work done by the project control method.

2 Application

The requirements of this procedure shall apply:

1. When the procedure is called up in a contract or is referred to in other documents which are themselves called up in contracts or when it is called for by a jurisdictional authority.

2. To the operations carried on within the company in respect to project work.

3. When project work underway is to be assessed and this procedure is being used.

2.1. When conflict arises between the requirements of this procedure and other quality system requirements in a contract, the requirements of the contract shall prevail.

3 Definitions

Terms specifically applicable to this work are defined here. For other terms, see "Glossary of Terms Used in Quality and Reliability," Sec. VII, Chap. 1 of *Quality Control Systems.**

audit	A documented activity aimed at verifying by examination and evaluation that the applicable elements of the quality program have been established, documented, and effectively implemented in accordance with specified requirements.
characteristic	A distinct property or dimension of an item, process, or service that can be described and measured to determine its conformance or nonconformance to specified requirements.
company	The organization or individual who contracts with a customer to undertake and carry out a project.
construction	Fabrication, assembly, erection, installation, or joining and combining together of items by or of work involving a number of disciplines at a site by the party or parties performing the work.
customer	The party, or the representative of the party, who issues a contract for the purpose of procuring projects, products, or services.
inspection and test point	The location or stage in the production cycle, delivery phase, or erection process at which the inspection or test is performed by personnel who have the responsibility to determine the acceptability of projects, products, or services and to record relevant data.

---

*James R. Taylor, *Quality Control Systems: Procedures for Planning Quality Programs*, McGraw-Hill, New York, 1989.

jurisdictional authority	The governmental body or authority or agency which has the lawful right and power to interpret and exercise authority in the execution of the law and regulations in respect to the work.
manufacturing	The processing, production, fabrication, or assembly of items into subassemblies, assemblies, or systems.
objective evidence	Recorded results of measurements made by using calibrated measuring methods, instruments, or gauges.
positive recall	The release and use of items under conditions such that the items can be removed and repaired or returned if found unacceptable at a later date.
quality control	All the activities carried out for the purpose of ensuring that the product or service characteristics will comply with requirements.
service	Work done by other persons or machines for the party who is the recipient of the benefits of the work.
subcontractor	The individual or organization who is awarded a contract for relevant work by the company.
verification	Confirming that an activity, condition, or characteristic conforms to specified requirements.

4   The Company's Responsibilities

4.1.   The company shall carry the sole and final responsibility to meet all quality and reliability requirements for the project.

4.2.   The company is responsible for developing and implementing the quality program procedures and controls of this procedure to prevent nonconformance to contractual and jurisdictional requirements.

4.3.   The company is responsible for developing and implementing the procedures and controls for detecting and correcting nonconformance to contractual and jurisdictional requirements.

4.4.   The company shall satisfy the jurisdictional and customer requirements specified in the contract.

4.5.   The company shall, when required by the contract, prepare and submit a quality manual, plus system performance procedures, for review and approval by the customer in accordance with instructions in the contract.

4.6.   The company shall prepare and submit to the customer an inspection and test plan in accordance with instructions in the contract.

4.7.   The company shall be responsible for updating and maintaining the inspection and test plan, quality manual, and system performance procedure when necessary.

4.8.   The company shall be responsible for maintaining the configuration requirements of the contract and ensuring they are met in the finished item of works.

5   Jurisdictional Authority

5.1.   All construction work, and much other project work, must comply with various laws, regulations, and jurisdictional rulings. The requirements of all jurisdictional authorities, local, county, state, and/or national or federal, that apply to the project shall be met.

5.2.   When the jurisdictional requirements apply to the owner of the works and the customer is that owner, the customer shall take the necessary steps to obtain compliance with jurisdictional stipulations.

6   Quality Requirements

6.1   The quality program.   The company shall plan, establish, implement, and maintain a quality control program according to the requirements of this procedure. When quality control is to be implemented by subcontractors, the company shall plan, design, implement, and maintain a quality assurance program to meet the requirements of this procedure.

6.2   Organization.   The company shall:

1. Clearly define management policies, objectives, and responsibilities for quality control and quality assurance. The responsibilities of different contributors to the accomplishment of the project shall be defined. The responsibility and authority for quality delegated to the individuals and managers of organizations who must manage and perform the work, as well as those who must audit and verify conformance of the work to requirements, shall be defined and their relationships shall be shown on organization charts.
2. Appoint a quality representative who shall report regularly to management at a level which shall ensure that quality require-

ments are not subordinated to design, manufacturing, productivity, construction, or delivery and shall define the authority of the quality representative to obtain resolution of quality matters. This appointment shall be reported to the customer in writing, along with the person's qualifications.

3. Provide for regular reviews, by management of affected areas, of the status and adequacy of the quality control program and any quality assurance program responsibilities placed on subcontractors. These reviews shall cover the activities of those responsible for managing and carrying out the work in a quality-controlled manner, as well as those responsible for verifying conformance to quality requirements.

4. Define the responsibility and authority of personnel who are primarily responsible for controlling quality and the organizational methods used to:

   a. Identify and record quality problems.

   b. Initiate, recommend, or provide solutions to quality problems.

   c. Verify implementation and effectiveness of solutions to quality problems.

   d. Control the ongoing processing, fabrication, delivery, installation, or commissioning of items containing nonconformities through to the stage at which verification establishes the satisfactory disposition of the earlier-questioned items.

   e. Carry out, by personnel other than those actually doing or supervising the work on items being inspected, verification of work done. The inspection and test plan shall clearly indicate when personnel responsible for verification of quality may report to supervisors who are directly responsible for accomplishing quality. Typically, this shall occur only in mass-production situations and then only when there is verification of quality by an independent audit. Jurisdictional requirements in this respect shall override the inspection and test plan when conflict arises.

6.3 Audits

6.3.1. The company shall design, establish, and implement a documented plan for audits which will objectively evaluate and verify that:

1. All requirements of the quality control program are being complied with and work is proceeding in accordance with documented quality program procedures.

2. The quality control program is performing effectively.

3. Recommended corrective actions are being implemented in an effective and timely manner.

4. Areas of control previously found deficient are being reaudited.

6.3.2. The audit plan shall, as a minimum, define:

1. Assignments of personnel doing audits

2. Functional areas to be audited

3. Frequency of audits and whether aperiodic or not

4. Method of reporting findings and recommendations

5. The procedure for deciding on and implementing corrective actions

6.3.3. Audits shall, as a minimum, include an evaluation of:

1. Work areas, activities, and processes

2. Products and services being produced

3. Quality control practices being used

4. Documented quality program procedures and instructions

5. Documents, reports, and records

6.3.4. Personnel assigned to carry out audits shall be appropriately trained and experienced and shall not be directly responsible for the area being audited.

6.3.5. Audits shall be carried out in accordance with this procedure.

6.3.6 Management responsible for the area audited shall review and correct any deficiencies found and reported in the documented audit results.

6.4 Documentation

6.4.1 The quality manual

6.4.1.1. The company shall:

1. Prepare a quality manual and have it approved and signed by a senior management official of the organization. The quality manual shall contain a quality policy statement signed by the chief executive officer. It shall have organization charts showing the

lines of responsibility for all work under the contract. It shall contain quality procedures by which the work is carried out.

2. Submit the quality manual to jurisdictional authorities and to the customer for review and approval.

3. Periodically review and update the quality manual to include current quality control practices and any new or changed quality program procedures. Also, the company shall resubmit changes to the quality manual to the affected jurisdictional authorities and the customer for approval.

4. Implement the approved program according to the quality manual.

6.4.1.2. The quality manual shall contain, as a minimum, the following:

1. A statement of the company's quality policy signed by the chief executive officer.

2. Organization charts defining and showing lines of reporting and responsibility for all work done on the contract by the company and subcontractors.

3. A quality control plan, prepared in accordance with this procedure, identifying the management function responsible for the plan, and showing how the plan will be developed and implemented.

4. The quality system performance procedures called for in Art. 6.5 of this procedure. They shall be either included or cross-referenced, with the actual procedures being provided upon request.

5. Procedures for auditing the quality program shall be either included or outlined and cross-referenced and shall be provided upon request.

6. A procedure for reviewing and updating the quality manual.

6.4.2 The quality control plan

6.4.2.1. The company shall:

1. Plan in detail the quality control activities which will be used to ensure the total quality control of the project.

2. Document the quality control plan which describes the methods, sources, and results to be objectively obtained and recorded,

from which confidence that the entire project conforms to specified requirements will be gained. For each item specified in the contract, there shall be an individual plan describing the process controls, inspections, tests, and verifications to be carried out in respect to the item to provide objective evidence of conformance.

3. Submit the quality control plan to the applicable jurisdictional authorities and to the customer for approval. When inspection or test procedures are referenced in the plan, they shall be made available for review upon request.

6.4.2.2. The quality control plan shall be prepared in the format that best suits the company's documentation system, but it shall, as a minimum:

1. Identify each point in the manufacturing and construction cycle at which inspections, tests, process controls, tryouts, or other verifications are to be employed. These shall cover vendor items, incoming items, preservation of items, packaging, site inspections, and all commissioning activities. When the company chooses to carry out independent assessments not subject to verification for the customer's own control purposes, they shall be indicated in the plan.

2. Identify work to be done by subcontractors and describe how the results of the work will be verified.

3. Identify the characteristics to be inspected, tested, and verified at each point of (1) above and the inspection and test procedures to be used.

4. Include in inspection and test procedures, as applicable, those who are responsible for carrying out verification work, how and when the work is to be carried out, the materials, equipment, and documents to be used, and how the work will be controlled.

5. Indicate mandatory hold points established by jurisdictional authority, by the customer, or by both which are required so either or both may witness or carry out inspections or tests for verification of selected characteristics. Work shall not proceed beyond a mandatory hold point.

6. Define the extent of and standards for any statistical methods to be used, including any sampling procedures needed.

7. Specify the quality program standards to be applied to subcontractors and the items the subcontractors supply.

8. Detail the methods to be used in verifying the quality of items supplied by subcontractors.

9. Define how compliance with the output from special processes will be accomplished and documented.

10. Indicate the inspections and tests to be carried out during the manufacturing and construction cycle to verify preservation of items.

6.4.3 System performance procedures. The company shall prepare and issue documented procedures to provide instructions for work that is to be done. When forms are to be used for checking, verifying, recording data, etc., examples of the forms shall be included in or with the procedures.

Each procedure shall document, as applicable, such things as purpose; scope; who is responsible for what; how, when, and where all steps are to be performed; the resources to be used; and how the work is to be accomplished.

6.5 Quality system functions

6.5.1 Contract review and quality plan. At the earliest possible time, the company shall hold an organized review of the contract and its requirements in complete detail. It shall by such review reaffirm its ability to meet all contract requirements fully. Applicable functions within the company's organization shall be required to review the contract as it applies to them and to confirm that they can fully comply.

The company shall prepare, from the review of the contract, complete and comprehensive plans for the accomplishment of work needed to totally discharge the contract. The quality plans shall be prepared by all functions needed to contribute to the discharge of the contract, and shall be reviewed and agreed to by parties within the company's and subcontractor's organizations.

6.5.2 Design quality assurance. The company shall plan, establish, and implement procedures that assure all design activities are performed according to the requirements of the applicable chapters of Sec. II of *Quality Control Systems*.

When required, the designs shall be approved at the appropriate points of execution by the jurisdictional authorities and/or by the customer.

6.5.3 Documentation control. The company shall establish a drawing system which is consistent and standard for the nation in which the work is carried out or in accordance with the contractual requirements. The drawing system used shall be at least downward-compatible and be such that later designs can be used with earlier designs of the same system.

Documentation change shall be controlled in accordance with the procedure of Sec. III, Chap. 8 of *Quality Control Systems*. Only the latest documents shall be permitted to be used at work stations unless specifically authorized to the contrary by the appropriate authority.

6.5.4   Measuring equipment control.   The company shall ensure that all measurements made for the purpose of verifying or validating items or services against the requirements of the contract shall be maintained, calibrated, and used in such a manner as to ensure the full compliance of the project with the contract.

All measuring equipment, instruments, gauges, and devices, as well as materials used to perform measurements on the items used in the contract, shall be calibrated in accordance with "Calibration Control System," Sec. III, Chap. 9 of *Quality Control Systems*.

6.5.5   Purchasing control.   Purchasing activities cover two major categories of work done under contract outside the company's organization. These include (1) the purchase of goods or services for use by and within the company's organization and supplied by vendors who supply the products or services and (2) the subcontracting of work, which may or may not include the supply of products and services but which is for the purpose of use on the project and is provided by subcontractors.

6.5.5.1.   Quality assurance of vendors:

6.5.5.1.1.   Each purchase order, purchase contract, or other such document shall contain, for the products or services, the applicable specifications, drawings, quality levels required, inspection or test methods to be used, characteristics to be supplied and limits to be met, quantity to be supplied, and all other pertinent data needed to assure the quality of incoming products and services.

6.5.5.1.2.   The company shall nominate the quality program standard to be applied to the products or services purchased.

6.5.5.1.3.   Purchase contracts shall clearly indicate any requirements for qualification, life or reliability testing, or identification labeling of products.

6.5.5.1.4. Purchase contracts shall specify any requirements for approval by the company of procedures, processes, use of a quality program standard, and any special processes concerned.

6.5.5.1.5. Purchase contracts shall clearly indicate any rights required for the customer or a jurisdictional authority to review the subcontractor's documentation and quality system, have access to the subcontractor's premises, conduct surveillance, and verify compliance with legal or technical stipulations of the contract.

6.5.5.1.6. Purchase contracts shall contain instructions for the submission, retention, storage, or disposition of records which constitute the objective evidence concerning the products or services supplied under the contract.

6.5.5.1.7. Purchase contracts shall clearly communicate all requirements for labeling, packing, shipping, delivering, installing, or commissioning.

6.5.5.2 Subcontractor quality assurance. The company shall identify, during the planning and contract review phase, the products or services that are required by the contract but will be provided by subcontractors. Unless previously specified by either the jurisdictional authority or the customer, the company shall determine and justify to the customer and the applicable jurisdictional authority a quality plan by which the quality of subcontracted work will be controlled and assured.

When a quality program for the subcontractor is required, the company shall:

1. Determine which quality system standard shall be applied by the subcontractor.
2. Evaluate and select subcontractors based on ability to meet subcontract and quality requirements.
3. Establish and maintain a record of acceptable subcontractors.
4. Carry out surveillance and audit of subcontractor operations during the production of products or services, including construction at the project site as applicable.
5. Evaluate and verify all subcontracted items, both products and services, as necessary to ensure that all parts of the requirements of the contract are satisfactory and are in full conformance with

contract requirements. Source inspection and subcontractor surveillance shall be applied as is appropriate.

6.5.5.3 Amendments to purchase orders and subcontracts. All amendments to purchase orders and subcontracts shall carry the same degree of examination and relevant information in respect to the changed products or services as is applicable to the original purchase order or subcontract. All such amendments shall be numbered and controlled.

6.5.6 Vendor supplies control. Products or services supplied by vendors shall be reviewed for satisfactory quality as required in the contract, and shall, if not having been verified appropriately, be identified, labeled, controlled, inspected, and tested as required by the quality plan. In this respect, the company shall:

1. Check the objective evidence provided by the vendors, subcontractors, and auditor to determine if adequate quality control has been exercised.

2. When nonconformances are discovered, initiate corrective action with vendors or subcontractors as necessary to ensure that contract requirements are met.

3. Control incoming items until the required quality evidence is obtained and it is verified that the items are of quality satisfactory for use on the project.

6.5.7 In-process control. The company shall:

1. Establish and maintain control over items in process in accordance with the quality control plan. When appropriate, processes shall be brought under statistical control and verifying inspections and tests shall be conducted to provide objective evidence of conformance. Items shall be identified as to inspection and test status.

2. For operations such that process control is not statistically possible and the items cannot be inspected, monitor the process with adequate closeness to ensure the control of conformance.

3. Implement controls to prevent the use of items of an unknown quality until the items have been inspected or tested and the results are known.

4. Segregate nonconforming items from conforming items and pos-

itively identify nonconforming items for nonuse and appropriate disposition.

6.5.8   Final product inspection control.   The company shall:

1. Inspect or test and identify each final item in accordance with the quality control plan.

2. From the quality control plan, prepare a checklist of all objective evidence which should exist for the item as it and its components have passed through the various stages of production and verify from the records that the item has been inspected or tested at all required points and that the records are complete.

3. Provide the respective jurisdictional authority and the customer with the objective evidence of conformance prior to or concurrent with submitting the item for acceptance.

4. Submit for acceptance only items which are known to be in conformance with requirements and for which there is objective evidence of conformance.

6.5.9   Product identification and traceability.   The company shall:

1. Through the use of flow tags, stamps, labels, or other devices provide means whereby items that require inspection and test before acceptance can be shown to have had such inspections and tests prior to being submitted for acceptance.

2. Establish a control system which maintains continuity of identity and inspection or test status for all items throughout the production cycle.

3. Establish a system which provides positive indications of when items have passed their final inspection or test.

4. Provide identity of the company's inspector or tester on stamps or labels, or by other means for indicating the inspection status of items, and record all information on traceability.

5. Provide a program for the control of inspection or test status indicators and nominate the parties who can put such identifications on items and those who are authorized to remove them.

6.5.10   Handling and storage control.   The company shall:

1. Prepare procedures, promulgate them, and establish a program for handling, transporting, stacking, storing, preserving, and segregating all items as necessary to safeguard quality charac-

teristics and prevent the commingling of nonconforming items with conforming items.

2. Periodically inspect items held in stock for condition and shelf life expiry.
3. Periodically inspect tools, machines, and special devices as necessary to ensure that they are adequately maintained and will not damage the items or material on which they are used.

6.5.11 Manufacturing or construction control.   The company shall:

1. Ensure that manufacturing, construction, and inspection activities are all documented to define:
   - The sequence of production operations
   - Work methods
   - Acceptance or rejection criteria
   - State of equipment
   - The environments in which work is done
2. Carry out such process control and inspection as is necessary to ensure effective control of quality.
3. Ensure that all devices used in the production of items have known and proven capability prior to their use on items and that any such devices that are unknown, damaged, or out of calibration are repaired and recalibrated before use.
4. Make corrections to the quality plan, methods, or devices when found to be unsuitable.
5. Ensure that, by formal review, there has been no unacceptable alteration to the configuration of the end works or product.

6.5.12 Control of special processes.   When in a production process the result cannot be determined or examined to establish that it is fully conforming, the process shall be called a special process. For all special processes the company shall:

1. Use only fully qualified and experienced personnel to carry them out and establish fully documented procedures by which to assure that the processes are yielding satisfactory conformance. All equipment, personnel, documents, standards, specifications, criteria, and customer or jurisdictional requirements shall be used to achieve control over special processes.
2. Maintain documentation according to established codes and standards for the accomplishment of work on special processes.
3. Define all necessary special process procedures, personnel qualifications, and equipment when they are not defined in codes,

practices, or standards applying to the special processes and when quality requirements or characteristic limits exceed the requirements of established codes or standards.

6.5.13 Preservation, packing, and shipping. The company shall ensure that supplies are suitably protected during handling and shipment to preserve the quality characteristics. Cleaning, marking, preserving, packing, and shipping shall all be inspected and audited to ensure that quality characteristics are protected and contract requirements are met.

6.5.14 Quality records. The company shall:

1. Maintain records that objectively demonstrate that the quality system is effective. To this effect the records shall show that:
   a. Each item meets jurisdictional and contractual requirements when such requirements exist.
   b. The quality program meets the requirements of this procedure.
   c. Personnel, equipment, and procedures for special processes are qualified as required when used.
   d. Control of subcontractors is achieved and maintained as required.
   e. When nonconformances are found, corrective action is taken and is effective in meeting requirements.
2. Retain quality audit records for agreed-upon times and make them available to the jurisdictional authority or the customer upon request when they contain the following:
   a. Results of audits of the quality system or of goods or services supplied.
   b. Results of audits of quality program procedures.
   c. Results of analyses of audit data showing the use of audits in the achievement of effective corrective action.
3. Retain the results of measurements which objectively show conformance with requirements of goods or services and include with each such record:
   a. The date of inspection or test.
   b. The identity of the inspector or tester and data recorder.
   c. Evidence of any nonconformance.
   d. The reference drawing number, part number, or other part identification and the current revision number of any documentation.
   e. Test schedule, test specification, or other applicable requirements.
   f. The specific inspections or tests performed, the results of such

inspections or tests, and, when applicable, the basis for acceptance.

    g. Evidence of feedback and corrective action resulting from dis-
covery of nonconformances.

4. Identify, index, and file quality records for easy retrieval.
5. Make quality records available to the applicable jurisdictional
authority and the customer for analysis and review.
6. Provide suitable storage or archiving environment for quality
records to prevent deterioration and store such records for the
time required by jurisdictional authorities or the customer.

6.5.15 Control of configuration. A principal aspect of the quality control plan shall be the designed configuration of the finished work or
product constructed under the contract. The company shall prepare
plans for the periodic review of work underway to ascertain that the
configuration of the end work or product is being maintained. These
plans shall call for configuration assessment and review following
any change in design and also following any change in the materials, processes, methods of joining, or other change which may affect
the configuration of the end work or product.

   At all times throughout the project the company shall ensure that
the intended configuration of the finished work or product is being
met. Configuration assessment and review shall take place without
regard to the source of any request for change of design, process, material, methods of joining, etc.

   Any change that alters the configuration of the finished work or
product that occurs during the process of discharging the contract
shall be communicated to the jurisdictional authority and the customer, and the approval of each to such change shall be obtained
prior to continuing with the project including the configurational
change.

6.5.16 Control of nonconformance. The company shall prepare, issue,
implement, and enforce procedures for handling, segregating, and dis-
posing of all items found to be nonconforming during the course of
work on the contract. Such control shall extend to any nonconformances in contract material found in subcontractor's premises. To
that end, the company shall:

1. Plan, document, implement, and maintain procedures for the
control of nonconforming items. The procedures shall:
    a. Define the responsibilities and authority of the persons
who are responsible for the disposition of nonconforming
items.
    b. Provide for a technical material review board composed of re-

sponsible individuals from the design, production, construction, and quality functions.

c. Promptly detect, record, and segregate nonconforming items.

d. Place nonconforming items in a marked holding zone or in quarantine storage and prevent mixing with conforming items.

e. Reach a disposition decision which has the concurrence of all members of the material review board and, when applicable, submit the decision to the appropriate jurisdictional authority or the customer as required.

f. Implement the disposition decision, having due regard for any special rework or retest requirements.

2. Record for each nonconforming item the nature and extent of nonconformance, the disposition decision, and, when the item is reused, objective evidence that rework and reinspection procedures were followed and that the item was found to be satisfactory for use.

6.5.17 Control of customer-supplied items.   Where the customer supplies items for use on the project and those items cannot be satisfactorily inspected to assure their quality as delivered to the company, the customer shall be responsible for providing objective evidence that such items are conforming and satisfactory for use. The customer shall, when it is applicable, satisfy the jurisdictional authority as required concerning such items.

When customer-supplied items can be satisfactorily certified as to their quality by testing after delivery, it shall be the company's responsibility to provide objective evidence of conformance for such items unless otherwise agreed in the contract.

In any event, in respect to customer-supplied items, the company shall:

1. Examine all such items upon receipt for completeness, proper type, and any evidence of transit damage.

2. Ascertain if specific characteristic values are required for further use of the customer-supplied items and, when necessary, either measure the values or obtain such data from the customer.

3. Control all customer-supplied items, preserve them from damage, and use them in accordance with this procedure, the contract, and the needs of the project.

4. On a timely basis, report to the customer or to the applicable jurisdictional authority any safety-related matters concerning such items and to the customer any evidence of damage or unsuitability.

6.5.18 Control of corrective action. In respect to corrective action of any kind in work on the project under the contract, the company shall:

1. Investigate the cause of the nonconformance, accident, wrong material, or other such situation requiring corrective action and record all relevant findings.

2. Take necessary steps to prevent recurrence of such a condition or situation.

3. Report the matter to the jurisdictional authority, when that is applicable, and to the customer.

4. Promptly initiate and carry through corrective action as approved by the applicable jurisdictional authority and the customer.

5. When a jurisdictional authority or the customer notifies the company of any nonconformance or inadequacy in procedures etc. under the contract, promptly take corrective action to control and correct the matter.

7 Verification of Quality

7.1 Evaluation before work begins

7.1.1 The quality control program. The customer shall evaluate the quality control program of the company prior to the award of the contract. This evaluation shall examine in depth the suitability of the quality control program for the project work to be undertaken and carried out. It shall cover policy, organization, procedures, and any relevant previous performance on the part of the company.

As a part of the evaluation of the company's quality control program, the customer shall examine in depth the quality manual and any system performance procedures. When any procedures, manual, or practices are found to be unsatisfactory, the customer shall require the company to make such corrections, amendments, or additions as may be necessary to fully comply with this procedure before awarding the contract. The customer shall notify any applicable jurisdictional authorities in respect to any deficiencies found and corrective actions initiated and carried out and when the program is found entirely satisfactory prior to the start of relevant work.

The customer shall be responsible for completely detailing to the company, and to all jurisdictional authorities, complete project requirements, and all quality aspects which must be met during the contract which are relevant.

7.1.2 Facilities and physical resources. The customer shall be responsible for evaluating the company's facilities, including buildings, equipment, and measuring instrumentation and devices or the company's access to these as may be required for successfully carrying out the work on the project. The customer shall be satisfied that the company is competent in all respects to fulfill the contractual requirements prior to awarding the contract.

The customer shall ascertain that any physical resources required by jurisdictional authorities for the undertaking and carrying out of such work as may be required on the project are in the possession of or available to the company and that they fully meet the requirements of the relevant jurisdictional authority prior to awarding the contract.

7.1.3 The quality plan. The customer shall require the company to prepare and submit a quality plan by which it can be ascertained that all necessary inspections, tests, and control of special processes will be accomplished. The quality plan shall be approved by both the customer and the jurisdictional authority, when applicable, prior to the beginning of work on the contract.

7.2 Continuing evaluation and verification. The customer, or his quality assurance representative (QAR), shall carry out continuing evaluation and verification that the company is complying with all the contractual requirements and with this procedure throughout the work on the contract.

7.3 Access, accommodation, and assistance. The company shall provide the customer and jurisdictional authorities with access, accommodation, and assistance as may be necessary for work under the contract.

5

Quality Control by Inspection System Procedure

PART A.   REVIEW AND GUIDANCE

1   Review

Controlling quality by inspection means performing measurements on each required characteristic against specified limits by using calibrated measuring equipment to ensure that all characteristics, including performance, are within limits. Most products have some characteristics that get covered up during later production operations and hence cannot be measured at end-of-line or on completed items. Also, it is necessary to ensure that the materials and components going into a product are individually within their limits, so incoming inspection is necessary. For those reasons inspection stations must be located at incoming areas, at identified points along the production line where characteristics are brought into being, and at the end of the production line when the product is considered to be complete.

In the above respects this procedure differs from one intended for end-of-line completed product inspection. It also differs from the procedure in Sec. III, Chap. 2 of *Quality Control Systems** in that there is no allowance for all the in-line and ancillary controls that are necessary to ensure that quality is built into the product.

In a total quality control (TQC) system which is controlling quality by controlling the individual production processes, the in-line inspec-

---

*James R. Taylor, *Quality Control Systems: Procedures for Planning Quality Programs,* McGraw-Hill, New York, 1989.

tors are best assigned to the individual production foremen or supervisors for the management of their inspection activities. The quality manager then uses quality auditors for the collection of independent data.

It is desirable in systems as described in this procedure that the inspectors report to the quality manager, who in turn reports to the chief executive officer. This reporting chain of command is provided to ensure that objective decisions are made regarding product quality.

2   Guidance

When the quality of products is controlled by inspection, the production processes from which the products come are usually not controlled. Hence they will produce some good products and some that are outside tolerance. The out-of-tolerance products may or may not be capable of being reworked and made usable. When they cannot be reworked, they are scrap material and constitute a part of the loss which must be paid for by the customer in the cost quoted in the original bid or tender.

It has been found that the magnitude of loss will be reduced when the inspection of characteristics can be carried out as soon after the characteristics are generated as possible. This means that sometimes, in smaller companies, the production operator also uses gauges or test instruments and measures the product characteristics he or she produces. In these situations the production operator must report to the production foreman, but the quality manager must be responsible for the measurement of characteristics, including the choice and accuracy of measuring equipment used. Results of measurements must be recorded in such cases and provided to the quality manager for analysis and reporting.

PART B.   PROCEDURE

Quality Control by Inspection System Procedure

1 Scope

This procedure defines the requirements of the company in respect to quality control by product inspection.

2 Application

The requirements of this procedure shall apply:

1. When this procedure is called up in a contract or is referred to in other documents which are themselves called up in the contract.

2. To the inspection operations of the company.

3. When an intending contractor seeks to have an inspection system assessed and approved by the company.

2.1. When conflict arises between the requirements of this procedure and other inspection system documents and both are called up in the contract, the requirements of this procedure shall prevail. When this procedure is not part of the contract, the contract shall prevail.

3 Definitions

For the purposes of this procedure, the following definitions shall apply:

1. Terms listed in "Glossary of Terms Used in Quality and Reliability," Sec. VII, Chap. 1 of *Quality Control Systems*.

2. Terms as used in an alternate standard when that standard is called for in a contract.

4   Referenced Documents

The following documents form part of this procedure:

1. "Calibration Control System," Sec. III, Chap. 9 of *Quality Control Systems*.
2. "Glossary of Terms Used in Quality and Reliability," Sec. VII, Chap. 1 of *Quality Control Systems*.

4.1.   When referred to in a contract, the issue of any document current at the date of issue of the contract, unless stated otherwise, shall apply to work done under the contract.

5   Inspection System Requirements

5.1   Management

5.1.1   The management responsibilities

5.1.1.1.   The total responsibility for quality shall be vested in the most senior officer of the company, usually called the chief executive officer (CEO). Though this officer, who is normally the president or the managing director of the company, will usually report to a board which will have a chairman of the board, the chairman is not considered an executive officer for the carrying out of the day-to-day business.

5.1.1.2.   When, in smaller companies, there are only a small number of company officers to undertake and carry out the total duties of management, it shall be the duty of the CEO, insofar as possible, to separate the responsibilities for production and quality in the duties of different management employees of the company. The aim shall be to provide the quality manager with the ability to make judgments about the quality of products which are independent of the pressures of meeting production schedules, consistent with the financial well-being of the company in the longer term.

5.1.2   Organizing for inspection control

5.1.2.1.   When organizing to produce a product or range of products, the CEO shall ensure that balanced attention is given to organizing for production of quality characteristics of the products and to measuring those characteristics against their respective required limits.

In pursuit of this objective, the CEO shall ensure that an appropriate division of responsibilities is made in the delegation of duties to the officers and employees of the company.

5.1.2.2. The CEO shall ensure that an appropriate division of resources is made in organizing for equipment to produce quality characteristics in the product and to measure the quality characteristics when they are produced.

5.2 Inspection planning

5.2.1. The company shall have an orderly system for the review of all contractual requirements prior to the start of production. The same orderly review of requirements shall take place before starting production when there is no contract. The system shall identify inspection requirements when the quality characteristics will be generated in the course of producing the product and when the inspection of the quality characteristics can best be carried out on each of them.

5.2.2. The company shall plan for inspection capability to measure all quality characteristics required for discharge of the contract and for production of satisfactory product.

5.2.3. When appropriate, inspection shall be planned for the measurement of quality characteristics prior to their being masked by later production operations.

5.2.4. Inspection of incoming supplies shall be so planned as to be carried out either by approved vendor inspection or by the company's incoming inspection activity.

5.3 Inspection documentation. The company shall establish and maintain a documentation system which, as a minimum, will cover the following points:

1. Establish the locations in the manufacturing cycle of all necessary inspection stations and the extent of inspection to be carried out at each.
2. Provide operating instructions for all complex measuring equipment and for the more difficult inspections.
3. Provide instructions for the formation and identification of all completed product lots or batches.
4. Provide for the collection of inspection records and include infor-

mation on any reinspection carried out on products required to make valid the sampling principles used.

5.4 Inspection records

5.4.1. The company shall keep records of inspections made, and the results thereof, on products produced under a contract or for independent sale. Such records shall include the identification of the item(s) inspected, the nature and number of observations made, the number and types of deficiencies found, quantities accepted and rejected, and the nature of any corrective actions taken.

5.4.2. Inspection records shall provide for positive segregation of nonconforming material from conforming material.

5.4.3. Inspection records shall provide evidence of the repair and calibration of all measuring equipment used to directly determine conformance to the requirements for the product and shall establish the next required calibration date for each piece of measuring equipment.

5.4.4. Inspection records shall, unless stated otherwise by the customer in a contract, be retained in a readily retrievable form for a minimum of 3 months after satisfaction of any contractual or customer requirements so expressed or for such longer periods as the contract may prescribe.

5.4.5. Inspection records shall be made available to the customer for review and verification upon request.

5.5 Changes to inspection documentation

5.5.1. The company shall ensure that inspection documentation used to inspect the product is current and accurately reflects contractual requirements or, when no contract applies, production needs.

5.5.2. In order to carry out 5.5.1, the company shall prepare and establish a procedure defining the conditions under which all formal documents related to the inspection control of quality are issued or changed. These shall prescribe procedures for their preparation and authorization.

5.5.3. All temporary changes used to maintain the continuity of production activities shall be made on the relevant documents and shall be dated and signed in indelible form by authorized persons.

5.5.4. All documents with temporary changes shall be replaced by new-issue documents after a reasonable time, and all obsolete documents shall be promptly removed from their points of use in the organization.

5.5.5. No improperly changed documents shall be used.

5.6 Training of inspectors and testers. The company shall ensure that each person who inspects the characteristics of products against their requirements to determine their conformance to specification possesses the knowledge and skills necessary to perform the required measurements satisfactorily.

5.7 Measuring equipment

5.7.1. The company shall provide, calibrate, and maintain suitable inspection, measuring, and testing devices to demonstrate conformance of products and services to specified requirements.

5.7.2. All measuring equipment used to assure conformance of supplies to requirements shall be calibrated and used in such a manner as to give correct readings of characteristics measured.

5.8 Measuring equipment calibration

5.8.1. All measuring equipment, physical standards, and certified reference materials or physical constants used to perform measurements on the products shall be calibrated, and their known accuracies shall be traceable to the appropriate national standards.

5.8.2. All measuring equipment shall be calibrated, labeled, and used in accordance with Sec. III, Chap. 9 of *Quality Control Systems*.

5.8.3. No measuring equipment that does not have a valid sticker or label showing it is being operated within its planned recalibration interval and that the calibration state has been properly validated shall be used.

5.9 Inspection of customer-furnished items

5.9.1. All items furnished by the customer to be used in the products shall be received, counted, inspected for possible shipping or handling damage, and measured as necessary to ensure that all quality characteristics conform to the specified requirements.

5.9.2. All items furnished by the customer to be used in the products shall be stored in such a way that they are preserved from deterioration of quality characteristics.

5.10   Vendor materials inspection

5.10.1. The company shall ensure that all purchased materials and services conform to quality requirements.

5.10.2. Purchasing documents issued to vendors and to subcontractor shall clearly reflect the necessary quality characteristics for the products and services concerned as well as the quality levels required.

5.10.3. Purchased products and services received from vendors and subcontractors shall be subject to such additional inspection as may be necessary to provide the customer with evidence of conformance to requirements.

5.10.4. The company shall pay due attention to the possibility of damage to products resulting from excessive retesting and prevent such damage from occurring.

5.11   Production process inspection

5.11.1. All quality characteristics of the product shall be verified by actual measurement to a sufficient degree to provide evidence of full conformance with quality requirements.

5.11.2. Appropriate in-process inspection shall be carried out to provide objective evidence of quality characteristics whose values are required to be known and which will be masked from later measurement by subsequent production processing.

5.12   Inspection status identification

5.12.1. The company shall establish and maintain procedures and methods for identification of products, with the use of flow tags or other media, so that the inspection status of such supplies can be determined at any point during production.

5.12.2. Identification flow tags or other media used to establish inspection identity of supplies during production shall not be removed from such supplies before and until the supplies have been incorporated in further assembly so that the characteristics are masked and the items are no longer individually and separately assessable.

5.13 Segregation, storage, and handling

5.13.1. During the course of incoming, in-process, and final inspection and at each other such inspection, nonconforming supplies, when they are found, shall be segregated from conforming supplies and so labeled, marked, or otherwise indicated that, as a result of the segregation and indication, there can be no mixing of conforming supplies with nonconforming supplies.

5.13.2. Supplies shall be stored, either in in-line temporary holding stores or in permanent stores, in such manner as to preserve their quality characteristics from deteriorating and so as to prevent mixing of conforming with nonconforming supplies.

5.13.3. All supplies shall be handled while being worked on, while in transit, or during their storage in such ways as to protect and preserve their quality characteristics.

5.14 Sampling inspection

5.14.1. All sampling inspection shall be carried out by approved and statistically valid sampling plans and methods. When such sampling inspection is being carried out on contract supplies, the sampling plans shall be subject to approval by the customer.

5.14.2. When sampling inspection is used to determine the conformance of supplies, reinspection shall be carried out with full knowledge of the previous inspection and rework history of the supplies so as to make the further inspection valid.

5.15 Disposition of nonconforming material

5.15.1. All material found to be nonconforming shall be segregated from conforming material. The nonconforming material shall be placed in a quarantine store, where it shall be subjected to review by a suitably constituted material review board which shall decide what shall be done with the nonconforming material.

5.15.2. When the material review board decision is either to *use* or to *rework and use,* the material concerned shall be so identified that it

can be appropriately handled and treated in further processing and inspection.

5.16   Completed product inspection

5.16.1.   The company shall perform all inspection on the completed
product necessary to complete the evidence of conformance to quality
requirements as stipulated either in the contract or product specification, or in both.

5.16.2.   The procedure for final product inspection shall ensure that
the evidence of conformance from earlier inspections has been obtained and is satisfactory.

5.16.3.   The combined evidence from earlier inspections, when added to
that from completed product inspection, shall comprise evidence showing full conformance of the product to the total stipulated requirements of the contract and/or the product specification.

5.17   Purchased inspection services.   The company may purchase inspection services from another company provided that they meet the
requirements of this procedure and, when there is a contract, that
they are acceptable to the customer.

5.18   Marking and packing

5.18.1.   Marking, including labeling, of products for identification and
communication to the customer or user shall be such as to provide the
required degree of permanence, and communicate all necessary information, and preserve the quality characteristics of the products.

5.18.2.   Packing methods and materials used shall preserve the quality
characteristics of the products concerned through all reasonable hazards of shipping, handling, and transport.

5.19   Shipping and delivery.   The company shall use appropriate methods and carriers to protect and preserve the quality characteristics of
the materials.

6   Facilities and Assistance

6.1   Facilities.   The company shall provide the customer with reasonable access to the premises and such use of measuring equipment as

may be necessary to verify the conformance of supplies to stipulated requirements.

6.2   Assistance.   The company shall provide assistance, in the form of trained inspectors and testers as may be required, along with suitably operating and calibrated measuring equipment and facilities, to enable the customer to verify conformance of supplies to the stipulated and agreed requirements.

6

Quality Control
by Completed Item Inspection

PART A. REVIEW AND GUIDANCE

1 Review

Completed item quality control by inspection only screens good products from bad. The word "control" therefore connotes the degree of capability to prevent any faulty products from entering the next stage of application, and not the capability to control the characteristics which have already been produced in the products.

There have developed many situations in industry such that completed item inspection is essential to the successful conduct of commercial activities. Examples of these are:

1. When purchasing products from a distributor or other warehousing organization.
2. When completed items are received for use on some project and there is inadequate knowledge about the methods and degrees of control during production.
3. When developed products, prototypes, or completed items from normal production are to have their quality verified (e.g., incoming inspection).

Completed items from a great many suppliers, including almost all vendors to the company, are evaluated by incoming inspection. Retailers, on a sampling basis, and other customers who deem such activities necessary to their success also use completed item inspection. Services which use products as part of their successful delivery should

also integrate the steps of this procedure into their product acceptance
activities.

2   Guidance

This procedure sets forth the essential aspects of a system of control by
which the quality characteristics of products can be assessed and verified with confidence in the outcome. All parts of Art. 5 of this procedure are considered necessary for successful use of the procedure. If
any subarticle is to be omitted, careful consideration should be given
to the probable effects on the organization in both the short and long
term.

When practicable, and if it is desired to influence the characteristics
of the items of product at an early stage of manufacture, the procedure
in Sec. III, Chap. 5 of *Quality Control Systems* should be used in place
of this procedure. This procedure will only influence such characteristics in the long term as the company receives feedback about accep-
tances and rejections from completed item inspection.

PART B.   PROCEDURE

Quality Control by Completed Item
Inspection

1 Scope

This procedure defines the quality system requirements for an inspection system with which to obtain assurance that items of product on which all production operations have been completed will meet their requirements satisfactorily.

2 Application

This procedure shall be applied in the following situations:

1. To completed item inspections carried out by the company when some more comprehensive quality control system is not appropriate.
2. When the company contracts with a customer requiring the demonstration of the company's capability to detect and control the nonconformities in completed items or the deficiencies in operational services.
3. When some regulatory body requires the demonstration of a company's capability to detect and control the nonconformities in completed items or deficiencies in operational services.

3 Referenced Documents

The following documents from *Quality Control Systems** shall be considered a part of this procedure to the extent that they are called up in this document:

1. "Calibration Control Systems," Sec. III, Chap. 9.
2. "Glossary of Terms Used in Quality and Reliability," Sec. VII, Chap. 1.

4 Definitions

The quality and reliability terms used in this procedure shall be interpreted in accordance with the definitions found in the following documents:

1. "Glossary of Terms Used in Quality and Reliability," Sec. VII, Chap. 1 of *Quality Control Systems*.
2. Documents specified in a contract.

---

*James R. Taylor, *Quality Control Systems: Procedures for Planning Quality Programs*, McGraw-Hill, New York, 1989.

5   Quality System Requirements

5.1   Management control

5.1.1.   The company shall define and publish, over the signature of the chief executive officer (CEO), management policies on quality. These shall express the organization's commitment to and objectives for quality.

5.1.2.   The company shall ensure that the quality policy is understood by all employees, fully implemented, and routinely maintained.

5.2   Planning control

5.2.1.   The company shall conduct, at the earliest practicable time, a review of the requirements in respect to the inspection of the products or operational services.

5.2.2.   The company shall identify the measuring equipment, skills, and other requirements needed to fully assess the products and/or operational services for their quality characteristics. These shall be obtained or specific actions for their acquisition shall be planned.

5.2.3.   The company shall identify data to be collected to prove the absence of nonconformities in the products or services and plan for them, including the preparation of any necessary test documents, inspection schedules, or other documents or forms needed in the work. When they are appropriate, computer use and automatic data processing systems shall provide for data collection, storage, and retrieval.

5.3   Organization

5.3.1.   The company shall define the responsibilities and authority of all staff who must do work in respect to obtaining objective evidence that the products and/or services are free of nonconformances and deficiencies.

5.3.2.   All staff assigned to undertake and carry out work in respect to assessment and measurement of the products or services shall be competent in their work and have knowledge and skills adequate to successfully and objectively make the measurements and assessments necessary to verify that the products or services meet specified requirements.

5.3.3.   The company shall appoint a management representative who, irrespective of other responsibilities, shall have defined authority and responsibility for ensuring that the requirements of this procedure are implemented and maintained.

5.4   Quality system audit.   The company shall prepare, implement, and maintain a program for the systematic review and audit of the quality system established in accordance with this procedure. The review and audit shall ensure the continuing suitability and effectiveness of the quality system.

5.5   Inspection of customer-supplied items.   The company shall assume responsibility for the quality of all items provided by the customer for inclusion in or with the product to be delivered or constructed. Such customer-supplied items shall be examined for possible shipping damage and shall be handled, stored, and processed with the company-provided items in ways which will preserve and protect the quality characteristics.

5.6   Quality system.   The company shall establish and maintain an effective quality system for inspections and tests on products or services in their completed stages. This shall include documented procedures for final inspection and test operations, including workmanship standards and quality records.

5.7   Measuring equipment control.   The company shall establish inspection and test equipment which will perform all necessary measurements and provide for inspection of workmanship and the assessment of other quality characteristics of product. The inspection and test equipment shall have ranges, sensitivities, and other capabilities commensurate with the requirements for measuring the products.

5.8   Measuring equipment calibration.   The company shall establish a calibration program which will provide for periodic calibration of all inspection and measuring equipment. Such calibrations and the accuracies they convey shall be traceable to the national standards. Measuring equipment shall be sealed to prevent tampering. All inspection and test equipment shall be labeled with a tag which indicates the item, its status of calibration, and the time the equipment will be ready for recall for calibration again.

5.9   Document control.   The company shall prepare and provide for use by testers and inspectors, as well as those who carry out the remainder of the quality activities of the system, instructions and procedures by which to carry out the work. All documents comprising part of the inspection system shall be numbered and have issue control and shall be controlled within the change control system of Art. 5.10.

When the quality requirements specify that data shall be collected on the measurements made, these records, including the data sheets as appropriate, shall form part of the quality records over which the company shall maintain control.

5.10 Document change control. The company shall maintain control over all documents used in carrying out the final tests and inspections, including the collection of inspection and test results. Such documents shall be marked or changed in any way only by approved members of the company's management and operating team. All changes shall be marked with the date, change, and signature of the person authorizing the change.

5.11 Inspection and test control. The company shall carry out all final inspection and tests in accordance with the documented procedures to complete the evidence of full conformance of the product or service to the specified requirements. The final inspection shall include the verification of acceptable results of other inspections and tests performed to verify that requirements are met.

5.12 Product identification. The company shall provide for identification of all product so that it can be correlated with the inspection and test results. Such marking or labeling shall provide positive identification and information on the month and year of manufacture, as well as the company producing the product.

5.13 Nonconforming product control. The company shall provide for positive identification of all product, the segregation of nonconforming product from conforming product, and positive control to prevent unauthorized use, delivery, or mixing with conforming product.

5.14 Inspection and test records. The company shall maintain inspection and test records to substantiate conformance with specified requirements. Records shall be legible and identifiable as to the product involved. Records that substantiate conformance with the specified requirements shall be retained for an agreed-upon period and made available to the customer upon request. In the absence of any other agreement, such records shall be retained and stored for a minimum of 3 months following the completion of a relevant contract.

5.15   Statistical techniques. The company shall establish, when it is appropriate, procedures for identifying and using adequate statistical techniques required for verifying the acceptability of product characteristics. These may include:

1. Identifying and classifying the required characteristics
2. Selecting methods and plans according to appropriate statistical procedures
3. Verifying the results of statistical application to confirm that product characteristics conform to specified requirements
4. Selecting samples for inspection

When statistical techniques are not used, the company shall document the inspection and test methods used, and the results obtained therefrom shall comprise a documented inspection system which shall be made available for review and approval by the customer.

5.16   Handling, storing, packing, and delivering. The company shall provide for the protection of the quality of the product and its identification after finished product inspection and test. When contractually stipulated, the company shall be responsible for the packing and preservation of products for shipment.

Methods of packing, storing, transporting, and delivering shall be such as to protect the quality characteristics of the product and forward the inspection and test results to the customer when agreed to in the contract.

Nonconforming Material Control Procedure

PART A. REVIEW AND GUIDANCE

1 Review

This procedure has been prepared specifically to meet the requirements of the company for internal production activities and to meet the requirements of customers. The quality system established in accordance with this general procedure meets all the requirements of U.S. MIL-STD-1520 and other such contractual or purchase order requirements. It can also help control product quality during production.

In the course of design, development, production, delivery, and installation of products there can occur some items which do not conform fully with all requirements. It is essential in the control of quality that these items be clearly identified and segregated from good items and that disposition and corrective action take place in an orderly and controlled manner.

Following discovery, identification, and segregation of nonconforming items, it is necessary to make intelligent disposition of such items and take corrective action. In the course of this work there is great risk that items containing nonconformances will become intermixed with conforming items of a similar nature or that the corrective action taken may interfere with the achievement of quality in other items under production.

When it is economical and technically feasible, or when a customer so specifies in a contract, arrangements for repair and rework to correct nonconforming materials shall be separate from those used in new production. When separate facilities are not feasible, special procedures shall be used to ensure that repair actions will not jeopardize the quality of new production items.

The aim of quality control shall be to reduce the incidence of nonconformance to so low a level that it is not necessary to undertake repair and rework activities. The effort of the company shall always be to achieve full conformance on the first time through production.

2   Guidance

The implementation of this procedure shall be in accordance with and to the degree that customer requirements and the needs of the company dictate. Where implementation is being accomplished in order to meet the requirements of a contract or purchase order, the relative parts of the system shall be submitted to the customer for approval when required. It is the policy of the company to fully meet all customer requirements and to do so in the most economical manner that is compatible with meeting technical stipulations in contracts and purchase orders. All employees of the company shall therefore carry out their work in accordance with this policy.

PART B.   PROCEDURE

Nonconforming Material Control Procedure

1 Scope

This procedure defines and establishes the requirements of the company in respect to methods to be used concerning nonconformance of products or services with requirements.

2 Application

This procedure shall apply to all activities of the company in its manufacturing operations and shall be varied as necessary to meet any special requirements of contracts and purchase orders unless stated otherwise in the relevant customer documentation.

3 Definitions

The terms used in this procedure, and their definitions, shall be interpreted in accordance with "Glossary of Terms Used in Quality and Reliability," Sec. VII, Chap. 1 of *Quality Control Systems*.*

4 Organization

4.1. It is the responsibility of the total company organization and all of its divisions and departments to comply with the mandatory requirements in this procedure. To that end the quality organization shall provide detailed operating procedures and instructions as necessary to make this part of the total quality system fully effective. It shall provide employees who are fully qualified both technically and in quality work to provide chairpersons of the material review board and members of other boards and committees or teams which may from time to time become involved in work with problems of nonconformance of the products.

The organization of the company currently holding responsibility for the design of products in manufacture shall provide members of their technically qualified staff to carry out work on the material review board, the corrective action board, and other committees and teams as appropriate. All employees of the company shall carry out their work to the best of their ability in a manner designed and intended to prevent the occurrence of nonconformances and to make the products right the first time through each operation.

4.2. There shall be established capabilities for analyzing nonconforming items to determine their causes of failure and provide guidance as

---

*James R. Taylor, *Quality Control Systems: Procedures for Planning Quality Programs*, McGraw-Hill, New York, 1989.

to the most suitable courses of action in obtaining rectification of the nonconformances both in failed items and in the processes to prevent recurrence of nonconformance in new products. It shall be the aim of this capability to ensure that any causes identified, and recommendations for corrective action made, are compatible with both the economic situation and the technical and quality requirements stipulated for the products.

5 Documentation

5.1. The quality manager shall have prepared procedures which set forth the total program of control of quality in respect to nonconformance. These procedures shall identify the work to be done, the responsibilities for carrying out such work, and the goals to be obtained. The responsibilities shall be in accordance with the various delegations to each unit, and the organizations participating in the program in each category shall be given the opportunity to contribute to and agree with the assigned responsibilities.

5.2. The system of documentation used shall maintain records of all nonconforming material, the dispositions of that material, the assignable causes, the corrective actions, and the effectiveness of the corrective actions. The system of documentation established by the quality manager, and by other company organizations, shall provide specifically for the requirements of Art. 8.

6 Detecting and Identifying Nonconformance

6.1. Nonconformance may be detected by any person coming into contact with or working on matters concerning the product of the company. When detected, it is the responsibility of all employees of the company, and is specifically requested of all customers and other persons, that all such nonconformances be brought to the early attention of the quality manager of the company so that the corrective action processes of the company can be set in motion.

6.2. The company shall establish a program for handling complaints which shall be designed to receive complaints about any matter, and specifically about any product of the company, with a view to resolving the specific complaint and to taking corrective action which will prevent future nonconformance of that nature.

6.3. Nonconforming material, once identified, shall be clearly segregated from good material, identified by marking, labeling, or in some other suitable way, and transferred to the control of the quality organization for review, disposition, and corrective action.

7   Segregating and Identifying Nonconforming Material

7.1.   When material is found to be nonconforming, it may occupy any of several states or situations. It may, for example, be liquid which comes from a reservoir of conforming material and becomes nonconforming only in some later stage of flow. It may be some part already fixed irretrievably into or onto some larger subassembly or system, or it may be some part which, because of size or hazardous nature, cannot be readily tagged or marked.

Regardless of its nature or position, the material which is found to be nonconforming shall be so identified by segregation, quarantining, labeling, tagging, marking or in other ways controlled that it will be conspicuously different from similar conforming material or material it may harm in some way. When its size or nature permits, the nonconforming material shall be removed from the inspection or production area where discovered and placed in a controlled quarantine area for disposition. The controlled area shall be protected to preclude unauthorized removal of the nonconforming material or its return to the production area.

Progressive marking of nonconforming material shall indicate its status in the disposition processes used by the company. When position is used to segregate and control nonconforming material, the material shall be changed in position to indicate progress toward final disposition.

7.2.   When it is not possible to tag, label, mark, or otherwise directly identify some item or items of nonconforming material, the identification method shall involve placing the material in a container or other geometrical position which itself can be marked to indicate nonconformance. When containers or other identifiable bordered areas are used to indicate nonconformance, no conforming material shall be permitted to be in the same container or area with the nonconforming material. The position in the container of the nonconforming material shall be used to indicate progress toward disposition when appropriate.

8   Failure Analysis of Nonconforming Material

8.1.   There shall be established a program designed to find and report the causes of nonconformance in products of the company and, when specified in contracts, of suppliers. The program shall provide for disassembly of items and the carrying out of physical, chemical, mechanical, or other suitable methods of analysis to determine the causes of failure, including reproducing the mechanisms when necessary.

8.2.   The failure analysis program shall be linked with the preliminary review program of Art. 9.1 below so that both are maximized in their contribution to control of nonconformance.

9   Review and Disposition

9.1   Preliminary review of nonconforming items

9.1.1.   When material is initially found to be nonconforming, it shall be examined by a competent member of the quality organization, and, when necessary, competent members of production and engineering organizations, to classify the nonconformance according to whether the material:

- Can be reworked
- Must be scrapped
- Can be repaired by approved methods
- Will be returned to the supplier
- Falls in none of the above classes and will be referred to the material review board for action

9.1.2.   All material handled by the preliminary review method shall be subject to all the same controls of identification, segregation, and corrective action board (CAB) action as set forth in Art. 10.

9.2   Material review board (MRB): composition and authority

9.2.1.   The MRB shall be composed of staff representing the quality organization and other company organizations necessary to determine appropriate disposition for each item of nonconformance. Permanent members in each equipment area are as follows:

1. The quality representative, who shall be the chairman
2. The design organization representative
3. The production organization representative

9.2.2.   The MRB representatives shall be chosen for their technical competence in respect to the product area for which they are representatives. When necessary, personnel may be coopted to the MRB from other areas of the company's operations in order to reach the most appropriate disposition decision. Each permanent MRB member shall have detailed knowledge of this procedure and its requirements, as well as any requirements of the contractor or customer.

9.2.3. Only one MRB shall be established for each major product operation, but there may be as many MRBs in operation as there are production divisions making different kinds of products.

9.2.4. No customer representative may be a member of an MRB, but the supplier may request the customer to provide a co-opted member to the MRB considering his or her supplies for disposition.

9.2.5. The material review board shall have the authority to make positive dispositions of materials and supplies without recourse to higher management. When the fiscal value of such material or other supplies and the work contained exceeds the approval level of the MRB, financial authority shall be sought and obtained from the appropriate level within the company. When the material review board, after due consideration of the failure mechanisms and effects, makes a disposition decision, it shall be binding on other organizations within the company.

9.3 Material review board: activities

9.3.1. The material review board shall carry out independent disposition of material referred to it for these decision categories:

- Scrap
- Rework
- Return to supplier
- Repair

9.3.2. The MRB shall investigate in a timely manner all nonconforming material referred to it following preliminary review. This investigation shall proceed to sufficient depth to determine proper disposition.

9.3.3. When the disposition decision reached is use-as-is or repair by other than approved methods and there is a customer representative or the contract or purchase order so specifies, the decision shall be reviewed and be subject to approval by the representative of the customer. When the customer's representative is involved in disposition of nonconforming material, he or she shall be kept informed of progress in the matters so that more effective decisions can be made.

9.4 Disposition of nonconforming material

9.4.1. Nonconforming material shall be divided into two categories, according to the most serious nonconformance possessed by the item(s) concerned: *major* and *minor nonconformances*.

Major nonconforming material is that which has one or more nonconformances that will render the material incapable of meeting requirements for one or more of the following:

1. Performance, effective use, or operation
2. Reliability or durability
3. Interchangeability
4. Weight, volume, or appearance (when a factor)
5. Health or safety

Minor nonconforming material is that which has one or more nonconformances that do not affect (1) through (5) above but which is a nonconformance to the requirements in the contract, specification, drawing, or other approved product description.

9.4.2. All nonconforming material which has not been previously disposed of by the preliminary review program shall be disposed of by the material review board. The MRB shall make a decision to:

1. Scrap
2. Rework
3. Repair
4. Return to supplier
5. Recommend for use-as-is to customer, quality manager, or jurisdictional authority

9.4.3. The company shall prepare and implement repair procedures which carry the approval of the customer or jurisdictional authority when necessary. Reprocessing material shall be considered to be either a rework or repair activity, and instructions for this work shall be included in the standard repair manual when used. When required by

the contract or work order, all nonconforming material shall be pro-
gressed through the manufacturing processes only with the customer's
prior agreement.

9.4.4. In all cases when disposal is to use-as-is there shall be an examination of the relevant documentation which caused the rejection
or nonconformance observation to determine if there shall be a revision of any of the documentation covering the material or processing
concerned.

9.4.5. All scrapped material shall be conspicuously marked or labeled
to preclude its being further processed or used.

9.4.6. All repaired or reworked material shall meet technical requirements in complete detail, but it shall be recognized that rework de-
grades workmanship.

10   Corrective Action

10.1   Corrective action board: composition and authority

10.1.1. The company shall appoint a corrective action board (CAB)
which shall assure that causes of nonconformance are identified in
each area in which they exist. The CAB shall carry out its work in
conjunction with the activity of Art. 8.

10.1.2. The CAB shall have members who are best suited to ascertain
causes of failure by analyses, trends, and other data and who shall
identify areas of high potential savings through the comparative analysis of costs and the use of the quality cost program. The CAB shall
prepare and maintain records of analyses, findings, trends, and individual causes acted upon. It shall prepare individual records for sum-
maries of actions taken.

10.1.3. The CAB shall have the authority to assure that all corrective
actions necessary to satisfy the full range of MRB and preliminary review dispositions are made. It shall have authority to require investigations and studies to be carried out by any group within the entire
manufacturing organization in support of cost reduction associated
with scrap, rework, and repair, as well as the improvement of quality.
The CAB shall document or have documented summary data of
nonconformances and be able to undertake studies of potential highly
cost-beneficial areas of the manufacturing activity. The CAB shall as-

sure that all necessary process controls for quality achievement are implemented and monitored.

10.1.4. The corrective action board, which will normally consist of managers from the quality, engineering, and production organizations, with managers from other affected organizations being co-opted from time to time, shall, when process controls are used, have the authority to require process control studies and corrective action to be taken when it can be shown that established standards of work are not being met. The CAB shall periodically review the preliminary review and material review board decisions for their correctness, and it shall audit and review all nonconformance data from time to time in its role of overseeing the nonconformance activities of the manufacturing organization. (The CAB will normally consist primarily of staff from the quality assurance organization in the position of chairman, with supporting managers from the engineering and production activities as necessary.)

10.2   Corrective action board: activities

10.2.1. The corrective action board carries out a joint quality assurance and quality control job within the overall activities of the manufacturing organization. As such it shall:

1. Assure that corrective actions are identified, planned, designed, implemented, and made to work in respect to nonconformance.
2. Require that investigations are undertaken by the most appropriate company organizations. The investigations shall be designed to reduce costs associated with scrap, rework, and repair as well as the improvement of quality.
3. Assure that documentation is prepared and acted upon in accordance with all nonconformances.
4. Follow up all corrective actions to assure their timeliness and effectiveness in respect to the nonconformance concerned.
5. Assure that nonconformance summary data are analyzed and areas of high payoff performance are investigated and essential corrective actions are implemented.
6. Assure that a system of monitoring process controls and documenting nonconformances is developed and established.
7. Periodically review nonconformance data, preliminary review and MRB disposition decisions for their effectiveness in overcoming nonconformances.

10.3   Control through quality costing

10.3.1.   The quality organization of the company shall design, develop, and establish a comprehensive quality cost program for the activity as a whole. This program shall be in accordance with "Manufacturing Quality Cost System," Sec. VI, Chap. 2 of *Quality Control Systems.*

10.3.2.   The quality manager of the company shall assure that all cost requirements of contracts and purchase orders and other customer requirements in this respect are met.

11   Documentation Concerning Nonconformance

11.1.   The company shall prepare and maintain records of all nonconforming material, the dispositions thereof, assignable causes, corrective actions taken, and the effectiveness of such corrective actions. The conformance records shall be so organized and stored or maintained as to permit:

- Efficient retrieval
- Summarization
- Identification of relationship between successive dispositions
- Corrective actions taken and their effectiveness.

11.2.   Records made of nonconformances shall include:

1. Initiator of the document
2. Date of the document
3. Identification necessary for traceability
4. Specific part number of the nonconforming part or item
5. Details of the manufacturing process in which the nonconformance occurred
6. A detailed description of the nonconformance
7. Disposition of the nonconforming item
8. Identification of personnel responsible for the disposition decision
9. MRB disposition of the nonconforming item(s)

10. Signatures of the disposition authorities

11. A description of the assignable causes for the nonconformance

12. The corrective actions taken to preclude recurrence of the nonconformance(s)

13. Identification of the organization and individuals taking the corrective action

11.3. When corrective action on the particular nonconforming items is not necessary or appropriate but it is appropriate to correct the process which was not controlling adequately, the correction data, as well as any degree of correction achieved as measured by further study of the degree of control of the process, shall be recorded.

11.4. Costs associated with nonconformance shall be collected and acted on in accordance with the quality costing program of the company. The quality costs shall be retrievable in respect to specific costs concerning areas of major nonconformance.

12 Supplier and Subcontract Items

When the company is involved with nonconformance of material from a supplier, and in particular when the company is a prime contractor to some customer, the company shall assume responsibility for corrective action in respect to the nonconformance. A record of such nonconformance shall be prepared and maintained, on a supplier-by-supplier basis. Though the company may choose to delegate corrective action to suppliers, it shall assume responsibility for all such action to its customer. Subcontracted material shall, when found to have nonconformances, be treated in the same way as company-manufactured material. The subcontract prepared for use with the subcontractor shall clearly identify the company's right to pursue nonconformance causes and corrective action in conjunction with subcontractor personnel.

13 Compliance with and Assistance to Customers

13.1. The company quality and other personnel shall ensure that all customer requirements and needs are satisfied in strict and direct proportion to the seriousness of the matter and the nature of the product. When the customer requires assistance with verifying that products conform, this shall be provided within reasonable cost limits.

13.2. In all cases when customer requirements dictate that the customer representative shall have the right of approval of some area of work by the company, this work shall be integrated by the quality manager, or the design manager as appropriate, with other organizations becoming involved on a needs basis. Full cooperation shall be given at all times with customer representatives, and any questions shall be referred immediately to the respective area manager.

Chapter

8

Quality Control of Change System

PART A. REVIEW AND GUIDANCE

1 Review

High quality is the aim of all manufacturing activities. The objective is to produce products which are totally free of all forms of nonconformance. It has been found that the methods of doing that differ depending on whether only a few items are to be produced or the production situation calls for mass production of one product design.

In the case of high quality for single items of product it has been found to be necessary to carry the planning activity all the way through every single action which is going to be taken, think each action and material through, and ensure that all necessary aspects of all activities are covered not only in the planning but also in the doing. In this way a detailed plan is prepared and documented; it can be followed rigorously, and any deviation from it becomes a major item for high-level theoretical and practical investigation and resolution.

When the production of a large number of some item of product is planned, there is opportunity for the manufacturing system to be taken through the "learning curve." All feedback loops can be tried and proved, and finally a system whereby the production operation runs smoothly like an automated machine is evolved. Within all systems, however, it is necessary to establish control of change. For any one of a very large number of reasons, changes will occur during any production cycle, no matter how short or long. The essential management aspect of this knowledge is that such change be controlled and not be permitted to take place without effective review and control being implemented each and every time.

The scientific management of change is a statistical mathematical process whereby variance is anticipated, the extent of risk is determined, and the limits set are managed to prevent their being exceeded. This involves a theoretical approach to risk management; and even when such methods are applicable, the methods set forth in this procedure will be found useful. The methods and procedures set forth herein are those which have been found through the years to work in all kinds of manufacturing situations and at all levels of quality.

2   Guidance

When a design and development activity is managed, it will be necessary to have the quality of the activity and its output controlled in accordance with the respective procedures from Sec. II of *Quality Control Systems.** The specific procedure to use will depend on the type of product being developed.

When a production or services-providing activity or the construction of a project is managed, it will be necessary to implement this procedure throughout the activity. The implementation should be under the direction of the quality manager, who must integrate with all other organizational components and assure that the requirements of this procedure are met.

In any situation in which a change that could in any way affect the quality of the completed items becomes necessary, the managers and supervisors of all organizations affected shall be informed before the change and be given the opportunity to approve or object to the change. A particularly difficult aspect of change exists when the production activity is operating under the tight control of a dominant customer or jurisdictional authority. When that is the situation, it must be recognized that the needs and requirements of the customer and/or jurisdictional authority are to be met. Delays are costly to any production operation, and it will be necessary to maintain close supervision of the need for change in order to expedite necessary change through both the outside and inside change authorities.

---

*James R. Taylor, *Quality Control Systems: Procedures for Planning Quality Programs,* McGraw-Hill, New York, 1989.

PART B.   PROCEDURE

Quality Control of Change System

1   Scope

This procedure defines the requirements of the company in respect to methods of control to be used concerning control of change which takes place during the course of a design, development, production, providing, or construction activity.

2   Application

This procedure shall apply throughout the company and in any situation where it is called up in a contract or purchase order involving the company. When it is appropriate, this procedure shall be made a requirement of subcontractors, vendors, and others who may do business with the company.

The issue of this procedure which shall apply shall be that called for in any relevant contract or purchase order. In lieu of such a requirement, the latest issue of this procedure shall apply.

3   Definitions

The terms used in this procedure shall be interpreted in accordance with the definitions presented in Sec. VII, Chap. 1 of *Quality Control*

Systems, unless specifically required otherwise in a contract or purchase order.

4   Referenced Documents

The following documents are referenced in this procedure:

1. The contract or purchase order (if any).
2. "Glossary of Terms Used in Quality and Reliability," Sec. VII, Chap. 1 of *Quality Control Systems.*
3. All applicable jurisdictional regulations and codes.
4. "Quality Control System for Products," Sec. III, Chap. 2 of *Quality Control Systems.**

5   Control of Change during Design Phase

Design work on a new item, or a design change in an existing item, shall proceed according to an organized program of work involving the use of standards, known and developed materials, and approved methods. Each element of work output included in the design of the item shall be documented in a manner suitable for permitting review, audit, and later assessment. When some aspect of a product must be changed to achieve a difference in the product characteristics, the change(s) made to bring about such result shall be documented to the same or greater degree than the earlier design state was.

Design changes to items shall always be tested in working models of the items throughout all relevant item operational requirements before they are considered satisfactory. The results obtained from such tests shall be documented and made a part of the item design history file for later review when required.

Control of changes made during the design phase of an item shall be by the design manager who has control of the overall design project. When it is appropriate, design changes shall receive the approval of the customer or any jurisdictional authority.

6   Control of Change during Development Phase

All changes made during the development phase of either the item or the process shall be documented, tested, and proved to yield satisfactory results in full conformance with requirements. The testing of items shall consist of evaluation of working models of each type of

---

*James R. Taylor, *Quality Control Systems: Procedures for Planning Quality Programs,* McGraw-Hill, New York, 1989.

item against the operational requirements, with the recording of results and the proving of full conformance with those requirements. The testing of a process change shall consist of operating the process to generate the planned output and then evaluating that output against requirements to verify that full conformance with requirements has been obtained.

When only one or a few end items are to be produced, the activity shall be considered in the same way as item development. Control of change shall be maintained in the same way as when items are developed. When necessary, all changes made to items or processes in development, along with test results, shall be submitted to the customer and/or jurisdictional authority for approval.

Construction work carried out on projects shall be treated as development work, and the control of change shall be carried out in the same way as for product or service development. The project manager shall identify and delegate to the quality organization the responsibility for the control of change activities, with the responsible design organization having direct approval responsibility.

7   The Change Control System in Production

7.1   Planning for control of change

7.1.1. During the production or providing phase of a manufacturing activity, it is desirable to achieve stability in all areas of the operation. For best achievement of quality and productivity, it is desirable that fully conforming purchased goods and services come into the operation, all processes operate in control, and inspections and tests consistently verify that materials and subassemblies are fully conforming. Completed item testing shall show that outgoing items consistently and fully conform to operational requirements. In such an operation it is possible to operate at the highest profit level. Change shall therefore be naturally resisted and considered an undesirable aspect of mass production.

As manufacturing proceeds, however, things happen for any one or more of innumerable reasons. Sometimes these unanticipated happenings result in item nonconformance. When they do, it is necessary to make changes. The task of management is to ensure that all change occurs in an orderly controlled manner. It is the purpose of planning to make that happen.

7.1.2. In planning for the control of change it is necessary to anticipate all possible eventualities and devise ways of coping with them

and overcoming them in orderly controlled ways. This means understanding the ways the production processes generate their various
item characteristics and how control of each process is maintained. It
means full understanding of all inspections and tests of item characteristics and full control of the production environment and all other
aspects of the production operation. These controls are set forth in Sec.
III, Chaps. 2, 3, and 4 of *Quality Control Systems.*

Planning for control of change means devising plans for what will
be the procedure to follow when it is determined that any of the various production processes, or the following inspections and tests, fail to
result in confirmation that the correct product characteristics are being generated. This procedure sets forth all the things which shall be
done to control change in production. It shall be implemented
throughout the activities of the company and by contract or purchase
order with suppliers and subcontractors.

7.2 Organization and change control. The company shall establish a
documented and integrated management structure which shall manage the business activities of the company. There shall be managers
reporting to the chief executive officer of the company, managers who
are responsible for production, quality, purchasing, plant engineering,
product engineering, laboratories, accounting, sales, and marketing
(or corresponding activities in project and service companies).

The quality manager shall have delegated to him or her the responsibility for designing and implementing a change control system
which is in accordance with this procedure. He or she shall have responsibility for integrating all change control activities with the respective managers of the various areas in accordance with the management control needed to make the control of change most effective.

All managers in the company shall be fully acquainted with all
other managers and other activities with which they must work in
discharging the various responsibilities of their managerial areas.
There shall be available at all times a clear documented organizational chart, and full understanding shall be conveyed to managers of
all positional responsibilities on the chart. To that end there shall be
prepared and promulgated, as necessary, responsibility statements for
each managerial area of control.

7.3 Control of documentation changes. All documentation issued by
the company shall have issue and revision control facilities included
in cover sheets or control drawings. Facilities for determining the currency of issue shall be provided on all documents officially incorporated into the operation. Changes and approvals of changes shall be
made in accordance with the following clauses of this procedure.

7.3.1 Change approval. The issue of all new drawings and documents used by the company, and the revision or reissue of those drawings and documents, shall be reviewed by and shall receive the approval of all organizational managers who are responsible for discharging work affected by the issued document or by its reissue.

A document change form shall be prepared for use by the company, and this form shall act as a routing sheet to direct new and revised documents to all area managers responsible for performing work affected by the document or any change to that document. When approval of newly issued or changed documents and drawings must be obtained from a customer or a jurisdictional authority, provision shall be made in the approval process to obtain such an approval prior to implementation of the change.

The operating procedures for the company shall prevent the use of any newly issued or revised document which has not received the necessary approvals in accordance with this procedure.

7.3.2 Documentation change. Documents used by employees and managers of the company shall have their contents changed in a permanent manner only by indelible marking by personnel who have the authority for making such changes. To that end, each change shall be initialed or signed by the person making the change, and the date of the change shall be entered on the document alongside the signature or initials of the person making the change.

Documents and drawings carrying changes shall be subject to permanent revision and reissue at the earliest practicable time following the change. Under no circumstance shall documents or drawings, after changes have been made on them, continue in use for longer than three production periods and before reissue without special managerial approval. When a document change affects more than one operating area of the company, the change notice shall carry the signature or initials of the supervisor or manager of each such area affected, along with the signature or initials of the person authorizing the change.

When some process is duplicated one or more times in the operating activities of the company and a change is made to the documents located at one such station, all other documents bearing the same number shall be marked likewise at the same time or date on which the first such document is changed and approved.

Other than the original content of documents and drawings, there shall be no markings on such paperwork or other instructions than those made by authorized personnel. The personnel authorized to make changes to operating documentation shall have the requisite technical and managerial skills and knowledge to support their authority and right to mark such instructions and documents. Requirements of the same type shall apply to all instructions which can affect the quality of the output, regardless of the nature of such instructions. The documents may include paperwork, drawings, transparencies, computer programs, graphic representations, combinations of them, or any other form of communication by which instructions and guides may be promulgated to workers and managers in the company.

7.3.3 Control of documentation issue. All documents, in whatever form, used by the company in the performance of work on production shall have their issue numbers and dates entered on them in a clear conspicuous manner, and the person authorizing them shall enter his or her signature or initials in a place specially prepared for such purpose. Software programs, graphic representations, and other forms of documented instructions, procedures, specifications, guides, standards, and other forms of communications to those who must carry out the work of the company shall be controlled and protected against change and damage which would render them capable of causing an error or being misinterpreted.

Drawings, procedures, standards, and other official publications of the company shall be under the control of a document center or drawing office which shall ensure that all such documents are controlled for both their new issue and their reissue. When drawings are first issued, the document controller shall ensure that they carry the necessary authorizing signatures and the dates of issue. All revised documents shall likewise carry the authorizing signatures and dates and shall be provided to the points of use throughout the company in an expeditious manner.

When a document is reissued, the earlier issue shall be removed from all points of use simultaneously with providing the revised version to the point of use. When the earlier model of a product requires continued production minus the change, separate numbers for the basic drawings shall be used for document control. The document change control system shall not be used to differentiate between two similar but slightly different models of the same product.

When computer software comprises the instructions to be used by persons responsible for producing the product, this form of documentation shall be supported by hardcopy which shall itself constitute controlled documentation. Video tapes shall carry their own specific and individual numbering and issue control information as an integral part of the company's document control system.

7.3.4 Control of document use. The company shall issue instructions to employees and managers on the penalties for misuse of documentation. Specific and clear training in responsibilities in respect to use, maintenance, and care of documents shall be given to each employee. In respect to each and every document to which the employee may need access in order to carry out assigned work, he or she shall be instructed in the care of the document.

It shall be the responsibility of the supervisor or manager of each work area to ensure that the correct documents, and correct revisions of such documents, are the ones in use in that area at all times. At no time shall the supervisor or manager permit the wrongful marking, use, or other action which would defeat the purpose of this procedure or the intent of document control.

Special care shall be taken to ensure that employees are given adequate training in the reading and interpretation of documentation used by the company. When changes to documentation are made, the import of such changes shall be clearly communicated to employees who are affected, and any new skills needed for the implementation of such changes in the processing or inspection and testing of products shall be provided. Employees shall not be expected to remember complex or voluminous amounts of information. Documents shall, at all times, be readily available to employees needing access to their contents.

7.4 Purchasing input to change control

7.4.1. The purchasing manager shall have the opportunity to review and approve all documents and document changes which affect directly the carrying out of purchasing duties. When changes are made to documents which affect purchasing, the purchasing manager shall ensure that the changes affecting contracts, purchase orders, or new procurement are promulgated to suppliers at the earliest possible times and in sufficient time to ensure that the supplies concerned are in full conformance with their applicable documentation.

7.4.2. It shall be the responsibility of the purchasing manager to ensure that all requirements for materials, components, subassemblies, and completed equipment or items are fully communicated to suppliers in contracts and purchase orders. These shall include quality and reliability requirements as well as specific technical, quantity, or costing types of product requirements.

7.4.3. When necessary for the conveyance of technical matters, the purchasing manager shall provide opportunities for technical personnel to meet with suppliers for the purpose of communicating to them interpretations and related technical matters in respect to the supplies being procured. The same facility shall be provided to quality personnel in respect to quality and reliability information.

7.4.4. Purchasing records shall meet the same rigorous change control requirements as other documentation used by the company when changes can affect the quality of the produced product. Changes in goods made by suppliers which are beyond the control of the purchasing manager shall be brought promptly to the attention of responsible and/or affected managers of areas within the production plant. The purchasing manager shall provide for evaluation of proposed or actual changes so their impact on the production activity can be assessed and any needed adjustments can be made. The production manager, the quality manager, and other affected managers, as a minimum, shall be involved in such assessments and determinations.

7.5   Control of handling and storage change

7.5.1. There are changes in stock which affect supplies, and there are changes in supplies which affect stock. It shall be the responsibility of the manager responsible for stores to ensure that all changes to stock activities and capabilities which affect production are made only after they are fully promulgated to all affected areas and approval of such changes is received.

It shall be the responsibility of the employees or managers who first become aware of changes that will affect stock activity to notify the manager responsible for stock so these changes can be controlled and their effects can be kept within acceptable limits. Store managers shall control their stock in such a manner that change will always be brought to their attention and will affect the control and issue of supplies in a minimal manner.

7.5.2. Once the methods of handling and transporting supplies and material in process have been established, changes in such methods shall not be made without full awareness by those who receive and use or work on the material and other supplies.

7.6   Process change control

7.6.1. Changes which take place in processes are of two kinds: either they are planned or they occur without prior knowledge and control. When an accidental change in a process takes place and the material or item being processed has one or more of its characteristics so changed as to affect conformance, that material or item shall be controlled to prevent shipment of nonconforming items. When they are appropriate, concessions shall be obtained from customers prior to shipment. When concessions are not appropriate, the company shall ensure that nonconforming supplies are shipped to customers only with full customer knowledge and the nonconforming supplies are marketed or sold accordingly.

7.6.2. Planned changes in processes shall result in new process capability studies being made and in the changed effect on item characteristics being determined. Planned changes in processes shall be made only as a result of changed documentation concerning the processes. Following the planned change in a process, the new item characteristic(s) shall be documented in drawings and other company documents. These other documents shall reflect any changes in costs of production and pricing.

7.6.3. When the customer or a jurisdictional authority is affected by process changes, he or it shall be notified and appropriate opportunity shall be given for review and approval to be obtained.

7.6.4. When items have been changed as a result of changed processes, there shall be taken, from among the very first production samples made on production tools, a sample of the changed item(s) which shall undergo full evaluation in respect to any change resulting therein, and such item(s) shall be the subject of agreement by customer or jurisdictional authority as is appropriate.

7.6.5. Following a process change, the quality manager shall cause an audit of all affected documentation concerning the process to be made. That audit shall show that all documentation concerned has been brought up to date with the change and is capable of continuing to control the manufacture of fully conforming items.

7.7 Inspection and test change control. When it is necessary to make changes in the methods, types, accuracies, or other aspects of inspections and tests on items or related materials, it shall be the responsibility of the quality manager to ensure that such changes are fully promulgated to all affected areas, and principally to production managers who are affected. All such changes to inspection and test activities, facilities, personnel, and other parts of the inspection and test change control activity shall be fully documented as a part of the normal ongoing work of the company.

Changes to inspection and test activities of the company shall, when it is appropriate, receive the prior approval of the customer and/or jurisdictional authority.

7.8   Marking, packing, and delivery change control

7.8.1.   When changes are made in the marking, packing, and/or delivery of items, such changes usually affect the customer or recipient of the item. When a contract or purchase order is operative in the situation, approval of changes shall be obtained from the customer. In the case of transport of potentially hazardous items over the nation's roads, it is usually necessary to obtain the approval of packing and transport conditions from jurisdictional authorities. It shall be the responsibility of the company dispatch supervisor or manager to identify needs in respect to changes in packing and delivery and to ensure that each of the identified needs is satisfied. It shall be the responsibility of the quality manager to identify deficiencies in marking and to have them corrected.

7.8.2.   All marking, packing, and delivery changes shall be documented. When there exist documents specifying the methods and materials to be used for marking, packing, and delivery and the methods of use of the documents in protecting and preserving the product quality characteristics, the documents shall be altered by the use of the company document change methods of this procedure. All necessary approvals and authorizations shall be obtained prior to implementing any changed marking, packing, or delivery methods or materials.

8   Audit and Surveillance of Change

8.1   Audit of change.   The quality manager shall establish a frequent but random quality audit of the processes of change as required in this procedure. During the course of a contract which runs for less than a year, or for 1 year when the longer time is appropriate, a total audit of each area of control of this procedure's requirements shall be made. When auditing is in respect to a contract that runs for less than 1 year, all change conditions used to update activities and relevant documentation in respect to the contractual obligations of the company shall be made. This shall be a separate audit from the ongoing and continuing audit of the areas of change for the total activities of the production system.

8.2.   It shall be a responsibility of all managers, supervisors, and quality assurance staff to maintain ongoing surveillance of the processes of change taking place in the company and to ensure that they take place in accordance with the orderly manner set forth in this procedure. The surveillance activity shall be one of awareness and inquisitive data collection which is ongoing in parallel with the other duties of the management and quality staff concerned. All deviations from the requirements for orderly change control in accordance with this procedure shall be recorded and reported to the quality manager with a view to improving the learning and performance of the manufacturing activity as a whole.

Chapter

9

Calibration Control System

PART A. REVIEW AND GUIDANCE

1 Review

All human knowledge is relative. We are immersed in the environment of things we measure, and hence all our measurements are relative. We begin by defining certain things to be our basic standards and by deriving other things from them to become what we call derived standards. All our measurements are then made in terms of the basic and derived standards by referring unknown dimensions to our known dimensions of the standards.

Basic and derived standards begin in each modern nation at the national level, where a standards body is set up as the national source for measurement. All other measurements in the nation are then referred back to the most fundamental standards maintained by the national standards body. This leads to what we call traceability in calibration standards.

The value of a highly stable standard of good precision and bias is first determined by referring it to the national standard (the primary standard) of that type. This precise, or secondary, standard of known bias then becomes the single most accurate standard of the institution or company, where it is placed in a calibration laboratory. Other measuring instruments that determine the same quantity are then calibrated against the secondary standard. (The national standard is always the primary standard.) Other measuring instruments are calibrated by comparing them with the secondary standards and then become the university, institution, or company working standards or instruments and gauges.

The accuracy of measuring instruments comprises two principal components of uncertainty: bias and precision. If we put a measuring instrument in a stable environment and with it measure the same characteristic of a fixed item 1000 times, the mean of those measurements will lie at a point distant from the true value. It is this distance we call the bias. The bias may have the value zero or any positive or negative value about zero. The scatter of the individual measurements which yielded the 1000 values will, if plotted on xy coordinates, give a distribution—the precision—having a variance about the mean value. The tail of this distribution that lies farthest from the true value of the measured characteristic determines the actual accuracy of the measurement. The actual accuracy is equal to the absolute value of the bias plus the magnitude of the variance that extends farthest from the true value as determined by the secondary or primary standard.

Experience has shown that, when measuring instruments are used over time, their bias and precision change. The bias tends to become greater, i.e., shift farther from the true value, and the variance as measured in a characteristic tends to become worse, i.e., reduce the precision. Industry has found it necessary to establish two programs to counter the tendency of bias to increase and precision to become worse. Bias is ascertained by periodically calibrating the measuring instrument against a known standard; precision is maintained by implementing a program of preventive and repair maintenance. Both programs are necessary if a company is to have a continuing quality control program.

2 Guidance

This procedure is one of the essential documents in all quality control programs. It is equally necessary for the control of quality in the manufacturing of products, the providing of services, or the construction of projects. The procedure set forth here will work satisfactorily for each of the three industry categories. All the control elements are necessary.

The major variation found necessary in the three industry categories when applying this procedure arises when the magnitude of effort is assessed. The number of staff, amount and cost of equipment and standards, and overall operational cost of the calibration program are generally greatest in the manufacturing sector. There are major exceptions, however, such as when large construction projects that last a number of years are undertaken and dozens of subcontractors as well as numerous suppliers contribute to the outcome.

The application of the control in respect to calibration requirements is most difficult in the project industry. Here the diverse measuring instruments, their different ownerships, and the many sites and company plants where they are found and must be used makes it difficult to enforce the requirements clauses of this procedure. The need is nonetheless important and essential, if there is to be a high-quality outcome of the total work program.

PART B.   PROCEDURE

Calibration Control System

1   Scope

This procedure defines the requirements of the company for calibration systems. It defines the requirements for a system to be established and used in ensuring that measuring equipment, standards, and certified reference materials (CRMs) are properly calibrated or certified and that the company's measuring equipment and CRMs are satisfactory for use in verifying the conformance to contract of material designed, developed, produced, or repaired and services offered.

2 Application

The requirements of this procedure shall apply to:

1. Suppliers supplying materials or services to the company when the contract, purchase order, or associated documents make reference to this procedure or to the need for calibration when no other standard on calibration is specified
2. The company for all measuring equipment used by it in any of its work

3 Definitions

For the purposes of this procedure the definitions that shall apply are those contained in "Glossary of Terms Used in Quality and Reliability," in Sec. VII, Chap. 1 of *Quality Control Systems.**
    The requirements of this procedure shall take precedence over the calibration requirements of other standards or documents relevant to work done under contract for the company and to work done for, in, or by the company, unless specifically stipulated otherwise.

4 Calibration System Requirements

4.1 Supplier's responsibility for calibration

4.1.1. The company shall asume the responsibility for ensuring that all measuring equipment used by the producer of materials and services in support of contracts with the company has a known accuracy of measurement and that the accuracy used is satisfactory to ensure and control the quality of the supplies delivered. To this end the company shall establish, document, and maintain a system for the effective control and calibration of all measuring equipment and physical standards used in the fulfillment of the contractual requirements.

4.1.2. The measuring system shall contain detection methods and timely corrective measures which are designed to prevent inaccura-

---

*James R. Taylor, *Quality Control Systems: Procedures for Planning Quality Programs,* McGraw-Hill, New York, 1989.

cies occurring rather than correct inaccuracies found through material nonconformance.

4.1.3. The calibration and measuring equipment control system shall ensure that calibrations are performed by a staff that has the necessary knowledge and skills.

4.1.4. Objective evidence that the calibration system is effective shall show that calibrations are performed by staff that has the necessary knowledge and skills.

4.1.5. A calibration service may be purchased by the company's suppliers to support relevant contractual activities provided the service meets the requirements of this procedure and prior permission in writing is obtained from the company.

4.2 Planning

4.2.1. The company shall conduct, during the earliest phase of contract or purchase order performance, an extensive review of the technical requirements of the contract or order to ensure that measuring equipment and standards necessary for the successful discharge of the work are available and are of the required accuracy, stability, and range for their intended applications.

4.2.2. The supplier shall identify and report to the quality assurance representative of the customer as early as possible any measurement requirements which may prevent or unduly delay the satisfactory discharge of the contractual obligations on the supplier.

4.3 Calibration procedures. Documented procedures shall be provided and used for the calibration of all measuring equipment and standards which are used in the performance of work on any contract or purchase order. Calibration procedures shall include such documents as manufacturers' manuals, published standard practices, and any necessary written instructions of the company or the producer of the measuring instruments, including step-by-step calibration sequences documented for use by calibration personnel.

4.4 Calibration records. The company shall develop and maintain a comprehensive and complete set of records which document the accuracy, calibration methods, and history of all measuring equipment, standards and CRMs. The records shall cover maintenance, storage conditions, calibration, certification and use, and they shall be made available for review by the customer upon request.

4.5 Standards used for calibration

4.5.1. The company shall ensure that physical standards needed to transfer accuracy to measuring devices used in production are available for use in calibrating working instruments or gauges for each measurement to be performed to determine the conformance of product characteristics to contract or purchase order requirements.

The company shall, when using materials which can be calibrated only by reference to other materials or to some known physical process, ensure that such materials and processes conform to accepted processes traceable to a national authority on that area of measurement and that conformance is determined by comparison with known CRMs traceable to the national measurement authority.

4.5.2. Vendors and subcontractors, when purchasing a calibration service, may use the calibrating organization's standards and CRMs provided the standards, materials, and services used meet the requirements of this procedure and prior approval is obtained from the company.

4.5.3. Standards used to transfer accuracy to measuring instruments or gauges shall have their accuracy traceable in accordance with the requirements of this procedure.

4.6 Calibration traceability

4.6.1. All standards used to calibrate measuring equipment for acceptance measurements shall have their accuracies traceable along a documented path of currently calibrated standards to the national standards of the country in which the measurements are made or to international standards as approved by the company.

4.6.2. Accepted physical values of natural physical constants (e.g., the ice point and the wavelength of the red cadmium line) and calibrations derived by the ratio method of self-calibration techniques need not have traceability, but their use shall be subject to the approval of the company.

4.6.3. All CRMs used to determine values for materials used in products and to determine processes that control product characteristics shall have their sources in or be traceable to the national standards laboratory or other organization responsible for providing such materials in the nation.

4.6.4. All standards used to calibrate measuring equipment shall be known with sufficient accuracy to convey to the measuring equipment adequate capability to determine that contractual limits of products supplied are met (see Art. 4.7).

4.6.5. All standards used and calibrations performed in support of a contract or purchase order shall be supported by documentation showing dates, accuracies, and any special conditions prevailing at the time of their determination.

4.6.6. When a high degree of precision in the measurement of a characteristic of a product item that is produced by two or more source organizations is required, a program of comparison measurements using a single item of reference material of high stability shall be established.

4.7 Accuracy and cumulative errors. The cumulative contribution of inaccuracy components in a chain or sequence of calibrations shall be known and taken into account when the acceptability of materials or equipment supplied under a contract or purchase order is determined. The calculations of cumulative errors shall follow accepted methods which shall be subject to approval by the customer.

4.8 Environment control

4.8.1. The environments in which measuring equipment, standards, and CRMs are stored and used shall be compatible with the stated or intended accuracies for these devices and materials. When measuring equipment is transferred from one place to another, due consideration shall be given to any changes in temperature, humidity, cleanliness, or other environmental factors that may contribute to a change in the accuracy obtainable from the measuring equipment.

4.8.2. When measuring equipment is used, due attention shall be given to the effects of temperature, temperature changes, humidity, vibration, lighting, contamination and other environmental factors which can contribute to the accuracy of the measurements. Compensating corrections shall be made when they are applicable.

4.8.3. When corrections of the results of measurements are made, records of such corrections shall be kept, and they shall show the nature and extent to which they affect the conformance of products or services supplied.

4.9   Storage, handling, and transport

4.9.1. The company's documented program covering measuring equipment, standards, and CRMs shall give due attention to providing guidance for the storage, handling, and transport from place to place of the equipment so that equipment conditions and accuracies will be preserved.

4.9.2. Secondary and transfer physical standards that have major importance in the satisfactory discharge of contracts, and that may be damaged in transport, shall not be subject to the normal conditions of transport, but shall be carried by hand or have special transportation planned and used when they must be moved from one location to another.

4.9.3. When large computer-controlled measuring equipment is moved from one plant site to another, it shall be transported in padded vans or trucks or in other vehicles equipped with facilities or capability to prevent shock or damage. Reference standards and sources in such equipment shall be regularly subjected to determination of their values by use of this procedure.

4.10   Calibration intervals

4.10.1. The intervals between calibration of measuring equipment shall be determined by the tendency of the bias, precision, or both of the particular piece of measuring equipment (or measuring system) to become unacceptable for the measurement accuracy required. With time and use both the displacement of the mean of measurements (bias) and the spread of the individual measurements (precision) will change and thereby cause loss of accuracy in almost all cases. To control this, the company shall provide for periodic recalibration of all measuring equipment at prescribed intervals during its use, as well as the carrying out of preventive maintenance as required to contain the precision within acceptable limits.

4.10.2. Many CRMs used to determine the characteristics of product materials and processes have the tendency to decay in respect to their own characteristics. The supplier shall know what such decay rates are and shall allow for them in the use and storage of such CRMs.

4.10.3. New measuring equipment shall be introduced for use with increased frequency of recalibration until the accuracy stability has been determined. No measuring equipment shall be used until it has first had its accuracy determined. Guidance on recalibration intervals for new measuring instruments shall be obtained from the instrument supplier or manufacturer or from the national standards authority when it is appropriate. In all situations, the accuracy of measuring equipment shall be known before the equipment is used on production materials.

4.10.4. The documented calibration system shall provide for taking out of service immediately any piece of measuring equipment with an accuracy known or suspected to be unsuitable for its intended use or with an accuracy that is unknown and hence not documented. This may be done by using a conspicuous label when the equipment or instrument is to be left in position or by removing the equipment or instrument to a place where it will not be used.

4.10.5. All repaired measuring equipment shall be subject to recalibration before use after repair, after being in storage, or after being in a state of nonuse for a time comparable to the recalibration interval. Increased frequency of calibration shall be instituted immediately when any measuring equipment is found to be out of calibration on a recalibration date, and accuracy stability shall be reestablished and an appropriate new recalibration interval for that equipment shall be set. All measuring equipment shall be recalibrated following any repair or maintenance activity that can affect its accuracy.

4.11 Calibration labeling and sealing

4.11.1. All measuring instruments shall be clearly marked or labeled so that they can be identified with calibration records and their intended uses.

4.11.2. An authenticated label showing the date when the next calibration is due shall be attached to each piece of measuring equipment which can be independently calibrated and to combinations of measuring equipment which require joint calibration. When such device or CRM cannot be suitably tagged, the container of the device or CRM shall be so labeled.

4.11.3.   Calibration records showing the date of last calibration, by whom calibrated, and the date when next calibration is due shall be maintained and be readily available to the company's quality assurance representative.

4.11.4.   The company's calibration system shall ensure that measuring equipment or standards are not used after their calibration has lapsed and before recalibration has been done.

4.11.5.   When necessary to preserve the calibration of standards and measuring equipment, the relative movements of parts and accesses to adjustments shall be sealed against unauthorized alteration of the calibration settings.

4.12   Measuring equipment recall system.   The company shall establish and maintain a positive documented system which will ensure that all measuring equipment is calibrated. This system may be stored in the memory of a computer for maximum ease and efficiency of operation. All measuring equipment shall be recalled for calibration:

1. Before its current calibration expires
2. Before its use when new, just repaired, or just placed back in service
3. Before use when it has not been used for a period of time longer than the established calibration interval
4. When it is to be applied to a new measurement for which its accuracy is in doubt
5. When there is any reason to question the accuracy or correctness of measurements by the equipment

4.13   Calibration of subcontractor's measuring equipment.   All work subcontracted to another organization not under the quality control system of this procedure shall be measured on equipment which is calibrated in accordance with the requirements of this procedure.

4.14   Calibration of measuring equipment used in design and development.   When design or development work is to be done in support of a contract, including that in support of manufacturing changes, the company shall ensure that all measurements which determine specified characteristics are performed on measuring equipment calibrated in accordance with this procedure.

5 Quality Assurance Provisions

5.1 Audit of the calibration system. The company shall conduct a periodic audit of the calibration system to ensure that the calibration program is effectively implemented and in operation for all measuring equipment and is operating in accordance with the calibration plan.

5.2 Records of calibration audit. The company shall record the findings of the calibration audit, and such records shall show the frequency of the audit, the findings of the audit, and any corrective action taken as a result of such an audit. The records shall be made available to the customer upon request.

6 Accommodation and Assistance

6.1 Accommodation. The company shall provide the quality assurance representative of the customer with accommodation as necessary to permit the effective review and assessment of the calibration program.

6.2 Assistance. The company shall provide the quality assurance representative of the customer with assistance as necessary to carry out an independent audit of the calibration program upon request.

Chapter 10

Quality Audit Systems

PART A. REVIEW AND GUIDANCE

1 Review

An audit is a verification activity aimed at evaluating the degree of conformance to a standard, specification, or procedure of the design, product, service, process, or system. Quality audits have two parts, one of which is the examination of the system within which the items of product or service are brought into being and the other is an examination of the items themselves. The first is called the quality system audit, and the second is the product or service quality audit.

The quality system audit evaluates management systems, methods, equipment, facilities, and manufacturing processes as compared to product or service audits, which examine physical products and service attributes and their measurement. A product-manufacturing activity, a service-providing activity, or indeed a bringing into being of a project will be satisfactorily audited only when *both* the quality system and the item(s) being brought into existence by the system are evaluated and assessed.

The quality system will usually be defined in *two* documents. These are the quality manual, prepared by the company supplying the product, service, or project, on the one hand, and the quality system standard specified by the customer as a requirement for the company on the other. The quality manual will contain, in addition to a quality policy and organization chart, a broad range of general quality procedures such as are found in *Quality Control Systems.** Since the quality

---

*James R. Taylor, *Quality Control Systems: Procedures for Planning Quality Programs,* McGraw-Hill, New York, 1989.

manual must often embrace all the requirements of more than one customer-required standard, it will be considerably more comprehensive than any individual standard. The work of a nation is greatly alleviated if the number of quality standards for a given category of industry can be reduced to one. It is further alleviated by general procedures such as those in the book cited above.

Audits can be satisfactorily carried out only by independent persons who are not themselves directly responsible for the outcome of the work being audited. For that reason the task of auditing for quality is normally assigned to the quality organization of the company or by a customer to the customer's quality organization. It is the responsibility of each organization to draw upon such additional areas of knowledge, skills, and experience as may be necessary to carry out the audit correctly and make its results acceptable to the managements concerned. For example, the design staff may take part in audits of design and development activities.

The work of bringing into being the product, service, or project is normally performed in accordance with both general procedures and detailed procedures which are themselves derived from the various standards with which the work must comply. A compilation of the general procedures covering all activities usually comprises the quality manual, but the detailed procedures relating to the specific products, services, or project may constitute the quality manual so long as they derive from documented general procedures (which are policy-type documents).

Since human effort involved in following some given set of procedures will invariably deviate at times, and since the procedures themselves are evolving documents, it is desirable that a person, or persons, knowledgeable in the type of quality systems concerned carry out an audit of the work to detect and have corrected any deviations. Alternatively, the audits may be carried out by representatives of the customer. Usually both parties are involved. It has been found to be desirable for the quality manager of a company to have a continuing quality audit of the company's operations carried out against agreed standards and procedures. The customer will often carry out an audit just before placing an order or entering into a contract and thereafter at periodic intervals if the contract is a continuing thing or there are to be following contracts.

2   Guidance

The conduct of a quality audit will vary slightly, depending on whether it is an internal audit or is conducted on behalf of the customer. Though both parties are searching for precisely the same thing, namely, conformance to standards, procedures, and specifications, there are certain formalities which must be gone through by the customer's representatives that are not necessary when employees of the company being audited do the work. These differences fall primarily in the area of introductory formalities allowing outside person(s) to get acquainted with the company and its operations. In this latter case, it is normal for the company to provide assistance to the outside auditors. Those assisting perform a variety of tasks ranging from making appointments with various company managers for the outside auditors to guiding them through both the quality manual and the premises of the company.

The conduct of the quality audit is carried out by examining the people, tools, premises, surroundings, and manufacturing or providing processes which collectively comprise the quality system. The examination is carried out against specific standards and procedures which should always be nominated prior to the start of an audit. Standards and procedures will contain both mandatory (i.e., requirements) clauses and advisory clauses which would serve in some cases to improve the activity. In addition, they will, from time to time, contain informative or instructive clauses that do not constitute part of the requirements of the documents.

Prior to carrying out an audit, it is desirable for the auditor(s) to have thoroughly examined the standard and/or procedure that will apply and to have turned the mandatory clauses into questions about the matters concerned. This is done by turning the structure of the "statement" sentence into a "question" sentence. Hence, the auditor will be seeking answers to the complete set of questions which will tell whether the quality system is in place and is operating satisfactorily.

The kinds of data needed, and the statistical processes that must be performed on the data, often dictate the adequacy of data and how the data are collected. It is a principal task of the audit team to examine available data obtained by independent audits (e.g., by auditors from other customers of the company). It may be found to be satisfactory to use the entire audit results of a respected auditor, under which condition the total amount of auditing needed, and also the cost, is reduced. The U.S. aerospace companies were among the first in the world to combine their efforts and establish lists of approved auditors so that duplication of effort at vendors' plants could be minimized.

Planning a product or service audit involves the use of sampling tables, the specifications against which the items were made or performed, and a knowledge of the measurement system from which data are collected. The system may be, and usually is, a subject of the audit. In addition to the foregoing, planning an audit requires setting times and obtaining agreement with suppliers (or, in the case of in-house auditors, with the area managers concerned). Audit work can be considerably facilitated by approaching the task in a professional manner.

It is essential to plan audits in detail before undertaking the work. This will incur the preparation of checklists setting out the matters and areas of work to be audited, as well as the sequence in which the audit work can most satisfactorily be carried out. The audit should take two quite general, but essential, lines of investigation. These consist, on the one hand, of questioning the managers, supervisors, and workers as necessary to elicit answers to the questions referred to above.

The questions asked of a particular person should relate to the work that he or she either manages or does, i.e., to his or her work area. This will yield a series of answers to questions that can then be used to move to phase two of the audit. In this second line of investigation, it is necessary to verify that the answers given are correct. This is done by going to the workplace and examining the work underway on the production floor, in the service-providing establishment, or at the project construction site.

It is necessary to carry out *both* phases of the investigation, since only then is it possible to assess the knowledge of the managers and supervisors, as well as the skills and abilities of the workers about what they say they are doing. Each manager or supervisor should have detailed knowledge about each of the surrounding work areas with which he or she must interact in getting the job done, in addition to a more detailed knowledge of the individual's work areas.

When entering a manager's or supervisor's area of control, it is necessary to get the permission of that person, and often necessary for him or her, or a representative, to accompany the auditor. These arrangements should be made by the outside auditor working through the quality representative assigned by the company. This requirement is less stringent when the audit is being carried out by an internal auditor who is an employee of the company. At no time, however, should an auditor enter an area without making the person supervising that area aware of his or her presence and purpose.

Quality audit work is usually done to:

1. Qualify a company prior to awarding a contract.
2. Gain or maintain confidence in a company's work.
3. Ascertain that changes have not adversely affected product configuration or performance.
4. Assess existing and prospective vendors for approval listing.

When the audit is being carried out by a team of auditors from outside the company, it is necessary that it begin with a meeting between the audit team and representatives of the company management and that the audit be terminated by a similar meeting at which the auditor(s) brief the company management on their findings. This meeting will be followed by a formal report from the audit team.

At no time should an audit be terminated prior to its completion without mutual agreement between the audit team and the management of the company being audited. It is usually best for the audit to be carried through, with detailed deviations from conformance with standards and procedures being presented to the company management regardless of the state of the quality system or its output. Only in that way can the company concerned objectively work to correct the deviations to the satisfaction of the customer. Though the audit may not result in the company getting the contract the first time, it can serve to give both the company and the customer a better quality system in the future.

PART B.   PROCEDURE

Quality Audit Systems

1   Scope

This procedure defines the requirements of the company in respect to audits of quality control systems, products, and services.

2   Application

This procedure shall apply in all business sites and activities of the company, including both in-house activities, as well as through contracts with suppliers from whom products and services are purchased. The accompanying standard and/or general procedure against which audits shall be conducted, as specified in internal documentation or as called up in contracts and purchase orders, shall be considered part of these application requirements.

There shall be conducted a continuing quality audit of the company's quality systems. This audit shall be carried out in accordance with this procedure and shall be the responsibility of the quality department of the company. When it is required by customers, assistance shall be given to customer representatives in carrying out quality audits.

3   Definitions

For definitions of terms used in this procedure, see "Glossary of Terms Used in Quality and Reliability," Sec. VII, Chap. 1 of *Quality Control Systems.**

4   The Quality System Quality Audit

4.1   **Introduction.**   The quality system audit will begin in one of two ways, depending on whether it is an internal audit or an audit conducted by the customer's quality assurance representative (QAR). The

---

*James R. Taylor, *Quality Control Systems: Procedures for Planning Quality Programs*, McGraw-Hill, New York, 1989.

internal audit, carried out by personnel from the quality department of the company will normally be a continuing thing, with the activities and documentation of the company being assessed against requirements throughout the year.

The quality system audit conducted by the QAR will normally begin with a phone call, or other communication, seeking a suitable date on which to visit the premises and begin the audit. The QAR's audit of the quality system can take from about 2 days minimum to several weeks embodied in one or more visits to the company's premises. The time taken will depend on the complexity and size of the system to be audited, the geographical location of activities, and the comprehensiveness of the audit. It will be in the best interests of the company to ensure that an adequate examination of the system is made to bring out the facts needed to engender confidence on the part of the customer, on the one hand, and in senior management of the company, on the other. To this extent, the company shall provide all assistance and guidance seen to be needed.

Unless otherwise instructed, the QAR shall work through the quality department of the company in all matters associated with the conduct of quality system audits.

4.2 Planning the quality system audit. There are seven major steps to be taken in respect to carrying out a quality system audit prior to beginning the audit:

1. Study and thoroughly understand the quality system standard that applies.

2. Examine the quality manual in detail and ensure that it is current and contains all necessary procedures and other information pertinent to the system and audit.

3. Prepare a list of the questions to be answered during the audit by examining the quality system standard and ensuring that all mandatory requirements are examined and met during the audit.

4. Prepare a checklist of all the things to do during the audit, including the principal areas to audit and the sequence in which they will be examined.

5. Prepare a schedule of the audit activities, including communications with the company or supplier, needed to conduct the audit.

6. Assemble the audit team and brief the members on the duties of each during the audit. Provide each member with the paperwork he or she will use in carrying out the audit, so he or she can make detailed prior study of the information.

7. Estimate the time required, arrange a suitable time with the

managers of the quality system to be audited, and make any necessary hotel or motel reservations, travel arrangements, etc.

When the planning, examination of the documentation, or some other matter to be used in the audit is unsatisfactory, it is usually desirable to have it corrected prior to beginning the audit, or at least to reach agreement with the other party on steps to be taken in that respect. The plans for the audit shall cover each of the above seven steps, as well as rectification of initial deficiencies.

4.3   Audit timing and management contact

4.3.1   Audit timing.   It will be necessary to time the audit of the quality system in relation to other matters. Such an audit may be conducted to determine if a particular potential supplier shall be given a contract to provide supplies or services. When that is the case, the audit shall be carried out before the contract is awarded.

When the audit is being conducted as a result of deficient products being delivered or in respect to known delivery problems, it shall be conducted at the appropriate time to resolve the difficulty most effectively. An audit carried out in one of these matters may involve considerably less than the entire quality system. When that is the case, only areas affecting the problem shall be audited.

When the quality system audit is being conducted as a routine confidence update concerning the ongoing activities of a supplier or other operator of a quality system, the full audit shall be conducted and the entire system shall be evaluated. An audit of this type can be made less frequently by using the ongoing audit results of the company's in-house quality system audits.

When a particular supplier has been evaluated and the quality system has initially been found to be satisfactory, ongoing confidence in that system can be largely derived from objective reports of in-house quality system audits conducted by members of the supplier's quality staff. By wording these reports appropriately and giving each control area of the system a rating of 1 to 10 for adequacy of control, accompanied by statements of nonconformances found and corrective action taken, considerable confidence in the ongoing control capability of the supplier's quality control system can be enjoyed by the customer without additional cost. This principle shall be used by the company to the maximum appropriate extent. When such a method of gaining confidence is used, it should be the subject of clauses in contracts and purchase orders.

4.3.2   Management contact.   At no time shall quality system audits be conducted without full knowledge of and concurrence by the management of the company being audited. In this respect, both audits to be carried out by QARs from customer organizations on the company and those carried out on suppliers by the company's quality staff shall begin after communication with the company or agency concerned has taken place and concurrence has been received.

The initial contact with a company shall be made with the nominated quality manager unless communications to the contrary have been received from the company to be audited. It is then the responsibility of the company's quality manager to see that other company personnel are informed of the impending assessment.

4.4 The quality standard and the quality manual

4.4.1 The quality standard. The quality system standard will be the principal requirement setting the levels and degrees of control throughout the activity concerned with producing a product, providing a service, or constructing a project. It is usually in the form of either a national standard published by the country's national standards body or a standard compiled and published by a professional quality organization or the customer. In the United States, a typical quality standard used is MIL-Q-9858, published by the Department of Defense. In Australia an example would be Australian Standard AS-1821; in Canada it might be CSA Z299.2. A civilian quality standard issued in the United States and frequently called up in contracts is ANSI/ASQC Z1.15-1979. The quality system to be audited must meet the requirements of the quality system standard called for in the contract or purchase order.

When there is conflict between the quality system standard specified by a customer and the company's quality manual, the quality system standard shall prevail.

All the controls called for in the quality standard required in a contract or company document shall be included in the design and implementation of the quality manual. When the quality system to be evaluated and audited is that of a supplier or other company, this requirement for compatibility of the quality standard and quality manual also shall apply.

4.4.2 The quality manual. Quality manuals compiled by companies and presented to QARs for audit take many forms. Some contain compilations of the actual operating procedures used throughout the manufacturing plant concerned. Others contain the flow tags and labels, procedure sheets and forms, procedure documents and software, and other operating documents used in the actual carrying out of the work. A third form taken by some quality manuals is that of a compilation of the policy documents of the company on quality and related work. The latter, taken alone, are not satisfactory as a quality manual. It is essential that policy-type quality manuals are supported in the production area by all the general procedures and detailed procedures and forms which implement the policies in the workplace.

Unless specifically stated otherwise, each quality manual (i.e., that, for each plant site) of a company shall be composed of the information from operating procedures setting forth the work done to control quality. All procedures used in the quality manual shall draw their authority from the respective policy documents of the company or those of the company to which the quality manual applies.

Sufficient copies of the quality manual shall be prepared to support the business activities of the company, and copies of this manual shall be made available to QARs on written request and to others as is appropriate.

4.5 The general procedures of quality control. General quality procedures, like general procedures of other areas of company activity, shall be documents that stipulate what is to be done without being product- or service-related in a specific way. The procedures tend to be useful for long periods of time without change. The details of how to produce some product or provide some service appear in a company's detailed quality procedures, which normally are included in the quality manual. The general procedures found to be useful in a company are set forth in *Quality Control Systems*.

4.6 The quality system audit divisions

4.6.1 Vendor audits. The audit of vendor quality assurance shall examine all aspects from the placing of a purchase order through the quality control called for and used at the vendor's premises, the delivery, handling, and temporary storage, incoming inspection and test, and the main stocks until issued for use. All procedures applying to these activities shall be examined for adequacy and the degree of control established.

The combined control of quality reflected and confirmed in the vendor quality control activities plus the incoming inspection and test shall be assessed for total adequacy of confidence transfer. This assessment shall be carried out in the audit, without regard to whether the company division being audited sells principally in the products market or the services market. Both types of suppliers require the quality control of products used, and it shall be a principal aspect of the quality audit to ascertain that adequate control exists throughout this area of activities.

When considered necessary, the quality audit shall be extended to a vendor's premises to examine evidence of quality control necessary to establish adequacy. When the audit is being performed by a QAR of a customer of the prime contractor, the agreement of both the quality manager and the purchasing manager of the company shall be obtained before visiting the vendor's plant. It shall be the responsibility of the quality assurance employee representing the company to get this agreement and make all necessary arrangements for such visit when vendors must be examined.

The audit shall examine the control trail all the way from what went into the wording of the procurement contract or purchase order specifying levels of control of the quality characteristics of supplies, as well as the limits of those characteristics, through production, testing, handling, packing, delivery, unpacking, labeling, storing, sampling, inspection and testing, disposition procedures for material found to be faulty, procedures for passing satisfactory material and delivering it to stock and then to point of use, and the preservation of quality characteristics during such activities. The trail of control shall be continuous throughout the above entire sequence of activities. Any points of weakness in the controls or of loss of continuity of control shall be examined in detail with a view to recommending corrective action.

4.6.2   Quality audit of production or providing

4.6.2.1   Subcontracted work.   When it is necessary to subcontract work in a production or providing activity, the subcontracted work shall be examined in detail to assure the existence and continuity of control throughout the entire sequence of subcontracting activities. Clear and complete specifications of what work is to be done shall be communicated to the subcontracting authority; the level of quality that is to be achieved shall be stated; and methods and means for proving the levels of quality in work done shall be covered in the audit.

It shall be the responsibility of the company, i.e., of the prime contractor (when a supplier to the prime contractor is the subject of the audit) to ensure that the work performed and supplies provided by subcontractors are of satisfactory quality. To that end, the contract with subcontractors shall include ways and means for packing and preservation during delivery of quality characteristics generated in the subcontracted work.

4.6.2.2   Control during production of products.   Two principal activities are underway simultaneously within a production facility: (1) the processing activities, which change existing characteristics in the production materials or generate new characteristics and (2) the measurement activities, which ascertain the degree or value of characteristics after processing. Both activities shall be audited throughout the entire production operation.

Particular care shall be taken in auditing manufacturing processes that are being operated under a system of statistical control. Both the system of control and the degree to which the control maintains the variability within limits shall be audited. Special attention shall be given to balance between productivity and quality being maintained.

The manner of auditing shall constitute examination of the processing and measurement (appraisal or inspection and test) activities against the requirements of the general and detailed procedures which apply. In the absence of a general procedure within the company being audited, the applicable general procedure from *Quality Control Systems* shall be used. The applicable procedure will be the one most suitable for the kind of work underway. Hence, procedures from the above book would be:

- For products, "Quality Control System for Products," Sec. III, Chap. 2.
- For services, "Quality Control System for Services," Sec. III, Chap. 3.
- For projects, "Quality Control System for Projects," Sec. III, Chap. 4.

The audit of the providing of services will entail many different methods and approaches from the audit of the manufacture of products. Similarly, the auditing of projects will entail many approaches that are different from the more practiced auditing of a product-manufacturing industry. We shall next examine some of the differences that shall be used when these other two categories of industry are audited.

4.6.2.3 Control during providing of services.

In general, the providing of services will result in either the transfer of ownership of a product-type commodity to the customer or the use of the product in carrying out the service. In either case it is necessary to carry out a thorough audit of the quality assurance system as it covers the production and delivery of products used in providing the services. This is covered in 4.6.1 above, and is equally applicable to the services industry. A comprehensive audit of the quality assurance system of the service company's vendors shall be carried out.

Auditing of the actual performance of the service sold as the primary commodity of exchange or of the service provided in support of the manufacture and delivery of some product category shall constitute examination of the performance of the service in a randomly sampled and statistically valid number of instances. The examination shall compare the performance of the service against the procedure specifying how the service is to be performed. Conformance or nonconformance shall be determined by the degree of agreement between the way the service is performed and the requirements in the operable detailed procedure.

Further, when the transfer of some product as a part of providing the service is involved, the quality of the product transferred shall be examined against individual specifications. Conformance or nonconformance shall be determined by the degree of agreement between the characteristics of the product delivered and the characteristics required in their individual specifications.

4.6.2.4 Control during construction of a project. The construction of a project will usually include the acquisition of both products and services from vendors under normal contractual processes. The major difference in project work from that in mass production activities lies in the great variety of small-quantity individual item purchases and the one-time very high total cost of the project. The risk of project-type work, depending as it does on the interdependence of many hundreds of individual items, many of which are supplied only as single items for that project, is very high, and great care shall be exercised in the audit to ascertain that the methods used to specify and obtain the required quality in each of these necessary items are adequate. Here, the entire "Quality Assurance of Supplies Audit," Art. 4.6.1, shall apply.

Similar to the many and diverse products used in the construction of major projects, many individual services of different types require the application of highly developed skills on the part of workmen to assemble and join the products together to make the project a success. These services are to be examined in the manner set forth in Art. 4.6.2.3.

Auditing of both the products delivered for use on a project and the services performed in assembling and building the project shall be randomly sampled, and with adequate severity, to obtain positive evidence of the effectiveness of the quality system being used. When necessary, the audit shall make use of both observation of the performance of services and the measurement of the quality characteristics of products delivered.

4.6.2.5 Audit skills and knowledge. Great care shall be used to ensure that the persons who audit quality systems are themselves experienced and knowledgeable in the type of production work, provision of services, or measurements made. Since observation and interpretation constitute an essential though subjective part of the work of auditing quality systems, it is essential that auditors be chosen from among the most highly qualified individuals available. The acceptance of the audit team by the organization being audited and the credibility of the team's reports will rest largely on the confidence which can be placed in the individuals carrying out the audit.

When the members of an audit team are employees of the company applying this procedure and they are shown not to possess some necessary type or range of skills or knowledge, such skills or knowledge shall be sought in persons from outside the company and those persons shall be recruited to carry out the audits. There is no requirement that auditors of quality systems consist only of staff from a quality organization, although the leader of an audit team shall come from the quality organization of the company.

4.6.3 Delivery and installation quality audit

4.6.3.1 Delivery. Auditing of delivery work, when items of product are transferred from one geographic location to another or when items of product are simply moved within a single plant or group of plants, consists of auditing services work. As such, the audits shall be conducted in accordance with the requirements of Art. 4.6.2.3.

Much delivery work is also subcontract work, and when that is true, the requirements of Arts. 4.6.2.1 and 4.6.2.3 shall be combined and complied with in carrying out the audit. When necessary, the audit shall also evaluate the quality characteristics of the products after their delivery, as well as the service-type activities performed in effecting the delivery.

4.6.3.2 Installation of products and systems of products. This work is similar to that done in erecting a project such as a power station, large building, or airfield. Installation work requires that the workers have skills and knowledge that are often unique to the particular items being installed. Both the services-type installation work and the products used in carrying out the installation work shall be audited for their quality.

The final test for success and quality of installation work consists of evaluating how well the installed products perform their intended functions and determining how long those functions are likely to continue being performed. Assessment of performance shall consist of operation or observation of the item in its intended use and observation and measurement of the degree of conformance of such operation to the specified requirements. Assessment of the reliability shall be of a predictive kind, and it shall, when possible, be required of the company supplying the installation service being audited.

4.6.3.3 Installation involving commissioning.

When the installation of some commodity includes the requirement that the item, such as a turnkey installation, be in an operational state when turned over to the customer, that aspect of the installation shall also constitute an essential part of the quality audit. When the commissioning of some complex commodity such as an electric power station, telephone exchange, ship, or dock loading facility is audited, the quality audit shall, for cost reasons, be carried out in conjunction with the commissioning tests conducted by the installation contractor.

During commissioning tests, the types of quality problems, their degrees of seriousness, the number of occurrences, and the recording, methods of correcting, and updating of documentation following corrections of faults shall be items which are audited.

4.6.4 Audit of quality costing.

The control of quality costs in industry, although capable of being extended to both service and project industries, will be found principally within the mass production industry. It shall be a requirement of the audit of any product, service, or project company's quality system that the control of quality costs is investigated. When the company being audited is engaged in the production of a product, it shall be expected that the use of quality cost control principles are being used.

The audit of quality cost control activities of the company and of any supplier to the company shall consist of examining the cost control methods used against either the in-house quality cost control procedure adopted or, in the absence of such a procedure, against the "Manufacturing Quality Cost System," Sec. VI, Chap. 2 of *Quality Control Systems.*

The actual costs incurred in doing business are of a highly proprietary nature; and when the company being audited chooses to keep its actual costs secret, that right shall be respected. Such a company shall, however, be expected to permit the examination of the methods used in collecting, analyzing, and applying quality costs in the manufacture of products, providing of services, or construction of projects. It shall be a requirement of the audit activity that the quality cost control methods are examined and determined to agree with generally accepted practices and also the standard or procedure required.

4.6.5 The calibration system quality audit.

In the field of national and international trade, dimensions of product characteristics and service characteristics must be assigned and controlled to units of magnitude that are common from one manufacturer to another and from one country to another. For this to be so, the instruments used to perform measurements on product and service characteristics shall have known accuracies which are traceable to the national system of standards in the country where the products are manufactured or the services are provided. It is a principal aspect of quality audits to verify that all measuring instruments used to determine and prove the characteristics of commodities made and offered for sale have known degrees of accuracy traceable to the national standards in the country of their manufacture or supply.

The audit team shall carry out the audit against the agreed standard, which shall be the one specified in any relevant contract or purchase order when such a commercial agreement exists. In the absence of an otherwise agreed-to calibration standard, the procedure in "Calibration Control System," Sec. III, Chap. 9 of *Quality Control Systems,* shall be used.

The audit shall examine the use of instruments for any lack of calibration currency, the instrument recall system for preventive maintenance and calibration methods and effectiveness, the calibration frequency practice in use, the method of initial setting of calibration frequency, etc. in accordance with the calibration standard. In addition to the above, the calibration audit shall examine the conditions of use and the environments of measuring instruments, the instrument handling and storage procedures, and the methods which can have a bearing on instrument accuracy. A particular area of the audit shall consist of examining the calibration system to determine that calibration intervals are shortened when it is found that instrument accuracy has changed outside limits at the time of periodic recall.

4.6.6 The audit of change control. The system of procedures used by the company or a supplier to the company to control changes of all kinds throughout the manufacturing or providing operation shall be a principal item for audit. There shall be some documented procedure of a general nature which sets out the required steps to be taken prior to introducing any change of stated nature or magnitudes. Generally, there are two levels of change in industry: (1) the degree or type of change that will affect the customer in some way and (2) the degree or type of change which will not affect the customer but is needed for production or providing. A change of the first level requires that the agreement of the contractual-type customer shall be obtained prior to introducing the change. A change of the second level may be made without customer agreement. Rigorous adherence to that principle shall be an item of examination during the audit.

When there exists a standard or general procedure specifying the activities that shall exist during operation and control of the process of change, it shall be the document against which the audit is performed. When there is no such document, the change control system in use shall be audited against the general procedure in "Quality Control of Change System," Sec. III, Chap. 8, of *Quality Control Systems.*

4.7   Quality audit reporting and follow-up

4.7.1   Reporting.   Careful transcriptions of observations made, inspection or test results obtained, conformances and nonconformances found, and other matters derived from the quality audit shall be made in a suitable manner and recorded during the course of carrying the audit out. The records shall be used at the end of the audit to compile a report of the entire audit findings and to relate each area of nonconformance to the specific area of control and activity where it was found.

Following the audit, a meeting with the management of the company or with the management of a supplier organization being audited shall be arranged. At the meeting, the findings of the audit shall be presented and discussed to gain agreement on resolution or rectification of any items or areas of nonconformance discovered during the audit. The time when such corrections will be in place and operating shall be agreed to.

The report of the audit shall then be published and made available to the managements of both supplier and customer, as appropriate, so that both may have their confidence reinforced and the ongoing activity may be made more satisfactory.

4.7.2   Follow-up.   The audit team shall arrange a follow-up examination of the nonconforming areas or items needing correction. This shall coincide with, or follow, the agreed date of resolution of those items or areas of inadequacy of control. A partial audit shall then be performed to examine only the items affected by the corrective actions.

Following the follow-up audit, the final report of the audit shall be issued; it shall show the degree of control found throughout the quality system audited.

5   The Product or Service Quality Audit

5.1   Scope.   The second part of this procedure sets forth the requirements of the company for quality audits which are to be performed on the products produced and/or services provided for customers.

5.2 Application. This procedure shall apply when called up in contracts and purchase orders. It shall also apply when work of this type is required within the company and when it becomes necessary to audit the products or services being produced or provided by suppliers to the company.

5.3 Definitions. The definitions of terms used in this procedure shall be those given in "Glossary of Terms Used in Quality and Reliability," Sec. VII, Chap. 1 of *Quality Control Systems*.

5.4 Product or service audit divisions

5.4.1 Customer requirements. When the customer requires the performance of quality audits of work done under contract, such audits shall be carried out in accordance with this procedure. When it is practicable to combine the work of auditing for assurance of the quality system or for confidence transfer purposes with the work of carrying out a product or service quality audit, such combining shall be done.

There is sometimes confusion concerning the purpose for which quality audits are conducted. It shall be a central principle of the performance of quality audits that the method and purpose shall be clearly identified when the audit project or work is justified. When it is appropriate, the results of quality audits shall be communicated to the customer in order to transfer confidence in the work being carried out.

5.4.2 Planning the product or service quality audit. Planning for a quality audit of products or services shall involve the same general principles and methods as planning for inspection of those items for acceptance purposes. Statistical sampling tables and methods shall be used; independent auditors shall do the measuring and evaluations; and all inspection and test equipment used shall be calibrated and operated in correct manner.

Before a quality audit is undertaken, the work shall be examined thoroughly, in respect to both purpose and method. Plans according to which the work shall be performed shall be made. The plans shall be coordinated with the quality organization staff that works in the areas to be audited, but they may be entirely unannounced so far as the production or providing staff is concerned.

The amount of quality auditing planned into a production or providing program shall be compatible with the complexity, cost, and difficulty involved. Specifically, sufficient quality auditing shall be planned to transfer to the customer adequate confidence in the quality of supplies. This principle shall apply, without regard to whether the company is the customer or the supplier.

5.4.3 Audit timing and management contact

5.4.3.1 Audit timing. Product or service audits shall be conducted with appropriate consideration of their purposes. In general, it will not be possible to perform quality audits of products or services until after the products or services have been produced for or provided to the customer. Normally, product audits shall be performed on completed items. Although in the case of products the audits can be performed at any time after the products are complete, within reasonable time limits, that is not true of services. The latter must be audited as they are being performed for the customers. Hence, there will be a tendency to draw conclusions when only a partial service has been delivered. Specific resistance against such a tendency shall be used to prevent drawing incomplete early conclusions. Often the manner of delivering a service is not readily apparent as to quality until after the delivery is complete.

Whereas tangible results can be obtained by assessing products in isolation from the customer, that is not true of services. Often it is necessary to obtain information from customers in order to audit the quality of services effectively. When that is so, specific plans as to the time and range of customers to be interrogated shall be made, always with the prior knowledge of the manager responsible for the site where the services are being provided.

5.4.3.2 Management contact. Whereas it is necessary to go through a formal program of contact with company management in the performance of the quality system audit, that is not true of product audits. In fact, products may often be audited after delivery to the customer's premises in complete ignorance of the supplier.

The auditing of services, however, is different from the auditing of products. Since it is usually necessary to be on the supplier's premises during business hours and to observe the performance of work in providing the service to the customer, it will be necessary to obtain the full cooperation of the supplier management. This is true when the auditor is a member of the customer's staff or a representative of an independent organization representing, for instance, the regulatory authority.

The degree to which contact with the supplier's managers is formalized will depend on the nature of the audit being conducted and the commodity being delivered to the customer. Care shall be used to arrange management contact commensurate with the degree of use of supplier facilities and staff in carrying out the audit.

5.4.4   Product or services specifications and the audit.   All audits of products or services shall be performed by comparing the quality characteristics with the respective specifications. In the normal audit, it shall be assumed that the specification for the commodity being supplied is satisfactory and that the product or service shall comply with it. Conformance or nonconformance is then ascertained by comparing the items and their characteristics against the values and limits specified for them. It is one of the tasks of the quality systems audit to ascertain the adequacy and correctness of the specifications.

5.4.5   The use of company facilities and personnel.   Sometimes in the auditing of products, and always in the auditing of the quality of services, it will be necessary to make use of the facilities and personnel of the supplier. When that is so, care shall be taken to ensure that the remeasurement of characteristics does not simply repeat the earlier faults that caused the items of product or service to appear to be conforming. A trap into which some auditors may fall is the repeating of unsatisfactory measurements. For that reason it shall be a particular aspect of the audit that the validity of remeasurements of products or services is investigated and validated as a formal part of the audit.

Arrangements for the use of a supplier's facilities and personnel shall always be made with the management of the supplier. When practicable, this work shall be covered in the contractual agreement between customer and supplier.

5.4.6   The analysis of product or service audit data.   The analysis of data acquired in audits shall be carried out by persons knowledgeable in statistics as well as in the technical requirements for the items being audited. Although audits normally involve fewer items than acceptance testing would, it shall be a requirement of audits that sufficient numbers of either products or services (or of repeated characteristics in complex products) are examined to gain confidence at an acceptable level that the product, service, or other audited aspect is conforming with requirements. Particular care shall be taken to ensure that the assumptions made in performing analyses on audit data are valid. In particular, the assumption that the audited items were randomly selected and that the data obtained were indeed representative of the population of product or service items from which the sample came shall be valid.

At no time shall audited items and their data be combined without due regard for the variance exhibited by the individual populations of items represented. Only data from populations with substantially similar variances shall be combined for analysis and reporting purposes.

5.4.7 The product or service quality audit report. All product or service audits shall be formally reported after suitable analysis. These reports shall be presented in forms suitable for conveying their message to the intended audience. For example, detailed reports of data shall be made only to work-face-level supervisors, and the reports to senior management shall normally follow the graphic presentation format.

Reports of product or service audits shall always contain exception report categories for items found to be nonconforming. When practicable, exception reports shall be accompanied by explanations of the reasons for nonconformance and a statement of the appropriate corrective action that is being taken.

5.5 The quality audit report and follow-up. All quality audits of products or services shall be reported formally to the management staff who are:

1. Responsible for producing the products or services and for implementing corrective action when any items are found to be nonconforming. This shall include the chief executive officer or his delegate at the plant site concerned.
2. Responsible for having the quality audit performed (e.g., the management of the customer organization).

Individual nonconforming items that directly affect quality of production underway, if the nonconformances are serious, shall be brought immediately to the attention of the responsible area manager so that corrective action can be planned and implemented at the earliest possible time.

When a product or service quality audit discovers nonconformance and the nonconformance is of a nature requiring corrective action, there shall always be follow-up to ensure that recommended or agreed-to corrective action has been taken. This follow-up shall be with the organizations responsible, and it shall take the form of a partial reaudit of the area to ascertain that the nonconformance previously found no longer exists in the product or services being produced.

Quality Control of Purchases

Source Quality Assurance System

PART A. REVIEW AND GUIDANCE

1 Review

In total quality control there is the concept that a production facility shall have a consistent supply of fully conforming materials from which to produce its output. With a totally controlled production operation, there will then be fully conforming products at the end of the production lines. There is considerable truth in the concept, but the system requires detailed planning and implementation, along with continuing control of the various activities needed to obtain the result.

This procedure is primarily concerned with obtaining fully conforming supplies from various vendors. Several principles must be woven together into an operating system, and the many variables must be dealt with and controlled so that each is prevented from getting out of control. Questions of great business importance to both the company and to the various suppliers arise in respect to how much control should be placed in the supplier-customer relationship and where it should be placed. In this procedure we discuss those questions and recommend the most suitable location for each area of controls.

2 Guidance

The spectrum of suppliers who satisfy the needs of a mass manufacturer, services provider, or project manager for the many raw materials, processed parts, and subsystems needed to generate the final outputs will be found to represent the full cross section of human industry. There will be large and small companies, and among them will be some with good quality control systems and others with little or no quality control. Some companies will control the quality of their output by inspection, i.e., by screening the good from the total population and rejecting or correcting the remainder. Other companies supply only an insignificant part of their output to a customer, who then has little or no leverage when corrective actions are sought. Still other suppliers will have excellent quality control systems and will deliver fully conforming items on a consistent basis.

It is far better to develop one good-quality supplier and keep that source of supply, rather than call for bids each time and place orders on the basis of price alone. What good does the purchase of unsatisfactory products at a lower price do a company that is trying to improve or maintain its quality?

The task of designing a source quality assurance (SQA) system consists of finding out all there is to know about each supplier and weaving together an SQA system that compensates for the weaknesses of each supplier and can ensure that all supplies delivered to the company consistently conform to their respective specifications. That calls for thorough evaluation of each supplier against agreed standards and procedures and the careful design and implementation of plans for coping with each supplier's weaknesses and assisting each to meet the assigned quality targets.

The concept of where the SQA system starts and finishes varies from company to company. For the purposes of this procedure we shall consider that the control of quality starts with the preparation of the purchase order and the selection of a supplier for the item needed. This part of the total quality control system will end with the properly run main material store from which the various production lines or other activities draw their raw and processed materials with which to produce the products or provide the services. These areas and all the sequential activities between are covered in this procedure.

PART B.   PROCEDURE

Source Quality Assurance System

1 Scope

This procedure contains the requirements of the company in respect to the control of quality of supplies purchased from suppliers or provided by customers for use in products of the company.

2 Application

This procedure shall be used and complied with in designing, establishing, and operating a system of source control for the supplies used by the company. When it is an essential aspect of the control system that suppliers also control their supplies and their production quality in a similar degree, the procedure shall be called for in contracts and purchase orders.

3 Definitions

Terms used in this procedure, unless stipulated otherwise in a contract, shall be interpreted in accordance with the definitions contained in "Glossary of Terms Used in Quality and Reliability," Sec. VII, Chap. 1 of *Quality Control Systems.**

4 Referenced Documents

This procedure shall be used in conjunction with one of the following procedures from *Quality Control Systems.*

1. "Quality Control System for Products," Sec. III, Chap. 2.
2. "Quality Control System for Services," Sec. III, Chap. 3.
3. "Quality Control System for Projects," Sec. III, Chap. 4.

5 Planning for Source Quality

Planning the source quality control system involves (1) detailed study of the items to be produced or provided and the individual item quality

---

*James R. Taylor, *Quality Control Systems: Procedures for Planning Quality Programs,* McGraw-Hill, New York, 1989.

needs and (2) devising a quality plan by which materials for each product arrives at the main in-house storage with the required quality. This quality plan shall identify the nature and degree of inspection to be used by the supplier, the extent of process control to be used in manufacturing the item, and all special considerations to be used, such as method of delivery or transport and critical handling or storage requirements. All of these factors identified as necessary to control the quality of supplies, on the part of the supplier, and to transfer confidence that such control was in fact carried out, shall appear in the contract or purchase order. The most important among these matters to be communicated to the supplier is the quality level required to ensure the needs of the company are met in its products.

An essential part of the quality plan shall be a review of the technical requirements for the items being purchased. These shall be communicated to the supplier as a part of the purchase order or contract, along with any necessary delivery schedules and points of supply.

The quality plan for each purchased item shall be a formal process on the part of the quality department of the company. The preparation of the plan shall be a specific duty of an identified individual employee, who shall be responsible for progressing the quality aspects of the purchased item through to the final storage prior to manufacturing use.

The detailed procedures for the quality planning and their execution shall be a formal part of the company's quality manual when they exist as documents separate from this procedure. The audit trail of controls applied to the items purchased for use in the company's products shall be continuous from planning, purchasing, production, delivery, receipt, acceptance inspection, and through storage to the point of issue and use.

6 Supplier Selection

The company shall select suppliers on the following bases:

1. Past and current quality performance
2. Financial soundness
3. Delivery performance history
4. Capacity to meet projected needs
5. History of cooperation with the company or other customers
6. An evaluation of the supplier's quality system and production capacity
7. Evidence of ability to meet the company's technical requirements

Collection of information and data on which to base judgments in respect to the above criteria shall be by supplier surveys, contacts with other customers, evaluation of samples of supplies, consultations with supplier's management, supplier's Dunn & Bradstreet rating, and evaluation of supplier's quality system, among others.

It shall be the policy of the company to work with known good suppliers to overcome difficulties, etc. rather than randomly call for bids and search for changes. To that end the purchasing organization and the quality organization shall work closely together in resolving matters affecting the quality and delivery of supplies.

7 Supplier Quality Control vs. Customer Quality Assurance

When seeking to assure the quality of supplies to the company, it will be necessary for the quality planner to make a decision as to what effort is to be expended at the vendor's plant toward controlling quality and what effort the company, as the customer, must expend to verify that the supplies do indeed have the quality levels specified in the purchase contract. This balance of effort is usually determined by the quality cost optimization being sought at the time.

There are three principal types of supplier material quality assessment, and one or a combination of them shall be used. They are:

1. Supplier quality evidence

2. Inspection at the source

3. Inspection at receipt by customer

To the extent that the supplier's efforts have been successful, the customer's efforts shall be curtailed. It is therefore necessary to have the supplier forward objective evidence of control during production. This frequently takes the form of (1) an assessment of the supplier's plant and quality system against the specified quality standard called for in the purchase contract and (2) data independently obtained directly from the quality characteristics of the items sampled for measurement by the vendor's quality organization.

In no case shall a certificate of compliance be accepted as objective evidence of conformance, although such a document may be accepted when quality of supplies is corroborated in other ways.

The control of quality of supplies shall always be placed first as a responsibility on the supplier. This is due to the fact that the supplier can only ensure that the supplies have the correct quality. Such arrangements also provide the opportunity for quality improvement and more effective and economical resolution of quality problems when they arise. These situations and circumstances are not available when it is decided to control the quality by product inspection at the customer's premises.

There are times, however, when inspection by the customer shall be performed. An example is when, for any reason, adequate control or confidence of control cannot be provided by the supplier for an economic price or in the time constraints which must be used. When adequate assurance of quality can be obtained in objective form from the activities of the supplier, there shall be no incoming inspection of those items of supplies, which shall be shipped direct to stock.

8   Source Quality and the Purchasing Function

The purchasing organization of the company shall discharge an essential and vital role in all purchasing of materials in respect to quality. Specifically, it shall be the responsibility of the purchasing organization to:

1. Ensure that the quality organization is informed each and every time a purchase is to be made from a new supplier or under a new contract from an existing supplier.

2. Ensure that the purchase contract contains all necessary technical and quality information as required by the quality plan for the particular item.

3. Select suppliers who have the approval of the quality organization of the company.

4. Bring to the attention of the quality organization all information relating to matters which may affect quality, i.e., matters that arise during the course of materials procurement.

5. Integrate its efforts with those of the quality organization to a sufficient degree to assure that all supplies purchased will have the required quality.

9   Delivery Preservation of Supplier Quality

Specific reviews and actions shall be used to examine the manner of packing, shipping, handling, transporting, identifying, and protecting materials and equipment obtained from suppliers. Such reviews shall be made with a view to assuring that those quality characteristics designed and constructed into the product items are in fact preserved throughout the entire process of packing, delivery, receiving, inspection, and storage.

When long-distance transport is necessary, particular attention shall be paid to such matters as:

- The vibration to which the items will be subjected
- The temperature extremes and durations to which the items will be subjected
- The variations in humidity involved, particularly when the items must be transported by ship across the equatorial regions
- The impacts or shocks, as well as the accelerations to which the items will be subjected during shipment
- Special precautions, such as shipment in close proximity to magnetic devices or radiation

There shall be specifications in all purchase contracts, when, after the above reviews, they are considered necessary. They shall state the requirements to be met in the delivery phase of supplier items. All items shall be appropriately labeled as to identity, source, quantity, or amount and all special handling instructions.

10 Receiving, Unpacking, and Handling Purchased Material

In this procedure the term "item" is used to mean products. Although services are required to have their respective levels of quality, this procedure seeks to stipulate the controls and activities which must be carried out in order to assure the quality of the items after delivery. The controls are, of necessity, applied on the material delivered.

For any one premises or plant location, one and only one point or area shall be designated for receiving material. That, of course, is contingent upon the area's meeting safety or security requirements (e.g., hazardous materials may be received away from occupied premises). Even when the physical location and handling of hazardous materials requires physical isolation, the paperwork and its processing shall be handled through the same office as that for nonhazardous production and nonproduction materials.

Care shall be used in handling and unpacking all materials so that their quality characteristics are preserved. Specific aspects to be aware of, and which shall be taken into consideration during handling and unpacking, are:

- Volume or physical size (for large objects)

- Special packing to preserve configuration or finish
- Fragile items requiring delicate handling
- Keeping designated top side upward
- Protection from rain and wet conditions
- Weight, for massive objects
- Hazardous nature of the materials

The receiving area shall, at all times, be kept in a neat, clean, and tidy manner. Packing materials, cartons, boxes, etc. shall not be permitted to accumulate and clutter the receiving area. The supplies being handled shall be kept free of dust, dirt, and foreign materials.

Attention shall be paid to the labeling of materials. When lots or batches of shipped materials are unpacked and separated, the sublots shall be relabeled so as to maintain continuity of identity. All items such as electrostatically sensitive materials, delicate mechanisms, fragile assemblies, and hazardous materials, shall receive special handling and labeling commensurate with their individual natures and requirements.

11   Incoming Inspection and Test

All material coming into the site or premises, whether for design use, housekeeping, or nonproduction use or for use in manufacturing products shall be subject to control through incoming inspection and test by the quality organization at its sole discretion. Such decisions shall be made following discussion with the ordering organization. It shall be the responsibility of the purchasing and the ordering organizations, acting in accordance with documented procedures, to notify the quality organization of the impending arrival of all materials whatsoever. Under no circumstances shall materials be permitted to enter the premises of the company in such a way as to bypass the incoming inspection and test area.

The incoming inspection and test activities shall be under the control of the quality organization of the company. They shall be integrated with the remainder of the quality activities of the company, and they shall meet all the requirements such as calibration, data accumulation, reporting, and other such management requirements as may be delegated to them.

All quality plans for purchased materials shall be reviewed by the incoming inspection and test area with a view to any required inspections or tests needed. They shall be carried out and the results shall be provided in accordance with the plans.

Care shall be used with materials held during inspection and test activities to ensure that identity, ownership responsibility, segregation of good from bad material, and repacking for storage, forwarding, or return to vendor are adequate. Records shall be created for all materials inspected or tested; they shall show the identity of the items, the number or quantity of material, the purchase order, the number found good and bad, and any disposition decided upon as a result of this activity.

When material intended for design use only is involved, the quality organization shall take the necessary steps to:

1. Ensure that surplus items from such orders do not become used in production in an uncontrolled way.

2. See to it that inspections and tests requested by design personnel are carried out.

3. Assist design personnel in accelerating delivery of the material to points of use.

When material is intended for housekeeping use only, the quality organization shall examine each such item to ensure that its use will not adversely affect produced items. When material is intended for use in the production process but is not to become part of the completed product, care shall be taken to ensure that appropriate cleaning processes are used to remove any material that may be deleterious to the product (e.g., cutting oils and cleaning solutions).

12   Storage of Received and Inspected Supplies

The main storage area(s) of the company on the premises shall possess the following characteristics and manner of operation:

1. The main storage shall be secure. It shall be enclosed and secure against unauthorized entry or access to the stored supplies.

2. Production materials shall be positively separated from nonproduction supplies.

3. All stored materials shall be labeled or otherwise positively identified as to material, type, class, category, or other characteristic needed to ensure correct use.

4. All production materials shall be issued on a first in, first out (FIFO) basis, except when it is necessary to keep production going or when a just-in-time (JIT) program is used, and then the ma-

terial movement through the storage area shall be on a direct needs basis.

5. Suitable handling, storage means, and other special requirements unique to the character of the materials being stored shall be provided.

6. The stored materials shall be periodically audited with respect to the continued maintenance of stored material characteristics. Special attention in this respect shall be paid to unprocessed plastic materials and other materials subject to rapid deterioration of their characteristics with time.

7. The storage environment, i.e., temperature, noxious or contaminated air, dust, dirt, grease, oils, and other potentially harmful substances, shall be planned as to their presence and effect on stored materials.

13   Control of Nonproduction Materials

All nonproduction materials purchased or brought into the production or construction environment or premises shall be examined with a concern for their potential adverse effect on the products or works of the company. Such nonproduction materials shall be kept segregated from production materials to a degree adequate to give confidence they will not become part of the product or construction works.

Nonproduction materials fall generally into three categories:

1. Materials intended to be used in designing new or changed products.

2. Materials intended to be used in or as a part of the production process. These materials include such items as cutting oils, production equipment, lubricating oils, wash solutions, degreasing compounds, and trace isotopes.

3. Materials, such as housekeeping materials or food for workers, which are not to become part of the process.

It is essential that the quality characteristics of all materials in category 1 be determined prior to use of the materials. Therefore, such materials shall be subject to oversight by the quality organization with the cooperation of the responsible design personnel. These materials shall be kept segregated from mass-production materials and shall be labeled at all times. Design material may, in project-type work, become part of the completed product, but it must have its quality characteristics determined prior to or in parallel with use.

2

Wholesaler's
Quality Control System

PART A.   REVIEW AND GUIDANCE

1   Review

In the world of commerce, manufacturers and the wider range of customers have need of sources from which parts, subsystems, and systems can be purchased on short notice, and with suitable quality and reliability, for a large number of purposes. Sometimes manufacturers will discontinue production of a model and spares for that model, leaving the customers with a continuing need which can be filled only by wholesalers. At other times, wholesalers fill a customer role for manufacturers who need to level-load their production facility when there are no immediate user orders for the products concerned. Wholesalers provide an important source of supply for a wide range of customers who need materials and components not readily obtainable from manufacturers at economic cost in small quantities and with quick delivery.

In some customer-supplier contractual relations, as when a supplier is to manufacture a certain model of equipment for a stated number of years, it is necessary to include a clause requiring the manufacturer to become a wholesaler for parts for that equipment for an agreed number of years following the discontinuance of manufacture of the equipment model concerned. This procedure will also apply to that type of supplier.

When parts are purchased from a wholesaler and the nature and application of the parts are important to quality and reliability or safety of the end product, the purchasing authority, whether government, industry, or an individual person, must be assured of the quality of the supplies. It is the responsibility of the wholesaler to furnish certified evidence of quality to customers when that requirement is stipulated in the contract or purchase order. To satisfy this requirement, wholesalers must either purchase supplies of assured quality supported by documented and objective evidence or establish the capability to prove the quality of supplies they sell. This requires the creation of a quality system capable of maintaining the quality and identity of supplies and verifying them when called upon to do so by the customer.

2   Guidance

In order to comply with the requirements of government and industry customers in respect to materials, components, and systems, wholesalers will need to develop, establish, and maintain a quality system in accordance with this procedure. The wholesaler may be a division of a manufacturing company, under which conditions it may be possible to transfer to the wholesaler's operation the necessary aspects of a quality system already in use in the manufacturing organization. If a wholesaler operation is being established as a separate company activity, it will be necessary to consider it in isolation from other industrial activities and to create a quality system independent of other activities.

The part of the wholesaling activities which will be new to existing wholesalers not practicing quality control are set forth in this procedure. They include such things as training, documented inspection and test, and equipment calibration. In particular, the wholesaler will need to develop the ability to verify quality and certify it to customers.

PART B.   PROCEDURE

Wholesaler's Quality Control System

1 Scope

This procedure establishes quality system requirements for wholesalers. It identifies the elements of a system to be established and maintained by the wholesaler to ensure that supplies conform with contract or purchase order requirements.

2 Application

This document applies to all supplies ordered on a contract or purchase order in which it is referenced. If there is any inconsistency between the contract or purchase order requirements and this document, the contract or purchase order requirements shall prevail.

3 Definitions

In the United States the term in common use for the activities of stocking and supplying various product items for sale to industrial or business customers is "wholesale operation." In Europe and Australia the term used is "stockist."

1. A wholesaler is an organization which acquires supplies and holds them in stock in anticipation of providing them to prospective purchasers mainly for resale or business use.

2. A retailer is an organization which acquires stocks of supplies in anticipation of selling them to the ultimate consumers for personal or household use. (*Note:* Some organizations or companies may operate both wholesale and retail operations in a manner similar to the manufacturing companies that both manufacture and provide wholesaler services.)

3. For other terms used see "Glossary of Terms Used in Quality and Reliability," Sec. VII, Chap. 1 of *Quality Control Systems.**

4 Referenced Documents

The following documents form a part of this document to the extent specified herein: "Calibration Control System," Sec. III, Chap. 9, and "Glossary of Terms Used in Quality and Reliability," Sec. VII, Chap. 1 of *Quality Control Systems.*

5 Organization

5.1. The wholesaler shall develop, establish, and maintain an effective quality control system to ensure that only acceptable supplies are consigned to the purchaser. The wholesaler shall furnish certified evidence of quality meeting the requirements of the contract or the purchase order. To achieve this, the wholesaler shall either purchase supplies of assured and verifiable quality with objective evidence thereof or prove conformance to contract or purchase order requirements by inspection and testing. The wholesaler shall create an organization capable of maintaining the quality and identity of such supplies prior to dispatch to purchasers.

The wholesaler shall establish and maintain adequate procedures for appropriate control, documentation, inspection, or testing and certification of all supplies purchased, held in stock, or consigned to a customer ordering supplies in accordance with this procedure.

5.2. The quality control system shall be satisfactory to the quality authority designated in the contract or purchase order or its authorized representative, hereinafter called the quality assurance representative (QAR).

5.3. The wholesaler shall appoint a management representative with the authority necessary to resolve matters pertaining to quality to the satisfaction of the QAR.

---

*James R. Taylor, *Quality Control Systems: Procedures for Planning Quality Programs,* McGraw-Hill, New York, 1989.

6 Planning

6.1. The wholesaler shall so plan the quality control system that all supplies dispatched against contracts or purchase orders will comply with the respective requirements. In this respect, the wholesaler shall plan acquisition programs and methods to ensure that items added to stock will be of verifiable quality and reliability. When possible, objective evidence shall be obtained along with supplies which are acquired proving the quality of the supplies against standards and specifications. Such objective evidence shall be maintained with the items of supply so they can be provided to customers as evidence of conformance.

6.2. When supplies for which there are no objective records of conformance to specifications or standards are acquired, the wholesaler shall plan inspection and test capabilities with which to verify the conformance of such supplies. The plans shall include programs for training of inspection and test staff, procurement of inspection and test equipment, and facilities or sources for maintenance and calibration of inspection and test equipment.

6.3. The wholesaler's plans shall encompass the entire operation in respect to each area and activity and the capability to contribute to or detract from the objective evidence of quality of supplies. The plans shall include programs for receiving, handling, storing, acquisition and maintenance of records, and review and audit of the system and supplies.

7 Quality System Review and Audit

Regular reviews and audits shall be conducted in a progressive manner by the wholesaler to demonstrate the effectiveness of the entire quality system. Procedures shall be established to detail the methods and frequency of reviews and audits. They shall cover the records to be made and maintained, the responsibilities for analysis of the review and audit data, and the use to be made of the data for corrective action purposes.

The wholesaler shall promptly correct deficiencies identified by reviews and audits. The QAR shall be advised of any changes made to the wholesaler procedures or to the quality system when the QAR's company is a current or regular customer who may be affected by such changes.

8 Limitations on Supplies

Unless specific authorization to the contrary is given in writing, supplies of unknown specification, history, or origin and supplies which have been previously placed in use shall not be provided in satisfaction of a purchase order or contract.

The wholesaler shall not supply items obtained from another wholesaler or from government surplus stocks unless so authorized in writing or in the purchase order or contract. Supplies shall be reconsigned in the condition in which they were received as meeting the order requirement unless otherwise authorized by the purchaser.

Whether obtained from verifying inspections and tests by the wholesaler or acquired with the supplies when they were procured from their earlier source, data representing objective evidence of conformance of supplies shall be provided with the supplies at their time of shipment.

The wholesaler may, with the approval of the customer or contractor, purchase inspection and test services from an outside organization.

9 Quality System Documentation

9.1 Procedures. The wholesaler shall have available all necessary procedures of both the general kind available from *Quality Control Systems* and the detailed procedures needed to establish and maintain the quality system.

9.2 Inspection and test instructions. When the wholesaler carries out in-house testing of items of product to prove their quality against specification, the tests shall be carried out in accordance with documented instructions which cover the operation of test instrumentation and the relevant inspections and tests performed thereon.

9.3 Records. The wholesaler shall develop, publish, and maintain such records as are necessary to provide identification for and traceability of supplies of assured quality and to ensure the effective working of his quality system. Examples of relevant records are the following.

1. Records of information about the supplies, including their:
   a. Identification
   b. Type, class, style, grade (and batch number), casting, etc.
   c. Source
   d. Place and date of manufacture

2. Information providing positive identification, including title, applicable issue of specifications, drawings, process instructions, inspection requirements and results, and other relevant technical data
3. Evidence of the wholesaler's compliance with the purchase order or contract
4. Records of inspections and tests carried out by the manufacturer or by or on behalf of the wholesaler
5. Copies of purchase orders, contracts, and related documents placed on the wholesaler as requirements
6. Rejection notes received or issued
7. Copies of all certificates of conformity received by or issued by the wholesaler
8. Records of the results of quality system reviews and audits

Records shall be retained and kept in a safe and retrievable manner and shall be produced for the QAR upon reasonable request.

10   Inspections and Tests

10.1   Inspections and tests by the wholesaler.   When the criteria necessary to provide certified objective evidence of quality of supplies are not fulfilled by data provided with the initial purchase by the wholesaler, the wholesaler shall, when the necessary inspection and test equipment and staff are available, carry out such inspections and tests as are necessary to provide the additional objective evidence. These shall be carried out to the satisfaction of the QAR.

10.2   Additional evidence.   When additional objective inspection and test evidence is required beyond that purchased by the wholesaler with the supplies and the wholesaler does not have the necessary inspection and test equipment, the wholesaler shall, with the written agreement of the purchaser or customer, have the inspections and tests carried out by a test house or laboratory acceptable to the purchaser or customer.

10.3   Inspection and test equipment.   The inspection and test equipment shall be capable of demonstrating conformance to the stipulated requirements of the purchase order or contract. All inspection and test equipment used to obtain objective evidence of conformance of supplies shall be maintained and calibrated in accordance with the procedure "Calibration Control System," Sec. III, Chap. 9 of *Quality Control Systems.*

11   Training

All staff members used by the wholesaler to carry out the duties which are necessary for the proper functioning of the quality system shall be suitably trained for their respective duties. In particular, staff members assigned to carry out inspections and tests on supplies shall be trained in the operation and use of the inspection and test equipment they must use.

12   Storage and Handling of Supplies

12.1   Storage facilities.   The wholesaler shall provide adequate storage facilities to segregate and maintain the quality, identity, and integrity of supplies of proven quality. Facilities for lifting, transporting within stores, and handling supplies in individual or bulk quantities shall be such as to protect the quality and identity of supplies.

12.2   Storage practices.   The storage facility shall be operated in an orderly and prescribed manner in accordance with procedures prepared for the purpose. Supplies, unless stipulated by the customer to be otherwise, shall be entered into and withdrawn from stock on a first in, first out (FIFO) basis. All supplies shall be assessed periodically to determine their condition. Supplies which have deteriorated or are suspected of having deteriorated or for which there is no objective evidence of conformance shall be treated as nonconforming supplies pending confirmation of their status by appropriate inspections and tests.

When supplies have a limited shelf life, the wholesaler shall determine the remaining shelf life and notify the customer accordingly at the time of shipment.

12.3   Handling.   Equipment and facilities with which quality characteristics of supplies can be preserved and protected during handling, movement, and storage shall be provided by the wholesaler. All handling shall be carried out by qualified personnel and no supplies which contain known or apparent damage due to handling shall be delivered to the customer without written permission.

13   Control of Nonconforming Supplies

The wholesaler shall ensure that all nonconforming supplies are segregated from known conforming supplies. At no time shall the wholesaler deliver nonconforming supplies against a purchase order or contract unless specifically permitted to so do by the customer in writing.

This requirement shall apply to supplies which do not have objective evidence of conformance.

Procedures of the wholesaler for controlling supplies which do not conform to the purchase order or contract shall provide specific provisions for the identification, segregation, and disposal of the nonconforming supplies. The procedures shall prevent mixing or shipment of such nonconforming supplies with conforming supplies.

Clear identification of nonconforming supplies, the nature and extent of such nonconformances, and the disposition of such supplies, shall form part of the records of the wholesaler.

14 Sampling Procedures

Statistical quality control methods, including sampling procedures used by the wholesaler, shall be as stated in the purchase order and/or contract or shall be subject to agreement by the QAR. When sampling procedures are used, a sampling standard acceptable to the customer shall be used.

15 Certification of Reconsigned Supplies

All supplies reconsigned by the wholesaler in satisfaction of orders requiring compliance with this procedure shall be accompanied by a certificate of conformity (see Art. 18). The certificate shall include, as appropriate, details extracted from the relevant incoming certificate of conformity or from the records retained in accordance with the provisions of this procedure.

16 Packing, Preservation, and Marking

When the purchase order or contract so stipulates, the wholesaler shall ensure that all packing, preservation, and marking of supplies complies with requirements. When any such requirement is not stipulated in the purchase order or contract, the wholesaler shall ensure that the terms and conditions of packing, preservation, and marking are such as to protect all quality characteristics of the supplies.

17 Accommodation and Assistance

17.1 Accommodation. The wholesaler shall provide the QAR with adequate accommodation and facilities needed to carry out his or her duties while on the wholesaler's premises. Any such special requirements shall be as stipulated in the purchase order or contract.

```
┌─────────────────────────────────────────────────────────────────────────┐
│                                                                           │
│         C E R T I F I C A T E   O F   C O N F O R M I T Y                 │
│                                                                           │
├───────────────────────────────────┬───────────────────────────┬─────────┤
│ REFERENCE NUMBER:                  │ ORDER REFERENCE:          │NO. PAGES│
├───────────────────────────┬───────┴───────────────────┬───────┴─────────┤
│ WHOLESALER'S NAME & ADDRESS│ DATE AND PLACE OF MFR.:    │ SHIPPED TO: (CONSIGNEE)│
│                            │                            │                 │
│                            │                            │                 │
├────────────────────────────┴───────────────┬───────────┴─────────────────┤
│ INCOMING CERTIFICATE OF CONFORMITY NO.:     │ PURCHASE ORDER OR CONTRACT NUMBER:│
│                                             │                             │
├─────────────────────────────────────────────┼─────────────────────────────┤
│ BATCH NO.:                                  │ CAST OR OTHER IDENT. NO.:   │
├─────────────────────────────────────────────┼─────────────────────────────┤
│ INSPECTION/TEST REPORT NO.:                 │ SHIPMENT NO. OR BILL OF LADING:│
└─────────────────────────────────────────────┴─────────────────────────────┘
```

I CERTIFY THAT THE WHOLE OF THE SUPPLIES DETAILED HEREON, UNLESS OTHERWISE STATED BELOW, CONFORMS IN ALL RESPECTS TO THE ORDER/CONTRACT REQUIREMENTS AND IS RECON-SIGNED IN THE CONDITION STATED ON THE INCOMING CERTIFICATE OF CONFORMITY, OR HAS BEEN INSPECTED AND TESTED IN ACCORDANCE WITH THE CONDITIONS OF THE ORDER/CONTRACT.

DATE: SIGNATURE: PRINTED NAME:

DETAILS OF SUPPLIES:

CONTRACT ITEM NO.:	STOCK/PART NO.&NAME:	QUANTITY:	SPECIFICATION AND/OR DRAWING NO. & ISSUE:

CONTINUE LIST ON SEPARATE PAGES IF NECESSARY:

Figure 2.1 Certificate of conformity.

17.2 Assistance. The wholesaler shall provide the QAR with access to inspection and test equipment, trained personnel as required, or additional necessary facilities for the purpose of verifying supplies to requirements. The wholesaler shall provide assistance required by the QAR in verifying the adequacy and effectiveness of the wholesaler's procedures. At the request of the QAR, the wholesaler shall provide and dispatch to a nominated authority any technical data and test pieces (or samples) needed for verification purposes. Costs for such services and assistance shall, when called for in the contract or purchase order, be to the customer's account.

18 Certificate of Conformity

The certificate of conformity provided with supplies delivered against purchase orders or contracts shall be in the format of and shall contain the information shown in the sample certificate of conformity provided with this procedure. The sample is set forth in Fig. 2.1.

When additional space is required to enter all the relevant data and supporting information, additional sheets having the general format following the official certificate format shown herein (Fig. 2.1) may be used.

Quality Control during Product Use

1

Product Recall System

PART A. REVIEW AND GUIDANCE

1 Review

Meeting consumer demand for safe products has become a world-wide requirement for all manufacturers. It is generally accepted that consumers have a right to be sold products which will be safe to use or, if in the food category, to consume. To that end, many manufacturing companies have designated their quality managers to be their product safety or liability managers also. In any event, without regard to the area of delegation, there is a need for a product recall program to be designed and established if the company sells some product which may be capable of harming the user.

The kind of a company, even in the services or project areas of business, is irrelevant in respect to whether a recall procedure is needed. *All* companies need such a procedure. Fast-food companies can be saddled with the greatest and most difficult recall problem when their foods prove to be contaminated or otherwise harmful to the consumers. That is because the foods are consumed so rapidly that there is little time in which to carry out a recall; accordingly, the risk is much greater. The risk to other companies, however, is also great.

The problem is no longer left up to the producer or supplier of some goods to the public or to other users. Most governments have adopted codes of performance which require the manufacturer or supplier to provide safe goods and to guarantee the consumers that the goods are safe. When something goes wrong, the producer or supplier will find that a government agency or several agencies will become involved at a very early date. That brings into the picture the need for a company to be aware of the local laws, codes, and regulations and the authorities who enforce them.

2 Guidance

Regardless of whether the matter of product safety is considered from the viewpoint of safety or liability, it is necessary to design, establish, and promulgate a product safety program which will both engender the production of safety in the items to be supplied and a program to provide for recall when the system permits some unacceptable characteristic to slip through.

There are a multitude of things which come up during a product recall, and each situation is different from other recalls which may have occurred in the industry. Each company is organized along different lines and will therefore require different interrelations during a product recall.

A product recall may not always be necessary, and it may be satisfactory to provide customers with some minor part they can add to make the product safe without returning it to the manufacturer. If a product recall does become necessary, the following actions will make it more effective:

1. A completely documented and promulgated product recall procedure is made available at the time of the recall and is strictly adhered to throughout the implementation of the recall.

2. The decision to implement the recall is made quickly following assembly of the product recall committee and its reaching a decision that recall is necessary.

3. The statutory authority responsible in the product area is invited to participate in the recall and is kept fully informed throughout the activity.

4. Statutory authorities, the media, and the company's insurers are kept informed as soon as possible after the recall decision is made, and throughout the remainder of the activity.

5. Following the decision to recall, the company's communication systems within the distribution network are activated quickly and information as to the course of action to be taken by each is relayed verbally to all distributors, warehousers, and retailers, as well as company-owned depots and sales outlets.

6. An accurate log of all events is kept by the company executive responsible for managing the recall.

7. An inventory detailing all product returned to the central production or processing plant is prepared and progressively maintained.

8. All returned product is sampled for the fault to determine the magnitude of the problem. This information will be needed when future insurance decisions are made, as well as for confirming the validity of earlier decisions.

9. The company ensures that all necessary resources are made available to the product recall committee for direction and use in the recall.

10. All product is *date-coded!* This makes a recall possible, once the fault has been identified, without involving the total amount of product shipped. The recall can be isolated to items which contain the fault, and the others can be left to be used by customers and to maintain the good name of the manufacturer. Liquids, gases, and raw materials shall be batched.

Two central problems will occur each time a product recall becomes necessary: (1) the need to identify the exact items which are faulty as to type, date code, and, when appropriate, serial number and (2) to find out where in the far-flung distribution system the items of product happen to be over some relatively short period of time. (In a distribution system the items keep moving from point to point until they are finally in the hands of the customers.)

It is essential that the company develop and establish a standard simple and clear method of complaint submission and recording. This method should be oriented toward obtaining from the customer a specific statement of *how* or *why* the product is unsatisfactory, what the product does or does not do, and how the product affects the customer. This will assist in identifying the recall items which contain the fault.

A further need within the company is for all communications to employees about the recall to be clear, concise, standard, and simple. Since recalls are, hopefully, an unusual occurrence and all company employees will naturally be concerned, it is necessary that the employees be kept informed to the appropriate degree. When employees who must participate in the recall receive communications about what to do, the communications must be clear and overriding even though they come from some outside person such as the recall coordinator.

PART B.   PROCEDURE

Product Recall System

1   Scope

This procedure defines the requirements of the company in respect to products which are found to be unsafe. It sets forth procedures to be followed in the event a product of the company which is unsafe or should be returned for other liability reasons is delivered, shipped, distributed, or sold.

2   Application

This procedure shall apply throughout the company and in all situations in which it or a standard method for conducting recalls is called up in a contract or purchase order.

3   Definitions

Terms used in this procedure shall be interpreted in accordance with the definitions given in "Glossary of Terms Used in Quality and Reliability," Sec. VII, Chap. 1, *Quality Control Systems.**

4   Referenced Documents

1. A code of practice for recall of unsafe goods or any law or other regulatory requirements document issued by a jurisdictional authority.

---

*James R. Taylor, *Quality Control Systems: Procedures for Planning Quality Programs,* McGraw-Hill, New York, 1989.

2. "Glossary of Terms Used in Quality and Reliability," Sec. VII, Chap. 1, of *Quality Control Systems.*

5 Organization

The company shall appoint from among its management a person who shall be called the recall coordinator and who shall be responsible for coordinating all activities concerning matters related to recall of products which the recall coordination committee shall decide are to be recalled. The recall coordinator shall occupy a position in the company within its management structure, and shall have the support of the chief executive officer in matters related to recall of product.

The company shall identify from among its members persons who, because of their positions in the organization or because of their unique abilities and external relations, are specifically suited to participate in the recall committee. They shall be appointed members of the recall committee, and the recall coordinator shall be the chairperson of that committee.

6 Planning

The company shall prepare plans which are to be used in the two major areas of product liability and hazard control and in the activity of product recall. Unless specifically delegated otherwise, the quality manager shall also be the product liability manager. It shall be the responsibility of the product liability manager to ensure that the characteristics of the various products of the company are identified and classified and to specifically measure, assess, and control the characteristics which could be hazardous to customers or to those who handle, install, apply, or use the products. This shall be carried out as a normal part of the quality assurance activities of the company. Control of product hazards shall be the direct responsibility of management personnel who are responsible for production, and the degree of control shall be measured and reported by the product liability manager.

The company shall prepare and publish documented proceedings to be followed in the event of a recall decision. The procedures shall be in accordance with the guidelines of this procedure. As part of the planning for prevention of product hazards, all members of the company shall receive communications on what will be expected of them in the event a recall becomes necessary. In particular, employees who must participate directly in a recall, such as distribution personnel, shall receive specific instruction from planned and documented recall procedures.

7   Jurisdictional Authorities

The recall coordinator shall identify the federal, state, and local government and regulatory authorities who may have an impact on product recall. He or she shall compile, in cooperation with the quality manager, a file of all laws, standards, codes, and regulations which apply to the products in respect to any potential hazardous conditions the products may present to customers or users. This file shall be kept up to date as new codes and regulations, or laws, are issued. Products manufactured shall meet their respective legal codes and regulations.

A unique part of the above jurisdictional file shall be the names, addresses, phone numbers, and, when applicable, telex numbers of the authorities who must be contacted on matters of product hazard and, in particular, of product recalls. It shall be the responsibility of the product liability manager, in conjunction with the recall coordinator, to maintain the jurisdictional file and keep it current in all respects.

8   Achieving Product Safety

8.1.   Product safety shall be a central and mandatory requirement of all work done by or for the company. Although the personnel safety program will normally receive equal emphasis from management, it will usually be run as a separate program within the company. Product safety will originate, for each product category, with the very first design concepts, and be carried through all design work, production, quality control, delivery, and customer education activities.

8.2.   When the product is designed, safety shall be a mandatory and integral objective of all work on the design. The three major design objectives shall, for all products, receive importance of attention in the following order:

1. Safety
2. Performance
3. Reliability

8.3.   When characteristics are classified for quality control purposes, safety shall be the most important classification and all products shall be given thorough review and examination to ensure that all potential product hazards are controlled or eliminated. All inspection and tests performed on the products shall be oriented to examine 100 percent of products for safety.

8.4. The company employees who are responsible for product safety, including those involved in design, production, and quality assurance, shall be knowledgeable in all aspects of standards, codes, and regulations as they pertain to their responsibility for product safety. Employees shall ensure that products manufactured comply with all requirements in this respect.

8.5. Among the activities and areas important to control in respect to product safety, the following shall receive specific attention:

1. Prototype and off-tool testing
2. Material and component integrity to specifications
3. Quality control procedures during manufacturing
4. Transit conditions and possible damage to product or vehicle
5. Dumping of products manufactured in other countries which cannot meet local safety codes and regulations
6. Disposal of product materials under conditions which may present a hazard to people under any conditions

9   Identifying Unsafe Products

9.1. In order to identify unsafe products, it is necessary to be able to identify each individual product. This means that part of the planning for product safety and control shall be the preparation of mandatory procedures for identification of products. Unless specifically required otherwise, every item of product manufactured by the company shall carry an indelible *date code* which shall, as a minimum, clearly show the month and year of manufacture. When it is important, the date code shall also show the day of manufacture.

9.2. When it is important that the product be handled in a certain manner, kept in a specific controlled atmosphere (e.g., refrigerated below a certain temperature), or used or operated in a certain manner, the handling instructions shall be clearly communicated on either the item itself or on the container for that item.

9.3. When product materials or items can be used, taken internally, or in other ways be hazardous to humans or their possessions, clear and obvious warnings shall be given on either or both the item or the container for the item or material. As appropriate, information on possible treatment for or antidotes to be taken or used in the event of injury shall be clearly communicated on the product item or its container.

9.4. Discovery that an unsafe product has been produced and delivered shall be a principal and mandatory requirement of procedures used by the company. To that extent and for that purpose, procedures shall provide for careful review and analysis of:

1. Customer complaints
2. Accident reports
3. Employee comments concerning product hazard or safety
4. Repair agency reports and complaints
5. Independent test and analysis reports
6. Trade organization and publication reports

10   Making the Recall Decision

10.1. Making a recall decision can be one of the most difficult decisions a company's management ever has to face. The recall of a product is very expensive in immediate and direct impact on income, additional expenditure, and longer-term customer and public acceptance of the company's products. Because of the cost in money, goodwill, and morale terms, there shall be a full review of the need for a recall made by the company's management at the highest levels. When necessary or advisable, the view of an independent body shall be obtained, once it is ascertained that a possible recall situation has arisen.

10.2. When a possible recall situation has arisen, it shall be the responsibility of the recall coordination committee to:

1. Determine the degree of the hazard.
2. Determine if a recall is necessary.
3. When a recall is considered necessary, determine if it is to be partial or total and, if partial, what items are to be recalled or repaired in the field.
4. Determine whether the situation can be rectified by the supply to customers or field depots of additional material or part(s) and what instructions are needed to use them.
5. Determine what expert advice from outside the company is to be obtained in such matters as possible severity of the hazard, or any injury therefrom, or special technical knowledge or tests required to reach a recall or no-recall decision.

10.3. The company, whether a manufacturer, wholesaler, or retailer, shall not be considered liable for recall of some product when one or more accidents occur through bizarre methods of use or illegitimate use of the product. The recall coordination committee shall consider the products of the company from that viewpoint. When, however, the hazard arises from some unforeseen, but legitimate, method of use which might cause injury, even when no injury has been reported, the recall coordination committee shall consider that grounds for possible recall exist.

11 Tracing Unsafe Products

11.1. The ability to trace unsafe products will depend on the existence of a rigorously maintained program of product date coding, identification labeling, and making and maintaining records adequate as to distribution and location. In view of that, it shall be a principal responsibility of the company to carry out a routine program of recording all matters concerning product identification, distribution, storage, and sales which may be needed in a recall situation.

11.2. Specific data which shall be recorded and preserved with retrievability shall include:

1. Specific batch numbers and quantities, serial and model numbers related to changes in formulation, designs, or modifications. Any unique identification information which may assist customers in identifying the product, should that become necessary, shall be noted and recorded.

2. Production and quality control records, including results of tests and inspections.

3. Shipping information, distribution network, and storage records.

4. Names and addresses of purchasers when a warranty system or similar source of data exists.

5. In the case of export products, the overseas agent(s) and their distribution network information available to the company.

12 The Recall and Repair or Replace Actions

12.1. The sequence of recall and repair or replace actions that shall apply is as follows:

Receive complaint(s).	From customers, employees, and others.
Analyze complaint(s).	Complaint supervisor and product recall committee.

Identify hazard, degree, and scope.	Recall coordinator convenes product recall committee.
Determine recall is necessary.	Transfer to recall coordinator to control and follow.
Halt production and notify authorities; recall coordinator prepares log.	Halt production of offending items; notify of hazard and its nature; enter all known data to date on problem; and maintain log.
Publicize recall; notify customers and distributors.	Product recall committee reviews and approves media communications; customers and distributors are notified.
Locate hazardous product; halt further distribution and any sales.	Determine locations of all known hazardous products; send notices to each; stop distribution and sales.
Recall product; determine storage and disposal of returns.	Place recall orders, with replacement instructions, to relevant recipients; and arrange transport, receipt, storage, and disposal of returns.
Update reports to authorities and to customers and public through media.	Keep authorities informed of all major decisions and acts. Keep customers informed to maintain their confidence in products.
Analyze causes of the hazard problem; apply corrective action.	Pass the hazardous items through the material review board for disposal and corrective action. Recall coordination committee reviews and approves.
Monitor recall and corrective action.	Monitor ongoing program of retrieval and application of corrective action.
Keep management and employees informed.	Keep company management and employees informed of progress toward solution.

12.2.   The above flowchart of actions to be taken during a product recall is applicable when there is to be product returned to the company for reasons of safety or hazardous condition. Other situations requiring action on safety matters can arise.

12.2.1.   Items of product minus a part which would have rendered them safe have been sold. Deliver the additional part as soon as possible.

12.2.2.   Items of product which are not wanted to be returned and may be safely disposed of by the recipients have been delivered or sold. Issue instructions for disposal.

12.2.3. Individuals have been injured, with various degrees of seriousness, by products of the company. Invoke the services of the company's legal department or lawyers and pursue a mutually agreeable solution.

12.2.4. Complaints about product safety which are not valid have been made. Quickly stop such untrue rumors by all available means, including legal action when it is appropriate.

12.2.5. In recall situations when the product, such as a food item, is delivered on a daily basis, the retail outlet can produce high levels of customer dissatisfaction with the product and subsequent loss of future market segment. This results when poor communications and poor supplier-retailer relationships exist. It shall be a principal responsibility of the recall coordinator to ensure that all customer outlets for the recalled items of product are kept suitably informed at all times so as to minimize the negative effects of the recall and maintain the best possible customer relations.

One major aim of all communications, after alerting customers to the hazard, shall be to maintain customer confidence in the company's products. This can be best accomplished by projecting a company image which gives customers confidence in all products and actions of the company.

12.3. Once a recall decision has been made, the recall coordination committee shall give full consideration to the problem of repair or replacement of the hazardous items of product. If time permits, the recall coordinator shall review the needs for additional production. If it does not, he or she shall delegate responsibility for a full review of the needs for additional production of safe items of product to be used as replacements or the provision of spare parts for a major repair program to make the items returned by customers safe to use.

The quantity of either new production material or the unanticipated larger quantity of spare parts needed to make returned product safe will be a major cost item in most cases. The management of this activity shall be carried out within the normal organizational structure of the company, the work being carried out by the organizations normally assigned to it. All items of product repaired, or those replacing returned items, shall be inspected 100 percent for absence of the hazard which brought about the recall.

Repaired or replacement items of product shall be provided to customers as rapidly as possible in order to prevent customers incurring any more inconvenience from being without their items of product than is necessary. Once again, all efforts shall be made to maintain customer confidence in the company and satisfaction with its products.

13   Unsafe Product Retrieval

13.1.   The following action sequence shall be followed, and each step shall be considered essential and be carried out to the degree necessary.

1. Identification.
   a. Identify the cause of the defect or nonconformity which presents the hazard.
   b. Isolate and locate by batches or lots and serial numbers the items of product involved.
   c. Ascertain the quantity of material or number of units involved.
2. Notification.
   a. If a breach of government regulations is likely or has occurred, notify the responsible government agencies.
   b. Notify the company's branches, distributors, and retailers.
   c. Notify consumers or customers.
3. Discontinue production and shipments of the faulty product until the defect or nonconformity is rectified.
4. Legal and costing.
   a. Discuss legal liability and arrange any action with advisers.
   b. Estimate total cost of recall and repair or replacement activity.
5. Replacement or modification.
   a. Allocate financial and worker resources to provide replacement parts or units or to modify returned items.
   b. Ship replacement parts or units or return modified items.
6. Monitor and report.
   a. Monitor recall process, maintain log, report to the responsible authorities, and keep employees and customers appropriately informed.
7. General.
   a. Do not launch a recall that covers only part of the items distributed and/or sold while leaving some unsafe items in the pipeline or in customers' hands.
   b. Review and make decisions on *all* necessary rectification activities needed to correct the unsafe condition, including repair of built-ins, etc. at customers' sites.

13.2.   In recalls, as in most other areas of work in industry, it is by effective and resourceful follow-through that a recall is made almost totally successful, and with little or no loss of customer confidence. In fact, a well-managed recall, with due regard for customer safety, can enhance the company's standing in the marketplace. That shall be the aim and objective of the recall activity.

14 Publicity

14.1. Though there may be a temptation to carry out a "secret" recall and carefully avoid any public statement about the hazard, that is not an acceptable method, and it will always backlash on the company when it is tried. Accordingly, all recalls shall be publicized to the extent necessary to engender customer confidence in the professional methods and behavior of the company.

14.2. The recall coordinator shall give due consideration to the amount of publicity required by the recall. When only a few items have been shipped and they present no lethal or serious hazard, such items being easily retrievable from customers, there may be no need for media publicity. It is necessary to provide information to the media (newspapers, television, radio) only when that form of publicity will provide greater protection of the customers and/or is considered necessary to effect a complete recall of all faulty items. All media announcements shall be kept in a positive and objective vein and shall be prepared for quote rather than permit the uninformed members of the journalist corps to couch the announcements in their less-informative words.

14.3. A careful review of affected government regulatory bodies and agencies shall be made. It is more important not to leave out some government body that may feel it should have been informed than it is to inform one agency too many. Accordingly, the recall coordinator shall ensure that all affected authorities are informed and are kept informed throughout the recall.

14.4. When announcements for publication are made, there shall be provided a telephone number and address from which customers can obtain additional information. Communications can easily become garbled, and the customer will often receive only enough of the intended message to become worried or have the hazard greatly magnified by some other uninformed source.

14.5. All organizations likely to be approached by the public for additional information shall be informed of the recall and, when it is appropriate, of details of the hazard. Each of these organizations, such as manufacturer or retailer associations, shall be provided an awareness plus information on whom to contact for additional information.

14.6. Other, distant divisions, and when applicable, parent organizations shall be informed of the recall. They can often be of assistance, and the parent company will have to be informed sooner or later. The earlier information is provided the better the overall effects can be controlled.

15   Costs Associated with Recalls

15.1. Costs associated with product recalls fall generally into the following cost areas:

1. Recompense to customers who have been injured or disadvantaged
2. Cost of parts and labor for product modification
3. Cost of product items used to replace recalled items
4. Cost of recall activity, including disposition of recalled items and delivery of replacements

15.2. Liability for damages in connection with product hazards shall always be discussed at the earliest opportunity with the company's lawyers. All correspondence with threatening customers shall be cleared with the company's legal representatives.

15.3. Products sold or offered for sale, must, in law, be of merchantable quality and be fit for the purpose intended, provided that purpose can reasonably be assumed or is known. The ultimate consumer is normally entitled to legal redress for breach of contract from the retailer, and the retailer is entitled to redress from the manufacturer and wholesaler. At times the manufacturer of parts supplied to the company for inclusion in some item of product will also be at risk. To the extent deemed appropriate, each organization in the sequence of activity leading to the hazardous product shall be informed of the hazard, and those contributing directly to the existence of the hazard shall be informed in detail so they may protect themselves.

15.4. All reasonable costs of modifying or remedying a defect or nonconformity shall be borne by the company, including transport of bulky items and, when appropriate, repair of defects at customers' premises. When the hazard is the fault of some supplier to the company or a deliverer or installer not a part of the company, the costs shall be borne by that body.

16   Disposition of Recalled Products

16.1.   Recalled products will fall into various categories, and their disposition will depend on the categories as well as the natures of the hazardous faults. The company has a material review board with a duty to review all products found to be nonconforming and dispose of such products. Accordingly, all recalled products shall be collected by the recall coordinator and then turned over to the material review board for disposition.

16.2.   The material review board shall, in reaching a disposition decision, take into consideration the need to provide customers with suitable nonhazardous products at the earliest possible time.

17   Termination of the Recall

17.1.   Although litigation about a recall situation can continue for years, it will be necessary that each specific recall reach a termination date as soon as practicable. To that end the recall coordinator shall maintain a log of recall actions and monitor the degree of recall of *all* hazardous items of product with a view to terminating recall when the appropriate time has been reached. This time will depend on when three critical stages have been reached:

1. When all known hazardous products have been retrieved or repaired at site.
2. When all customers have had their hazardous products replaced.
3. When the hazard has been analyzed and eliminated from future production.

18   Legal Implications of the Recall

18.1.   Customers who have been injured by hazardous products may choose to initiate litigation after extended periods of time have passed. Most countries and states have some statutory limitation beyond which such litigation may no longer be initiated in the civil courts. This may range from 3 to 6 years in typical cases. It sometimes takes seriously injured customers a long time to regain their health to a sufficient degree to begin legal proceedings. The recall file shall be maintained in or be accessible to the company's legal representatives following termination of the recall by the manufacturing facility.

18.2.   The company shall make arrangements to meet the demands of any legal situations anticipated from the results of the recall. To that end, the company shall insure itself against damages and other effects of hazardous product liability to the extent deemed appropriate.

18.3.   The quality manager shall prepare for litigation in respect to product quality involving hazard situations by ensuring that all statistical sampling and inspection or testing of products are conducted in a rigorous scientific manner which will be defensible in court.

19   Recall Review and Adjustments

The recall coordinator shall be permanently assigned. Before disbanding, the recall coordination committee shall hold a review of the recall with a view to preparing for any future similar situations or minimizing the recurrence of such situations.

Risk can be minimized but never completely eliminated. The recall coordination committee, co-opting any other members of management or outside consultants found necessary, shall determine the desirable and tolerable level of risk to be borne by the company and shall establish the necessary internal mechanisms to continue operations within the defined range of acceptable risk.

Employee Participation Programs, Quality Costs, and Just-in-Time

Chapter

1

Employee Participation
Program Quality System

PART A. REVIEW AND GUIDANCE

1 Review

The total activity of a company involved in manufacturing some product, providing some service, or constructing some project is ordinarily organized into a number of divisions, departments, and lesser components. These are managed by a hierarchical structure that culminates in a president or managing director. The various organizational components are joined together at interfaces across which components interact and receive or transmit inputs and outputs.

Each organizational component is comprised of a manager and the workers who report to him or her. It tends to resolve its internal problems more easily and effectively than when problems occur at interfaces between components. Therefore, it is necessary to provide special management procedures which will help achieve resolution of people-to-people and component-to-component problems. That calls for integration that will naturally break down barriers and result in cooperation between and concerted action of organizational components.

In the past, methods devised to improve employee motivation have tended to improve either quality or productivity, but a few programs have given balanced attention to both. Typical among them are:

1. The *zero defects* or zero nonconformities program, designed to improve quality

   prove quality

2. The *worker incentives* program, designed to improve productivity by paying higher rates for more output

(*Note:* A formula which gives equal weighting to productivity and quality can be devised. It increases pay in proportion to increased output and decreases pay in proportion to decreased quality. This arrangement shall be adopted if an incentives program is used.)

While the Japanese were developing the now-recognized quality circles, early programs to relax the rigid control over workers in industry were developing in the west. One example is Flexi-Time, which is now widely introduced in western industry. Flexi-Time allows employees to adjust their work schedules within controlled limits so they can do such things as take children to the dentist and do shopping in stores that are closed when they normally get off work. Although Flexi-Time programs do not greatly increase either productivity or quality, they are representative of the increasing awareness that western workers have too long been subjected to a dominance style of management.

Also recognized is the untapped reservoir of employee knowledge about the products being produced. The Japanese were the first to take full advantage of this vast potential for productivity and quality improvement through their quality circle programs and integrated management styles.

One criticism which may be leveled against this book is the lack of a chapter on quality circles. Such an inclusion was considered unwarranted in view of the far more comprehensive and advanced approach represented by the employee participation programs (EPP) that are the subject of this chapter. In fact, the EPP action teams are the equivalent of the less comprehensive and effective quality circles practiced in many western companies for several years. The methods and techniques of this chapter are required to bring a western company into line with Japanese counterparts that have been practicing the totally integrated form of management for years. There the quality circle was only the action team part of the whole program.

Gradually the rigid planned worklife of employees laboring within the Frederick W. Taylor scientific management system is beginning to be varied in ways that are favorable to both workers and management. This greatest approach to maximizing the contributions of employees and managers has evolved from the 1970s and is still evolving in most western companies. Following GE's discovery of the brainstorming method of synergistically maximizing the discovery of solutions of problems by gathering managers and workers together in a room for a set period of time and giving the group one problem to work on, the Japanese developed a full-blown program of management-employee participation in problem solving and cooperative manufacturing.

2   Guidance

Workers in industry have the same motivation matrix as management has. Each worker seeks:

1. Material well-being
2. Prestige well-being
3. Physiological well-being (which includes spiritual well-being)

It is a search for both material and intangible things in their lives that motivates workers. In industry the worker seeks more than just a pay envelope every week or two. That is particularly true once the worker's material requirements have been met. Workers can be divided into several different groups in respect to motivation. Here let us consider the short-term worker and the long-term worker seeking a lifetime of employment.

The short-term employee will most often be working to purchase some commodity that he or she desires. Company loyalty, working conditions, etc. are therefore of less concern to the short-term worker. The long-term employee will see the workplace as an important part of his or her life and will seek a much broader range of benefits. We can categorize the more important things that motivate long-term workers as follows:

1. *A pleasant workplace.*   It is important to workers to be members of an organization that provides a work environment and fellow workers that together make the workplace desirable.

2. *An adequate level of pay.*   Workers expect to receive reasonable rates of pay for the work they do. They compare with fellow workers; and when they feel they are being taken advantage of, they will rebel against management.

3. *Security of employment.*   Workers want to feel they are contributing to their work security. In a world of turmoil, most workers seek security of employment above most other things. That is why the EPP programs are proving to be so successful.

4. *Pride of contribution.*   Workers like to gain prestige among fellow workers when they make a suggestion or some other contribution that is to the advantage of the company and adds to their and their fellow workers' security.

5. *Respect by management and fellow workers.*   Workers have usu-

ally put a great deal of personal effort into their educations in and out of the workplace. They overcome the same difficulties as management in getting to work each day. They are trying to do the right thing; and whereas a kind word or a word of praise will evoke magnificent efforts, the slightest evidence of dominance by management will cause rebellion and reduce effort.

6. *A feeling of belonging.*   A worker needs to feel that he or she is a wanted member of the work team. It is important to the worker to be greeted pleasantly and to be encouraged by use of words that are designed to motivate rather than degrade and criticize. Even when the employee accidentally does something wrong, it is better for the business if the manager encourages rather than criticizes.

2.1   Introducing EPP into a company.   When a program of employee participation (EP) is introduced to a company for the first time, great care should be used in the planning. Specific effort should be made to incorporate in the program each of the following characteristics to an appropriate degree:

1. Training for members of management who will participate on each team and especially those serving as mentors

2. Specialized training for the facilitator, moderator, or coordinator assigned to program the team and keep it working on relevant problems

3. Inclusion of a cross section of workers and management staff who are from areas familiar with the problems to be solved

4. Inclusion of all workers and management in some area of the management-employee participation teams

5. Extension of the employee participation program to all company locations and to all areas of each such location

In general terms, what is sought in this new and expanding partic-ipation of workers in the management of company activities is very far-ranging indeed. When F. W. Taylor worked in a foundry, the sep-aration between skilled tradesmen and the average worker with little or no education was very great. That gap has been closed; and in some countries such as Japan and the United States, many workers have college or university degrees.

We can call the new approach by the name "team management," be-cause both managers and workers are given the opportunity to con-tribute to the success of the activity. We recognize in team manage-ment one of the managerial styles from the recent past rising to the top. Autocratic management is replaced by worker loyalty, enthusiasm, understanding, and motivation on a more durable basis.

Threats, fear, deprivation of privileges, and similar negative motivators of the past must be replaced by counseling, reeducation, imaginative transfer policies, and a readjusted reward system for workers in industry. If management is to be successful in introducing the highly productive new team management style in industry, with workers also being members of the team, the general approach set forth in this procedure is recommended.

It is strongly urged that companies seeking to implement the employee participation program style of management for the first time secure the services of a consulting agency specially trained in implementing this type of managerial change. Most company managements in western countries would not have the skills and planning experience necessary in this essentially human relations area.

PART B.   PROCEDURE

Employee Participation Program Quality System

1   Scope

This procedure defines the requirements of the company in respect to a comprehensive employee participation program (EPP) that shall be adopted, implemented, and operated within the company at its various locations.

2 Application

Employee participation programs shall be introduced and used at all business locations of the company in accordance with a planned program as set forth in this procedure. When the company engages in project work, EPPs shall be used and they shall involve members of each of the several participating organizations who can constructively contribute to the solution of quality problems. This shall be made a condition of the contract and subcontracts.

A particular effort shall be made to include members of union leadership on EPP teams when such inclusion can materially contribute to the depolarization of work situations and the achievement of higher quality and productivity. All employees and managers shall be included in EPP activities at the appropriate times and for each work location.

3 Definitions

brain- storming	A method of problem solution identification in which a group of people who have diverse backgrounds and educations and are believed to have capabilities related to the problem are assembled in a room with a moderator and a recorder. The problem is presented, and a time limit, typically 30 minutes, is set. The members of the group then individually and synergistically seek to state as many solutions as possible to the problem without regard to the practicality of each solution offered.
quality circles	A program in which teams of people, usually consisting of members from the management and workers involved with a defined area of work, meet regularly for the purpose of improving all aspects of the company's operations which now or in the future may impact on the team's or company's activities. The establishment of such a team implies that it has the full support of senior management and that its recommendations will be considered and acted upon.
industrial democracy	The overall program of industrial relations which promotes employee participation throughout the entire activities of industry in a nation. Because of differences in resolution of industrial relations matters, the industrial democracy will vary from nation to nation.

employee participation	The program of activities in which employees take part in any or all of the activities of the company for which they work. The activities range from highly restricted participation in suggestion programs to full self-determination of duties, work rewards, and in some cases partial or full ownership of the company.

For other terms used in this procedure and their definitions see Sec. VII, Chap. 1, of *Quality Control Systems.* *

4 Requirements

4.1 The strategy. The introduction and use of an employee participation program is a total strategy for the company. It shall include everyone who is paid by the company for work performed as an employee of the company in any capacity. The EPP shall be used to develop people through training and personal initiatives and focus their energies and thoughts on helping themselves through their contributions toward making their company a better place to work. The strategy shall be to:

1. Identify and specify the challenges open to solution by the EPP approach.
2. Construct and publicize the strategy for meeting the challenges.
3. Detail the structure of the EPP and its sequence of events.
4. Plan for periodic surveys of EPP activities.
5. Refine the EPP to ensure its continuity and effectiveness.

4.1.1 Identifying and specifying the challenges. The challenges are to:

1. Develop for each employee the image of the company as a family of people whose loyalty to and identification with the company is stronger than the identification with and loyalty to individual work areas or suborganizations of the company. (Each employee must see his or her personal family as included within the loyalty group.)
2. Involve employees in defining and developing an understanding of personal ownership of the values and vision necessary for success of the company.
3. Develop in each employee a full appreciation of the importance

---

*James R. Taylor, *Quality Control Systems: Procedures for Planning Quality Programs,* McGraw-Hill, New York, 1989.

of customers and their satisfaction to the future well-being of the company and all its employees.

4. Convince all employees that they will be provided the opportunity to make their maximum contribution to building the company by meeting the challenges and obtaining for each the maximum benefit when their work contributes to success.

5. Improve the role, scope, and importance of training in the company and enhance the development activities of the company with particular emphasis on customer satisfaction and company development.

6. Involve the union(s) representing the company's employees in the participation program when defining the values and vision for the future and developing the commitment to achieve them.

7. Develop among the company's employees and managers at all levels a corporate understanding of the role of profit and market share necessary to the success of the company and imbue each with a profit-for-value-of-service and quality-of-product culture.

8. Develop a corporate family imbued with an appreciation of the customer's needs for timeliness and quality of service and product.

9. Substantially enhance the perception, efficiency, and effectiveness of management of the company through employee activities and employee participation.

10. Keep employees at all levels well informed and ensure that the communications are dealt with at least as effectively as are matters concerning production of products or provision of services.

11. Enhance, through advertising and actual quality of output, customer's perceptions of the excellent value for money obtainable in products and services from the company.

12. Ensure that employees are given recognition for their contributions throughout the company and that such recognition of and by employees and managers of the company is a fundamental corporate objective integrated into the company's way of doing business.

13. Develop employee commitment to all areas of corporate activity through providing a working environment characterized by trust, respect, and corporate caring for employees.

14. Encourage innovation and entrepreneurship within the corporate goals and objectives and foster a positive and objective at-

titude for success as a team on the part of all corporate family members.

15. Foster and support research, design, and development in all areas in which they can improve the strength, posture, and position of the company in the marketplace.

4.1.2 Other industrial experiences. Experience in western industry has shown that corporations which have strong corporate cultures, with which their employees are imbued and which are aligned to their overall corporate purposes, are able to consistently achieve a distinct competitive advantage in times of change. All top-performing companies recognize their human assets as vital to their success and treat those assets accordingly.

Several university-connected leaders have made major headway in breaking down the barriers so common throughout industry. Chasms that would normally impede day-to-day industrial activities have been bridged to clear ways for improved communications and the more effective carrying out of work. Those areas and others of a similar nature provide the most important auspices for quality and productivity improvements. Many of the more successful corporations have used employee participation to improve their market strengths.

It shall be the strategy of the company to make maximum use of experiences gained in other industrial companies in the implementation of employee participation programs.

4.1.3 Leading up to employee participation. The following general steps shall be followed in introducing employee participation programs in the company for its different form of management.

4.1.3.1. Prepare an employee questionnaire. This questionnaire shall seek to discover the viewpoints and ideas of a broad cross section of the company's employees on such matters as their:

- Views of the company as a place to work
- Concept of their relationships to the company management
- Feelings of security gained from working in the company
- Perceptions of values gained from the workplace
- Perceptions of improvements that would enhance their working lives
- Views on the form the EPP should take
- Views on the extent of a need for reshaping the corporate internal relationships and loyalties (i.e., culture)

4.1.3.2. Analyze the answers to the employee questionnaire (4.1.3.1) and provide the results of the analysis to all employees.

4.1.3.3. Circularize all employees on the upcoming EPP, its importance as seen by them and their coworkers, and some ideas of how it can affect their working lives.

4.1.3.4. Have local area managers identify the members from their organizations who will participate in the first EPP team meetings. Collect the names and, in collaboration with the area supervisors, schedule meetings for each area. (Ideally, team sizes should be between 5 and 15 members, and the first teams should consist of employees who have the most enthusiasm for the program or have a consistently objective outlook.)

4.1.3.5. From the introductory sessions collect the best ideas on:

- How to build the company in the future
- How to develop corporate culture growth with EPPs
- How to build quality and productivity through EPP activities

4.1.3.6. Select the best ideas from each department's EPP team meetings and the departmental forum. Forward them to the management oversight forum for review and expenditure approval. The selected ideas become starting-point ideas which will be used as the kickoff action items.

4.1.3.7. Publish the ideas chosen as the kickoff ideas and give recognition to the committees and team members who generated them. Solicit total employee participation in the EPP and ensure that all employees are invited to participate in one of the future teams and workshops.

4.2   Employee participation

4.2.1   EPP operation. The broad operation of the EPP is as shown in Fig. 1.1. There it may be seen that a management oversight forum is to be established for the EPP. This forum consists of the senior heads of the departments of the company; there is one management oversight forum for each business or plant location.

Operating under the oversight forum is a departmental forum for each department in a division. This second-level forum is made up of the departmental head and his senior managers. From them a depart-

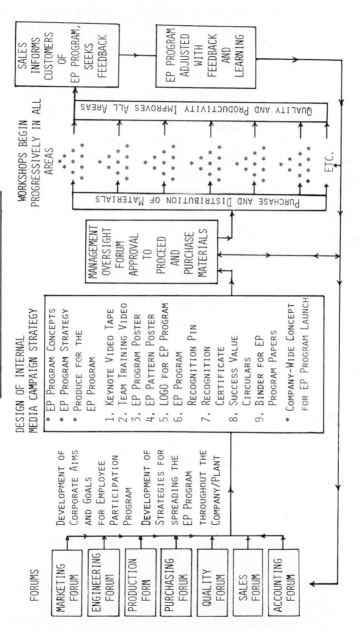

Figure 1.1 Organization chart for EPP teams in a manufacturing company division.

mental monitor is chosen for each of the department teams to be established. For each department, there shall be sufficient numbers of teams to include all employees of the company in that department. The teams consist of the mentor, a facilitator, and a cross section of employees and supervisory staff from work areas related to the types of problems on which they will be expected to work.

The teams should remain more or less constant in composition for many meetings so they can see the total working of their areas and synergistically contribute their maximum input to the solution of problems in the area as well as growth of the area. It is not desirable to move team members en masse from one work area to another, but it is appropriate to transfer individual team members from one team to another so as to take maximum advantage of any special skills and make synergistic interactions possible.

It will be necessary to make arrangements for keeping the team mentors well informed and up to date on the decisions of higher management as well as problems being worked on in peripheral and related areas of activity. That is necessary in order to make the mentors' guidance more effective and prevent duplicate or unauthorized activities. It shall be a policy of the company that circulation of team decisions and publication of decisions reached by the management oversight forum shall be regularly carried out so mentors are kept informed. It may be found that an intracompany publication specially compiled for this purpose will be the best means of ensuring awareness of those who are responsible for the progress of the EPP.

Figure 1.1 shows the structure of an EPP for a typical manufacturing company producing a range of products. A similar program structure following the general company structure would be found effective for the EPP in either a services company or a company whose principal work is on project-type contracts. As can be seen in Fig. 1.1, each company department (the largest organizational subdivision at the site) has a departmental forum made up of its departmental manager and other senior managers. In that way the departmental manager acts as the link with the management oversight forum headed by the company's or plant's chief executive officer. (*Note:* Large companies are usually divided into several divisions, one for each business site or location. Within those divisions the companies are further subdivided, usually into departments and lesser components.)

As shown in Fig. 1.1, the departmental forum provides a departmental mentor for each of the several facilitator-coordinated committees that may be established within a large company or plant site. A facilitator and a mentor from the departmental forum are assigned to participate in the meetings of each employee participation team. At plants where there are large numbers of employees, a departmental forum mentor may have to participate in the meetings of more than one team. It is important that the workers see direct participation with the more senior company managers through the team process, and each such team shall contain representation of direct in-line employee supervision to prevent bypassing those people when more senior management members are involved.

Figure 1.1 shows the general information flow lines within the company's manufacturing plants when the plants are operating EPPs. Since the work carried out by the EPP committees is the same as the work with which the company management and employees are routinely concerned, the information flow will not be at variance with the ongoing operation of the company. Some additional communication that is specially attuned to the EPP will be needed, but the major difference will be that, through the EPP activities, the skills and knowledge of the employees will be drawn upon to manage the ongoing work programs. The employees will see themselves as being more a part of the company and able to contribute in concrete ways toward their future security. This will build greater company loyalty, higher morale, and pride of membership in the company family.

4.2.2   Team activities: their extent.   The concept of EP action teams is developed to provide for early action as the EPP is getting underway in the event that introduction and establishment of the program identifies either (1) a particular opportunity to introduce or make some drastic or major change or constructive contribution to the company's output or welfare or (2) a particular obstacle needing early removal to ensure that the EPP successfully emerges.

The activities of action teams are confined to building and implementing the EPP so that it involves all employees and managers of the company. The teams take responsibility for tasks for which solutions can be achieved within 6 months when the importance of reaching solutions is a major consideration. At least one action team shall be established for each department at each plant of the company, and a forum shall be established for the company. The number of such teams within a department shall be determined by the volume and variety of short-term major problems which need solution.

The action team consists of the head of the department or other organizational component concerned and members of middle management and more senior employees who are mature and able to grasp the importance of the EPP concept to the company. Action team members shall participate on other EPP teams with employees at all levels.

When an EPP team that is under the oversight of a mentor and is coordinated by a facilitator has identified a problem that is in need of solution and the problem lies within the scope of activity of that team, the action team shall merge with the EPP team in working on the problem and reaching a solution. In no case shall the action team simply take away the problem first identified by an EPP team and work on it apart from the EPP team.

4.2.2.1   EP program team, action team, and customer analogy.   The relations between the activities of the action teams, the EPP teams, and the customers of the company can best be seen in terms of an analogy with primary industry. The action teams exist to clear away the large trees and rocks; the EPP teams exist to till the land, sow the seed, and cultivate the crops; and the customers exist to share the harvest of improved quality and productivity. The employees and managers of the company share in the harvest through improved quality of working life and greater job security in the future.

4.2.2.2   Action teams and their responsibilities

1. The corporate or division action team:

- *Upgrades internal company communications of all types.*   Ensures that staff members at all levels are effectively inducted into the EPP.

2. The departmental action team:

- *Identifies, in conjunction with EPP teams, problems of major importance with short-term solutions.*   Develops the internal/external presentation skills improvement program for managers and supervisors.

- *Identifies opportunities to eliminate unnecessary or wasteful operations and develops appropriate solutions.*   Develops designed experimental models for the successful launch of new products, acquisition of new business, or commissioning of new works.

- *Implements internal/external communications media and methods identified and needed to run the EPP.*   Develops a program to orient employees to business values and an understanding of the role of profit.

- *Develops departmental and company forum recognition processes for distinctive contributors to the success of the EPP.*   Develops programs and methods which engender and enhance employee loyalty to the company.

- *Develops communications with customers and enhances customer awareness of the EPP benefits.*

4.2.2.3 Action team ongoing responsibilities. As can be seen from the above tasks, the duties of the action teams within the company are of great importance: They identify needs which have early importance in the successful introduction and operation of the EPP. Although the majority of the tasks should be attacked and satisfactorily achieved and be in continuing operation, there are some which will either be recurrent or will need further or ongoing nurture and guidance to ensure total success. It is therefore intrinsic to the action team concept that the workload will be particularly heavy early in the EPP but will become less onerous during the ongoing period of the program.

Of particular importance to the ongoing standby role of the action teams is the need to ensure that the financial aspects of the EPP are adequately provided for and accounted within the company's total fiscal activity. Since the action teams will always gain the immediate attention of senior management, it is appropriate that the teams should be responsible for keeping senior management aware of their activities and achievements and failures.

It shall be noted that the action team responsibilities listed in 4.2.2.2 are in two groups; certain of the actions fall more within one department than another. When that is true, it shall be the role of the departmental action teams, in conjunction with the overseeing management forum, to ensure that there is minimal duplication and that work assignments go to appropriate departments.

4.2.3 Internal team communications. Figure 1.2 provides a graphic example of the internal communications leading up to the establishment of the first EPP team workshops. The individual departmental forums shall develop the corporate aims and goals appropriate to each department for the EPP. These forums shall also develop and document the strategies for progressively extending the EPP throughout the company and each company plant location.

It will be necessary for the departmental forums, with action team participation, to develop the EPP concepts and strategy and to arrange the production of all necessary media and EPP identification and recognition material. It is the joint role of the departmental forums and the senior management forum to develop and communicate the company-wide concept for the EPP launch.

4.2.3.1 The internal media campaign strategy. The purpose of the internal media campaign (IMC) strategy is to create changes in the attitudes and behavior of the company's employees as necessary to create self-identification with and personal feelings of ownership of the EPP and the company. The aim of the IMC is to provide the company with

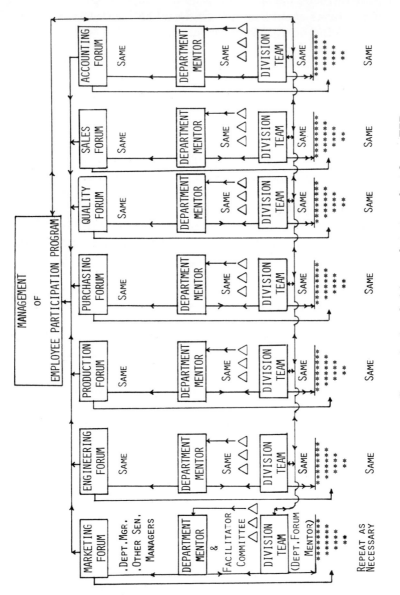

Figure 1.2 Communication, decision, and strategy chart for an EPP.

powerful communications tools which will foster the realization of the desired distinguishing character and future of the company.

The principal objectives of the IMC are to:

1. Build pride in self and in the company by contributions through work and membership on the team.
2. Provide a clear, convincing, and powerful picture of the distinguishing character and future desired for the company.
3. Provide all company employees and customers with evidence of positive company change.
4. Provide employees with both awareness and recognition of individual and group achievements.
5. Communicate to all employees and customers the nature, philosophy, and purpose of the EPP.

The EPP has a number of core values which are of prime importance and which must be transmitted to the employees through the company. Principal among them are:

- Customers always come first.
- Employees of the company make success possible.
- Business success builds customer confidence and security for the employees.

It shall be central to the IMC to imbue, in each employee and manager:

- A positive outlook
- A positive belief in the worth of the company family, including staff members and their families, customers, suppliers, and vendors
- A positive belief in the distinguishing character and future envisioned for the company
- A positive belief in the benefits derived from change
- A positive belief in the vital link between personal, team, and corporate pride and personal productivity
- A positive belief in the vital link between corporate success and individual success within the company
- A positive belief in the link between friendliness and helpfulness on the one hand and good customer relations on the other
- A positive belief in the vital link between the success of the com-

pany and customer satisfaction with the company's products, services, and works

- A positive belief in the link between personal pride and the performance of each employee and manager
- A positive belief that the contributions of each person employed by the company are important in the success of the company and its members
- A positive belief in the mutual best interest of employees and management working together and having respect for each other's roles and their concerted efforts on behalf of the company

4.2.3.2 Internal media campaign (IMC) functions. The internal media campaign has the following as its principal functions:

- It develops in the employees and managers a similar high degree of ownership of the distinguishing character of the company.
- It provides communications that can be related to by employees of the company at all levels and in all work areas independent of social background, economic background, geographic location, and company operational differences.
- It possesses the flexibility to act as the communicator of the overall EPP thrust.
- It communicates the urgency and reality of the actual changes taking place and maintains an ongoing awareness of changes as they are occurring.

In summary, the strategy of the IMC is to take the necessary sequence of steps to get the EPP up and running with the necessary ongoing growth of positive thinking and affirmative beliefs essential to eventual overall program success. Each of the following steps shall be taken:

1. Achieve positive staff acceptance of the beliefs, values, and behaviors of the EPP.
2. Launch the EPP with its concepts and purposes.
3. Design, procure, and establish the internal media campaign.
4. Introduce and establish early the achievement and recognition awards for employees and announce the awards to other employees.
5. As shown in Fig. 1.2, communicate the benefits of the EPP to cus-

tomers via the sales staff and to the company's vendors via the purchasing staff.

4.2.4 Launching the employee participation teams.

As shown in Fig. 1.2, the various EPP team workshops are to begin progressively in each department and eventually involve all employees and managers. The timing of the actual launch depends on education and supplies.

Unless specifically designated otherwise by the senior management forum, all workshops shall be held during normal working hours. It will be necessary to reschedule all work activities so that the EPP workshop activities become a natural ongoing part of the company production effort. The actual times when workshop meetings are held and the availability of meeting space or rooms will depend to a large extent on what has been made available. It may be necessary to alter area layouts to provide for workshop activities. Such an expenditure will be part of the normal budgeting and implementation program, but sympathetic consideration shall be given to requests for urgent needs, when they are identified, in order to get the EPP up and running.

4.2.4.1 Communications in the launch.

The launch of the EPP shall take place by senior managers briefing the middle-level managers who report directly to them, the managers briefing supervisors who report to them, the supervisors briefing staff members, and so on down the ladder until all company staff are informed. A time limit of 2 months shall be imposed on the process so that not longer than 2 months elapses between the first and last briefings. No departure from the vertical communication chain shall take place, so that all staff will see the introduction of the EPP as an orderly evolution from the past.

Note. In action team and EPP workshop meetings, two, three, or more levels of management may take part, but communications shall continue along the normal organizational channels of the company except when altered by the management forum's need to implement, measure, and make decisions concerning the EPP.

4.2.5 Forums for senior and key managers.

It can be expected that the employment of a consulting agency to assist in the introduction of the EPP will impact to the greatest degree, initially, on the senior and key managers of the company. That is because it is with those managers that the consultants will work directly in implanting their ideas and concepts. The general contribution of the consultants should fall in the area of assisting managers to accept, understand, and adopt the positive outlook toward employee participation in their decision-making processes and in wording and compiling communications documents, award certificates, and other media forms at which they may be specialists.

A special part of the senior management forum shall be concerned with the staff members who work in or directly support the senior management offices. These staff members shall be included in the EPP and shall, when appropriate, participate in EPP team workshops concerning their areas of work.

Areas of a workshop nature of particular concern to be considered by and acted upon by the senior management forum are:

1. Review of general policies for the company and the publication and promulgation of those to all staff members.

2. Review of general operating procedures emanating from the general policies with a view to adapting them to operation within the sphere of the EPP activities.

It shall be a responsibility of the headquarters EPP workshops that all matters of budgeting, finances, expenditure authorizations, EPP material procurement, etc., shall be reviewed with respect to their appropriateness, adequacy, timeliness, and allowance within the current fiscal budgetary status of the company. The headquarters EPP workshops falling within the EPP shall ensure that communications from action teams are received and promptly referred to the appropriate senior managers for action. When appropriate, they shall be added to the agenda of senior management forums for review and consideration.

All changes resulting from EPP workshops shall be introduced and shall progress through existing structures and communication channels, with new channels being opened only when they are found to have thorough justification. Links shall be established between the various headquarters workshops and their mentors and facilitators so that awareness of interdependent activities will develop and remain current at all times.

A special emphasis shall be given to developing the corporate ethos with motivation and commitment among the sales staff. To support it, there shall exist a senior key management forum to oversee the sales activities and workshops. All sales staff of the company shall be imbued with the vision, team spirit, and pride of membership in the company necessary to achieve the optimum result. Effective communication links shall exist with operating areas of the company.

4.2.6 Planning expanded employee involvement. Detailed planning shall be carried out on a plant-by-plant and a department-by-department basis for the company. The plans shall develop criteria for involvement of all staff in the EPP. Special plans shall be made for staff members who indicate an initial unwillingness to participate. Although participation is on a voluntary basis, personnel who are unwilling to participate are often encountered upon the introduction of an EPP. They represent impediments that must be overcome. It will be necessary to seek out the reasons for these impediments and to devise ways of either removing them or resolving their causes. These areas shall be a matter of special attention at the senior management forums.

Although it is ultimately desirable that all company staff members take part in the EPP, initial team composition and criteria shall be planned to better ensure the success of the program. Accordingly, the following major aspects shall apply:

1. Each initial team shall consist of approximately 60 percent staff and 40 percent managers and supervisors.

2. Each initial team shall consist of a cross-functional mix of staff and managers and supervisors who are chosen for their positive outlook and are key individuals in influencing opinions in their areas.

3. The criteria for team composition and meetings shall be cost-effective.

4. Each team shall be overseen and controlled by a mentor from the senior management forum.

5. Each team shall have a facilitator who shall call meetings, guide the activities at meetings, and carry out all the other duties involved in keeping the meetings productive and ongoing.

All EP action teams, including initial EPP teams, shall make reports to the senior management forum for review and action as necessary.

4.2.7 Start of the long-term program. Following the initial planning and formation of the forums, EP action teams, and initial EPP team workshops, it is desirable to implement a controlled time period program during which some measure of achievement and degree of success can be had. At the beginning of some definite time period, the degree of implementation of the internal media campaign and the known state of the EPP implementation shall be used as a starting point of a 1-year measurement period. In addition to knowing the point of starting the 1-year measurement interval, it shall be determined what accomplishments will be aimed at during the 12 months. They shall derive from the findings of the senior management forum and the departmental forums. The initial action team projects shall normally be completed before the end of the 1-year measurement interval.

The aim of the 12-month corporate EP effort shall be to make significant, measurable, and visible progress toward improving quality, productivity, and profitability while enhancing pride and positive outlook of employees.

Specific objectives at the corporate level for the 12 months shall be to:

1. Build a distinguishing character for the company while creating an ongoing awareness by employees, vendors, and customers of the benefits to each from this evolving character of the company.
2. Progressively enable participation by staff members, supervisors, and managers at all levels to participate in and contribute to the EPP.
3. Realign organizational structures, systems, functions, and processes of work for a better fit with the emerging distinguishing company character.
4. Establish employee identification with the company as the family of which each is a member and thereby engender company loyalty higher than to local areas.
5. Establish supplier and customer identification with the accomplishment of the distinguishing company character and show how each contributes and will benefit.
6. Build esprit de corps among the corporate family members, each having developed:
   a. Pride in the company
   b. Pride in the team
   c. Pride in self
   d. Pride in individual contributions

4.2.7.1 The aim and objectives for employees during the 12 months. The aim of employees shall be to develop and optimize their levels of success and well-being derived from their work in conjunction with their capacity to achieve results both at work and away from work. It is a particular responsibility of managers and supervisors to establish climates which will foster employee objectives.

The objectives of employees shall be to:

1. Develop their interpersonal relationships for interacting with other people productively and effectively over a range of positive

and negative situations so as to accomplish tasks and achieve results.

2. Develop personal skills and tools (including thought) to help in creating opportunities, overcoming obstacles, and achieving results.

3. Develop the ability to set and achieve realistic goals.

4. Learn the skills necessary to develop positive, helpful, and supportive attitudes in handling people, situations, and circumstances.

5. Develop and enhance personal tools such as lateral thinking, creative option-seeking, and possibility analysis.

6. Increase each employee's level of self-esteem, motivation, energy, and well-being and thereby enhance each one's capacity to handle stressful situations, tension, and difficulties while working toward a better future.

7. Work toward developing each employee's capacity for achieving his or her individual goals and aspirations.

8. Provide recognition for deserving individuals and groups so employees can have a feeling of pride through the success of others.

9. Enable employees to be involved in structural, value, work, judgment, and other realignments brought about by EPP activities.

4.2.8 Increasing the scope of employee participation. A particular part of the EPP shall consist of identifying special staff areas needing unique attention and approaches to ensure success. The unique features and characteristics of these areas shall be identified and factored into the EPP planning, design, and implementation. Such unique areas may be identified as the sales area, militant union members, areas of manual labor, etc. Each such area shall be studied, and a plan for including its members in the EPP activities shall be devised.

Special care shall be taken to ensure that the sales workforce is provided with all necessary support to enable it to develop the highest ethos and motivation for success; for on that the corporate success will depend to a very large degree. Specialized action teams shall work out of the sales areas to provide training and opportunity for each member of the sales staff. Any areas of staff or individual members of staff who are unable to adopt a positive attitude shall be assessed in respect to their individual needs, and those needs shall be specific items of consideration for the industrial relations department, personnel department (or, if combined, the human relations department). Efforts shall be made to develop the positive attitudes and ethos needed in all staff members to ensure success of the EPP and the business.

4.2.9   EPP training and development.   Corporate training staff shall be involved from the outset in the planning of the EPP to ensure that appropriate staff-training facilities and opportunities are factored into the plans to ensure their successful achievement. In this aspect of the program the gains to be made by the training staff as well as from their contributions shall be considered. The EPP's positive and objective needs and methods will identify strategy concerning elements such as:

- The identification and selection of special staff-training members possessing unique skills required by the EPP
- Assignment of the special staff-training personnel to the EPP team and workshop activities in which their skills are most useful
- Ongoing maintenance of liaisons between staff training and the continuing EPP activities

4.2.10   Review of staff involvement and commitment.   Following the 12-month measurement period of the EPP, and for successive measurement periods, it will be necessary to develop measurement points and methods by which to:

- Assess staff attitudes and their changes resulting from participation in the EPP.
- Assess the effects on customer and supplier perceptions made by the change in the corporate ethos.
- Assess the improvement in quality, productivity, and profit stemming from the EPP.
- Identify any areas or activities in which special attention is needed because of the ongoing program.

Appropriate points of measurement and methods of measurement shall be identified and incorporated in the EPP to enable the above to be carried out.

5   Annual Survey of EPP Activities

An annual survey of the ongoing EPP activities shall be carried out to provide corporate management with data with which to retune the program and identify new or developed areas of need and opportunity.

When the latter are identified, they shall be given early attention to ensure that a lapse in attitudes is not permitted and that ongoing programs of recognition, reward, and promotion are adhered to in the operation of the company.

6 Refinement of the EPP

It shall be the responsibility of the senior management forum to meet with sufficient regularity to review ongoing programs, assess and recommend change, and measure and achieve profit margins acceptable to shareholders and to the employees and managers of the company while operating to the highest aspirations of the new company ethos.

2

Manufacturing Quality Cost System

PART A. REVIEW AND GUIDANCE

1 Review

The expenditure of money in manufacturing industry can be divided into two categories from the viewpoint of the types of products and related activities. One category comprises modifications and improvements made to products currently being produced; the second category comprises products which have not before been manufactured by the company. The first is called cost-optimization expenditure; the second is called income-expansion expenditure. It is usually desirable to keep the financing and costing of the two activities separated in order to manage each one effectively.

Although we shall, in this procedure, discuss quality costing as that science relates to both the design phase and the production phase of the manufacturing effort, we shall here principally be addressing the control of quality costs during the production phase. Costs incurred during the production phase can be divided into two categories called processing costs and quality costs. The control of processing costs has been a constant aim of management in industry since the beginning of modern manufacturing industry early in the twentieth century. In fact, the science of accounting for business developed in parallel with, and for the purpose of, managing the costs of doing business. Cost ac-

Acknowledgment and appreciation are extended to the Standards Association of Australia for permission to follow the format of its standard AS-2561-1982 in the preparation of a procedure by which to control quality costs.

counting developed primarily for the purpose of controlling the costs of processing in manufacturing industry. Accordingly, it has been found that the structure of cost accounting taught in universities and colleges around the world has been specifically designed to segregate the individual cost centers in processing activities for visibility and control.

When, in the latter half of the twentieth century, quality costing came into prominence, it was necessary to restructure the cost accounting practices in order to identify, extract, and manage quality costs. Most textbooks on accounting practices in use in the late 1980s still do not provide guidance for quality cost accounting. When the modern company seeks to implement quality science from a cost control viewpoint, it is often found necessary to restructure the cost accounting activity of the manufacturing company before control of quality costs can be implemented.

Manufacturing industry has as its goal the design and production of products which will have the design characteristics and production quality needed to satisfy customers throughout the lifetime of the products. Products have those attributes within an overall economic system that will suit the customer's ideas of quality for a reasonable price and provide the manufacturer with an acceptable profit. The manufacturer who can successfully control all the costs and adjust them so as to maximize quality and profit will, for a given product design, prove more successful in the business world.

In the traditional methods of accounting, costs are grouped under one or the other of two general headings: capital costs and operating costs. The exact division between the two is heavily influenced by tax laws in the country of manufacture. Generally, however, long-life items, such as buildings and major general-use equipment, come under capital costs and short-life items, such as tools and/or equipment specifically adapted to making one kind of product and the general costs of day-to-day operations, make up the operating costs. Salaries and wages are often the largest single operating cost item in labor-intensive operations.

2 Guidance

For balancing, optimization, and control purposes, quality costs have been divided among three areas of activity related to production. For the purposes of this procedure we may consider that the production phase begins following the acceptance of the design prototype and freeze of the design. Design quality costs will already have been incurred in reaching an acceptable manufacturable design. The three areas of production quality cost activity are called prevention, appraisal, and failure. The latter area is further subdivided into internal failure and external failure. Failure cost subdivisions are separated at the point where ownership is transferred from the manufacturer to the customer (who may be a wholesaler, retailer, or end user).

There is no limit to the size of production activity which can benefit from the use of quality cost control in addition to processing cost control, nor is there a limit to the type of production activity which will benefit. All companies who process raw materials into finished goods, assemble parts into finished systems, or, through project activity, assemble systems into operational utilities of major proportions will be able to use the principles of quality cost control to their profitable advantage. In project companies, however, as well as in services companies, there will have to be some adaptation of the standard presentation set forth in this procedure to best fit the production programs.

It will be necessary for the quality organization to work with the accounting organization to separate quality costs from processing costs. The former must be collected, recorded, analyzed, and reported separately from processing costs. The accounting organization will not normally have separated costs in the way set forth in this procedure. It will be necessary for the quality manager and the accounting manager to work closely in separating processing and quality costs, recording each, and analyzing and reporting these costs of doing business. It is a principal responsibility of the quality manager to coordinate the adjustment of quality costs by other organizations so that optimum cost distribution and minimum total cost of operation are achieved in respect to quality activities.

When quality costs are reported it will be necessary to constantly review the use of various bases for reporting and to adjust them to maintain true relevance to the ongoing production activities. Activities change with time and the varying degrees of maturity of certain related company functions. For example, cost reporting on a basis of direct labor dollar expenditure will be changed when new automated machinery is installed in the plant and the number of process operators in that area changes.

By following the general methods and meeting the specific requirements of this procedure, it will be possible to design, implement, and apply effective quality cost control to most company activities.

PART B.   PROCEDURE

Manufacturing Quality Cost System

1 Scope

This procedure defines the requirements of the company in respect to the identification, collection, recording, analysis, and use of costing information for the purposes of adjusting quality costs and minimizing total manufacturing costs.

2 Application

This procedure shall apply throughout the company and shall be called up in relevant purchase orders and contracts with vendors and subcontractors, in which the use of quality costing principles can provide for a more economically produced product or acceptable quality.

3 Definitions

The terms used in this procedure shall be interpreted in accordance with the definitions given in "Glossary of Terms Used in Quality and Reliability," Sec. VII, Chap. 1 of *Quality Control Systems*,* unless stipulated otherwise in a contract or purchase order. Terms specifically related to the subjects of this procedure are discussed in the following articles.

3.1 **Process operating costs.** All the costs, other than capital costs and quality operating costs, incurred in producing the product, service, or project are called process operating costs. They are divided into:

1. *Direct labor costs.* Wages paid to any persons who perform a process operation on product material or processes. These costs are recorded by accounting personnel according to specific job orders.

2. *Direct material costs.* The costs of all materials that are intended to become parts of the end product. These costs are re-

---

*James R. Taylor, *Quality Control Systems: Procedures for Planning Quality Programs,* McGraw-Hill, New York, 1989.

corded by accounting personnel according to specific work orders or cost centers from invoices, requisitions, etc.

3. *Indirect processing costs.* All costs which are not directly identifiable with specific work orders but which are incurred in the general operation of the processing activities. They are also called overhead or burden, and they are further subdivided by accounting as follows:

- *Indirect labor.* All labor, other than labor associated with the quality function, which is not directly applied to the production of the product

- *Indirect material.* All material used in production that is not intended to become a part of the product

- *Indirect expense.* All costs of operating the factory which cannot be correctly applied as indirect labor or material costs

3.2 Quality operating costs. All costs, other than capital costs and process operating costs, necessary to produce the product with a given quality.

Note. Quality cost is the difference between the actual cost to a company of making and selling products and the cost which would exist if there were no failure, and no possibility of failure, of the product to conform to the specifications during manufacture and use.

The quality operating costs are comprised of prevention, appraisal, and failure costs as defined below:

1. *Prevention costs.* The costs incurred in planning, documenting, implementing, and maintaining the quality system, including quality assurance of vendor or subcontractor supplies, necessary to ensure product conformance to quality requirements.
2. *Appraisal costs.* The costs incurred in performing measurements and audits on designs, products, components, and materials in order to establish the degree of conformance with quality requirements.
3. *Failure costs.* Costs as defined in two subcategories:
   a. *Internal failure costs.* Costs that arise as a result of products, components, or materials failing to conform to quality requirements prior to transfer of ownership to the customer
   b. *External failure costs.* Costs incurred when products, components, or materials fail to conform to quality requirements after transfer of ownership to the customer

4   Referenced Documents

"Glossary of Terms Used in Quality and Reliability," Sec. VII, Chap. 1 of *Quality Control Systems.*

5   Cost Identification

5.1   Introduction

5.1.1. In the manufacturing industry, several different kinds of costs are incurred in undertaking and carrying on business. On a gross scale they divide into design costs, production costs, and marketing costs. The production costs further subdivide into process costs and quality costs. Each of the process and quality cost areas further subdivide into capital and operating costs.

5.1.2. For accounting purposes, in both process costs and quality costs, the capital portion further subdivides into three areas: depreciation costs, interest costs, and opportunity costs. Depreciation costs of plant and buildings are readily understood accounting cost cells. Similarly, interest costs on money borrowed, invested, and used for manufacturing are normal areas of expenditure and accounting. Opportunity budgets reflect the nearness of any new product production or major improvements and the magnitude of effort by the relevant cost center for those activities. Early in new product activities, marketing, design, and sales carry larger opportunity budgets. Then, as the production schedule is planned, the opportunity budget will decrease and the operating budget will increase to handle the new effort.

5.1.3. The operating costs of processing subdivide into direct labor, direct material, and indirect cost. Indirect cost further subdivides into labor, material, and expense. In certain companies other names may be used for the same categories of expense incurred in doing business. The effect is the same, however, and should not alter the task of separating quality costs from process costs.

5.1.4. Some operations involve both quality cost and processing cost. For example, a production engineer may plan both the processing station and the inspection gauges with which the process worker ascertains the success or failure of the process operation on the part or material. Each of these, the engineer and the process worker, is doing part quality work and part process work, and it is the responsibility of the quality planner to determine which part of the cost incurred for the entire activity is to be charged to each area. It will be found that there are people throughout all manufacturing operations who usually expend process-type funds but at other times are required by their duties to expend quality funds. For convenience, one cost center may carry both types of budgeted monies, and the assignment to process or quality work is made in accordance with the actual time spent on each type of work. Those factors shall be kept in mind when expenditures are being classified as to the reasons for them.

5.2 Prevention costs. Prevention costs are incurred with a view to minimizing failure costs while optimizing appraisal costs. Whereas it is usually most appropriate to minimize failure quality costs, it is sometimes more appropriate to optimize appraisal costs with prevention costs in order to achieve lower overall quality costs. The usual categories of costs included in prevention are discussed in the following articles.

5.2.1 Quality planning. The activity of planning quality systems and translating product designs and customer quality requirements into measures that will ensure the attainment of the requisite product quality is called quality planning. This cost area includes the broad array of activities that collectively bring into being the total quality system and its individual plans unique to the various product types. It also includes the preparation and issue of the quality manual, quality procedures, and related quality instructions. Employees and managers from outside the quality organization may contribute to this category.

5.2.2 Assuring vendor and subcontractor quality. The initial assessment and subsequent audits and surveillance of vendor and subcontractor organizations and quality systems, methods, and processes are for the purpose of ensuring that the vendor and subcontractor are able to meet and maintain the required quality of work and supplies. This category also includes work done by the quality organization in respect to contracts and purchase orders, as well as reviews of tenders or bids.

5.2.3 Reviewing and verifying designs. This category includes work by the quality and other organizations in monitoring activities during design phases of products, as well as quality assurance work performed during development. It also includes work by the quality organization in design reviews, design verification activities, and tests and verifications carried out during product development for adjusting and verifying reliability and maintainability during the design phase.

5.2.4 Design and development of quality-measuring equipment. This category includes all costs of designing, developing, documenting, and other such work carried out in proving that the inspection and test equipment is suitable for the intended application of each item. (It does not include the capital cost of such equipment.)

5.2.5 Quality training. This category includes all costs associated with training employees to reach a given level of quality proficiency.

5.2.6 Process control engineering. This category includes engineering and management effort and the costs associated with the part of process control engineering needed to achieve defined quality goals.

5.2.7 Quality auditing. This category includes all work involving the appraisal, assessment, evaluation, and analysis associated with ascertaining the existence and capability of the quality system used by the company or by another company.

5.2.8 Acquisition, analysis, and reporting of quality data to prevent failure. This category includes the part of all work carried out in acquiring, analyzing, and reporting quality data which is defined as being for the purpose of preventing future product failure. (It is not to be confused with the acquisition, analysis, and reporting of inspection and test results for appraisal of existing quality.)

5.2.9 Quality improvement programs. This category includes nonconformity prevention programs, quality motivation programs, and such other activities as are directed toward achieving new levels of quality performance. It also includes design improvement of products in current production.

5.2.10 Planning of product recalls. This category includes the preparation and modification of plans for product recalls.

5.2.11 Product liability insurance. This category includes the premiums paid to minimize the cost of product recalls and liability litigation and damages. (See Art. 5.4.2, item 3 of this procedure.)

5.3 Appraisal costs. Appraisal costs are incurred for the purpose of ascertaining the degree of conformance of the product to quality requirements. (Costs of rework or reinspection following failure are not included in these costs.) The usual categories of appraisal costs are as follows:

5.3.1 Design appraisal. This category includes costs associated with the testing and evaluation of preproduction models for the purpose of verifying the conformance of the design to the quality requirements.

5.3.2 Receiving inspection. This category includes the costs of inspection and testing of incoming materials, components, and parts. It also includes the cost of inspection staff of the customer at the vendor's plant.

5.3.3 In-process inspection and testing by production and quality personnel. This category includes costs of inspection and testing work performed on any part of the product, components, or materials to and including the final testing of the completed product which were not included in receiving inspection. It includes the costs of carrying out product quality audits and product checking by production operators and supervision, as well as the costs of clerical support for those activities. (It does not include additional inspection and testing made necessary by failure or rejection because of inadequate quality.)

5.3.4 Materials consumed by inspection and test activities. This category includes all production materials, components, and equipment consumed or destroyed during the course of inspection and testing as a necessary adjunct of such work.

5.3.5 Analysis and reporting of inspection and test results. This category includes all the costs associated with establishing whether quality requirements have been met, and promulgating that information, when such work is carried out prior to the transfer of ownership to the customer.

5.3.6 Field performance testing. This category includes the costs of testing activities carried out at the customer's site prior to release of the product for customer acceptance.

5.3.7 Inspection and test equipment. This category includes the costs of depreciation of inspection and test equipment and support facilities, as well as the costs of setting up and providing for maintenance and calibration of such equipment.

5.3.8 Stored material evaluation. This category includes the costs of carrying out inspection and testing of stored materials, components, and equipment for the purpose of assuring that quality characteristics adequate for use are being maintained.

5.3.9 Approvals and endorsements by outside authorities. This category includes the costs of any approvals or endorsements required by authorities from outside the company, including, in the case of international trade, those in another country.

5.3.10 Quality records storage and standards. This category includes the costs incurred by the storage of quality control results, as well as the costs of providing and maintaining approved reference and calibration standards and certified reference materials.

5.4 Failure costs. Failure costs include all the costs incurred as a result of the product materials, components, or finished items failing to meet quality requirements at the first test or inspection following some product operation or upon product completion. These costs are divided into two groups for control purposes depending on whether they are incurred on the product prior to transfer of ownership to the customer or afterward.

5.4.1 Internal failure costs. This group includes the costs incurred because of inadequate quality discovered prior to transfer of ownership to the customer:

1. *Scrap.* This category includes the costs incurred from loss of parts, components, assemblies, materials, formulations, product, and items which fail to conform to quality requirements and which cannot be economically reworked. As well as the material costs, it includes the labor and labor overhead associated with the scrapped items. (Accidental or unavoidable material wastage is not included here.)

2. *Rework, repair, and replacement.* This category includes the costs incurred by replacing or rectifying product which fails to meet quality requirements. It includes the costs of both material rectification and any planning and procurement activities that make rectification possible.

3. *Reinspection and retesting.* This category includes the costs incurred as a result of subsequent testing of previously failed product items following rework, repair, or material review board action.

4. *Diagnosis of nonconformances.* This category includes the costs

incurred by analyzing failed items of product to determine their failure mechanisms so causes can be established and corrective action to overcome quality failures can be applied.

5. *Failed-item disposition determination.* This category includes the costs incurred by operation of a material review board, or other activity, established to review and make disposition determinations concerning failed items of product, components, or materials. It includes ancillary testing and evaluations necessary to reach disposition decisions, but it does not include reinspection or retesting following rectification of faults.

6. *Downtime.* This category includes the cost of idle facilities, equipment, and personnel resulting from failed product items, components, or materials. It also includes the costs of related disruptions to production schedules.

7. *Downgrading.* This category includes the costs incurred as a result of having to lower the price of nonconforming products and all losses therefrom which are traceable to quality.

5.4.2 External failure costs. This section includes the costs incurred because of inadequate quality discovered after transfer of ownership by the company to the customer:

1. *Complaints.* This category includes those costs incurred as a result of complaints received, investigations undertaken, and compensation or replacements provided as a result of confirmed inadequate quality.

2. *Warranty or guarantee claims.* This category includes the costs incurred by work, materials, and overhead associated with repair, replacement, or refunds arising from liability incurred under the terms of a warranty or guarantee.

3. *Product liability claims.* This category includes the costs incurred as a result of customer rejection of product because of quality deficiencies. The costs may be incurred by the customer sorting, reworking, returning, or otherwise transferring costs to the company as a result of poor quality. Costs of shipment, handling, rework, repair, or replacement incurred by the manufacturer are included.

4. *Concessions.* This category includes the costs incurred as a result of discounting product to a customer because of nonconforming characteristics accepted by the customer.

5. *Loss of goodwill and sales.* Loss of profit because of reduction or cessation of orders from prior market segments which are due to poor product quality are costs included in this category.

6. *Product recall costs*. This category includes all the costs incurred as a result of having to recall from the marketplace, or repair at site or dealer, some unsafe, hazardous, or suspect product. Replacement products as well as repairs carried out at the customer's premises are included in this category.

Note. This category will raise some difficulty with the ownership division of costs. In that case all product which has left the company-owned premises and come under control of other organizations shall be deemed to have transferred ownership.

6 Collecting and Recording Quality Cost Data

6.1 Collection procedures

6.1.1 Identifying quality cost elements. The first step in establishing a quality cost data collection system is to identify the quality cost elements. The elements used shall be those identified in Art. 5 of this procedure to the extent they apply. They shall be separated into prevention, appraisal, and failure segments of the total quality cost.

6.1.2 Correlating quality cost elements with accounting cost centers. The second step in establishing the quality cost data collection system involves identifying the quality cost elements with the respective accounting cost centers which have been, or will now need to be, established for control throughout the manufacturing company. Data for a given quality cost element may come from more than one cost center. For example, data in respect to product recall may come from every cost center in the company, whereas the data associated with the receiving inspection element may come only from the receiving inspection cost center.

It is necessary to be comprehensive in identifying the cost centers from which cost data for each element will come. It will also be necessary to communicate to each cost center how quality cost data are to be segregated from processing cost data and recorded separately or differently so accounting personnel can effectively record and report their accumulation. Work involved in this step shall include personnel from the accounting as well as the quality organizations.

6.1.3 Quality and accounting cooperation. The third step in establishing the quality cost data collection system involves close cooperative working relationships between the quality and accounting organizations to arrange the corporate cost accounting accounts for ease of recording and extracting quality cost data.

6.1.4 Involving cost center management. The fourth step will involve all cost center managers and supervisors receiving communications about and adjusting their individual recording of budgets, labor times, and other changes necessary to record and extract quality costs in accordance with the identified quality cost elements for which each is responsible. This is an extensive program when quality costing is being introduced into the manufacturing company, and it will involve considerable learning and adjustment of work done. As such, it will take time, and several accounting periods should be allowed before effective extraction of quality costs can be expected.

6.1.5 Quality cost reporting. The fifth step involves the accounting organization implementation of quality cost reporting on a periodic basis. The success of this stage will depend on the success of the program to introduce the recording of quality costs by the involved supervisors and managers throughout the manufacturing company. The identification of quality costs, as distinct from process costs, within the overall costed operations of the organization requires a detailed understanding of the operating and accounting procedures. The salary and overhead percentages of each worker's wages or salary which comprise quality costs shall be segregated from the portion comprising process costs and recorded and reported to accounting accordingly.

6.1.6 Non-cost-center quality costs. There are many quality costs which must be identified and costed separately from the cost centers involved, i.e., those with which the cost center manager does not become involved. They include such costs as overhead or burden, which are added on a percentage or other adopted basis by the cost accounting organization when the costs to be assigned to each cost center are computed.

At other times costs which would have been normal process costs become quality costs because of the reason for which they are incurred. Examples of this are product manufactured to replace failed products in the field or recalled from the marketplace for quality reasons.

6.1.7 Costing special activities. Sometimes, as when the organization is involved with a product recall, the quality-costing effort becomes a major program of collecting, recording, reporting, and analyzing data in order to cover the organization-wide activities. Then it shall be the responsibility of the quality representative on the responsible committee or board (e.g., recall coordination committee) to see that all necessary costing activities are identified, noted, and recorded for later use in computing the quality cost of the activity.

6.2 Sources of quality cost data

6.2.1 General.
Recording and reporting, as well as collecting and analyzing, quality cost data are just as necessary as the similar activities with process cost data. Together the two comprise the operating costs of the organization as a whole; and without due attention to both there can be no in-depth understanding of and control of the economic operations of the company.

There are as many sources from which data can be obtained to assist in compiling the quality cost record of the organization as there are areas performing work that affects quality. Some data sources are:

- Organizational and cost center budgets
- Wages and salary sheets
- Unit cost records and scrap reports
- Material review reports and rework job sheets
- Manufacturing expense sheets and product cost information
- Production times and operator performance records
- Purchase orders and receiving reports
- Inspection and test records
- Sales, service, and field reports
- Personnel movement and data transmission records

All of the above will provide quality cost data, and the list is not exhaustive. The quality organization shall review and identify all significant sources of quality cost data to be used in the collection process.

In some cases it will not be obvious which cost elements are associated with observed expenses, i.e., whether the costs belong in the process or quality areas or are related to some other cost element. When necessary, such costs shall be collected for a time and other related cost sources shall be observed to ascertain the true nature of the expenses incurred. When necessary, estimates shall be made and used until more objective data are available.

It will be found that the quality costs associated with the range of cost elements in each of the prevention, appraisal, and failure areas exhibit a Pareto relationship in respect to the cost magnitude distribution. In each group of quality cost elements there are costs which are greater and others decreasingly small. All quality costs vary with time and work programs. It shall be a principal purpose of quality-costing activities to influence those costs and cause them to adjust to the desired values.

6.2.2 Sources of prevention cost data. The sources of data on prevention costs are listed in Table 2.1.

6.2.3 Sources of appraisal cost data. The sources of data on appraisal costs are listed in Table 2.2.

6.2.4 Sources of failure cost data. The sources of data on internal failure costs are listed in Table 2.3, and the sources of data on external failure costs are listed in Table 2.4.

TABLE 2.1   Prevention Cost Data Sources

Quality cost element	Cost contributors and data sources[1]
(a) Quality planning	Salaries[2] (planning, production, quality assurance, and quality control) Travel and accommodation Telephone, telex, and correspondence
(b) Vendor and subcontractor quality assurance	Travel and accommodation Salaries (purchasing, quality assurance)
(c) Process control engineering	Salaries (production engineering and quality control engineering)
(d) Design and development of inspection and test equipment	Design salaries (instrument design engineers, quality assurance, laboratory, and drawing office)
(e) Acquisition, recording, analysis, and reporting of quality data	Salaries and consumables (QA and QC) Data processing costs
(f) Planning for product recalls	Preparation and promulgation of recall procedures (salaries and consumables) Establishment and maintenance of product distribution records Legal consultations
(g) Insurance against product recall and liability	Premiums
(h) Quality training	Salaries (instructors and students) Purchase orders and training aids
(i) Quality audits	Salaries and resources used
(j) Quality improvement programs	Salaries and consumables (motivation prizes)
(k) Design reviews and verifications	Laboratory salaries and consumables Salaries of design reviewers (designers, production, quality, production engineering, research and development staff)

1. The list of quality cost contributors is not exhaustive.
2. For "salaries" read also "wages."

TABLE 2.2   Appraisal Cost Data Sources

Quality cost element	Cost contributor and data sources[1]
(a) Preproduction model, appraisal of designs	Costs of models Laboratory and testing costs Salaries[2] (quality, laboratory, production engineering, research and development)
(b) Inspection and test equipment	Equipment maintenance and calibration Salaries Replacement parts Inspection and test equipment register Internal rent, leasing, depreciation and interest charges
(c) Inspection and testing (first time)	Salaries (quality control, quality assurance and production
(d) Receiving inspection	Salaries (purchasing, stock, laboratory, quality assurance, and quality control) Consumables and destructively tested items
(e) Materials consumed during inspection and testing	Purchase orders, invoices, bills, and stock requisitions
(f) Approvals and endorsements	Laboratory invoices, purchase orders, approbation costs, salaries (QA and QC)
(g) Field performance testing	Salaries (QC and QA), transportation and travel costs
(h) Analysis and reporting of inspection and test results	Salaries (QC and QA) Consumables
(i) Stock evaluation	Salaries (stock, QC, and QA) Inventory records
(j) Record storage and retrieval	Salaries, storage facilities, and maintenance of records

1. This table of cost contributors is not exhaustive.
2. For "salaries" read also "wages."

7.   Analysis of Quality Cost Data

7.1   Introduction.   The major purpose of identifying, collecting, recording, and analyzing quality costs is to provide the managers and supervisors of the business with the informational tools by which their budget centers of the business may be controlled. Without access to those costs, each manager or supervisor of a budget center can see only part of the ongoing expenses in a visible manner.

Cost control reports from the accounting organization have traditionally contained only process costs, within which have been buried a portion of the quality costs, intermixed and misunderstood. It is a necessary condition for the management of any endeavor that the various details shall be visible and be subject to manipulation, adjustment, and control in order to ensure that a desired outcome will eventuate. Analysis of quality costs is an essential part of that capability, and it

TABLE 2.3   Internal Failure Cost Data Sources

Quality cost element	Cost contributors and data sources[1]
(a) Scrapped product, parts, and raw materials	Material review board reports, salvage reports Material and product disposal reports Salaries[2] (production, material review board, material control, quality assurance) Cost accounting reports on wastage
(b) Product replacement	Product costing reports for replacements Salaries (production, sales, quality assurance, material control)
(c) Repair or rework of product, components, and materials	Reports of parts and materials usage Salaries (production, quality assurance, and material control)
(d) Reinspection and retesting	Materials usage reports Transportation and handling Salaries (production, quality control, and quality assurance)
(e) Fault diagnosis	Salaries (laboratory, quality assurance, production and material control) Equipment operation costs (for both tests and dismantling)
(f) Disposition determination	Salaries (material review board, quality assurance, material control)
(g) Downtime	Salaries (production, quality control, material control, purchasing, stock)
(h) Replacement procurement	Materials and parts cost reports Salaries (purchasing, stock, quality control, and quality assurance)
(i) Downgrading	Sales reports Income returns and allowance reports

1. This table of cost contributors is not exhaustive.
2. For "salaries" read also "wages."

shall be carried out in sufficient detail to permit effective management of the business.

7.2 Quality cost indices. Quality costs, by themselves, are not adequate for conveying their individual degrees of significance. A sum of money on its own, without someone's ability to view it relative to some chosen base of overall monetary control, does not convey its importance. It is necessary to be able to see the individual quality costs in terms of the various cost standards chosen for the business. Those cost standards, or bases, are chosen measures of business performance such as standard sales dollar, standard dollar of direct production labor, standard hour of direct production labor, and standard dollar of processing cost. Typically, the ratio or percentage relationship of a quality cost to one of the related measures of business performance

TABLE 2.4   External Failure Cost Data Sources

Quality cost element	Cost contributors and data sources[1]
(a) Complaints	Sales and service reports
	Market research on customer opinions and user costs
	Allowances or composition and consequential costs
	Field failure reports
	Travel and accommodation costs
	Salaries[2] (field service, complaint investigation, stock, sales, marketing, quality control, and quality assurance)
(b) Product rejected by customer and returned	Materials loss or write-down
	Replacement materials, parts, or equipment
	Rework or repair
	Salaries (production, transport, stock, accounting, quality control, and quality assurance)
(c) Concessions	Sales reports of product discounting
(d) Warranty claims	Materials or parts cost or reimbursement, and consequential costs
	Materials used for testing
	Salaries (quality assurance, quality control, field service, sales, stock, product development)
(e) Product recall	Stock transfer records
	Transport and handling records
	Material or product usage (for verification and testing)
	Advertising and mailing
	Salaries (of personnel involved in recall)
(f) Loss of sales	Sales reports
(g) Product liability	Legal fees
	Court awards
	Salaries (quality assurance, product liability)

1. There may be other cost contributors and data sources not listed here, e.g., records providing information on listed cost contributors.
2. For "salaries" read also "wages."

comprises what is called a quality cost index. It is usually the total quality cost, or the quality cost of one of the areas such as prevention, appraisal, or failure, which is compared to the reference base in order to give the sum of money a suitable significance or meaning.

There is no reference base which is always best for use with quality costs. Indeed, the bases themselves change and must be regularly reviewed in order to make the quality cost reports relevant. Accordingly, it is necessary to provide interpretive explanations along with the quality cost indices, and that shall be done whenever it is found to be necessary. The reference bases chosen shall always be closely related to the quality cost area concerned.

The bases shall be chosen for their sensitivity to the business activity and the quality cost area being considered. Individual bases, on their own, will not reflect sufficient sensitivity to changes which are unusual. As a result, a sufficient number of bases for each quality cost category shall be chosen to provide clear visibility of the ongoing business activities and their changes. Typically, this shall constitute a minimum of three or more bases in use at all times. Eight quality cost indices are commonly used in business. They are discussed in the following articles.

7.2.1   Per dollar of sales.   This index is particularly suitable for senior management. Care shall be used to identify areas of undue influence stemming from variations in sales policies, marketing expenses, sales markdown or markup, etc.

7.2.2   Per hour of direct production labor.   When the business activity is highly labor-intensive, this index shall always be used. Direct production hours constitute a readily available base which is highly useful as a short-range measure of business activity. Care shall always be used to factor into the quality cost reports any influence of automation being added to the production activity. The inclusion of automatic machines can rapidly erode this base and make the reports erroneous through the reduction of direct labor staff.

7.2.3   Per dollar of direct production labor.   This quality cost index shall be used to provide a base for neutralizing inflation factors. It is readily available from accounting, and, as in 7.2.2, it is dependent on such factors as degree of automation and amount of subcontracting.

7.2.4   Per dollar of processing cost.   This index is useful for making comparisons between production lines or between different production plants in a multiple-plant company. When this index is used, care shall be taken to allow for the degree of material intensiveness of the activity, since a high material-to-labor cost can make this index misleading.

7.2.5   Per dollar of standard manufacturing cost.   When the production activity is undergoing a change to automation, this standard index shall be used. With its content of materials costs, factory overheads, etc. this base is more stable than 7.2.3 and less influenced by small introductions of automation.

7.2.6 Per unit of product. This index provides a figure which is meaningful when the item of product is in mass production and there are relatively few types of the item. For job shops and when there are frequent changes in the type of product manufactured, or when a great variety of product is made, it will be necessary to carefully distinguish, in the quality cost report, the unit of product concerned.

7.2.7 Per equivalent unit of product. When the variety of items being produced is considerable, this standard base shall be used. The quality cost per equivalent unit of product is the ratio of the quality cost to the unit of product obtained by taking the most common aspect of the multiproduction line and standardizing all others to it. For example, the most standard unit of product may be the product which is manufactured most of the time, and other units of product are then equated to it. Alternatively, there may be some operation or product characteristic, such as material content, which can be chosen as the base, and all other item costs are then equated to it. The quality cost for the total activity (i.e., total quality cost, prevention quality cost, etc.) is then the ratio of that cost to that standard base.

7.2.8 Per dollar of value added. This index has particular value to members of higher management and in situations such that the product taxation scheme operates on a value-added basis. It shall be used when it is found to be appropriate, and it will provide a weighting factor that allows comparison between different product items.

Quality cost reports issued by the company, or in situations in which this procedure is required, shall provide information about such costs in terms of indices as above. The indices used shall be those which will provide the greatest visibility of the business activity and provide management with the greatest appreciation of and sensitivity to the ongoing costs of doing business in each area.

7.3 Distribution, variation, and use of costs

7.3.1 General. Experience has shown that, when a quality cost control scheme is introduced in a manufacturing company, the total quality costs are found to be much higher than anticipated. Not only have some quality costs been previously ignored but others have been wrongly reported as part of the production cost control system when no meaningful corrective action program could be introduced.

Quality costs, expressed as dollars and as ratios or percentages of defined and understood bases, demonstrate the value of analysis of properly calculated quality costs. Analysis of quality costs cannot be governed by a rigid unchanging system. They must take into consideration the day-to-day alterations, changes, and progressive actions taking place in a company using this procedure. From the very beginning, and then on throughout the remainder of the time quality costing is carried out, the effort must support an ongoing quality improvement program.

Quality and productivity are joint responsibilities of every employee of the company; neither is the domain of only one organization. For example, quality costing is not something done to assist the quality organization, nor are quality staff members disinterested in productivity. The two, quality and productivity, are the principal objectives of senior management, and hence they must be the principal objectives of all employees. Although many companies tend to view the two in a productivity first–quality second relationship, that has been found to work against their success. Such companies finally come to realize, after loss of market share, that the two must be treated as equal partners. If they conflict, quality must be placed ahead of productivity.

The specific types and ranges of analyses found to be most suitable by a company will depend on many factors. For example, if quality costing has been underway for some time, the program will be continually updated to stay current with the changing situation. If quality costing is being introduced, basic and new factors must be introduced into the operations of all organization components associated directly with producing and selling the products as well as accounting for what is done. The following articles of this procedure will describe some approaches which will be found useful in many situations.

7.3.2 Distribution of quality costs. An initial study, or one seeking to update or appraise the quality cost situation, shall seek to establish the current situation. As time progresses, the actual costs change, and so do the bases with which they are compared. For the purposes of such a study, the following areas shall be included.

7.3.2.1 Distribution of quality costs among the quality cost elements. The study shall ascertain the quality cost of each element identified in Art. 6.2 of this procedure. The importance of each cost element shall then be determined by calculating the cost as a percent of the total quality cost, which is the sum of the cost of all quality cost elements.

7.3.2.2 Distribution of quality costs among cost centers. Each supervisory or management person in the organization will usually also manage a budget, which is called the cost center for that part of the total activity. The product, which is brought into being through the successive activities of a number of cost centers, will contain quality costs from each. Each stage of manufacture represented by a cost center contributes to the final quality of the product. It is now necessary to segregate, for each cost center, the part of the expenditures which contributed to quality vs. the part which contributed to processing.

This analysis is important, and it shall be carried out to provide information from which to draw conclusions when it is found that various quality deficiencies are traceable to a given cost center. It also shall be used to indicate which cost centers are overexpending in comparison to their quality contributions. Care shall be used to separate cost center costs on a product basis.

7.3.2.3 Distribution of quality costs among products.
An essential task in the collection of quality costs is to separate the costs according to the various products, components, and materials involved in the production process. This collection shall be meticulously carried out with a view to clearly apportioning costs only to the product category concerned. When common materials or components are involved, they shall be separated into cost cells representing the amount or number of each used in the product.

Although the overall quality costs are necessary when the effort is to provide a report of the state of the business, they cannot be used to make quality improvements in specific areas. It shall be an integral aspect of the quality cost collection program to separate the costs from centers into costs allocatable to specific products. This separation of costs will provide evidence of where corrective action and quality improvements are most needed.

7.3.3 Variation of quality costs.
It will be found that quality costs are a continuously changing variable. Costs of doing business change as a result of many influences. Although some costs appear to remain unchanging for several months at a time and it is necessary to seek a balance or optimum in the costs of quality, it will be found that these costs are ratios or percentages of some reference base (such as the magnitude of sales for a given month) which itself is changing. It shall be an objective of the quality organization to seek the best possible interrelationship of composite quality costs among the various products being produced while recognizing that all effort requires expenditure. The aim of the effort to control quality costs is to eliminate unnecessary costs while making those which are necessary more effective in producing quality in each product.

Quality costs vary with product type, time, cost center, parts and materials, processes, and quality improvement programs. It is also necessary for the quality organization to ensure that quality costs vary with the efforts to optimize such expenditures. The management of quality costs in a manufacturing operation may be defined as causing to happen that which should happen.

7.3.4   Cautions on quality costs

7.3.4.1   Analyzing for corrective action. Normally, investigation of quality cost origins shall proceed from an analysis of the quality cost elements. It must not be assumed, however, that the reason for unusual levels of quality cost will always be found there. Specific reasons for unusually high quality costs may come from such diverse areas as an initial proving of some new process, introduction of some new part or material, and excessively high outside laboratory test costs of some equipment item. Human error, such as unsatisfactory contractual agreements with suppliers or customers, will also be found to be the causes of high quality costs.

Considerable detective work will often be required to trace elusive but intensive quality costs to their true sources. High laboratory costs, at first the apparent cause of high quality costs, may be found to be the result of situations beyond the laboratory's control, and so the actual cause may lie outside the laboratory.

7.3.4.2   Unusually high quality costs. It shall be the aim of the quality organization to study areas of unusually high quality cost with a view to achieving the required quality at a lower cost. The aim shall be to find the areas in which quality assurance or quality control is inadequate and cost-intensive weaknesses exist. Specific subdivisions of quality costs by types of product failure shall be used to identify high quality cost failures with a view to using the Pareto principal for attacking the most important areas first.

Great care shall be used to apply good human factors principles in all attempts to get quality costs into optimized control. Introduction of employee participation programs to the manufacturing plant's activities shall be a central objective in achieving higher productivity at lower quality cost.

8   Reporting of Quality Costs

8.1   Introduction. In the reporting of quality costs an effort shall be made to satisfy two principal aims:

1. To enable senior management and those managing cost centers to monitor the ongoing expenditures being made for quality.

2. To enable those receiving the report to identify areas needing corrective action and to provide them with the initial information within the sphere of relevance of the report for that action.

Reports shall be structured for and directed to specific recipients with a view to communicating to the areas the necessary information relevant to the detailed, as well as the overall, company quality programs. Particular care shall be used to so structure reports that they are relevant to the level of the recipient and to the controls which the recipient can effectively act upon. They shall also contain detailed information relating to the activities of the recipient when corrective action is to be taken.

8.2 Responsibility for quality cost reports.   There are two aspects of responsibility in this situation: responsibility for the analysis, preparation, and issue of the report and responsibility to take action on the report once its contents are known. Clearly, it is the responsibility of the cost center manager or supervisor to take direct corrective action when the quality costs for that cost center are demonstrated to be improper or in need of adjustment. Correspondingly, it is the responsibility of line management above the cost center manager to see that the respective actions are taken.

Responsibility for cost analysis and report preparation and issue is best divided between the accounting and the quality assurance organizations. The basic collection, recording, and processing of cost data is commonly carried out by, or under the guidance of, the accounting organization. This makes best use of the expertise of the accounting staff, avoids jurisdictional disputes, and adds to the credibility of the figures obtained. Members of the accounting staff are generally considered to be less biased in quality matters than members of the quality organization are.

When the report comprises the publication of tabular presentation of cost figures related to specific product codes, again the work is best done by accounting. Other organizations, including quality, production, and production control, shall participate in determining the formats of each report and, to the extent needed by each area, its content.

In comparison with accounting-issued reports, the quality organization is best equipped by training, accessed data, and overall responsibility to prepare and publish data presented in graphic format, including trends, and data representing modified or supplementary evaluations and interpretations. Reports of those types shall be issued by quality personnel.

8.3 Frequency and orientation of quality cost reports.   Each quality cost report shall be designed to communicate specific and pertinent results to categories of management and staff who are directly responsible for the areas covered in the report. Quality cost reports shall be timely and shall, to the maximum extent practicable, be integrated with the ongoing schedules of expenditure and thereby make it possible to influence the expenditure to the desired degree.

Reports forwarded to managers and supervisors responsible for direct control of operational areas shall be designed to assist the recipients in the discharge of their day-to-day activities. Reports for such areas shall be issued daily or weekly, depending on the costs covered and the rate of flow of work through the area. Managers of operational areas covering several cost centers shall receive condensed reports that reflect the entire scope of their areas but with less detail except in problem areas.

Quality cost reports for senior management shall be in graphic or trend format (so as to use the least amount of the recipient's time) and shall reflect the ongoing state of the business, on an operational basis, as well as the costs related to major product categories. The contents of quality cost reports for divisional and more senior management shall contain details which permit them to concentrate on broad review, planning, and action. Specific, more detailed, reports shall be provided as required and break down the information about cost elements of concern at the time.

Quality cost reports related to quality improvement programs shall be prepared with specific data related to the results being obtained by the program. These reports shall be circulated to all levels of management and supervision, with details being provided to those cost center managers who must make the program a success.

When the company is operating an employee participation program (EPP), quality cost reports that relate to specific EPP workshop problems shall be designed to yield the information needed by the employee-management workshops and shall be circulated on a timely basis to the relevant workshops. Such reports shall also be forwarded to the in-line management forum which is responsible for overseeing the workshop activity.

8.4 Cost reports for cost center managers. Cost reports shall cover the scope of the manager's cost center. They shall consist of the detailed and comprehensive presentation of individual data from the report period each time that is necessary for the most effective management of the cost center. They shall focus on the individual quality costs. Failure quality costs in particular shall be clearly attributed to the department and cost center incurring them. It is a clear responsibility of the quality assurance organization to identify such failure responsibilities through fault analysis programs and to see that their costs are reported to the areas where corrective action can be taken.

When specific desirable actions are known, they shall be included in the quality cost reports as recommendations. The actual content and format of quality cost reports shall have consistency and regularity to permit ease of understanding and highlighting the costs of most significance.

Table 2.5 shows a typical format for quality cost reports to cost center supervisors.

8.5 Cost reports for middle management. Quality cost reports prepared for middle management shall contain breakdowns of costs consolidated according to the cost center under each such manager's control. A further breakdown of costs according to product type shall also be provided, along with costs of areas with which the cost center interfaces. Quality cost reports to middle management shall contain listings of the recommendations made to cost center supervisors reporting to the respective middle managers. These reports shall be compiled from the contents of cost center reports.

8.6 Cost reports for senior management. These quality cost reports shall contain a combination of graphic and tabulated data summarizing the more relevant details for the report period and highlighting the action areas and results. Quality costs presented in tabular form shall present the current picture for each of the cost areas: prevention, appraisal, and failure. When particular problems with either internal or external failure exist, the relevant area shall be highlighted in the senior management report.

Quality cost reports to senior management shall present the total cost figures, with expenditure trends, and identify the results obtained. Projected future trends and forecast target results shall also be presented to senior management to enable the managers to be better prepared to approve budgets and take needed action.

8.7 Cost reports for quality assurance use. The quality manager shall plan for, collect data for, and compile quality cost reports as necessary to provide for routine assessment of the ongoing total quality system operation. These reports shall be specifically structured to present data for use by quality staff in adjusting quality costs and optimizing the total quality cost system.

Quality cost reports shall, when applicable, be used to assist in the motivation, improvement, and solution of quality matters in the production area. The reports shall be used in all situations in which competition between operating areas is used.

TABLE 2.5   Typical Cost Center Supervisor's Report

Statement of Scrap Cost Details (in $)   Cost Ctr. *232*   Mo. *11* Year *1989*

Report No.	Defect code	Part number	Oprn. no.	Qty.	Mate-rial cost	Wages	OH	Total costs
3122	04	21-484-139951	200	19	5.96	7.21	15	29.17
3125	04	21-493-139955	205	11	16.15	6.97	27	49.12
3126	04	21-485-139947	215	6	21.55	14.72	49	85.12
3120	04	21-481-139942	220	211	3.35	86.22	92	181.57
	04				47.01	115.12	183	344.98
3152	09	21-481-139845	320	55	14.28	22.96	39	75.24
3153	09	21-488-139965	322	29	5.97	14.22	28	48.19
3158	09	21-485-139941	320	19	26.50	27.11	51	104.61
3161	09	21-484-139988	315	44	88.00	43.10	92	215.10
	09				100.75	107.39	210	443.14
3185	12	21-489-139881	410	6	15.90	15.15	41	72.05
3189	12	21-489-139884	410	9	9.18	6.60	21	36.78
3190	12	21-489-139888	410	13	33.30	32.00	89	154.30
3193	12	21-489-139882	410	2	5.66	2.28	19	26.94
	12		410		64.04	56.03	170	290.57
					211.80	278.54	563	1078.69

9.   Minimizing Total Quality Costs

9.1   The economic perspective

9.1.1   General.   Quality costs shall not be viewed as some aspect of doing business which is totally undesirable. The undertaking and carrying out of any work will carry a cost of some magnitude. The task for the managers of a business is to find the most economical combination of work methods, personnel, equipment, and operational relationships which produces the highest-quality product with the highest productivity for the lowest total cost.

The preceding articles of this procedure presented terms and their development related to areas of activity needed to produce products. This spectrum of costs must now be examined with a view to optimization and minimization in ways that are compatible with maintaining productivity and quality.

The supervisor or manager who is responsible for building quality into products must find ways to do so while keeping productivity high and yet ensuring that the company will make a profit. Ultimately, the business problem in the market resolves itself into two considerations: the manufacturing company's economics vs. the customer's total costs related to the product. In the consumer market, the usual result is the optimization of the manufacturer's costs and the corresponding development of a service and replacement industry. By comparison, government-related bodies and industry customers, to meet their particular needs, require a guaranteed life, low maintenance costs, and a controlled total life cycle cost. The latter customer needs are reflected in higher quality and reliability requirements. They, in turn, dictate a need for better control of quality costs. In the latter case it is necessary to optimize both the manufacturer's costs and the customer's total cost by careful design and production of appropriate quality products.

Production costs include process costs and quality costs. In production operations, a large part of the total cost is usually incurred by the processes which build quality into the product rather than from inspection, which measures the quality produced. The extent to which processes can be planned and used to achieve first-time conformance of product characteristics has an important bearing on quality costs incurred from nonconformance during production and after sale in the field.

It matters little whether the customer or the manufacturer dictates the degree of product conformance to specifications. An economic problem is presented to the quality organization which involves a choice of alternative combinations of possible process methods, degrees of inspection or test, and investment of resources. Although this procedure is primarily concerned with quality of conformance, the quality of design is also of great importance and must be considered in achieving an optimized quality cost balance for the manufacturing operation.

9.1.2 Costs related to new products. Expenditure in manufacturing industry is concerned with the two principal categories of products. One consists of the products which are new to the operation and represent attempts to expand the company's income, i.e., income expansion expenditure. The other consists of the cost of searching for ways to make more profit from the existing products being produced, or cost reduction expenditure. In this part of the activity the search is for ways to reduce the costs of producing products of suitable quality in sufficient quantity to meet schedules and the market demand.

For new products readily identifiable stages are involved in designing, developing, and producing a product. Ensuring that the quality is built in the first time through for each stage is an integral part of this activity. The marketing or sales organization will usually carry out market studies to determine what the market wants and what it is willing to pay for a given quality product. It then becomes the task of the designer to design a product that, when produced in optimum conformance to the design, can be produced at a profit and will have the value of quality for which the customer is willing to pay. These steps shall be taken and the product shall be designed to achieve the value of quality for a given cost of quality as set forth in Fig. 2.1 unless some

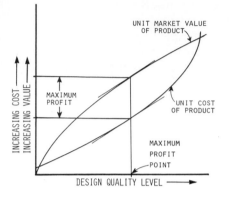

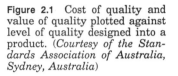

Figure 2.1 Cost of quality and value of quality plotted against level of quality designed into a product. (*Courtesy of the Standards Association of Australia, Sydney, Australia*)

other value of design quality is specified in a contract or purchase order.

9.1.3 Costs related to existing products. When a product is made to an existing design, it is the task of management to identify areas of excessive or unnecessary costs and minimize or eliminate these. In this program of cost reduction, it is necessary, and shall be a target of management, to ensure that the product quality or reliability is not permitted to suffer unduly from cost-cutting exercises.

When the customer's specification permits, the company shall aim for minimum total production cost. This is the condition which is reached at specific points on the quality cost curve and the process cost curve (Fig. 2.2).

9.2   Adjusting quality costs

9.2.1 Introduction. The quality of product is particularly sensitive to the expenditure of money to achieve that quality and to where within the spectrum of such costs the expenditure is made. In this way the quality of products can be both favorably and adversely affected, depending on what is done in adjusting these costs. For example, taking funds away from an activity which is already performing marginally will only worsen the performance unless some compensating action is taken elsewhere within the cost spectrum. It shall be a prime purpose of the quality manager to ensure that changes to the quality budgets of cost center managers are made in an orderly and controlled manner.

9.2.2 Prevention cost adjustment. Expenditure made on prevention cost elements acts as a balance against the costs of appraisal and fail-

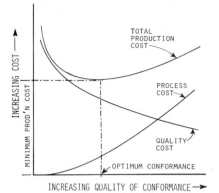

Figure 2.2 Increasing cost of production plotted against increasing quality of conformance to design, showing minimum cost of production.

ure elements. More is involved than just catching a failure or cause early in the production cycle when applying prevention strategy to the manufacturing exercise. Although the order of magnitude cost escalation from vendor to production to external failure (i.e., $1 saves $10 saves $100) bears no direct relation to the savings from early detection, it is definitely in the right direction and is often of the correct proportions as well.

Several factors influence prevention cost expenditures. Some of these are discussed in the following articles.

9.2.2.1 Employee attitudes, loyalty, and alertness.
Employee attitudes are determined to a great degree by the work atmosphere and company employee programs used to engender loyalty and correct attitudes. Alertness is not solely a result of freedom from boredom and tiredness; it can be awakened and nurtured by encouragement of employees to think and recommend, see their ideas being included in the products, and gain prestige with management and their fellow workers. This is a major benefit derived from the introduction of employee participation programs (see Sec. VI, Chap. 1 of *Quality Control Systems*). The commitment of senior management to the improvement of quality must be visible to all employees if the employees are expected to support first-line supervisors in quality achievement. The steps to be taken include the following:

1. Employees shall be made aware of all aspects of the work program affecting them. Planned graphic, written, and verbal communication, as well as training, shall be used to inform employees.

2. Opportunities shall be provided for each employee to present his

or her ideas and suggestions for overcoming problems and improving quality. The company shall display early evidence of action taken as a result of employee suggestions and recommendations.

3. When appropriate, employee participation in the setting of goals shall be used in conjunction with the planning of orderly programs for their achievement.

9.2.2.2 Prevention program development. A program aimed at the prevention of deficiencies in products shall be planned, developed, and implemented. This program shall encompass the activities designed to prevent the occurrence of nonconformances in the products.

Thorough and successive design reviews shall be conducted. Designs shall be reviewed and carefully examined for possible causes of internal or external failure, poor reliability, testability, maintainability, etc. Specific actions in respect to design reviews shall include:

- Make a detailed analysis of customer requirements.

- Thoroughly review design vs. customer specifications to ensure that design accurately reflects customer requirements.

- Identify areas of product not covered by customer specification and develop quality standards to cover them.

- Ensure compatibility of design with production drawings and requirements, as well as testing, production, maintainability, reliability, and other needs.

- Ensure that the developed product contains all the characteristics and capabilities identified above.

- Participate in or conduct product verification tests, including the full environmental program.

- Follow up design change decisions and ensure they are made fully effective.

9.2.2.3 Minimizing failure cost. Through quality assurance develop and implement a program of quality effort which will minimize the incidence of failure during and following production. The most effective cost strategy shall be devised to provide quality products of defined value while ensuring that the cost of quality throughout the life cycle is controlled.

9.2.2.4 Prevention quality costing. Prevention quality costing shall be introduced to the sales and marketing activities aimed at better-defined customer needs, better customer education, and improved product field performance.

9.2.3 Appraisal cost adjustment.

Although the greatest cost savings frequently stem from attention to prevention quality costs, the appraisal cost area can yield major benefits; and appraisal shall be given primary attention when optimizing quality costs. There will be a continuing tendency to misinterpret as appraisal costs the things done during production to prevent failure. Care shall be used to minimize this source of quality cost reporting error.

9.2.3.1 Quality measurement strategy.

Planning is an essential function when a quality appraisal measurement system is being established. Great care shall be used by professionally trained staff to ensure that measurement stations under the control of trained inspectors and testers operating from professionally prepared instructions are positioned throughout the production process line at all essential points.

Preparation for optimum appraisal shall begin with the design reviews, in which essential points of measurement shall be identified and the first flowcharts prepared to show the progressive construction of the product through the successive processes, each followed by appropriate appraisal of the quality obtained. Determination of the points of control and the amount of inspection and testing required shall be integrated with the planning of the processing, with feedback loops being shortened to the optimum degree and the cost of making each measurement being analyzed and reduced to a minimum consistent with the needs of the product.

After the flowcharts covering processing, inspection, and testing have been prepared, they shall be jointly analyzed with a view to eliminating unnecessary appraisal. It may be best to perform a number of processing operations on one piece or one area of a product before performing a measurement on it. It may be better to have the operator who controls a process with large operator input also perform the inspection or test. It may be cheaper to integrate the measurement apparatus with the processing apparatus and thereby eliminate the need for separate test equipment. Automation of the inspection or test may be included in the design of the processing equipment and thereby further eliminate the cost of appraisal. All these techniques and more shall be considered and adopted as they are found to be appropriate.

The in-process controls shall be so chosen as to minimize the manufacture of defective products. Finished product inspection and testing shall be integrated with the amount of in-process measurement of quality characteristics so as to optimize the amount of each. In the ongoing program the finished product inspection and test requirements, as well as the instructions for them, shall be thoroughly reviewed along with the amount of in-process measurement. The reviews shall consider not only the amount but also the orientation and purpose of each measurement with a view to balancing them with the amount, purpose, and types of prevention measurements.

9.2.3.2 Equipment and method improvement. There are many steps which can and shall be taken not only to reduce the costs of appraisal but also to make appraisal more effective. Some areas of measuring equipment improvement which shall be considered and used as appropriate are:

1. Constructing processing equipment with measuring instruments built in.
2. Using ergonomics and other industrial engineering techniques to improve the inspection and test stations.
3. Providing greater degrees of automation in testing, recording data, and reporting to central points.

Stations dependent on an inspector or tester for highly repetitive and rapid output are usually candidates for cost reduction exercises. These, as well as other higher quality cost measurements of quality, shall be attacked first in the program to reduce appraisal costs. Following closely shall be reviews to eliminate unnecessary inspection and testing. When elimination is not possible, alternative methods of lower cost shall be considered and tried.

Computer controls, as well as recording, sorting, analyzing, and even reporting by computer shall be used when they are found to be suitable and cost-beneficial. In carrying out any or all such improvements, careful attention shall be given to the risks involved relative to the achievement and proving of the agreed quality levels in the product.

9.2.3.3 The use of statistical methods. Stochastic methods, as well as the statistical methods for data manipulation, are tools which shall be used in the appraisal of product. In particular, the application of statistical mathematics shall be used in:

1. Process capability studies and process adjustments
2. Acceptance sampling programs and techniques
3. The preparation and use of process control charts
4. The analysis, arrangement, and reporting of data

9.2.3.4 Accuracy of inspection and test. Great care shall be used to ensure that all instrumentation and aids used to measure product quality convey the required accuracy. In particular, attention shall be routinely given to the subjective or sensory methods of measurement. Methods of improving those methods such as the following shall be used.

- Providing better training for inspectors
- Providing better permanent physical or pictorial standards
- Providing of objective inspection and test devices
- Reducing the labor content by using better decision methods

9.2.4   Failure cost adjustment.   See Art. 6 for the elements and sources of failure quality costs. The methods identified here for adjusting them apply in different forms and degrees to both internal and external failures.

9.2.4.1   Reporting.   A formal system shall be established for reporting failure at all stages of production and during product use. The program shall consist of a number of stages divided into an internal fault reporting system and an external customer complaints system. Other methods of reporting nonconformance, wherever found and regardless of by whom reported, shall be provided for. Emphasis shall be placed on reports that identify to a maximum degree the nature of, cause for, and other pertinent facts about the failure. These systems shall be oriented toward stimulating corrective action within the company.

9.2.4.2   Failure analysis.   A formal program, staffed and equipped and adequate to the needs of the organization, shall be established for the purpose of carrying out analytical investigations on failed products, materials, and components to establish the modes and causes of failure. The output of this program shall be keyed to the production process and to customer services for appropriate corrective action implementation.

9.2.4.3   Corrective action and follow-up.   A program of corrective action whereby each failure report receives due attention and action in direct proportion to its seriousness to the customer and the company shall be prepared, documented, and implemented. This program shall provide for follow-up after the implementation of corrective action to ensure that the solution implemented did in fact work satisfactorily and the failure cause was either removed or ameliorated to an acceptable degree.

Formal reporting to management of the results of managing the area of product failure shall be an essential part of the quality assurance program of the company.

9.3 Optimizing quality costs

9.3.1 General. The management of quality costs requires the balancing of prevention costs on the one hand against the net sum of appraisal and failure costs on the other. To a lesser degree, appraisal costs can be used to modify failure costs; and this will be discussed below. In the latter case, appraisal is normally combined with prevention to gain the most effective control of failure mechanisms. Optimization decisions rely on accurate and timely cost data collected and reported in exact agreement with instructions and definitions provided in documentation to the company's personnel. It shall be a central purpose of quality management to ensure that, to the maximum extent, all the personnel of the company speak the same language of quality in a cooperative and concerted drive toward the same ends.

9.3.2 Optimizing prevention vs. appraisal and failure costs. It can be seen in Fig. 2.3 that, with expenditure of money on prevention of nonconformance, less expenditure is needed for appraisal and failure. It is shown in Fig. 2.3 that there is some relationship of the three areas such that the least possible total quality cost is reached. In the absence of other constraints, such as contract or purchase order, the minimum total quality cost point shall be the aim of company management.

Doing more things right to get the materials and components entering into the production process to be in full conformance and stable in their characteristics will lead to less inspection and testing in process and on finished product, as well as to less failure of products. The relationship between prevention and failure is so sensitive that, in a plant experiencing high failure rates, only a small expenditure in key prevention areas will be required to get a major drop in failure rates.

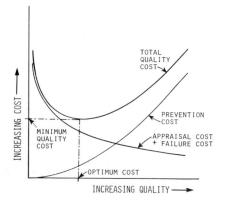

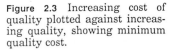

Figure 2.3 Increasing cost of quality plotted against increasing quality, showing minimum quality cost.

Great care shall be taken to integrate all changes in both the processing and the quality activities in order to prevent benefits from one area being canceled by changes in other areas (see Fig. 2.4).

9.3.3 Optimizing prevention vs. appraisal costs. When control of required quality characteristics in materials and components is inadequate, there develops a need to apply greater expenditures in appraising, screening, and sorting produced items in order to obtain items acceptable for shipment. This type of activity is accompanied by a high level of scrap and rework activity going on in parallel. It has been found that the application of greater attention to prevention of defects and nonconformance in raw materials and components will reduce the need for great amounts of appraisal consequent to the lack of such preventive effort.

It shall be a principal function of the quality manager to work in conjunction with other concerned managers in the company to achieve an optimum balance between the expenditures on appraisal of quality being achieved and prevention of nonconformance of purchased materials, components, and services.

9.3.4 Optimizing prevention vs. failure costs. Two factors influence the degree of optimization to be sought in this area. One is the economics of the overall production operation; the other is the matter of safety and liability incurred by the company in this respect. In the absence of a safety problem, the aim of management shall be to achieve a balance between expenditure on prevention of faults and nonconformance throughout the total activity and the expenses incurred through product failure. This will mean that, at some point, further expenditure on prevention is no longer justified because it will outweigh costwise the costs of rectifying the failure.

When jurisdictional regulations, company liability, or other considerations relating to safety of people and goods dictate, the expenditure on prevention shall not be balanced against the costs of failure alone. Rather, an effort shall be made, within acceptable risk levels, to prevent the failure. To that extent, the manager responsible for liability risks shall play a major role in determining the goals to be sought in all types of quality cost optimization.

9.3.5 Optimizing appraisal vs. failure costs. It will sometimes be found that prevention costs are fixed. For example, the items purchased may be off-the-shelf followed by screening, and nothing further can be done to improve incoming supplies. For a fixed prevention cost, it may be found that significant improvement in failure costs can be achieved by adjusting expenditure on appraisal.

The costs of appraisal come from a vast range of company activities involving employees in engineering, science, laboratory, process, and

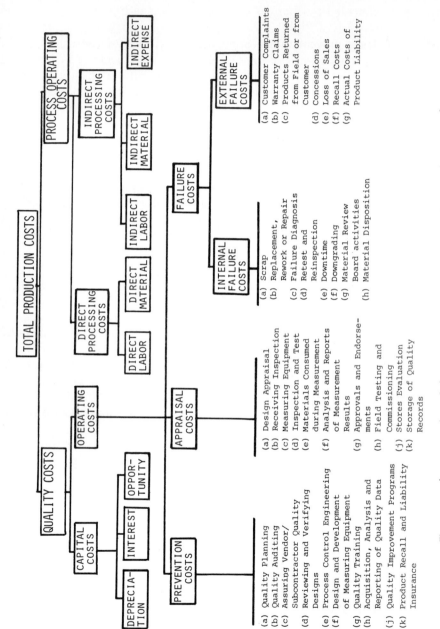

Figure 2.4 A presentation of the total production costs required to produce a product. (*Courtesy of the Standards Association of Australia, Sydney, Australia*)

quality engineering areas as well as the direct employees who produce the product. Because it is not always simple to quantify these varied sources of cost, it is best to follow a strategy of quality education and awareness, with all staff members making appropriate contributions from their various areas. Because appraisal does not prevent failure but only finds it and may find it earlier in some cases than others, there is no unique relationship between appraisal and failure. The company shall have as its goal the development and implementation of an appraisal strategy, in this type of situation, which will maximize the cost effectiveness of changes or increases in appraisal expenditure so that, for each, there is a consequent reduction in failure expenditure.

In general, in appraisal work, it is better to carry out inspections and tests early rather than late in the production cycle. The concept of fixed prevention cost shall also remain constantly under examination, because that activity will have the greatest effect on failure.

9.3.6 Optimizing prevention and appraisal vs. failure costs. There is a positive or direct relation between expenditure on either prevention or appraisal and the degree of product conformance achieved. Correspondingly, there is an inverse relation between failure cost and conformance. It can be seen, therefore, that combining appraisal and prevention on one expenditure curve will, when graphed with failure expenditure, yield a minimum total quality cost point at some level of conformance. It is that point which the optimization program shall seek.

In general, the introduction of such an optimization program will find the failure costs high and the expenditure on prevention and appraisal either low or poorly distributed. It will therefore be found that the goal becomes the reduction of failure costs with rising prevention and appraisal costs until the point of minimum total quality cost is reached. This shall be the aim of the optimization program in newly introduced quality control programs.

3

Just-in-Time
Quality Control System

PART A.   REVIEW AND GUIDANCE

1   Review

Many techniques in the field of quality control have evolved over the
years, some to wane and disappear when their sponsors changed jobs
or moved to new ideas. Other techniques remained to be fostered and
followed by succeeding quality engineers and managers. Some of them
were:

1. *Data analysis.*   In this work, yield and failure data are analyzed
   to determine the most important areas on which to concentrate
   the resources of the company for solution of the failure problems
   concerned.

2. *Failure analysis.*   In this technique, the failed items of product,
   disassembled as necessary, are analyzed to determine what the
   basic failure mode was.

3. *Assembly of management teams.*   In manufacturing industry
   there are many occasions requiring the assembly of management
   teams from several operating sectors. Some teams remain designated indefinitely; others function once or only a few times.

Just-in-time (JIT) is a colloquial U.S. term for a management approach and associated techniques used to accomplish quality and productivity improvement. JIT programs are a company-wide approach to
problem solving which quality engineers have practiced at their individual levels for years. The cookbook approach to problem solving involves the following five steps:

1. Study information and define the problem.
2. Search for and identify all possible solutions within the time constraints available.
3. Select from among the possible solutions the one to be applied.
4. Apply the chosen solution to the problem.
5. At a later time review the problem area to confirm that the defined problem was solved.

The JIT approach is to follow the same route to problem solution and quality and productivity improvement as in the above five-step approach to problem solving. It does so within the modern framework of employee participation programs, management steering committees, and use of statistical methods.

2   Guidance

JIT is a teamwork approach to problem solving and hence quality and productivity improvement. As such it can and should become an ongoing quality improvement program. As in the conduct of any ongoing program, a program coordinator will be needed. Typically, this person should be a quality engineer or an industrial engineer trained in the techniques of quality control.

Teamwork will be the key to success in applying the JIT approach. It is essential, therefore, that the program coordinator be a person who has excellent interpersonal relationships and gets along well with workers and management on all levels. He or she should have a good general understanding of the product categories to be improved and should understand the use of statistical methods in analysis and decision making.

There are other benefits besides quality and productivity that can be derived from an ongoing JIT program. One major benefit is the potential such a program offers for reduction of inventory. When there are a large number of quality problems, it is necessary to carry excess stock to meet corrective actions and replacement production runs. If poor quality is being received from vendors, it may be necessary to issue typically 1 to 5 percent overruns to ensure having adequate product to meet shipment requirements. These are areas that should be helped by the JIT program.

Inventories cannot be reduced until the manufacturing process is improved to such a degree that the generation of high levels of faulty products or services is reduced or stopped. The JIT program will start, therefore, with an examination of the current situation.

The JIT program should be coupled with the ongoing quality control efforts of the company, and management committees and others involved in JIT should not displace or do the work of established committees such as the material review board and the design organization. Rather, the JIT program coordinator should utilize those activities when they are called for.

PART B.   PROCEDURE

Just-in-Time Quality Control System

1   Scope

This procedure contains the company's requirements for establishing and operating a just-in-time quality and productivity improvement program.

2   Application

This procedure shall be implemented and operated throughout all divisions of the company and shall, when applicable, be a requirement placed on vendors supplying materials to the company.

3   Definitions

Definitions of terms used in this procedure are from "Glossary of Terms Used in Quality and Reliability," Sec. VII, Chap. 1 of *Quality Control Systems.**

4   Choosing the JIT Program Coordinator

A JIT program coordinator shall be chosen by the company. The coordinator shall be experienced in the use of statistical methods for the purpose of identifying and solving quality and production problems. He or she shall have a knowledge of the company and the products and/or services it produces and sells.   Particular care shall be taken to select a person who has good interpersonal relationships and possesses the ability to integrate well with all levels of management, as well as all other employee levels within the company. The coordinator shall possess personal drive that will ensure the dynamic and aggressive pursuit of the objectives of the program.

The JIT program coordinator shall report at a level in the company that will allow him or her to ensure the effective solution to quality and productivity problems, as well as the overall success of the JIT program.

5   Choosing the JIT Program Statistician

The person selected by the company to be the JIT program statistician shall have academic training in the mathematical sciences and specific education and experience in the field of industrial statistics. This person shall have sufficient experience in the use of industrial statistics to be capable of performing the detailed analyses needed to identify variance and control problems of a complex nature.

The statistician shall have the ability to instruct and lead others in the use of statistical methods in solving quality and productivity problems in industry.

6   Planning for the JIT Program

6.1   Planning program communications.   The JIT program coordinator shall, in cooperation with other staff in such organizations as quality engineering and production engineering prepare plans for obtaining data, communicating the results of the analyses of the data, and com-

---

*James R. Taylor, *Quality Control Systems: Procedures for Planning Quality Programs,* McGraw-Hill, New York, 1989.

municating with the various levels of management throughout the company.

Specific plans shall be prepared for keeping members of management teams informed of ongoing work in their areas, as well as the steering committee of management on the overall operation of the program.

6.2 Planning for review of current situations. The JIT program coordinator shall, in conjunction with other staff as needed, prepare plans for:

1. Collecting data

2. Analyzing data collected

3. Identifying quality, productivity, and inventory problems

4. Preparing flowcharts depicting the time and space sequence of events taking place and locating identified problem areas on these charts

5. Preparing priority listings of the problems identified to be used by the respective management teams

6.3 Planning for JIT program resources. The JIT program coordinator shall prepare a budget, obtain monies, and otherwise establish a financial base for the JIT program. He or she shall obtain materials, forms, etc. and all the texts, reference notes, background information, and communication materials needed by the statistics instructor to teach the statistics course to the planned number of staff on the management teams.

Arrangements shall be made for meeting places and for any other requirements which the management teams may need for the effective carrying out of their roles of analyzing and solving the problems identified and chosen.

7 Implementing the JIT Program

The JIT program coordinator shall begin by giving a general presentation to the company management concerning the concepts of the JIT program. He or she shall outline the statistical methods training course to be taken by members of the JIT management teams and the manner of working of the teams. When such data are available, details of success of similar programs at other facilities shall be provided.

The coordinator shall next hold a meeting with each individual organization head throughout the plant or work sites. The kinds of problems to be found in each manager's work area shall be discussed. During these discussions the coordinator shall assemble a résumé of the kinds of problems being encountered by management. The problems may include market analysis difficulties, sales volumes, purchased material variances, existing inventory levels, quality rejections, scrap and rework costs, equipment changeover times, equipment utilization levels, and customer complaints.

Problems identified shall next be discussed with the managers in a second meeting. This information shall be used to identify the plant's problems and establish a priority listing to be worked on by the management teams.

7.1 Familiarize the statistician with products. The statistician shall be given a thorough introduction to the range and types of products produced at the site and shall be provided with a scale of magnitude in each area as needed to permit him or her to acquire detailed knowledge of the operation.

7.2 Establish a management steering committee. By working with the chief executive officer, or the most senior plant manager, the JIT program coordinator shall select the members of a steering committee for the program. These members shall come from senior management at the site, and then shall collectively possess the stature and knowledge to ensure cooperation from other managers and enhance the chances of success for the program.

7.3 Establish the management study teams. Working with senior management, teams of managers and other staff members possessing the diverse disciplines needed to solve the plant's problems are identified and established. Each member is notified, given a timetable of meetings and a schedule for training in statistics and problem-solving techniques, and the management teams are established.

A facilitator or team leader shall be chosen for each team. This person shall carry the responsibility for calling the team members together, and shall communicate the results of the team activities to the program coordinator and the steering committee.

7.4 Train management study teams in statistics. The several members of each management team, which is not a quality circle but a problem-solving team, shall acquire training in statistical methods of identifying and analyzing problems and in the use of statistical methods for problem solution. These shall be taught by the statistician selected, who shall then continue supporting the various management teams as they pursue their objectives of improving quality and productivity.

7.5   Prepare current situation flowcharts.   The management teams shall collect data from their respective areas. These data shall be used to compile situation flowcharts which, collectively, shall cover the entire plant's operations.

7.6   Statistically analyze flowcharts.   The management teams, with the assistance of the statistician as necessary, shall analyze the situation flowcharts and identify the magnitudes of specific problems and the potential for their solution and for quality or productivity improvement. Special care shall be taken to ensure that productivity is not increased at the expense of quality. In all areas, quality shall be given a weighting equal to or greater than that given productivity. At no time shall quality of conformance be decreased in order to obtain productivity.

7.7   Make assignments to management study teams.   After reviewing the results of the situation flowcharts provided by the management study teams, the program coordinator shall review them with the management steering committee. Together, the coordinator and committee shall determine a program of work including priorities for each management study team.

The program coordinator shall make assignments of agreed-upon areas of work involving the problems identified by the analyses of the situation flowcharts and in accordance with priorities set by the steering committee.

7.8   Establish goals for management study teams.   Goals shall be established by the members of each management study team. These goals shall be subject to agreement by the management steering committee. They shall also be in accordance with budget planning of the program coordinator. Hence, work which involves the expenditure of funds shall not begin until the necessary communication and approvals are complete.

7.9   Identify problems needing solutions.   Within the broad overall scope of the situation flowcharts and the system of priorities established for each management study team, specific quality, productivity, equipment utilization, or other problems needing solution shall be identified.

7.10   Identify problem root causes.   By using statistical methods, measurement of characteristics, or other methods, the necessary data to identify the failure modes or other root causes of the problems being worked on shall be obtained. The details of the problem and its root causes shall be prepared in written form for later reference when solution methods have been applied. This is necessary in order to ascertain whether solutions applied do indeed result in correction of the problem or removal of the anomaly.

7.11 Identify and apply solutions to problem(s). The management study team shall identify the various possible solutions to the problem under study. From among the possible solutions one shall be then chosen for application to solve the problem. Cost studies shall be made before applying the solution to ensure that such solutions are either quality- or cost-beneficial. Problem solutions shall be cost-beneficial at the current financial break-even point stipulated by the company's finance department. Authorization from the steering committee via the program coordinator shall be obtained prior to applying solutions that involve expenditure of monies outside the delegations of the management study team members.

7.12 Introduce statistical process controls. When the introduction of a solution to a production problem involves production processes and permanence of the solution is dependent on the statistical control of such processes, steps shall be taken to ensure that the statistical controls will continue. The appropriate quality assurance staff shall be involved and provision for continued monitoring of the control shall be made.

7.13 Review and adjust inventory levels. Material inventory levels shall be reviewed as a part of the ongoing effort of each management study team following the implementation of any solution that results in:

1. Greater equipment utilization
2. Less product loss through variability of processes
3. Any other cause that alters the justification for stocking materials at previous levels

When reviews as above demonstrate that adjustments in inventory levels are justified, steps shall be taken to make such adjustments. In this situation, the respective members of the accounting, purchasing, storage, and other affected organizations shall be provided with the details necessary to adjust their work accordingly.

7.14 Prepare new situation flowcharts. Following the introduction of problem solutions that alter the detail of previous situation flowcharts, new charts to show the new current situation shall be produced. These new charts shall then be studied in conjunction with corresponding charts of contiguous operating areas with a view to ensuring that uniform progressive improvements take place throughout the entire production activity on each product.

Care shall be taken in product flow or equipment utilization situations to prevent solution of a problem at one point by shifting the problem further along the production line.

7.15 Analyze and establish new team goals. When the several management study teams have completed a round of analyses and problem solutions which have lifted the quality and/or productivity throughout an area, the new situation flowcharts shall be analyzed and a new set of team goals for each management study team shall be established. In this way the product quality improvement program is made an ongoing activity of the company.

Glossary of Terms Used in Quality and Reliability

1

Glossary

PART A. REVIEW AND GUIDANCE

1 Review

In each specialized field of human effort there develops a unique language which expands the field of lexicography and is characteristic of that particular field. In the field of quality, extending as it does into all human endeavor, we should expect to find, and indeed do find, the most extensive of such languages. It is necessary to understand the language of each field in order to work in that field. In quality work, the more precise the language the less the variance of communications and the more scientific the work done.

In accordance with the stated need for better uniformity in quality and reliability communications, this glossary is primarily based on the International Standards Organization (ISO) standard ISO 8402 and its definitions. It is compatible with the ANSI/ASQC standards on inspection, quality systems, etc., and also with the European Organization for Quality Control multilingual standard for terms and definitions. Further, the Australian Standards Organization (SAA) standard on quality and reliability terms and their definitions will be found to be in general agreement with the definitions given here. Perhaps the areas of greatest difference that will be noted in this attempt to provide a universal language for the essential activities of quality and reliability are:

1. The adoption of the ISO definitions for *defect* and *nonconformity* and their extension throughout related definitions.

2. The treatment of the area of *causality,* which has been divided into *assignable cause* and *uncorrectable cause.* Earlier works

---

Note: Terms marked ASQC reprinted with permission of the American Society of Quality Control.

have tended to perpetuate the myth that some causes do not occur on a random basis.

3. The treatment of *projects* and *services* on an equal footing with *mass manufacturing*. The latter area has, in previous works, been the only endeavor given significant treatment, with services being a minor subset and projects being largely ignored.

We must seek to achieve quality and productivity in all that we do. Whether we are producing some item of product, providing some item of service, or constructing some major project work, the total endeavor in bringing it into being must be approached with a view to carrying out each task in the most correct manner the very first time and each and every time. Since communication is perhaps the greatest impediment encountered in achieving first time through conformance of products, it is essential that all who work in industry speak the same language of quality and reliability as they work together toward the same goals and objectives.

This glossary of quality and reliability terms is intended for use by all people in industry without regard for the area or position in which they work. It is a revision and expansion of a glossary first published only in Australia by the author in 1972. Having been used extensively and found to be effective in all areas of quality and reliability work, and having been brought into line with modern usage, those terms and more are now published here as a comprehensive glossary of quality.

2   Guidance

Many glossaries of terms used in quality and reliability work exist. They will be found in all modern developed nations and in many languages. It is to be expected, therefore, that there is a great need for a quality glossary which can provide universal definitions for all the terms used in this field of work. When glossaries in different countries have similar definitions for the same term, those differences can introduce confusion in international communications on quality and be very real barriers to international trade. The universal use of this glossary on quality should help to overcome differences that exist between countries. The terms defined in the glossary are entered alphabetically in accordance with the English language.

PART B.   GLOSSARY

1 Scope

This glossary contains the terms and their definitions which are used in the management and practice of the science of quality and reliability.

2 The Glossary

absolute frequency   A term used alternatively to **frequency**. *See also* **relative frequency**.

accelerated life test   A life test in which the stress is raised above the specified maximum for the characteristic of the item under test. Also, a cyclical life test in which the frequency of the cycle is increased above that for the specified maximum frequency of operation for the characteristic of the item under test.

accelerated test   A test in which the applied stress level is chosen to exceed that stated in the reference conditions in order to shorten the time required to observe the response of the item to the stress or magnify the responses in a given time. *Note:* To be valid an accelerated test must not alter the basic modes and/or mechanisms of failure, or their relative prevalence.

acceleration test   An environmental test in which the item is subjected to a specified rate of acceleration in a specified directional sense along a specified axis for a specified time. The item is then measured to determine if damage or change has occurred.

accept [ASQC]   To decide that a batch, lot or quantity of product, material or service satisfies the requirement criteria based on the information obtained from the sample(s).

accept number   Not a preferred term; see **acceptance number**.

accept reject criteria   The sampling inspection accept or reject numbers, the specification limits, the contract conditions, or other criteria against which products or services are assessed for acceptance or rejection.

acceptable   A condition wherein products or services satisfactorily meet the requirements specified for them.

acceptable component failure level   A level of component failure occurring in systems under life test which is considered acceptable by the customer in consideration of reliability and maintenance.

acceptable mean life   A life value so chosen that it corresponds to the mean value of a distribution which represents a spread of life values that can be tolerated.

acceptable quality level (AQL) [ASQC]   The maximum percentage or proportion of variant units in a lot or batch that, for the purposes of acceptance sampling, can be considered satisfactory as a process average.

acceptability criterion (variables sampling)   (1) For a single lower specification limit, the condition that the quantity $\bar{x} - L/\overline{R}$ shall be equal to or less than the acceptability constant K obtainable from the variables sampling tables; (2) for a single upper specification limit, the condition that the quantity $U - \bar{x}\,\overline{R}$ shall be equal to or greater than the acceptability constant K obtainable from the variables sampling tables; (3) for double specification limits, the condition that the total estimated percent failing meets the condition obtainable from the variables sampling tables.

$\bar{x}$ = mean value of x for the sample of n units
$\overline{R}$ = average of the ranges of the subgroups of units
L = lower specification limit
U = upper specification limit acceptance

acceptance   The agreement to take items as offered and the related activities accompanying such agreement.

acceptance inspection   The inspection of products or services for the purpose of collecting data on which to base acceptance decisions.

acceptance number (attributes) [ASQC]   The maximum number of variants or variant units in the sample that will permit acceptance of the inspected lot or batch.

acceptance procedure   The prescribed method, involving supplier and customer, by which ownership or control of products or services is progressively transferred to the customer from the supplier.

acceptance sampling [ASQC]   Sampling inspection in which decisions are made to accept or not accept products or services; also, the methodology that deals with procedures by which decisions to accept or not-accept are based on the results of the inspection of samples.

acceptance sampling plan [ASQC]   A specific plan that states the sample size or sizes to be used, and the associated acceptance and nonacceptance criteria.

acceptance sampling scheme [ASQC]   A specific set of procedures which usually consists of acceptance sampling plans in which lot sizes, sample sizes and acceptance criteria, or the amount of 100 percent inspection and sampling are related. (*Note:* A scheme normally contains rules for switching and operating the scheme.)

acceptance sampling system [ASQC]   A collection of sampling schemes together with criteria for selection of a scheme.

accreditation [ASQC]   Certification by a duly recognized body of the facilities, capability, objectivity, competence and integrity of an agency, service or operational group or individual to provide the specific service(s) or operation(s) needed.

accuracy   A qualitative term describing the degree of closeness with which the indications of an instrument approach the true value of the physical quantity, property, or condition which is measured. *Note:* For quantitative use, the term "uncertainty" replaces "accuracy."

accuracy components   The sources of uncertainty involved in a measurement that determine the two parts of "accuracy," i.e., precision and bias. *Note:* A number of measurements of the same characteristic made by using the same measuring equipment yields a distribution of values whose scatter represents the *precision* and whose mean value displacement from the true value represents the *bias.*

accuracy in the mean   The closeness between the true value and the mean value obtained from a number of measurements.

accuracy of data   The closeness of existing data to that which correctly relates a situation.

action limits   Control limits set on quality control charts such that a prescribed course of action must be taken when points fall outside the limits.

action point   The point plotted on a quality control chart, usually in relation to an action or warning limit after which corrective action on the process is required.

active preventive maintenance time   That part of the preventive maintenance time, including technical delays inherent in the actions, during which preventive maintenance actions are performed on an item either manually or automatically.

active redundancy   A state of redundancy wherein more than one means of performing a given function is operating at the same time.

active repair time   That part of the maintenance time in which corrective maintenance actions are performed on an item, including the time due to delays inherent in the repair operation. *Note:* Active repair time does not include (1) repair time for replacement items or (2) administrative, waiting, or access times. Active repair time may be stated in terms of a mean value and a maximum repair time associated with a stated percentile.

additional processing   Processing above and beyond that normally required to generate the relevant characteristic(s) required.

adequacy of standards   The condition existing in a manufacturer's plant when properly calibrated standards of suitable accuracy are available to support all measurements of characteristics required by specifications.

administrative time   The period of time during which an item has failed and corrective maintenance actions are pending or are being prepared but have not yet been initiated.

advanced measurement   Measurement involving specialized technical skills and measuring instrumentation of a highly sophisticated or complex nature.

analysis of variance (ANOVA)   A technique by which the total variation of a set of data is subdivided into meaningful component parts each of which is associated with a specific source of variation for the purpose of testing some hypothesis on the parameters of the model or estimating variance components.

analysis sample   A number of items or a quantity of material taken for analysis purposes.

application for quality system approval   An application made by a manufacturer or wholesaler to a customer or other approving authority to have the quality system evaluated and approved against a nominated standard.

appraisal   An assessment or determination of values of a thing or situation against a specification or standard for some purpose.

approval, capability   An approval granted to a supplier for a range of products or services for which it has been demonstrated that the total quality system (covering design and/or manufacturing) is capable of supplying products or services the quality of which meets the specified requirements.

approval, qualification   An approval given to the production system of a manufacturer whose product has been demonstrated to meet all the requirements of the product specification and quality plan.

approval, type   An approval given to a design that has been shown by type tests to meet all the requirements of the product specification and is therefore suitable for some specific application.

approved component   A specific manufacturer's component, designated by a unique part number, which has been evaluated against specified performance requirements and approved by the design authority for use in a particular application.

approved supplier   A company that is operating and controlling an evaluated and approved system of effective controls under a defined and documented management control structure, thereby giving it the capability of ensuring that fully conforming items will be produced and delivered.

approved supplier program (ASP)   A program—planned, implemented, and carried out by a customer—whereby vendors who develop adequate systems of quality control are evaluated against an adopted and agreed-upon standard and given qualification approval. It reduces the amount of incoming quality assurance effort required by the customer.

arithmetic mean   The average value of a quantity of data; it is calculated by dividing the sum of n observed values by n.

assessed failure rate   The failure rate of an item determined as a limiting value of as limiting values of the confidence interval with a stated confidence level. It is based on the same data as the observed failure rate of nominally identical items. *Note:* When the limit is single-valued, it is usually the upper value.

assessment   The procedure by which the acceptance or rejection of some item or system is determined.

assignable cause   A determinable cause of a variation in a characteristic.

assignable cause (process)   A detectable and identifiable cause of nonuniformity in a process.

attribute   A characteristic (e.g., go or no go) which is appraised in terms of whether it meets or does not meet a given requirement.

attributes, method of [ASQC]   Measurement of quality by the method of attributes consists of noting the presence (or absence) of some characteristic or attribute in each of the units in the group under consideration, and counting how many units do (or do not) possess the quality attribute, or how many such events occur in the unit, group or area.

audit   A verification activity aimed at evaluating the conformance of the design, product, process, or system.

audit, inspection   The systematic examination or inspection of products or services for the purpose of ascertaining that specified acceptance inspection of the items has been correctly carried out.

audit, product quality   A quantitative assessment of the conformance of product characteristics to the requirements.

audit, quality   A systematic and independent examination to determine whether quality activities and results comply with planned arrangements and whether those arrangements are effectively implemented and are suitable to achieve objectives.

audit, quality system   A documented activity performed to verify, by examination and evaluation of objective evidence, that applicable elements of the quality system are effectively implemented in accordance with specified requirements.

audit of calibration system   A planned and periodic assessment of the carrying out of the activities of a calibration system against the specified or agreed standard.

audit of inspection system   The regular and planned verification of the existence and proper operation of an inspection system.

audit of product quality   Inspection of product at a lesser frequency and/or severity than that which is carried out for normal quality control and acceptance purposes as an aid to assessing the effectiveness of the quality controls.

audit trail continuity control   The maintenance of traceability along the path or sequence of actions constituting the activities underway as a result of requirements for traceability in respect to certain system controls.

availability [ASQC]   The ability of an item to perform its designated function when required for use. (*Note:* Availability may be calculated for an instant of time, or over a defined period of time.)

availability, instantaneous   The probability that an item can perform required functions under stated conditions at a stated instant of time.

availability, mean   The mean of the instantaneous availabilities of an item in a stated interval of time.

average   *See* **mean**.

average amount of inspection   In a given sampling plan, the average number of items expected to be inspected per batch in order to reach a decision for a certain batch quality.

average life   The arithmetic means of the lives of the items in a quantity of life test items.

average number of defects or nonconformities per item   The number of defects or nonconformities observed in a given number of items divided by the number of items inspected.

average outgoing quality (AOQ) [ASQC] The expected quality of outgoing product following the use of an acceptance sampling plan for a given value of incoming product quality. (*Note:* Computation of the AOQ depends on decisions taken regarding variant units and sample units, and their disposition.)

average outgoing quality limit (AOQL) [ASQC] For a given acceptance sampling plan, the maximum AOQ over all possible levels of incoming quality.

average quality protection A procedure for keeping the average proportion of nonconforming items in deliveries of a product (if necessary after inspection and rectification) at or below some specified limit. It is to be expected that occasionally individual batches may exceed that limit.

average run length (ARL) (sample sense) [ASQC] The average number of times that a process will have been sampled and evaluated before a shift in process level is signaled.

average run length (ARL) (unit sense) [ASQC] The average number of units that will have been produced before a shift in level is signaled.

average sample number (ASN) [ASQC] The average number of sample units per lot used for making decisions (to accept or reject).

average sample number curve A graphic representation of the average sample number as a function of quality.

average sample size Not a preferred term; see **average sample number**.

average total inspection (ATI) [ASQC] The average number of units inspected per lot based on the sample size for accepted lots and all inspected units in non-accepted lots.

band chart A graphic representation of time-related quantities wherein the record of observations during successive intervals of time is represented as bands across the chart.

bar chart A chart portraying relative magnitudes by the lengths of bars of uniform width.

basic physical standard Not a preferred term; see **primary physical standard**.

basic size A dimension in relation to which all limits of variation are specified. Alternatively, the **nominal value**.

basic standard A reference document from which other documents derive their authority.

batch (or lot) An identified quantity of a commodity manufactured by one supplier under conditions of manufacture that are presumed to be uniform.

batch fraction defective or nonconforming The total number of variant units in a batch divided by the total number of units in the batch.

batch inspection The inspection of material in batches or lots, as compared with other methods, e.g., continuous inspection and 100 percent inspection.

batch percent defective or nonconforming The total number of variant units in a batch divided by the total number of units in the batch and multiplied by 100.

batch size   The number of units of product or services in a batch.

batch variation (within the batch)   The maximum variation, among units from the batch, of the characteristic under consideration.

batch variation (between batches)   The difference between similar points on the distributions of the batches being considered. The points represent the same characteristic from each batch.

bathtub curve   A composite curve constructed by joining the early failure rate and constant failure rate curves for a product to the normalized curve of wear-out failure rate of the product. *Note:* The early failure and constant failure curves constitute exponential functions; the wear-out normal distribution normalized curve represents the progressive reciprocal of the cumulative number of wear-out failures.

beginning of stress   That point in time at which a specified stress is applied to an item for the first time.

bias   A property of a measurement or a statistical estimate such that the result of repeated measurements or estimates have a systematic error in relation to the true value of the estimated parameter as distinct from random errors which are attached to individual measurements or estimates but balance out on the average, i.e., have zero mean value.

bias of estimate   The deviation of the expectation of an estimate of a parameter from the true value of the parameter.

biased sample   A sample which, for the characteristic under consideration, has a systematic error component that is different from that for the batch or population from which the sample came.

biased test   A test which gives a lower probability of rejecting the hypothesis under test H_1 when an alternative hypothesis H_2 is true than when H_1 is true. Alternatively, a test which gives a higher probability of accepting the hypothesis under test H_{1a} when an alternative hypothesis H_{2a} is false than when the hypothesis H_{1a} is false.

binomial distribution   The distribution of the number of occurrences X of an event in n independent trials when the probability p of the events occurring in each of the trials is constant. This is expressed mathematically as follows;

$$P_{r\,(X-x)} = \frac{n!}{x!(n-x)!}\,p^x(1-p)^{n-x} \qquad (1.1)$$

where $0 < p < 1$ and x is an integer.

bond store (or warehouse)   A store, capable of being sealed against ingress and egress, which is used to hold items under bond, usually for customs purposes.

branding   Not a preferred term; see **marking**.

breadboard model   Not a preferred term; see **design model**.

breakdown inspection   Not a preferred term; see **disassembly inspection**.

bug   A variant which causes or can cause operational difficulty.

build standard   A list of records at a defined issue status for an item of equipment. It comprises all the drawings and lists of instructions necessary for the manufacture, overhaul, and reconditioning of that equipment and, when appropriate, for testing, packaging, and installation. *Note:* Also known as *master work record* or as *master record index*.

build state   The actual build of an item of equipment as produced.

bulk sampling   The sampling of materials available in bulk quantities. *Note:* Often used when raw materials or materials from mining or agricultural sources are sampled.

bump test   Not a preferred term; see **shock test**.

burn-in   The initial operational stressing of an item within its design limits under operating conditions for the purpose of eliminating early failures.

c (count)   The count or number of events of a given classification occurring in a sample. *Note:* More than one event may occur in a unit or area of opportunity, and each such event throughout the sample is counted.

calculated value   A value arrived at from first principles with the aid of mathematics and without the use of measurement.

calibration (comparative sense)   The process of comparing or measuring an instrument or gauge of known accuracy, called the standard, with a second instrument or gauge for the purpose of obtaining, through observation and adjustment as necessary, correlation of indications between the two and thereby enabling a statement of accuracy to be made for the second measuring instrument or gauge.

calibration (analysis sense)   The process used in determining the values of the errors of measuring instruments, physical standards, and, as necessary, other metrological properties such as influence quantities.

calibration accuracy   The maximum difference from the true value of a characteristic which can be obtained by a measurement using a calibrated instrument or gauge.

calibration error   Not a preferred term; see **error of measurement**.

calibration identification   The label or tag attached to a calibrated instrument or gauge; it should show when the device is due for calibration next time, the date of last calibration, and the mark of the authorized person.

calibration interval   The period of time beginning with the calibration of an instrument or gauge and terminating with the next successive actual time of calibration. Also called *calibration period*.

calibration labeling system   The program used to provide calibration status identification of instruments or gauges.

calibration period   *See* **calibration interval**.

calibration procedure   The documented sequence of actions, with associated equipment and standards, used to carry out a calibration.

calibration program   The planned and documented system of effort and equipment, including standards, recall system labeling, etc., used in an organization to keep the measuring equipment calibrated.

calibration records   The objective evidence maintained in the form of documents, labels, data, and other filed information which shows the calibration status of all measuring equipment.

calibration seal   A means of preventing tampering with or accidental altering of the adjustment of parts on an instrument or gauge which has been calibrated. *Note:* Sealing is used to ensure the lasting integrity of the calibration.

calibration security   The system of sealing and controls used to maintain the integrity of measuring equipment calibration.

calibration source   The calibration standard, personnel, and organization which imparted to the measuring equipment its degree of known accuracy.

calibration standard   Any physical object, quantity, or material used to compare with an unknown but related object or instrument for the purpose of transferring a state of known value or indicating ability to the second object or instrument.

capability   Not a preferred term; see **process capability**.

capability approval   Approval granted to a supplier for a range of products or services for which it has been demonstrated that the supplier's declared design rules, manufacturing process, and quality control are capable of producing products or services the quality of which meets or will meet the specified requirements.

catastrophic failure   Failure which is both sudden and complete.

central line [ASQC]   A line on a control chart representing the long-term average or a standard value of the statistical measure being plotted.

certainty   The degree of probability with which some quantity may be estimated.

certificate of acceptance   Documentation of an acceptance decision given to a supplier by a customer concerning some item or quantity of products or services.

certificate of compliance [ASQC]   A document signed by an authorized party affirming that the supplier of a product or service has met the requirements of the relevant specifications, contract, or regulation.

certificate of conformance (certificate of conformity)   A document signed by an authorized party affirming that a product or service has met the requirements of the relevant specifications, contract, or regulation.

certificate of receipt   A document, issued by a customer or receiving organization, providing objective evidence of the receipt of some item or quantity of products or services.

certification [ASQC]   The procedure and action by a duly authorized body of determining, verifying, and attesting in writing to the qualifications of personnel, processes, procedures, or items in accordance with applicable requirements.

certification body   An impartial body or organization, a regulatory body or organization, or the quality organization of a supplier that possesses the necessary competence and integrity to provide the specified services and/or required operation.

certified reference material (CRM)   Material in any chemical or physical state or form that has had one or more of its characteristics determined by the national calibration laboratory and is used for the purpose of a standard or reference material in the determination of corresponding characteristics in production material.

chain sampling plan [ASQC]   Sampling inspection in which the criteria for acceptance and nonacceptance of the lot depend in part on the results of the inspection of immediately preceding lots.

chance causes (random causes) [ASQC]   Factors, generally numerous and individually of relatively small importance, which contribute to variation, but which are not feasible to detect or identify.

chance variation (random variation) [ASQC]   Variation due to chance causes.

change control   A documented system whereby changes in a product are either prevented or introduced in a controlled manner.

change notice   A document notifying each manager in an organization who will be affected by a change of the intention to introduce the change. It is usually used to obtain the approvals and signatures necessary to authorize the change.

characteristic [ASQC]   A property of items in a sample or population which, when measured, counted, or otherwise observed, helps to distinguish between the items. (*Note:* Products or services have features each of which have one or more characteristics. It is the characteristics that are measured, not the features.)

***c* (count) chart**   A control chart for evaluating a process in terms of the count of events c of a given classification occurring in the sample. *Note:* A unit, or area of opportunity, may contain more than one event.

D chart   A control chart for evaluating a process in terms of a demerit score.

***np* chart**   A control chart for evaluating a process in terms of the total number of units (i.e., areas of opportunity) in a sample in which an event of a given classification occurs.

***p* (fraction defective) chart**   A control chart for evaluating a process in terms of the fraction defective p of the total number of units in a sample in which a given event occurs. *Note:* A unit is counted only once, regardless of the number of events having the classification which occur.

Q chart   A control chart for evaluating a process in terms of a quality score.

R (range) chart   A control chart for evaluating the variability within a process in terms of the subgroup standard deviation S.

S (sigma) chart   A control chart for evaluating the variability within a process in terms of the subgroup standard deviation S.

u **chart**   A control chart for evaluating a process in terms of the average count of events of a given classification per unit occurring within a sample.

$\bar{x}$ **(x bar) chart**   A control chart for evaluating the process or subgroup differences in terms of the subgroup average x. *Note:* Usually used in conjunction with an R chart.

chi-squared test   A mathematical test performed on two sets of data of the same random variable to determine if the two distributions are different at a given level of significance.

class (as a set)   An arbitrarily defined set or group of items having some common attribute.

class (for variates)   A class formed by an arbitrarily defined part of the range of variate values.

class boundaries   The extreme possible magnitudes or values which can occur in a class. *Note:* In statistics the class boundaries of 0.210 to 0.232 have the extreme possible magnitudes of 0.20950 to 0.23249 (to five decimal places), whereas in engineering usage the class boundaries of 0.210 to 0.232 have the extreme possible magnitudes of 0.21000 to 0.23200 (to five decimal places).

class interval   In a frequency distribution having equally wide classes, the difference between any two consecutive midvalues.

class limits   The values defining the upper and lower bounds of a class. *Note:* The limit belonging to the class should be specified.

class variate limits   The observable or recorded variate values which determine the upper and lower limits of a class.

classification   The act of grouping items into classes.

classification of defects or nonconformities   A procedure whereby each of the measurable characteristics of a feature of an item, product, or service is noted, listed, and then classified as to its seriousness should it fail, according to some division of the 0 to 100 percent seriousness range.

clearance number [ASQC]   As associated with a continuous sampling plan, the number of successively inspected units of product that must be found acceptable during the 100 percent inspection sequence before action to change the amount of inspection can be taken.

clearance sample   The number of successively sampled units that must, in a continuous sampling plan, be conforming or nondefective in order to switch to random sampling.

coding   Mathematically modifying observed values or data in order to simplify statistical computations thereon.

coding for control   The process of identifying a number of items according to some prescribed code for the purpose of controlling them, usually in later processing.

coefficient of variation   The standard deviation when divided by the arithmetic mean; it may be multiplied by 100 to express the coefficient as a percentage.

cold solder joint   A solder joint wherein the solder does not wet one or more of the adjoining surfaces and therefore does not provide low-resistance electrical continuity. The nonwetting may be due to inadequate heating, contamination, chemical incompatibility, or movement of the workpieces while the solder is soft.

cold test   A test conducted on an item to determine the capability of the item to endure for a specified time a specified temperature below ambient without unacceptable change.

commercial in confidence   Information or knowledge imparted or gained which is the property of one or more parties and is not to be communicated outside a stated limited sphere of activity.

commodity   Anything of value which is traded in commerce, normally referred to as a product or service.

company confidential   Information which is of high commercial value to a company and which demands protection by those who come into possession of it.

company quality policy   An expression of the belief and intent, usually by the chief executive officer of a company, concerning the quality of products and/or services supplied by the company.

compatibility   The suitability of products and/or services to be used together under specified conditions to fulfill the relevant requirements without causing unacceptable interactions.

complete failure   Failure resulting from deviations in characteristics beyond specified limits such as to cause complete lack of the required function. *Note:* Normally, special limits are specified for this purpose.

compliance [ASQC]   An affirmative indication or judgment that the supplier of a product or service has met the requirements of the relevant specifications, contract or regulation; also the state of meeting the requirements.

component   Any single identifiable part of a whole.

compression test   A test in which a material or item is subjected to a specified compressive load stress along a stated axis for a stated time and then examined for damage or for the determination of the failure point.

concession (waiver)   Written authorization to use or release a quantity of material, components, or stores that have already been manufactured but do not conform to the specified requirements. *Note:* Concessions (waivers) should be for limited quantities or periods and for specified uses.

conditional probability of failure   The probability that items taken from initials will fail before a given instant of time.

conditioning   The planned exposure of an item to a stress or sequence of stresses prior to carrying out specified tests on or using the item for a specified purpose.

conditioning monitoring   The practice of making and assessing measurements of physical quantities on operating plant for the purpose of judging the fitness of the plant to continue in service.

conditions of use   The conditions which must be fulfilled in order to use a measuring instrument correctly, taking into account the design, construction, and purpose of the instrument.

confidence (inspection)   See **confidence (quality assurance)**.

confidence (quality assurance)   Belief, based on knowledge, experience, and statistical inference, in the outcome of some particular result.

confidence coefficient (level)   Not a preferred term; see **confidence level**.

confidence interval   The interval of θ between T_1 and T_2 such that

$$P_{(T_1 < \theta < T_2)} = 1 - a \qquad (1.2)$$

where T_1 and T_2 are functions of the observed value, θ is the population parameter to be estimated, and a is a positive fixed number less than 1.

confidence interval, one-sided   An interval of θ at the confidence level wherein T is a function of the observed values such that, θ being a population parameter to be estimated, the probability Pr $(T < \theta)$ or the probability Pr $(T > \theta)$ is equal to a stated confidence level, the interval from the smallest possible value of θ up to T or the interval between T and the greatest possible value of θ. *Note:* The limit T of the confidence interval is a random variable and as such will assume different values in every sample.

confidence interval (two-sided)   The interval between T_1 and T_2 for θ at the confidence level wherein it is possible to define two functions T_1 and T_2 of the observed value such that, θ being a population parameter to be estimated, the probability Pr $(T_1 < \theta < T_2)$ is equal to a stated confidence level. *Note:* The limits T_1 and T_2 of the confidence interval are random variables and, as such, they will usually assume different values in every sample.

confidence level   The value of the probability associated with a confidence interval or a statistical tolerance interval.

confidence limit(s)   The end points of the confidence interval that is believed to include the population parameter with a specified degree of confidence. *Note:* These are normally expressed as the upper confidence limit (UCL) and the lower confidence limit (LCL).

configuration   The functional physical and interrelational characteristics of a product or system delineated in supporting documentation.

configuration change control   The systematic evaluation, coordination, approval, or disapproval of changes and implementation of all approved changes in the configuration of an item after the initial definition of the configuration.

configuration management   The discipline within an organization that applies technical and administrative direction and surveillance to identify and document the functional and physical characteristics of an item, control changes to those characteristics, and record and report processing and implementation status of changes.

conformance [ASQC]   An affirmative indication or judgment that a product or service has met the requirements of the relevant specifications, contract, or regulation; also the state of meeting the requirements.

conforming material [ASQC]   Material which is found by measurement to be within the specified limits set for each of its characteristics.

conformity   The fulfilling of specification requirements by a product or service.

consignment   A quantity of some commodity shipped or delivered at one time.

constant failure rate period   The period of time during the life of an item in which failures occur at an approximately uniform rate. *Note:* Also known as the *chance failure rate period.*

consumer's decision risk   Not a preferred term; see **consumer's risk**.

consumer's risk   The probability of accepting a batch or lot whose fraction or percent nonconforming has a value stated by the given sampling plan as rejectable.

contingency table   A tabular form of presentation having data in rows and columns so as to display clearly the relations between various factors.

continual use   The uninterrupted operation of some item or device.

continuous sampling plan [ASQC]   A plan intended for application to a continuous flow of individual units of product that (1) involves acceptance or nonacceptance on a unit-by-unit basis and (2) uses alternate periods of 100% inspection and sampling depending on the quality of the observed product.

contract   A legally binding agreement between two or more parties for the transfer between the parties of something of value. *Note:* A contract must comprise two parties dealing at arm's length wherein there has been a meeting of the minds concerning what is to be exchanged. That which is to be exchanged must have value. Also, if the agreement is illegal, the contract is not valid.

contract quality requirements   The clauses in a contract which specify and/or stipulate the degree(s) of conformance with which products and/or services supplied must meet the specified requirements and the methods whereby objective evidence of such is to be obtained and communicated.

contractor   One of the parties to a contract, usually the supplier.

contractor assessment (evaluation sense)   A process whereby a contractor's (supplier's) organization, facilities, plant, and capabilities are studied in depth against established standards, contract requirements, and the quality manual to determine the ability of the contractor (supplier) to meet the requirements of these. *Note:* The assessment should ascertain the ability of the contractor to make a product of the required quality and deliver it on time.

contractor's quality control system   The system of management controls that comprises all the things which have been and will be done to ensure that products and/or services of specified quality will be supplied on time.

control   The methods by which some desired result is ensured.

control chart   A chart on which limits are drawn and on which are plotted values of any statistic(s) obtained from successive or sequential samples of products or services.

control chart factor [ASQC]   A factor, usually varying with sample size, to convert specified statistics or parameters into a central line value or control limit appropriate to the control chart.

control chart method [ASQC]   The method of using control charts to determine whether or not processes are in a stable state.

control file   A distinct place where records of control systems and activities are kept.

control limits [ASQC]   Limits on a control chart which are used as criteria for signaling the need for action, or for judging whether a set of data does or does not indicate a "state of statistical control."

control system   The system of controls by which control of some desired result is achieved.

controlled process   A production process involving ensuring the stability of one or more item parameters the variance of which is controlled within specified limits.

coordination activity   A program activity designed to achieve a planned sequence and order of results from the effort underway with due attention to each facet of the work in respect to its importance.

correctable cause   A cause of nonconformance in products or services such that it can be assigned to a tangible source and positive action can be taken to eliminate it.

corrective action   Measures taken to rectify conditions adverse to quality.

corrective action board (CAB)   A contractor or supplier board consisting of management representatives of appropriate contractor's organizations with a level of responsibility and authority sufficient to assure that causes of nonconformances are identified and corrective actions are effected.

corrective maintenance   The maintenance carried out after a failure has occurred in order to restore the item to a state in which it can perform its required function(s).

corrective maintenance time   The part of the maintenance time, including that due to logistics delays, during which corrective maintenance is performed on an item.

cost of quality   The cost of achieving a specified level of quality in a product or service.

count [ASQC]   The count or number of events of a given classification occurring in a sample. *Note:* More than one event may occur in a unit, and each such occurrence throughout the sample is counted.

count per 100 units [ASQC]   The average count, or average number of events of a given classification, per 100 units occurring within a sample. *Note:* It is common to count the average number of nonconformities per 100 units.

critical defect   A defect that judgment and experience indicate is likely to result in hazardous or unsafe conditions for individuals depending on, using, or maintaining the product or service or to result in harm to other products.

critical defective   A unit of product or service which contains one or more critical defects and which may also contain other defects or nonconformities.

critical failure   A failure which is likely to cause injury to persons or significant damage to material.

critical nonconforming unit   A unit of product or service which contains one or more critical nonconformities and which may also contain other nonconformities.

critical nonconformity   A nonconformity that judgment and experience indicate is likely to result in hazardous or unsafe conditions for individuals depending on, using, or maintaining the product or service or to result in harm to other products.

critical variant   A variant that judgment and experience indicate is likely to result in hazardous or unsafe conditions for individuals depending on, using, or maintaining the product or service or to result in harm to other products.

critical variant unit   A unit of product or service which contains one or more critical variants and which may also contain other variants.

cumulative   The process of increasing in value, magnitude, or number by successive additions.

cumulative distribution   Not a preferred term; see **cumulative frequency probability function**.

cumulative error   An error which is systematic and unidirectional and which increases with successive use or application.

cumulative error effect   The algebraic sum of all the error effects (i.e., uncertainties) upon which a statement of value is dependent for its accuracy.

cumulative failure frequency   The sum of the failure frequencies up to a given point in time.

cumulative frequency   The total frequency of values less than or equal to a class boundary.

cumulative frequency (probability) function   The function $G(x)$ of a variate θ, i.e., the number of occurrences of members with variate values less than or equal to θ.

cumulative frequency curve   A graph of cumulative frequency along the ordinate against the variable value along the abcissa.

cumulative frequency polygon   A diagram in which the tops of the ordinates representing the values of cumulative frequency at the corresponding class boundaries, e.g., of the variate, are linked by straight lines.

cumulative normal distribution   The cumulative frequency function of the normal distribution.

cumulative result   The aggregate sum of a succession of items or values.

cumulative time   The sum of the times in a stated period, during which all the individual items under observation have been subjected to the stated stress conditions, excluding any downtime.

curtailed inspection   An inspection program which has been stopped for any reason.

customer   The party to an exchange of ownership or control of some commodity who is the recipient of the commodity or control. In a contractual situation, the party who receives the benefit of the product or service provided under the contract.

customer feedback and corrective action   A program of feedback and corrective action based upon customer-supplied data and including activities which embrace the corrective action.

customer inspection   Inspection of a product or service by a customer as opposed to inspection of the same commodity by the supplier.

customer-supplied material control   Control by a product or service supplier of any supplies furnished by the customer and usually intended for inclusion in or with the product or service or for supportive use. *Note:* The primary purpose of such control is preservation and protection of the quality characteristics of the customer-supplied material.

cusum chart   A chart on which are plotted values of some statistical measure for a series of samples, the ordinate of each point plotted being composed of the ordinate of the immediately preceding point plus the value of the statistic from the last sample. *Note:* "Cusum" is an acronym of "cummulative sums."

cycle time   The time between two points of equal value and direction.

cycling test   A test wherein the method or methods of stress applied to an item are cycled one or more times and the item is then tested for change.

data   Information stored or communicated in any form; specifically, statistics obtained from measurements and observations.

date code   A set of data, normally placed on the item, indicating the year-month-day on which the item of product reached its completed stage of manufacture and acceptance testing and from which time the life of the item is reckoned.

debugging (hardware sense)   A process whereby items of equipment are operated for a time prior to their use for the purpose of identifying, removing, and replacing parts or characteristics which are found to be defective or nonconforming and to correct other errors and weaknesses.

debugging (software sense)   A process whereby software programs are progressively examined by people or equipment and then applied in their intended applications for the purpose of identifying, removing, and correcting elements which are found to be defective or nonconforming and to correct other errors and weaknesses.

decision function   A rule which, at any given stage of a sampling investigation or designed experiment, shows whether sufficient information has been collected or further observations must be made and also what decision to make on the information at that stage.

decision point   In a sampling plan or designed experiment, a specified stage at which sufficient information should have been accumulated to make some decision about acceptance, rejection, or continuation.

defect [ISO]   The nonfulfillment of intended usage requirements. [*Note:* In the International Standards Organization (ISO) definition, the basic difference between "nonconformity" and "defect" is that the specified requirements may differ from the requirements for the intended use. See **nonconformity**.]

defect or nonconformity analysis   The analysis performed relative to a defective or nonconforming unit of product for the purpose of identifying and/or correcting the basic cause(s).

defect or nonconformity classification list   A list of the characteristics of the features of an item, arranged in accordance with a seriousness classification over the range from 0 to 100, whereby the values of the characteristics and their degrees of conformance are assessed for their significance to the use of the product or service.

defective [ISO]   An item of product or a service containing one or more characteristics that does not fulfill intended usage requirements.

defective (defective unit) [ASQC]   A unit of product or service containing at least one defect, or having several imperfections that in combination cause the unit to fail to satisfy intended normal, or reasonably foreseeable usage requirements.

defective material report   A report, provided from inside or outside a supplier's organization, containing information on a defective item for the purpose of providing awareness and the application of corrective action.

defects per 100 units   The number of defects or nonconformances as a limit or as measured in 100 units of the product or service concerned. *Note:* Used most often with complex products in which there is a large number of characteristic repetitions.

defects per item   The possible or actual number of defects in an item.

defects per item, average   The sum of all the defects in a number of items divided by the number of items.

degradation failure   A failure which is both gradual and partial.

degree of inspection   The severity with which a given quantity of product or services is inspected.

degrees of freedom   A whole number used for entering statistical tables of distribution. It is obtained by subtracting the number of independent parameters assessed from the sample size. For example, $S^2 = \Sigma (x - \bar{x})^2/(n - 1)$ has $n - 1$ degrees of freedom, since the mean is estimated from the sample.

deliverables Controlled software items found to be acceptable and to be delivered to the customer by the software developer. *Note:* May also be used with products of other types.

delivery (see shipment) The quantity of a commodity delivered at the one time. *Note:* A consignment may consist of more than one delivery or shipment.

delivery quality The quality of the product or service at the time of delivery.

demerit A numerical value assigned to a defect, nonconformity, or variant which is determined by the seriousness of the defect or nonconformance in respect to the function of the item. *Note:* The number of demerits often assigned is equal to the nearest whole-numbered reciprocal of the acceptable quality level (AQL).

demerit rating A numerical rating of an item based on demerits assigned in accordance with some prescribed weighting scheme which ties a demerit value to the seriousness of the defect or nonconformance found.

demerit report A report of an inspection, audit, or other assessment based on a scheme of demerit rating.

dependability [ASQC] The state of being counted on or trusted.

dependent failure A failure of a part which occurs as a direct result of an independent failure, i.e., one caused by an associated part or item.

dependent variable A characteristic of a feature of an item the magnitude or value of which is directly influenced by the magnitude or value of some other characteristic.

derating (adjustment sense) The lowering of stress applied to an item by one stress field in order to allow an increase in the stress that can be applied to the item by another stress field or add to the reliable operating life of the item.

derating (use sense) The use of an item in such a way that applied stresses are below rated strength values.

derating factor 1 minus the quotient of the actual stress divided by the maximum specified operating stress.

design The expression of ideas in drawn, written, or physical terms.

design approval authority The person or organization who or which has the authority for approving the design and making changes thereto. *Note:* During manufacture, the authority for changes in design often transfers from those doing the original design work to other technically qualified persons in the manufacturing or customer facility.

design authority The person or organization who or which has the responsibility for the design and the preparation, modification, or interpretation of specifications of products or services.

design documentation control The orderly development, standardizing, and promulgation of all necessary documentation related to the design function and its output.

design freeze   The stage at the end of the design phase and the start of the production phase during which it is progressively inappropriate to make any further change in the design because of the costs and delays which would be incurred. *Note:* A design freeze may be complete for mass production, or it may be limited in project situations in which the design authority continues active in the production or development of the small number of total products of the project.

design guide   A documented expression of general and specific design guidelines, limits, and requirements in a particular field.

design model   A physical construction representing the design idea. *Note:* The design model may be an actual laboratory-built working model, or it may be a prototype or a first-piece production sample from the factory.

design quality (or quality of design)   (1) When the design specifies the process, the degree to which the design defines the most economical manufacturing actions, equipment, and controls needed to produce a product that will be fit for the intended purpose. (2) When the design specifies only the product or service, the degree to which the design defines the most economical product which will best suit the purpose of the customer.

design reliability (or reliability of design)   (1) The part of the product reliability derived from the design specification of material, processing, methods, assembly configuration, limits, or performance. (2) The durability of the design expression making it possible to produce the product without changes.

design review [ASQC]   A formal, documented, comprehensive, and systematic examination of a design to evaluate the design requirements and the capability of the design to meet these requirements and to identify problems and propose solutions.

design safety factor   The ratio of the design safety margin to the range of the characteristic within the specified limits (for a stated design limit).

design safety margin   The portion of the range of any designed characteristic that lies outside the design limits but within which the product or service will still satisfactorily carry out its intended purpose.

design specification   A documented expression of the requirements which the process and/or the product or service must meet.

design verification tests   Tests performed for the purpose of verifying that the design intent, as expressed in the design specification, has been embodied in the material, equipment, or system.

destructive testing   Tests which stress one or more of the characteristics of the product or process beyond the point of recovery.

developer   A person who or organization which develops a design idea into an embodiment of the idea.

developmental model   A model of the product or service produced during the development phase.

deviation   Any departure from the specified range of a characteristic.

dimensional metrology   The field of metrology that has to do with length, angle, conformation and geometric relationships.

directional sample   In bulk sampling, a geometric sample taken in only one dimension related to a single axis of variability of material in a unit or quantity of product.

disassembly inspection   The inspection of a product which has been assembled to the degree at which the characteristic to be measured has been masked and disassembly is therefore necessary before the test can be performed.

discrepancy   Any departure from requirements.

discrimination ratio   The ratio of the specified MTBF to the minimum acceptable MTBF (or a similar ratio for other quantities).

dispersion   The degree of scatter shown by observation of a characteristic.

disposition   Actions in respect to a nonconforming product that are directed to be taken by a preliminary review or material review board.

distribution (logistics)   The delivery of products or services to wholesalers, retailers, or other customers.

distribution (statistics)   *See* **frequency distribution**.

distribution curve   The line enveloping a frequency distribution.

distribution-free (statistics)   Any of various analytical techniques the applicability of which is independent of the distribution of the random variable considered.

distribution function   A function $F(x)$, of a random variable x, the value of which is equal to the probability with which the random variable assumes values less than or equal to x.

distribution-independent   *See* **distribution-free**.

distribution of cumulative failure   The connection between the progressive failure sum and time.

document   Any physical expression of information or data.

documentation   The sum of the various forms of physical expression of information about an area of knowledge. *Note:* Documentation is increasingly taking the form of information stored in computer memories.

documentation change control   The system of management controls by which changes to documents are either prevented or carried out in a controlled manner.

domestic contractor   A contractor located in the same nation or state as the customer.

dot diagram   Not a preferred term; see **scatter diagram**.

double sampling [ASQC]   Sampling inspection in which the inspection of the first sample of size $n1$ leads to a decision to accept a lot; or not to accept it; or to take a second sample of size $n2$, and the inspection of the second sample then leads to a decision to accept or not to accept the lot.

double-sampling plan   An inspection plan for double sampling which specifies the lot, the sample size, and the accept, reject, and double-sampling decision numbers.

downtime   The period of time during which an item is not in a condition to perform its intended function(s). *Note:* The downtime of an item is made up of active maintenance time and delays that are due to the unavailability of labor, spares, facilities, movement, etc.

drawing   A graphic or pictorial expression of information.

drawing change   Any alteration to an issued drawing within a system of management control.

drawing change control   *See* **documentation change control**.

drawing freeze   *See* **design freeze**.

drawing of samples   The procedure by which sample items for inspection are withdrawn from a larger number of similar items.

drift   The change with time of the metrological properties of a measuring instrument used in accordance with stated conditions that result in variation of the instrument's indication or output characteristic(s).

drop test   Not a preferred term; see **shock test.**

durability   A generic term used to express the relative capability of an item to endure a given stress or wear condition.

duty cycle (general)   The ratio of the period of time during which an event or equipment item is in the on state to the total time between the beginning of one on condition and the beginning of the next. (Usually multiplied by 100 and expressed as a percent.)

duty cycle (life test)   The ratio of the time during which a stated stress is applied to the sum of the times when the stress is applied plus the time during which the item is free of the stress, usually expressed as a percent.

early failure   The chance failure, for any reason, of material, component, or equipment directly after production.

early-failure period   The period beginning immediately after a product is placed in use and extending through the time of a decreasing rate of failures until the constant failure rate period begins.

economic quality   The level of quality at which the cost of securing higher quality would exceed the benefits of quality improvement.

electrical integrity   The condition in an item of electrical equipment when all electrically energized parts are, or are capable of, operating correctly and reliably.

electrical metrology   The science measurement of electrical quantities.

empirical value   A value obtained by measurement rather than by deductive reasoning or calculation.

employee participation program   A program in which employees and management are fully integrated in identifying and solving problems of quality and productivity and building corporate morale for the joint benefit of the company and all its employees and managers.

end inspection   The testing or examination of some life-tested item against its end point requirements after the item has been subjected to life-test stresses.

end point limit   A required characteristic value of a product or service which has undergone the stress(es) of life test. *Note:* This value is often set outside the normal derated design limits in order to allow for wear.

endurance   The capability of an item to withstand a given stress for a stated period of time with no more than the permitted degree of change.

endurance test   A test of an item at stated levels of stress for a stated period of time with specified end point limits.

engineering change   A change to the specified technical or operational methods, materials, or procedures used to produce some item of product or service. *Note:* Usually done within a system of change control by using a change notice.

environment (life)   All the external physical conditions and quantities that may apply stress to and thereby influence the operation of an item.

environmental condition   The planned control of specified characteristics of an environment for the purpose of enhancing the achievement of a specific purpose.

environmental controls (calibration sense)   Things done to provide a stable and/or known operating environment in which to perform measurements or carry out calibration activities.

environmental effects   Variations of or errors in a measurement that are traceable to such factors as temperature, humidity, and vibration.

environmental testing   Testing of items under conditions such that one or more of the characteristics of the items are intentionally stressed by a controlled environmental factor.

equipment failure   The inability of a previously acceptable item to perform its required functions within previously established limits.

equivalent single-sample size   The number of items n in a theoretical sample used with the Poisson distribution to derive the equivalent sample sizes $0.631n$ and $0.025n$ for double and multiple sampling, respectively.

error of measurement   The maximum possible discrepancy between the result of a measurement and the true value of the quantity measured.

error of the first kind   In statistical testing, the error of rejecting a hypothesis under test when it is actually true. *See* **producer's risk**.

error of the second kind   In statistical testing the error of accepting the hypothesis under test when an alternative hypothesis is true. *See* **consumer's risk.**

error of the third kind   Error committed by establishing testing procedures based on incorrect assumptions.

errors   The components of uncertainty which determine the degree of departure from an exact or absolute accuracy in measurement.

estimate   The estimated value of a population parameter.

estimated process average   The average percent defective, or average number of defects per 100 items, whichever is applicable, of the product or services submitted for original inspection as assessed from a sample of the population. *See also* **true process average.**

estimator   The statistic usually intended to estimate an unknown population parameter.

evaluation (component)   The process of determining the numerical value of the characteristics or performance of some item, usually for comparison with a relevant standard.

evaluation (system)   A process in which the characteristics of the features of a complex product or quality system are examined and assessed against established standards and in specified environments.

evaluation model   The model of a product which is subjected to an evaluation.

evaluation of a calibration system   The assessment of a supplier's calibration system against established written standards.

event [ASQC]   An occurrence of some attribute.

examination   The careful study of some item, quantity, or system for the purpose of drawing a conclusion. Usually it takes place by comparing that which is examined with a documented standard.

expectation   *See* **expected value.**

expected test time curve   A graphic representation of the total time required to perform a specified test or sequence of tests when the equipment continues to function with no more than the allowable repairs.

expected value   The mean of a function of variate values in infinitely repeated sampling. *Note:* The expected value is not necessarily the most frequently occurring value or even a possible value.

experimental design   The planning of experiments such that statistically valid data will be obtained and will be capable of yielding valid results by statistical analysis when factors are varied under controlled conditions.

exponential distribution   For a random variable θ the exponential distribution has the density function

$$F(\theta) = \lambda\theta e^{-\lambda\theta} \qquad \text{for } \theta > 0 \qquad (1.3)$$

extension test   Subjection of an item to a specified tensile stress along a specified axis for a stated period of time and subsequent assessment of the end point requirement.

extrapolated failure rate   Extension by a defined extrapolation or interpolation of the observed or assessed failure rate for durations and/or stress conditions different from those under which the failure rate was observed or assessed.

extrapolated mean life   Extension by a defined extrapolation or interpolation of the observed or assessed mean life for stress conditions and/or times different from those under which the mean life was observed or assessed.

extrapolated Q percentile life   Extension by a defined extrapolation or interpolation of the observed or assessed Q percentile life for stress conditions different from those applying to the assessed Q percentile life and/or for different percentages.

extreme values   The largest or smallest values in a set.

factor (statistical sense)   A variable characteristic or condition which is likely to affect the yield of a single treatment or operation.

factorial experiment   An experiment designed to determine the presence or absence of interactions and the effects of one or more factors each of which is applied at a minimum of two levels. In a complete factorial experiment all combinations of all the levels of the factors are tested.

fail safe   A design characteristic of an item which minimizes the probability of a failure being a critical failure.

failure (functional)   The initial incapability, or the termination of the capability, of a completed item to perform one or more of its required functions.

failure (inspection)   The incapability of a characteristic of a feature of an item of product or service to conform to the requirement.

failure analysis   The analytical examination of a failed item to determine the independent and dependent failure causes.

failure cause   The basic cause system (material, process, procedure, control, etc.) which must be altered to remove the source of failure from a product or service.

failure criteria (inspection)   *See* **defect or nonconformity classification list.**

failure criteria (reliability)   The defined conditions and limits the exceeding of which constitutes failure of an item under life test.

failure density   The quotient of the failure frequency divided by the period of time concerned.

failure density distribution   The connection between the failure probability density and time.

failure frequency (over time)   The absolute difference between the number of survivals at the beginning and end of a period of time divided by the time.

failure frequency distribution   The connection between failure frequency and time.

failure mechanism   The physical, chemical, or other process which results in failure.

failure mode   The effect by which a failure is observed.

failure mode and effect analysis (FMEA)   The study of the potential failures that might occur in any part of a system to determine the probable effect of each failure on all other parts of the system, on other systems, and on probable operational success.

failure mode effect and criticality analysis (FMECA)   The quantitative study of the failures that might occur in any part of a system to determine the probable effect of each failure on all other parts of the system, on other systems, and on probable operational success, the results of which are ranked in order of seriousness.

failure probability distribution   The connection between failure probability and time.

failure quota   The quotient of temporary failure frequency divided by the relevant period of time.

failure rate   The number of failures of an item per unit measure of life expressed in such factors as cycles, time, miles, or events.

failure rate acceleration factor   The ratio of the accelerated testing failure rate to the failure rate under stated reference test conditions, both rates being relevant to the same time period in the life of the tested items.

failure rate level   A failure rate value chosen from a series of such values and used for stating requirements or presenting test results. *Note:* Normally this is the highest permissible failure rate stated in a life test requirement.

fault analysis   Not a preferred term; see **defect or nonconformity analysis**.

fault tree analysis (FTA)   The study, using the diagrammatic method of algorithms, of the possible sequence of events constituting the failure of a system.

feature   A functional aspect of an item, usually an aspect possessing one or more measurable characteristics. *Note:* Product or service items are composed of features which correspond to their functioning parts, and features are in turn composed of characteristics which are measured to ascertain item quality.

field data   Data obtained from observations made during field tests or use.

field inspection   Inspections or tests carried out on a product after delivery to site of use.

field performance   A generic term for the way in which an item functions when in use, usually as compared with the performance of the item in the factory or laboratory.

field service   The use, or length of time in use, of an item while under field conditions.

final test audit   The regular and planned measurement of finished product at a severity level below that of acceptance inspection, usually for the purpose of ensuring the validity and effectiveness of final inspection.

finished product   Items of product upon which all the manufacturing operations have been performed.

firmware   The program which controls the logic of a computer.

first off   *See* **first-piece production sample**.

first-piece inspection   An inspection carried out on items of product upon which some change has been made or which represent initial production. Usually it involves a verification that the documentation system has also been brought into line with the new product production or with design changes or verifies that the product meets the specifications.

first-piece production sample   A sample of one or more production units representing the first output from production tooling after a design change or new start-up. *Note:* Also called *off-tool sample*.

foreign contractor   A supplier whose base of operations or factory is outside the nation or state in which the customer is located. *See also* **domestic contractor**.

fraction defective   The total number of defective or nonconforming items divided by the total number of items.

free time   The part of the nonrequired time during which an item is in a condition to perform its required function.

frequency (statistics)   The number of occurrences of a given type of event or the number of members of a population falling into a specified class.

frequency density   The ratio of the relative frequency to the relevant class interval.

frequency distribution   The relation between the values of a characteristic and their frequencies or relative frequencies.

full operating time   The period of time during which an item performs all its functions in their respective modes of application.

functional characteristic   A characteristic of a feature of an item which determines the successful operation of the feature.

functional defect   The failure of a functional characteristic.

functional defective or nonconforming unit   A unit of product which cannot perform one or more of its required functions.

functional stress   Stress due to any cause which affects the performance of the item.

fundamental standard   *See* **primary physical standard**.

gate   The set of conditions, limits, or requirements through which a product or service must pass in order to be acceptable to the customer or the next stage of production.

gauge (noun)   A measuring device normally used to measure mechanical dimensions of a product.

gauging method   Not a preferred term; see **method of measurement**.

Gaussian distribution   *See* **normal distribution**.

geometric sample   A sample of specific geometric shape or form, taken from a bulk material population, the dimensions of which are related to the axes of variability of material in a unit or quantity of product.

goodness of fit (of a distribution)   A measure of the agreement between an observed distribution and a theoretical distribution. It is specified a priori or fitted to the observations.

grade   An indicator of category or rank applied to products, processes, or services intended for the same functional use but for an otherwise different set of needs.

gradual failure   A failure which could be anticipated by prior examination or testing.

guide   A document offering explanations, interpretations, or factors to be considered and suggestions as to what is regarded as good or standard practice.

handicap   A numerical value used in a sequential sampling plan to determine the starting point for keeping score when sampling under the plan.

handling   Any activity which causes the product or service to come under the influence of outside factors which can affect the item or alter its immediate environment.

handling effects   Changes in one or more of the characteristics of a product or service which result from handling.

high-temperature test   A process whereby the item is subjected to specified temperature stresses higher than those of the normal operating environment for a stated period of time and then examined to ascertain what changes, if any, have taken place.

histogram   A graphic representation of a frequency distribution in which the interval for each class is used as the base and a rectangle whose area represents the frequency in the interval is constructed.

hold points (mandatory)   Points beyond which the work may not proceed without review by the customer or other authority.

homogeneous   Having   similar   characteristics   uniformly   distributed throughout. Sample data from a homogeneous population also are assumed to be homogeneous.

homogeneous lot A lot or batch of material or items in which the similar characteristics are uniformly distributed.

humidity cycling An environmental conditioning process in which the item is subjected to environmental stressing from elevated moisture content in its surrounding atmosphere. The cycling is normally followed by examination to ascertain if there has been any effect on the item.

hypergeometric distribution The distribution of the number of occurrences X of a characteristic in n trials, where selection is made without replacement from a finite population of size N in which k members of the population have the characteristic. This may be expressed mathematically as follows:

$$P_{r(X=x)} = \frac{\binom{k}{x}\binom{N-k}{n-x}}{\binom{N}{n}} \qquad (1.4)$$

hypothesis A supposition made as a basis for reasoning or as a starting point for investigation.

identity That which characterizes a product or service.

identity continuity A process whereby there is maintained throughout a sequence of actions, or over time, sufficient characterization of an item to maintain item identity, or the identity of some related aspect.

impact test Not a preferred term; see **shock test**.

incidental defect or nonconformity A departure from good workmanship having no significant bearing on function, assembly, life, or interchangeability.

incidental defective or nonconforming unit An item which contains one or more incidental defects but no more serious defects.

increment A quantity of material taken at one time from a larger body of material. *Note:* The term "increment" is not applied when liquids are sampled.

incremental probability of failure The probability that an item of the initials will fail in the interval of time observed.

independence The property of an item or quantity whereby it is unaffected by other items or quantities.

independent variable A variable characteristic value of an item whose magnitude is independent of the magnitude or value of other characteristics of the item.

independent failure A failure of a characteristic which will independently cause equipment performance that is outside specified limits and is unrelated to the failure of associated items.

indifference point   A point on the operating characteristic curve corresponding to probabilities of acceptance and rejection equal to 0.50.

indifference zone   The region containing quality levels between the acceptable quality level (AQL) and the limiting quality level (LQL).

individual   Not a preferred term; see **item**.

inherent weakness failure   A failure of an item, when subjected to stresses within specified normal operating limits, that is due to an inherent weakness in design or production.

initial inspection   The first inspection, for the purpose of acceptance, of a new or modified item. *Note:* Not to be confused with **original inspection**, which has another meaning.

initials   The items in the sample which exist at the start of an observation or test.

in-line inspection   *See* **in-process inspection**.

in-process inspection   Inspection of product or services prior to final inspection and in sequence with processing.

inspect   The process of ascertaining the value of product or service characteristics or performance against a set of requirements or a standard.

inspecting officer   That person who performs inspection work.

inspection [ASQC]   Activities, such as measuring, examining, testing, gauging or one or more characteristics of a project and/or service, and comparing these with specified requirements to determine conformity.

inspection, curtailed [ASQC]   Sampling inspection in which, as soon as a decision is certain, inspection of the sample is stopped.

inspection, normal [ASQC]   Inspection that is used in accordance with an acceptance sampling scheme when a process is considered to be operating at, or slightly better than, its acceptable quality level.

inspection 100% [ASQC]   Inspection of all the units in a lot or batch. (*Also called* **screening inspection**.)

inspection, rectifying [ASQC]   Removal or replacement of variant units during inspection of all the units, or some specified number, in a lot or batch which was not accepted by acceptance sampling.

inspection, reduced [ASQC]   A feature of a sampling scheme permitting smaller sample sizes than used in normal inspection. (*Note*: Reduced inspection is used in some sampling schemes when experience with the level of submitted quality is sufficiently good, and other stated conditions apply.)

inspection, tightened [ASQC]   A feature of a sampling scheme using stricter acceptance criteria than those used in normal inspection. (*Note*: Tightened inspection is used in some sampling schemes as a protective measure to increase the probability of rejecting lots when experience shows the level of submitted quality has deteriorated significantly.)

inspection by attributes   An inspection in which the item is classified as either defective or nondefective (or conforming or nonconforming) or the number of defects or nonconformities with respect to a given requirement or set of requirements is counted.

inspection by variables   Inspection in which certain quality characteristics of the item are evaluated with respect to a scale of measurement and expressed as precise points along that scale. *Note:* Inspection by variables yields the degree of conformance or nonconformance of the item.

inspection diagram   A diagram of the production process showing the points at which inspection takes place.

inspection equipment   Any equipment, instruments, cables, or devices used in ascertaining the value of characteristics or performance of an item.

inspection level [ASQC]   A feature of a sampling scheme relating the size of the sample to that of the lot.

inspection lot [ASQC]   A collection of similar units, or a specific quantity of similar material, offered for inspection and subject to a decision with respect to acceptance.

inspection lot (general definition)   A collection of similar units or a specific quantity of material offered for inspection and subject to a decision with respect to acceptance.

inspection lot (quality control)   An identifiable quantity of material or items normally manufactured at one time by one process or production system.

inspection plan   A documented procedure setting forth the actions, methods, and criteria to be used in carrying out inspection on some item or quantity of material.

inspection record   A collection of objective evidence comprising the inspection plan, identifying the items or material inspected, and providing the data obtained, as well as information on the number or quantity found to be faulty and acceptable.

inspection report   A report of the findings of an inspection of some product or service.

inspection specification   A document setting forth the criteria against which some item or quantity of material is inspected and possibly also specifying the inspection method.

inspection station   The point at which the inspection equipment is located and at which the inspection takes place.

inspection status   The amount of inspection which has been performed on items of product or service or quantities of material.

inspection system   The documented program, together with personnel, equipment, and associated facilities and services, by which inspection of some product or service is carried out.

inspection system audit   An assessment of an inspection system carried out at a low level of frequency and stated severity.

inspection system evaluation   The detailed examination of an inspection system against the documented requirements for that system, including any relevant contract requirements.

inspector   *See* **inspecting officer.**

instantaneous failure rate   The instantaneous failure rate $z(t)$ at the instant t given by:

$$z(t) = \lim \bar{z}(t_1, t_2) \qquad (1.5)$$

as $(t_2 - t_1) \rightarrow 0$

instant of failure   The instant when the failure mode first appears outside limits.

integration   The process of combining software programs into an overall system.

integrity of calibration   The faithfulness with which the known state of calibration of some measuring device remains unchanged by any cause.

intensity of inspection   Not a preferred term; see **severity of inspection**

interaction failure   A failure occurring as a result of an interaction between two or more parts of the item or between two or more pieces of equipment or quantities of material.

interaction (feature)   An interaction between two or more characteristics of an item, usually during production or operation, such that the value of one feature's characteristic is affected by a characteristic of another feature.

interaction (population)   An interaction between two or more populations that results in the modification of one or more of the population parameters.

intermeshing   The provision of operation paths in a quantity greater in number than is necessary for the intended function. *Note:* Intermeshing may be essential for reliability.

intermittent failure   A failure of an item persisting for a limited period of time following which the item recovers its ability to perform its required function(s) without being subjected to any external correcting action. *Note:* Intermittent failures are often recurrent.

intermittent use   The nonperiodic use of some measuring device or item of product with long periods of storage or disuse occurring between the periods of use.

interval (inspection)   The separation in number, time, or space between two events, e.g., the number of product units between two successively inspected units in a continuous sampling plan.

interval (statistics)   A range occupied by a class.

invoice   A list of products or services shipped, delivered, or performed with prices and charges thereon.

inwards inspection   *See* **receiving inspection**.

inwards management control   The system of controls by which management ensures that received products will be preserved, protected from damage, and routed to the correct places in the company.

inwards measurement control   The system of management controls by which it is ensured that products received by the company will have their characteristics assessed and recorded prior to use.

isolated lot [ASQC]   A lot separated from the sequence of lots in which it was produced or collected and not forming part of a current sequence of inspection lots. Also a lot of units or material which is not part of a sequence of lots (based on knowledge of either the supplier or the customer, or both).

isolated sequence [ASQC]   A group of lots not forming part of a large sequence or continuous process. (*Note:* Switching rules do not apply when sampling isolated sequences of lots.)

item (measurement sense) [ASQC]   The result of making an observation on an object or quantity of material which is generally recorded.

item (object sense) [ASQC]   An observed value or test result obtained from an object or quantity of material and/or service.

kurtosis coefficient   The degree to which a distribution is flattened or peaked. A normal distribution has a kurtosis of $+3$.

labeling   The practice of affixing labels or tags, stamping, or otherwise fixing information to or on an item. *Note:* An example is the labeling of measuring equipment to identify its calibration status.

laboratory model   An item of product or quantity of material which was prepared in a laboratory as compared to production models constructed by using production tooling and procedures.

laboratory sample   A sample of some product or service chosen for analysis in a laboratory.

least aperture   The minimum granularity or value of a characteristic of the item being observed which it is possible to resolve with the measuring instrument or device used.

legal metrology   The part of metrology that deals with units of measurement, methods of measurement, and measuring instruments and the calibration thereof in relation to requirements imposed by law.

length of life   The interval of time that begins with the first operational use of an item after its conditioning and ends with the occurrence of a failure greater than that allowed in the specifications for the item.

letter of acceptance   A document representing an essential step in a procurement process whereby the requirements of the customer and those of the supplier are brought into agreement to yield one set of requirements.

level of quality *See* **process average**.

level of seriousness A degree of concern, expressed on a scale of 0 to 100 percent, about the potential or actual damaging effect of some possible defect or nonconformity in an item of product or service. *Note:* An essential aspect of the defect or nonconformity classification process.

level of significance The probability of committing an **error of the first kind**.

liability (product, process, or service) (1) The risk that a producer or others may have to bear the responsibility for personal injury or harm resulting from the use of a product, process, or service supplied. (2) The possible legal retribution by those responsible for supplying a product, process, or service that causes persons injury or harm. (3) The onus on a producer or others for the financial loss or other harm suffered by the users of a product, process, or service that it or they put into circulation.

life cycle cost (LCC) The total cost to the owner of an item over the item's full life.

life expectancy The mean value of item lifetime found by testing a number of the items.

life test A test or set of tests in which an item is placed under a specified set of stress conditions, usually in an operational state, and the time taken to reach the first failure that causes the loss of one or more functions is measured.

life test sequence The sequence in which a number of operational functions of some item is tested when all functions cannot be tested at the same time, the purpose being to minimize the occurrence of dependent failures.

life utility Not a preferred term; see **life expectancy**.

limit The maximum extent of the value of some required characteristic of a product or service which, if exceeded, will require some action to be taken.

limit number The cumulative total number of defectives in 10 or more preceding consecutive batches of accepted original product units on normal inspection which may not be exceeded if a switch to reduced inspection is to be made.

limiting quality (LQ) The limiting quality level that a customer is prepared to accept with a very small probability that a lot of this fraction defective or nonconforming will occur. *Note:* When expressed as a percent, this quantity is called the lot tolerance percent defective (LTPD) or lot tolerance percent nonconforming (LTPN).

limiting quality level (LQL) [ASQC] The percentage or proportion of variant units in a batch or lot for which, for the purposes of acceptance sampling, the consumer wishes the probability of acceptance to be restricted to a specified low value. [*Note:* The limiting quality level is sometimes referred to as the rejectable quality level (RQL) or limiting quality (LQ).]

limits, control The limits on a control chart between which the statistic under consideration will lie when the process is under control.

limits, warning The limits on a control chart beyond which increased supervision and attention are required, corrective action being taken as necessary. The warning limits lie inside the control limits.

limits of variation   The maximum range which the values of a random variable may take at a specified level of probability.

line inspection   *See* **in-process inspection.**

load test   An assessment of the capability of an item to carry out some intended function under one or more states of stress.

longevity   Not a preferred term; see **life expectancy.**

lot (batch)   A definite quantity of some commodity (product or service) accumulated under conditions that for sampling purposes are considered uniform.

lot inspection   The inspection of commodities assembled into lots or batches.

lot-by-lot inspection [ASQC]   Inspection of product or services submitted in a series of lots.

lot formation   The process by which product lots are assembled or so identified that valid statistical sampling can be performed.

lot percent defective   The quotient of the number of defective units in a lot divided by the total number of units in the lot multiplied by 100.

lot percent nonconforming   The quotient of the number of units with nonconformities in a lot divided by the number of units in the lot multiplied by 100.

lot quality [ASQC]   A statistical measure of quality of product or services of a given lot.

lot size (*N*) (inspection) **[ASQC]**   The number of units in the lot.

lot size (shipment)   The number of units, or quantity of material, comprising the total amount of product in one shipment.

lot tolerance percent defective (LTPD) [ASQC]   The percent defective considered unsatisfactory but which the consumer is willing to accept with a small probability of acceptance (usually probability of acceptance P_a = 0.10 is used).

lot tolerance percent nonconforming (LTPN)   *See* **limiting quality level (LQL).**

lot variation (between lots)   The difference between the distributions of values of a given characteristic in two or more lots.

lot variation (within a lot)   The degree to which the value of a given characteristic within the lot varies from other values of the same kind.

low-temperature test   Testing under conditions in which products or services are subjected to a specified temperature or range of temperatures below ambient for a specified period of time.

lower control limit (LCL)   The lower of two control limits or sets of control limits as on a control chart.

lower tolerance limit (LTL) [ASQC]   A tolerance limit that defines the lower conformance boundary for an individual unit of a manufacturing or service operation.

maintainability [ASQC]   The ability of an item, under stated conditions of use, to be retained in, or restored to, within a given period of time, a specified state in which it can perform its required function(s) when maintenance is performed under stated conditions and while using prescribed procedures and resources. (*Note:* Maintainability is a quality imparted to a product during design.)

maintenance   The combination of all technical and corresponding administrative actions carried out to retain an item at or restore it to a state in which it can perform its required function(s).

maintenance quality assurance   The application of quality assurance principles to a maintenance program.

maintenance quality control   The use of statistical procedures and related control methods in the designing and carrying out of maintenance programs.

major defect or nonconformity   A variant other than a critical variant that is likely to result in failure or reduce materially the usability of the item for its intended purpose.

major failure   A failure other than a critical failure which is likely to reduce the capability of a relatively complex item to perform its required function.

major nonconformance (disposition sense)   A nonconformance which cannot be completely eliminated by rework or reduced to a minor nonconformance by repair. Final decision for acceptance of material containing major nonconformances shall be made by the customer.

management control division   The organizational division, within a company, that is under the direction of a group of managers and supervisors who have been delegated responsibility for control of the production of some commodity.

manufacturer's quality manual   A document in which is assembled all the procedures, plus policy and organization charts, by which a company controls its quality.

manufacturer's recommended calibration interval   The period of time during which the bias and precision of some measuring instrument or device can be expected to remain within acceptable limits as recommended by the manufacturer. *Note:* In the absence of other information, this time is used as the interval between calibrations.

manufacturing quality system audit   A planned and regularly conducted audit of all management controls designed to contribute to the production of a conforming product with a specified quality.

margin test   A test carried out on a piece of equipment or product under conditions such that the stresses cause the item to operate in a reduced safety margin region.

mark of conformance   A mark attesting that a product is in conformance with specific standards, specifications, or regulations.

marking   The application of information on a product or its package principally for the purpose of identifying the product and/or its characteristics and providing handling and routing information.

material   A generic term for all kinds of items, including equipment, but primarily raw material or chemical materials in compounds or mixtures of any phase.

material measure   The quantity which characterizes a material.

material receiving   All the acts and procedures related to receiving material from the deliverer, holding it in temporary storage under controlled conditions, and then routing or delivering it to a designated destination, usually incoming material inspection and test.

material rejection advice   A document given to a supplier by a customer indicating that material is not acceptable.

material review board (MRB)   A contractor or supplier board, consisting of representatives of the relevant company departments, empowered to disposition nonconforming material referred to it.

material stores control   The proper management of all stored material, including that which is in line with production and temporarily under stores-hold status, so that quality characteristics are preserved, control of material is enhanced, and identity continuity is maintained. *Note:* A typical control mechanism in primary stores is to ensure that first in, first out (FIFO) principles are rigorously applied.

materials inspection   *See* **inspection**.

materiel   Equipment, stores, supplies, and spares that form the subject of a contract. *Note:* The term is most often used in relation to military supplies.

mean   The sum of a set of values divided by the number of such values in the set.

mean deviation   The arithmetic mean of the deviations from an origin when all deviations are given a positive sign.

mean life   The mean value of the lengths of time to failure of all items in a population under stated conditions.

mean range   The mean of the ranges of a set of samples of the same size.

mean time between failures (MTBF)   For a stated period in the life of an item, or a population of items, the mean value of the length of time between consecutive failures of the item calculated as the ratio of the cumulative time to the total number of failures under stated conditions.

mean time between maintenance (MTBM)   The average time between maintenance actions (preventive, corrective, or both).

mean time to failure (MTTF)   In a stated period in the life of a population of items, the ratio of the cumulative time to the total number of failures in the population during the period under stated conditions. *Note:* It is necessary to state whether the cumulative time is the chronological or the operating time.

mean time to first failure (MTTFF)   The mean value of the times to first failures of items in a population of items.

mean time to repair (MTTR)   The average corrective maintenance time of an item or a population of items. *Note:* It is necessary to state whether active repair time or total corrective maintenance time is used.

measurand   A physical quantity, property, or condition which is measured. *Note:* This term is used in calibration work and is seldom used in other work related to quality.

measure (noun)   The quantitative value of a characteristic of some item or commodity.

measure (verb)   To compare a characteristic of an item against a standard for the purpose of assigning a relative value to it.

measurement   The process of determining the value of a measurand in terms of the appropriate unit of measurement. Also, the result of a measuring process.

measurement category   The discipline of science, e.g., nuclear, chemical, physical, electronic, or mechanical, in which a particular measurement principle lies.

measurement documentation   All documents, such as inspection instructions and record forms, operating and maintenance instructions, calibration instructions, and classification instructions, used to carry out the quality function.

measurement standard   A measuring instrument, material measure, or given set of elements of a measuring system which physically defines, embodies, represents, reproduces, or conserves a unit of measurement or value of a quantity. *Note:* The purpose of a standard is to transmit, by comparison, some unit of measurement or value of a quantity to other measuring devices, products, or services.

measuring equipment   An assembly of one or more measuring instruments together with connection and indicating devices and other necessary ancillary features.

measuring equipment calibration   A process whereby measuring instruments are compared with measurement standards for the purpose of transferring known relative values to the instruments.

measuring instrument   A device intended for the purpose of making a measurement which can be used to transfer a comparative value to some unknown.

measuring system   The assembly of physical elements necessary to achieve the objectives of a measurement by the application of a measuring process in a given environment.

mechanical integrity   The condition existing in an item when all mechanical parts of the item are capable of or are properly performing their functions.

median   The value within a distribution above and below which an equal number of values lie. *Note:* If n values are arranged in increasing order of algebraic magnitude and numbered 1 to n, the median of the n values is the

$[(n + 1)/2]$th value if n is odd. If n is even, the median lies between the $(n/2)$th and the $[(n/2) + 1]$th values and is not uniquely defined.

method of measurement   The nature of the procedure used in the measurement.

metrology   The field of knowledge concerned with measurement.

midrange   Half the sum of the largest and the smallest of a set of values.

midvalue of a class   The arithmetic mean of the two class boundaries.

minimum acceptable MTBF   A value so selected that an associated and specified risk of accepting items of this value is tolerable.

minimum acceptable quality   The maximum level of variants existing in a quantity of product or service which, for sampling inspection purposes, can be considered satisfactory as a process average.

minimum inspection   A level of inspection which will provide the minimum acceptable confidence about a quantity of material offered for acceptance.

minor defect or nonconformity   A defect or nonconformity that is not likely to reduce materially the usability of the item for its intended purpose or is a departure from established standards having little bearing on the effective use or operation of the item.

minor defective or nonconforming unit   A unit of product or service containing at least one defect or nonconformity.

minor nonconformance (disposition sense)   A nonconformance to the requirements specified in the contract, specification, drawing or other approved product description which does not adversely affect performance, durability, reliability, interchangeability, effective use or operation, weight or appearance (when a factor), or health or safety.

misuse failure   A failure attributable to the application of stresses beyond the specified strengths of the item and usually associated with a wrongful application.

mode   The value within a distribution which has the greatest probability or frequency of occurrence.

model (mathematical)   A statement in mathematical form of events which it is deduced have occurred or will occur. The greater the correspondence between the mathematical statement and the physical event the better the model.

model (product or service)   A physical representation of a thing or commodity.

multilevel continuous sampling   Sampling inspection of consecutively produced units in which two or more sampling rates are alternated with 100 percent inspection or with each other, depending on the quality of observed product.

multiple sampling [ASQC]   Sampling inspection in which, after each sample is inspected, the decision is made to accept a lot, not accept it, or to take another sample to reach the decision. There may be a prescribed maximum number of samples, after which a decision to accept or not to accept the lot must be reached.

multistage sampling   Not a preferred term; see **nested sampling**.

multivariate quality control   A method of control of quality in which each item for inspection must conform to standards for more than one random variable.

national standard   A physical standard or method of measurement from first principles which is maintained at a national laboratory and used as the nation's primary standard.

nested sampling   A method of sampling whereby the sample chosen from successive stages is subsampled from larger sample groups chosen from preceding stages.

nominal value   A dimension, expressed in a product design specification or drawing, from which variations within tolerance limits are permitted.

nonassignable cause   An indeterminable cause of variation in a characteristic.

nonconforming material   Any item or quantity of material which has one or more known characteristics outside the specifications or which has a level of variants higher than allowed by the acceptable quality level.

nonconforming unit [ASQC]   A unit of product or service containing at least one nonconformity.

nonconformity [ISO]   The nonfulfillment of specified requirements. (*Note:* This definition covers the departure or absence of one or more quality characteristics from specified requirements. It also covers the departure or absence of an element of a quality system. The basic difference between "nonconformity" and "defect" is that specified requirements may differ from the requirements for the intended use.)

nondestructive testing   A class of inspection methods which are designed to obtain data about a product without disassembling, sectioning, or in any way destroying the product sample; usually it relies on some form of radiation or dye penetration or radiation reflection to produce the objective evidence.

nonparametric   Free of interaction with the parameters concerned.

nonrelevant failure   A failure that is to be excluded in interpreting test results or in calculating the value of a reliability characteristic. *Note:* The criteria used to justify exclusion should be stated.

nonrequired time   The period of time during which the user does not require that the item be in a condition to perform its required function.

normal distribution   The distribution of a random continuous variable such that the variability is due to the summed effect of many random independent causes. When plotted, this distribution has a single mode from which the curve falls away symmetrically on two sides, making the mode, median, and mean all one value. This is expressed as:

$$f(x) = \frac{1}{\sigma\sqrt{2\pi}} \ \exp - \frac{1}{2}\frac{(x-\mu)^2}{\sigma^2} \tag{1.6}$$

normal inspection   The severity of sampling inspection applied when there is no evidence that the quality of the product or service being submitted is better or poorer than the specified quality level.

normal production   The production of products in the established manner by using the established procedures, tools, and people in the usual time. Continuing production may be assumed unless stated otherwise.

numerical reliability   The probability that an item will perform a required function under stated conditions for a stated period of time. *See* **reliability**; the requirement for what constitutes a satisfactory function should be stated.

objective evidence   Inspection records of data taken from properly calibrated and operated measuring equipment showing that the item or quantity of material concerned meets its technical requirements.

observation   *See* **observed value**.

observational standard   *See* **physical standard**.

observed failure rate   The ratio of the total number of failures in a sample to the total accumulated test time on the sample. *Note:* Exclude any time when an item was not actually performing its functions.

observed mean life   The mean value of the lengths of observed times to failure of all items in a sample under stated conditions. *Note:* When one limiting value is given, it is usually the lower limit.

observed MTBF   For a stated period in the life of an item, the mean value of the length of time between consecutive failures computed as the ratio of the cumulative observed time to the number of failures under stated conditions.

observed MTTF   For a particular period, the cumulative time a sample is observed divided by the total number of failures in the sample during the period under stated conditions.

observed q-percentile life   The length of observed time by which a stated proportion (q percent) of a sample or population of items has failed. Note: The q-percentile life coincides with $100 - q$ percent reliability. It is necessary to state the criteria by which failure is identified.

observed reliability (nonrepaired items)   For a stated period of time, the ratio of the number of items which performed their functions satisfactorily at the end of the period to the total number of items at the beginning of the period.

observed reliability (repaired item or items)   The ratio of the number of occasions on which an item or items performed its or their function(s) satisfactorily for a stated period of time to the total number of occasions the item or items were required to perform for the same period.

observed value [ASQC]   The particular value of a characteristic determined as a result of an observation, test, or measurement.

obvious defect or nonconformity   A defect or nonconformity which can be observed without the aid of calibrated measuring equipment.

on-receipt inspection   Not a preferred term; see **receiving inspection**.

operating characteristic   A description of the behavior of a sampling inspection plan; usually it is reported as an **operating characteristic curve**.

operating characteristic curve (OC curve) [ASQC]   (1) (For isolated or unique lots or a lot from an isolated sequence): A curve showing, for a given sampling plan, the probability of accepting a lot as a function of the lot quality. (Type A). (2) (For a continuous stream of lots): A curve showing, for a given sampling plan, the probability of accepting a lot as a function of the process average. (Type B). (3) (For continuous sampling plans): A curve showing the long-run percentage of product accepted during the sampling phase(s) as a function of the quality level of the process. (4) (For special plans): A curve showing, for a given sampling plan, the probability of continuing to permit the process to continue without adjustment as a function of the process quality.

operating path   The logic combination of operations necessary and satisfactory for the function of the item.

operating time   The period of time during which an item is performing and is satisfactory for the function of the item.

operational cycle   One complete cycle of functional stress of an item.

operator control   The part of process control which is carried out by the operator.

order (logistics)   A quantity of a commodity ordered at one time from one supplier. An order may consist of one or more consignments.

order statistic   Variate values arrayed in order of magnitude. *Note:* Examples of order statistics are the median and the smallest value of a sample. Generally, any statistic based on order statistics in this sense is called an order statistic, e.g., "range."

origin   Any point used as a reference point for measurements as distinguished from inspection of a product that is resubmitted after prior inspection.

original inspection [ASQC]   The first inspection of a lot as distinguished from the inspection of a lot which has been resubmitted after previous nonacceptance.

outlier   An observation made on a sample which is so far separated in value from the remainder of similar observations as to suggest that it is from a different population or that the sampling technique is at fault. Also called *sport*.

overload test   Any test whereby the characteristic(s) of a test item is or are subjected to stress conditions exceeding by a stated amount those specified for intended use, e.g., high-voltage-overload test.

ownership of product   That which changes from the supplier to the customer when items offered by the supplier under contract are accepted by the customer and payment is made therefor.

p [ASQC]   Used in the sense of a proportion or fraction. The ratio of the number of units in which at least one event of a given classification occurs, to the total number of units sampled.

p (p.95, p.50, p.10, p.05, etc.) [ASQC]   The submitted quality in terms of the proportion of variant units for which the probability of acceptance is 0.95, 0.50, 0.10, 0.05, etc., for a given sampling plan.

pack (noun)   That in which an item is enclosed for protection.

pack (verb)   The process of enclosing or otherwise protecting the quality characteristics of some item against damage or alteration during assembly, handling, shipment, or storage.

package (noun, general sense)   That in which an item is enclosed for protection.

package (verb, configuration sense)   The relative geometrical and physical positions in which the various components, parts, or elements of an assembly are so placed as to achieve some objective, e.g., lack of interaction, greater density of components, smaller size, or functional performance.

packaging (configuration control)   The process of specifying or placing the elements of some assembly in specific relative positions on a geometrical or physical basis.

packaging (logistics)   The process of enclosing items of product in protective wrappings or containers.

packing (logistics)   The process of enclosing items of product in protective wrappings or containers.

parallax   A source of error in the value observed with any device which requires two or more points in space to be in line for accurate observation. *Note:* An example is the moving-indicator meter. The observer's eye should be in a specific position relative to the needle and scale of the instrument, usually in a line that is perpendicular to the scale and passes through the needle center.

parameter (population)   A quantity used to describe the distribution of a characteristic within a population, e.g., mean and standard deviation.

partial failure   An item which contains some defects or nonconformities but which continues to meet acceptance criteria, e.g., an item which continues to perform its function(s) during life test or use despite the failure of some components.

partial operating time   Operating time in which an item fulfills only a part of its intended functions.

patrol inspection   Inspection whereby an inspector moves along a specific designated route and performs inspections at a number of stations in sequence.

pattern failure   A type of failure whereby the same type of component, in similar usage throughout a system or in different systems, exhibits a higher than anticipated rate of failure.

peak (mathematics sense)   The observation in an ordered series (e.g., by time or sequence) that has a value greater than the values of the two adjacent observations.

peak (noun)   The maximum or highest value of some characteristic of a product or service.

peak (verb)   To reach greatest or maximum value.

penalty   A disadvantage and a handicap calculated and used in reaching a decision on the lot or batch in some sequential sampling plans.

percent defective   The fraction defective multiplied by 100.

percent nonconforming   The fraction nonconforming multiplied by 100.

percentile   A dividing value of a parameter under consideration when a frequency distribution of the parameter is ordered conventionally and divided into 100 parts. *Note:* It is customary to use certain conventions when dealing with samples; e.g., when there are n test results, the percentile of the rth result of an ordered array is given by the expression $(2r - 1)/2n \times 100$.

performance   The carrying out of specified functions by an item, a system, a person, or an organization.

physical metrology   That field of metrology which primarily covers the measurement of mass, volume, density, pressure, and temperature.

physical standard   Any material item, including an electronic instrument, a device, or a piece of product, or any specified physical or chemical process using material items which may be used as a known reference against which to measure (usually similar) unknown items or processes.

pilot line   A production line set up to gain experience on production tooling with a new or changed process.

pilot lot   A small batch or lot run through production tooling and processes at the start of production of a new or changed design or manufacturing system to gain experience and data about the product and system.

pilot model   Not a preferred term; see **tool-made sample.**

pilot run testing   Inspection of products produced on a pilot line, usually for the purpose of gaining experience and information.

point of control   A point of the operating characteristic curve, with its ordinate at 0.5, used as a rough summarizing quantity of the curve.

Poisson distribution   The distribution of a discrete random variable x with mean m when its probability function is such that

$$f(x) = \frac{e^{-\lambda}(-\lambda)^x}{x!} \qquad \text{for } \lambda > 0 \qquad (1.7)$$

Note: Although the Poisson distribution can be derived from first principles and be shown to apply to random events occurring with a small probability over short intervals of time on a continuum, in statistical quality control it is often derived and used as an approximation to the binomial distribution.

population parameter *See* **parameter (population)**.

population (universe sense) The set or aggregate of similar sets from which samples are selected for measurement and statistical assessment.

power (statistics) The probability that a statistical test of some hypothesis rejects the hypothesis under test when the hypothesis is false by some specified degree or amount.

preaward survey Not a preferred term; see **contractor assessment**.

precision (calibration) The six-sigma scatter of statistics obtained by using one measuring device and repeatedly measuring the same characteristic. The maximum extent of the data so obtained, within the six-sigma spread, is the precision of the measurement. *Note:* The bias of the instrument plus one-half of the six-sigma spread usually determines the accuracy of the measurement made by using that instrument to measure normally distributed data.

precision (statistics) The scatter of the variate within the distribution of results obtained by applying the prescribed procedure several times under the same defined conditions.

preconditioning The conditioning of an item prior to the start of a life test in order to get the item into the proper environmental condition or operating mode.

predicted failure rate For the stated conditions of use and the design requirements of an item, the failure rate computed from the observed, measured, or extrapolated failure rates of its parts. When computed, the basis used shall be stated.

predicted mean life For the stated conditions of use, and taking into account the design of an item, the mean life computed from the observed, assessed, or extrapolated failure rates of the item's parts.

predicted q-percentile life For the stated conditions of use and taking into account the design of an item, the computed q-percentile life based on the observed, assessed, or extrapolated q-percentile lives of the item's parts.

predicted reliability For the stated conditions of use and taking into account the design of an item, the reliability computed from the observed, assessed, or extrapolated reliabilities of the item parts.

preferred AQLs AQLs calculated and published in tables for sampling inspection. *Note:* Any AQL can be calculated from the continuous distribution functions used in sampling inspection, but certain AQLs have been adopted for common (preferred) use corresponding to discrete steps.

preliminary review (PR) A formal review, with competent contractor personnel taking part, held when material is found to be nonconforming to determine if the nonconformances can be reworked, must be scrapped, can be repaired by standard contractor repair processes which have been approved by the material review board, will be returned to the supplier, or meets none of these criteria and must be referred to the material review board for disposition.

preproduction model   Not a preferred term because of its multiple meanings. It may refer to **design model, prototype, tool-made sample,** or other models not in full production.

preproduction testing   *See* **pilot run testing.** May refer to **first-piece inspection** testing when there is no pilot run.

prevention inspection   The use of inspection prior to carrying out some process, the purpose being to ensure the success of the process to the extent that the material entering the process would have contributed variability. *Note:* Preventive inspection may take place at the vendor's plant, at incoming, or in-line, or during the carrying out of the process.

preventive maintenance   The maintenance carried out at predetermined intervals or corresponding to prescribed criteria and intended to reduce the probability of failure or degradation of performance of an item.

primary failure   The failure of an item not caused either directly or indirectly by the failure of another item.

primary inspection   The inspection of parts produced within a factory for use in other products produced in the same factory and subjected to inspection for control of quality.

primary physical standard   Any physical standard under the control of the nation's national standards authority for physical standards.

prime contractor   The person who or company that contracts directly with the customer for the supply of some commodity.

probability   A real number in the range 0 to 1 attached to a random event to infer its likelihood of occurrence. *Note:* Probability can be related to the relative frequency of actual occurrence or to the belief that an event will occur.

probability density function   A function $f(x)$ of an approximately continuous variate such that, for a continuous variate, the expression $f(x)\ dx$ is equal to the probability with which the values of the variate will fall in the interval from x to $x + dx$.

probability distribution   A function which determines the probability that a random variable takesany given value or set of values.

probability limits   *See* **confidence limits** or **control limits.**

probability of acceptance (P_a) [ASQC]   The probability that a lot will be accepted under a given sampling plan.

probability of rejection (P_r) [ASQC]   The probability that a lot will not be accepted under a given sampling plan.

process   One event or a succession of events wherein people, tools, material, and/or environment act in concert to perform operation(s) which cause one or more characteristics of the production material to be altered or generated.

process average (quality level sense) [ASQC]   The average value of process quality in terms of the percentage or proportion of variant units.

process capability   The limits of inherent variability within which a process generates characteristic values in the production material as controlled by the contributing control influences, e.g., operator, tool, tool setup, or management procedure.

process capability study   A controlled collection of statistics from a process for the purpose of statistically determining the capability of the process on specified materials under specified conditions.

process control   The part of quality control concerned with ensuring that the variability of characteristics from a process lies within specified limits.

process documentation   The documentation prepared and used to perform and control a process.

process equipment   The tools on which the product characteristics are generated.

process inspection   *See* **in-process inspection**.

process liability   The onus and obligation on the producer and/or wholesaler and seller for the proper capability of the process and, in particular, the aspects which may be safety or health hazards.

process planning   The preparation of documented methods, specifications, organizations, and facilities by which to accomplish some process capability.

process quality [ASQC]   A statistical measure for the quality of product from a given process.

process quality audit [ASQC]   An analysis of elements of a process and appraisal of completeness, correctness of conditions, and probable effectiveness.

process range   The largest minus the smallest of the variate values in the product population from the one process.

process spread   The total variability, arising from all causes, which exists in items produced by the process.

process surveillance   The unplanned but frequent oversight of process operations underway on production materials, including performance of process capability studies and review of workmanship and material-handling methods and procedures.

process tolerance   The tolerance allowed on the product from a process. *Note:* The process tolerance may be considerably tighter than the design tolerance in order to take into consideration such matters as remeasurement accuracies and the effects of further processing.

process under control   A process in which the various contributors to variability of the product are monitored and maintained within defined control limits.

producer   The person who or organization that produces some item of product.

producer's decision risk   Not a preferred term; see **producer's risk**.

producer's risk   For a given sampling plan, the probability of rejection of a batch whose defective or nonconforming proportion has a value stated by the plan.

product control   *See* **production control**.

product evaluation   The complete assessing of an item of product against an established set of requirements, including any stressing necessary, which is more severe than that in the application specification.

product flow continuity control   The establishment of control over the flow of production materials so as to minimize delays and disruptive influences which could be detrimental to meeting quality goals and delivery schedules.

product liability   The onus and obligation on the manufacturer of some commodity, including the similar responsibilities of material suppliers and those who store, distribute, and deliver the commodity for the aspects of the product which may be safety or health hazards.

product quality audit   A quantitative assessment of conformance to required product characteristics.

product recall   The action of a producer and/or a distributor to bring about the return or repair of products known or suspected of containing defects or nonconformities, especially those that are safety or health hazards, or to effect repair or replacement at the customer's premises.

product standard (class or quality)   *See* **grade**.

product standard (calibration or workmanship)   A product item, or part thereof, used as a standard example in respect to the production of the product.

product verification inspection   Inspection of product items carried out by a customer's QAR, or on his behalf, for the purpose of verifying that records of quality data submitted in support of a submission of product for acceptance are valid in respect to the material to be supplied.

production control   The control of production effort and material flow to achieve a given rate of production and product output at a given quality.

production gauging   The use of gauges in the inspection or verification of product characteristics.

production limits   The maximum range of variance over which the characteristic values of production material is permitted. It may be different and is usually smaller than the variance permitted by the design limits.

production model   Any sample unit of the product which is representative of normal production.

production permit (ISO)   A written authorization, prior to production or before provision of a service, to depart from specified requirements for a specified quantity or time. Also called *deviation permit*.

production population control   The control of all aspects affecting production, including people changes, procedural changes, and outside influences, so that the parameters of the population of products remain essentially unaltered or, if altered, ensure that changes take place within a planned system of controls.

production process   Any activity which is planned to alter one or more of the characteristics of a feature of the product.

production run   A quantity of products produced within one time span, and in one continuous production activity, without interruption and using the same tooling, production operators, etc.

production testing   *See* **in-process inspection.**

production tooling   The machines, equipment, fixtures, gauges, and other devices used to produce a product item or quantity of material.

proprietary information   Any information which is owned by a person or company and is considered by the owner to be prejudicial to the welfare of that person or the company were it to come into the possession of unauthorized persons or companies.

prototype   A complete functioning model of the product or service usually constructed or performed to be like the finished item but brought into being without the use of some or all of the facilities, tooling, people, etc. to be used in producing the product or providing the service.

prototype testing   Testing, inspection, and examination of a prototype against specified requirements to ascertain the degree of compliance with requirements.

provisional approval   Partial approval accorded a supplier's quality control system pending the correction of specified items.

pull test   Not a preferred term; see **tensile test.**

purchased material control   All the actions undertaken to identify, position, assess, inspect, test, store, and otherwise assure that the material purchased from vendors or subcontractors is controlled.

pyramidal tolerancing   A tightening of product tolerances nearer the start of a production line and widening toward the end of the line to allow for remeasurement accuracy.

qualification (component sense)   The entire process by which products are obtained from a manufacturer or distributor and then examined or tested against written standards and documented or identified as qualified products. *Note:* The qualification process usually implies a need for continuing control of production quality.

qualification approval   The approval given some component or material which has been assessed against a standard and approved or the approval given to a supplier following an assessment of his quality control system.

qualified component or material   A component or material which has met the requirements of an applicable standard and has been qualified to the standard.

qualified products list   A list of products, including components and materials when applicable, which contains the items that have been evaluated and approved against documented standards.

qualimetry   Methods for quantitative estimation of product quality.

qualitative data   Data which identify an item relative to some limit but do not give the value(s) of the characteristic(s) of the item's features.

quality [ISO]   The totality of features and characteristics of a product, process or service that bear on its ability to satisfy stated or implied needs.

quality (measurement sense)   The probability that the values of the characteristics of a product or service will lie within specified limits and impart to the product or service the ability to satisfy given needs.

quality assurance [ASQC]   All those planned or systematic actions necessary to provide adequate confidence that a product, process or service will satisfy given needs.

quality assurance authority   The customer or the organization, person, or group of persons authorized by the customer or his contracting authority to act in all matters related to the assurance of quality of the products or services detailed in the contract or production provisions.

quality assurance engineer   A person educated and designated as an engineer who possesses the disciplines of quality control and quality assurance in addition to his basic professional engineering qualifications.

quality assurance representative (QAR)   The person or organization designated by the customer to act in his behalf on matters concerning quality.

quality assurance surveillance   The procedure of carrying out surveillance on a supplier's production and/or supply activities in respect to the contribution of those activities to the quality of products or services.

quality assurance team   The team of individuals, comprised of representatives of the customer and accompanied by representatives of the supplier, who undertake the work of assessing and evaluating the quality system of a supplier.

quality audit [ISO]   A systematic and independent examination to determine whether quality activities and results comply with planned arrangements andwhether these arrangements are effectively implemented and are suitable to achieve objectives.

quality characteristic   Any aspect of an item which can be measured and which contributes in any way to the acceptability and/or functioning of the item.

quality characteristic classification   *See* **defect or nonconformity classification list.**

quality circle   An action team, composed of members of management, workers, and sometimes union representatives, that meets regularly with a leader called a facilitator to work on quality and productivity matters. *See* **employee participation program**, of which the *quality circle* is a part.

quality conformance inspection   *See* **inspection**.

quality control [ISO]   The operational techniques and activities that are used to satisfy quality requirements.

quality control chart   A chart, used to display quality data, on which are plotted limit lines defining the permissible range for the values of quality characteristics and data obtained from units of product.

quality control program   A management program planned, documented, and implemented for the purpose of controlling the quality of work and hence products or services.

quality control surveillance   The surveillance of work as it is performed in the creation of a design or the production of a product or the providing of a service.

quality control system   A system of management controls designed and documented in a quality manual containing the policy and procedures by which quality of production or services are to be obtained.

quality cost   Any expenditure made for the purpose of achieving or preserving quality in a product or service. *Note:* See for comparison the costs of processing the materials that become the product or providing the service.

quality cost optimization   The adjustment of different quality costs for the purpose of either minimizing the total quality cost or for balancing costs among the various operating areas.

quality engineering   The branch of engineering which deals with the principles and practices of product and service quality assurance and control.

quality information equipment   A term designating any measuring device used to ascertain the value of a quality characteristic.

quality level   *See* **process average**.

quality loop (quality spiral)   A conceptual model of interacting activities that influence the quality of a product, process, or service in various stages ranging from the identification of needs to the assessment of whether these needs have been satisfied.

quality management [ISO]   That aspect of the overall management function that determines and implements the quality policy.

quality manager   A person or organization assigned the responsibility and authority to design, develop, implement, and establish a quality system or to oversee such a system operation and make it work.

quality manual   A document in which is assembled the quality policy, organization charts, and operating procedures by which quality is controlled. *Note:* It is usual for the chief executive officer (CEO) to approve and sign the quality policy.

quality measure   A quantitative measure of the characteristics of the features of a product or service.

quality of conformance   A measure of the fidelity with which the product, taken at the point of acceptance, conforms to the design.

quality of design   A measure of the adequacy of the design in relation to the requirements.

quality of manufacture   A measure of the adequacy with which the product meets the customer's requirements.

quality plan [ISO]   A document setting out the specific quality practices, resources, and activities relevant to a particular product, process, service, contract or project.

quality policy [ISO]   The overall quality intentions and objectives of an organization as formally expressed by senior management.

quality program   The documented plans for implementing the quality system.

quality, relative [ASQC]   Degree of excellence of a product or service.

quality requirements   The entire set of characteristics and their ranges as defined by product specifications and including operational requirements.

quality standards   All physical standards and document standards used in the achievement of quality in products, processes, services, and projects.

quality surveillance [ISO]   The continuing evaluation of the status of procedures, methods, conditions, products, processes and services, and analysis of records in relation to stated references to ensure that quality requirements are being met.

quality system [ISO]   The organizational structure, responsibilities, procedures, activities, capabilities and resources that together aim to ensure that products, processes, and services (or projects) will satisfy stated or implied needs.

quality system audit   A documented activity performed to verify, by examination and evaluation of objective evidence, that applicable elements of the quality system are suitable and have been developed, documented, and effectively implemented in accordance with specified requirements.

quality system review [ISO]   A formal examination by management of the status and adequacy of the quality system in relation to quality policy and new objectives resulting from changing circumstances.

quantitative data   Data from measurements on some item which give the values of the characteristics concerned. *See* **variables, method of**.

quantity (quality sense)   An attribute of a phenomenon or item which may be identified and measured.

quantity (amount sense)   The amount of some material or item(s) as expressed in mass, length, or other dimensions.

quarantine store   A well-defined place used for the segregation of product, in terms of conforming, nonconforming, and questionable, to await a disposition decision.

quartile One of three values which, in a random frequency distribution, divide the distribution into four equal parts, the median being the second quartile and the first and third dividing the two halves into equal quarters.

random (general sense) A term generally used to imply that the process under consideration is in some sense probabilistic or that a process of selection applied to a set of objects is said to be simply random if each object has an equal chance of being chosen.

random cause The cause of a variation in a characteristic the occurrence of which is unpredictable.

random failure A failure of an item from a system composed of many similar items the result of which is part of a continuing constant failure rate. Also called *chance failure*.

random numbers Sets of numbers which are generated by a process involving a chance element.

random operating failure Not a preferred term; see either **random failure** or **intermittent failure**.

random sample A sample chosen in such a manner that each item in the population has an equal chance of being chosen.

random sampling [ASQC] As commonly used in acceptance sampling, the process of selecting sample units in such a manner that all combinations of n units under consideration have an equal chance of being selected as the sample. (*Note:* Though equal probabilities of being selected are not necessary, it is essential that the probability of selection be ascertainable as sample units are normally removed from the population as they are chosen. Sampling tables commonly assume random sampling with equal probability.)

random variable A variable which may take any one of the values of a specified set of values and with which is associated a probability distribution. *Note:* Variables which may take only isolated values are said to be *discrete variables*.

random walk A sequential sampling process in which sample items are chosen at random and are tested; the sampling process continues until some predetermined accept or reject number is reached.

randomization A process, used in sampling inspection or designing experiments, whereby the units in a population are drawn at random, each unit is assigned a number, and the population is then reassembled in the order in which the units were randomly drawn.

range The difference between the greatest and smallest values of a quantitatively observed characteristic in a population.

range chart The part of a quality control chart on which are plotted the values of the ranges of samples to provide a measure of the variability of the product and/or process.

ranking A method of classification in which a series of sample items is placed in the order of intensity or degree of some specified characteristic.

rated life *See* **length of life**.

rating The recommended limiting value of an operating condition or parameter.

rational subgroup One of the small groups within which it is believed that assignable causes are constant and into which observations can be subdivided in the carrying out of certain methods of statistical analysis. *Note:* In the operation of a control chart, a continuing test for significance of differences between a succession of rational subgroups and some reference value is implied.

raw material Any material, normally supplied in bulk form, which has not been processed through one or more production steps beyond the bulk material state. *Note:* Examples are metal in rods, bars, wire, sheets, etc., plastic in beads, liquid, feedstock, etc., chemicals in single element form or as processed into compounds.

readability The minimum value which can be reliably read from the indication in the region concerned on the scale of a measuring instrument. *Note:* Readability is accuracy-limiting, and on variable-scale instruments the readability will alter from point to point.

recall The process whereby an item or a group of items is recovered from the distribution system or from customers for a definite purpose justifying the expenditure. *Note:* Usually applied either in calibration systems or when a product is found to pose some safety or health hazard.

recall system The organized management system by which the recall of some commodity is effected.

receiving inspection Inspection carried out by a consumer or customer of items or material as delivered. *Note:* Also called *inwards inspection*.

reduced inspection Inspection severity at a level lower than that of normal inspection severity. It is used when the quality of a specified number of lots, at normal inspection severity, is better than specified.

reduction In bulk sampling, the process which reduces the quantity of a sample or the particle size of the sample.

redundancy The provision of more than one means of performing a given function.

reference material (RM) A substance or a device that has stable and readily measured characteristics and is used as a standard of measurement or in the calibration of measuring equipment. *See* **certified reference material**.

reference standards The most accurate and/or stable physical standards possessed by or available to a measurement or calibration program.

register An authoritative list of parts or systems which have been assessed or evaluated and found to meet the specified requirements; such parts or systems are approved entities.

registration system A program by which parts or systems, including contractor's quality systems, measuring instruments, etc., are recognized as approved by being listed in a register and are thereby available for further action.

regression equation   An equation relating the expectation of a variate to the value of one or more variables.

regression testing   Testing performed after a functional improvement or repair of a software item has been made.

regular audit inspection   A continuing program of auditing the quality of some product or service.

reject (noun)   A defective or nonconforming item which is unsuitable for use as offered.

reject (acceptance sampling sense) [ASQC]   To decide that a batch, lot or quantity of product, material or service has not been shown to satisfy the requirement criteria based on the information obtained from the sample(s).

rejectable quality level (RQL) [ASQC]   *See* **limiting quality level**.

rejection number [ASQC]   The minimum number of variants or variant units in the sample that will cause the lot or batch to be designated as not-acceptable.

rejects   The items of product or service which are not accepted because they fail to meet the requirement criteria.

relative frequency   The ratio of the number of times a particular value (or a value falling within a given class) is observed to the total number of observations.

relative slope of OC curve   A measure of the discriminating power of the sampling plan. The slope of the OC curve provides a comparison of discriminating power with that of other OC curves.

relative survivals   The quotient of survivals to the initials.

reliability [ISO]   The ability of an item to perform a required function under stated conditions for a stated period of time. *Note:* Quantitatively, reliability is the probability of success.

reliability assurance   *See* **quality assurance**.

reliability compliance test   An experiment to find whether or not a reliability characteristic of an item complies with the stated reliability requirements.

reliability engineering [ASQC]   That engineering function dealing with the principles and practices related to the design, specification, assessment and achievement of product or system reliability requirements and involving aspects of prediction, evaluation, production, and demonstration.

reliability growth   The replacement of an as-designed part in an operating system by a more reliable part for the purpose of improving the MTBF or other reliability characteristic of the system.

reliability growth testing   Testing carried out to ascertain the improvement in the reliability of a system by the inclusion of a more reliable part during the system's operating life.

reliability, numerical [ASQC]   The probability that an item will perform a required function under stated conditions for a stated period of time.

reliability of design   The part of the reliability of a product or service derived from the design specification when an item of such product or service is produced in complete conformance with the specifications.

relevant failure   A failure that is to be included in interpreting test results or in calculating the value of a reliability characteristic.

remeasurement control   A control documented in the quality system which ensures that due notice is given and appropriate action is taken in relation to inspection of nonoriginal products or material submitted for remeasurement.

repaired material   Nonconforming material subjected to a process designed to reduce but not completely eliminate the nonconformance.

repair time   The elapsed time period beginning with the start of actual repair effort and ending with the return of the failed item to a state of readiness for use. *See* **downtime.**

repeatability   A quantitative expression of the closeness of the agreement between the results of successive measurements of the same value of the same physical quantity, property, or condition carried out by the same method, by the same observer, with the same measuring instruments, at the same location at appropriately short intervals of time.

replacement inspection   Sampling inspection whereby each failed item or unit is removed from the population or batch and replaced by an acceptable one.

replication   The performance of an experiment or parts of an experiment more than once. Each performance, including the first one, is called a replicate.

representative sample   A sample chosen or assigned by any method to minimize the existence of bias between the sample and the lot or population from which it came.

representative sampling   The process whereby sample units are drawn from a batch of units or a population in such a way as to contain minimum bias between the value(s) of the characteristics of the units and the corresponding values of the units in the batch or population.

reproducibility   A quantitative expression of the closeness of the agreement between the results of measurements of the same physical quantity, property, or condition when the individual measurements are made under different defined conditons. *Note:* The results of individual measurements are assumed to be corrected as appropriate.

required time   The period of time during which the user requires the item to be in a condition suitable for the performance of its required function(s).

research model   A model of an item constructed in a laboratory which depicts some aspect or aspects of an idea in a physical manner.

residuals   Any or all of several lesser sources of uncertainty which contribute to the total error of a measurement.

response time   The time taken for the indication of an instrument to attain and remain within a specified deviation from its final value after a defined change in input.

restorable change   A change that can be reversed by a special measure, e.g., restoration stress.

restoration   Not a preferred term; see **replacement inspection**.

resubmitted lot [ASQC]   A lot or batch which previously has been designated as not-acceptable and which is submitted again for acceptance inspection after having been further treated, sorted, reprocessed, etc.

reversible change   A change in an item which is partially or completely self-correcting during further operational use of the item.

review   The examination in detail of a material, item, condition, or system by a competent body of individuals, usually for the purpose of deciding upon some course of action.

rework   Any process whereby defective material is altered in an effort to make it acceptable; also, the act of reprocessing.

reworked material   Material that was nonconforming but has been subjected to a process that restores all nonconforming characteristics to the requirements in the contract, specification drawing, or other approved product description. *Note:* Compare with **repaired material**.

risk, consumer's (β) [ASQC]   For a given sampling plan, the probability of acceptance of a lot the quality of which has a designated numerical value representing a level which it is seldom desired to accept. [*Note*: Usually the designated value will be the limiting quality level (LQL).]

risk, producer's (α) [ASQC]   For a given sampling plan, the probability of not accepting a lot the quality of which has a designated numerical value representing a level which it is generally desired to accept. [*Note*: Usually the designated value will be the acceptable quality level (AQL).]

rounding of numerical values   The practice, and the conventions used, in stating numerical values of characteristics to the last significant figure, which is adjusted to reflect the value of figures following in the sequence.

routine inspection   Periodic and continuing inspection of items, material, or systems from a repetitive or continuing production process.

roving inspection   *See* **patrol inspection**.

run   A quantity of product produced in a continuing sequence of operations through a production system within one (usually short) period of time.

safety factor (population sense)   The ratio of the mean strength of the items to the statistical mean stress to which the items will be exposed.

safety hazard   An item, quantity of material, or condition which possesses one or more characteristics having the capability to jeopardize the health or safety of persons using it, maintaining it, or depending on it.

safety management   The application of organizational and management principles in order to assure, with high confidence, the timely realization of the goal of optimum safety. *Note:* Safety management encompasses planning, organizing, and controlling the developmental and operational activities directed toward the goal of optimum safety, including coordination and evaluation needed to attain that goal.

safety margin (population sense)   The ratio of the difference between the mean strength of the items and the statistical mean stress to which the items will be exposed to the standard deviation of the difference.

sample (acceptance sampling sense) [ASQC]   One or more units of product, or a quantity of material, drawn from a specific lot or process for purposes of inspection to provide information that may be used as a basis for making a decision concerning acceptance of that lot or process.

sample division   A portion of a sample divided for some purpose such as inspection of different characteristics at different levels of severity or stress intensity.

sample fraction defective/nonconforming   The proportion of items or quantity of material in the sample which is defective or nonconforming.

sample median   The observation in a set of n observations arranged in increasing order which occurs as (1) for odd n, the $(n + 1)/2$ observation and (2) for even n, the arithmetic mean of the $N/2$ observation and the $(n + 2)/2$ observation.

sample number   The number of a sample, which may contain one or more units, when more than one sample item is chosen in succession from a batch or continuous production process.

sample point (probability term)   In probability theory, an event, in sample space, representing a possible result of an experiment.

sample point (quality control term)   In quality control theory, a point plotted on a control chart.

sample preparation   A process whereby a product or material has operations performed on it to make it measurable by some method while preserving the characteristics to be measured.

sample selection   The process, usually intended to be random, by which sample items of product or quantities of material are selected from a population for the purpose of determining the values of the quality characteristics concerned.

sample size   The number of units of product or services specified to be selected from the distribution or population for some purpose, such as inspection.

sample size code letter   A letter used in a sampling plan to designate the number of units in a sample selected in accordance with the plan.

sample size curve (average)   A curve used to show the average sample size which may be required for double or multiple sampling in order to reach a decision.

sample space   The space defined by the locations of all sample points.

sample statistic   *See* **statistic.**

sample unit or item   *See* **sampling unit.**

sampling   An arrangement for taking samples; usually it is qualified by a description of the type of sampling.

sampling distribution   The distribution of a statistic (characteristic value) in all possible sample units that can be chosen in accordance with a specified sampling scheme.

sampling fraction   The ratio of the sample size to the total number of units in the batch or relevant population.

sampling frequency   In a sequential or continuous sampling plan, the ratio of the number of units of product randomly selected for inspection at an inspection station to the number of units of product moving past the inspection station.

sampling inspection   Any method of inspection involving measurement of less than the total amount of a type of product or quantity or material in order to gain knowledge of the total quantity of items or material.

sampling inspection plan   A statement of the methods and criteria to be used in carrying out sampling inspection, including selection of sample units, sample size to be used, and the associated acceptance or rejection criteria, as well as the specification or standard against which to inspect.

sampling instruction   Any of the actions documented in some form which are used in a sampling procedure.

sampling interval [ASQC]   In systematic sampling, the fixed interval of time, output, running hours, etc. between samples.

sampling plan   A plan according to which one or more samples are taken from a batch or population.

sampling procedure   The method by which a sampling plan works.

sampling scheme   An overall system or procedure for sampling inspection which may contain a range of sampling plans.

sampling unit   One of the individual units into which a batch or population is divided, or regarded to be divided, for the purpose of sampling inspection. A sampling unit may contain more than one item or a quantity of material.

sampling without replacement   A method of sampling inspection by which units of a product or service, when found defective or nonconforming, are not replaced in the batch or population and the absolute size of the batch or population is thereby reduced.

scatter   The extremities of the location of sample points in a sample space or a distribution.

scatter diagram   A two-coordinate plot of sample points.

scrap Nonconforming material, components, or equipment that is not usable and cannot be economically reworked or repaired.

screening inspection Complete inspection, i.e., 100 percent examination, of a quantity of material or batch or population of units of a product for one or more specified characteristics and rejection and removal of all items or portions of material found defective or nonconforming.

screening test A type of screening inspection.

sealing A process used to minimize the possibility that a temporarily fixed setting of some adjustable control, usually on a calibrated instrument or device, will be altered.

secondary failure The failure of an item or quantity of material caused either directly or indirectly by the failure of another item or quantity of material.

secondary standard A physical standard calibrated by comparison with a primary physical standard.

self-calibrating principle Any of the recognized natural physical constants, such as the ice point, from which reference points are taken in the science of measurement. The term is also used to refer to the practice of including reference voltage, current, time, etc. sources inside a piece of electronic instrumentation for calibration purposes.

sensitivity (instrument sense) The relation of the change of the response to the corresponding change of the stimulus. *Note:* Sensitivity is normally expressed as a ratio.

sensitivity (noise sense) The value of the stimulus required to produce a response exceeding, by a specified amount, a response already present that is due to other causes, e.g., noise.

sentence The decision to accept, reject, or take other action, together with instructions for any subsequent action, resulting from an inspection, test, audit, evaluation, assessment, examination, or other such action.

sequential sampling [ASQC] Sampling inspection in which, after each unit is inspected, the decision is made to accept the lot, not to accept it, or to inspect another unit.

sequential sampling plan A plan stating rules for a particular sequential sampling inspection.

sequential test A test of significance for a statistical hypothesis which is carried out by using the methods of sequential sampling.

service life The period of time under service conditions for which specified performance and safety requirements are met.

serviceability The capability of an item to be inspected and maintained under stated conditions and by using prescribed procedures and resources.

settling-in period Not a preferred term; see **conditioning**.

severity of inspection The number, ratio, or percent representing the degree of inspection. *Note:* For example, a low AQL requires more severe inspection than does a high AQL.

shelf life (or storage life) The stated period of time during which items that exhibit deterioration are deemed to remain suitable for use.

shipment The quantity of a commodity delivered at one time. *Note:* A shipment may consist of an entire consignment or any part thereof.

shipping sample Items of product or quantity of material removed from a consignment or bulk lot prior to shipment.

shock test The arresting and bringing to rest of an item or quantity of material within a specified distance and while it is traveling at a specified rate along a specified axis with no more than a specified level of rebound. *Note:* The shock is usually required to conform to a specified impact curve relating travel with time.

shop standard A standard that has been calibrated against a secondary standard or subjectively selected for workmanship and is used in the production area to provide a state of known value to some instrument or item. *Note: See also* **transfer standard**.

significance *See* **level of significance**.

significance test A statistical procedure to assess whether some quantity which is subject to a random variation differs from a postulated figure by an amount greater than that attributable to random variation alone. Compare with **level of significance**.

simple random sample A sample of n items or individuals taken from a population of N items that have the same chance of being taken.

single-level continuous sampling Sampling inspection of consecutively produced units in which two or more sampling rates are alternated with 100 percent inspection, or each other, depending on the quality of observed product.

single sample A single item, group of items, or quantity of material taken from a lot, batch or population.

single sampling A type of sampling inspection by which a decision to accept or reject is reached by inspecting a single sample.

skewed distribution A distribution the curve of which is asymmetric. Positive skewness means greater scatter to the right of the mean; negative skewness means greater scatter to the left.

skip-lot sampling [ASQC] In acceptance sampling, a plan in which some lots in a series are accepted without inspection (other than possible spot checks) when the sampling results for a stated number of immediately preceding lots meet stated criteria.

sling shot A type of machine used for imparting very high velocities to some item of product so that a very high shock test may be performed on the item. *Note:* Several thousand Gs of force may be achieved.

slope of the OC curve A measure of the steepness of the OC curve indicating the discriminating power of the sampling plan represented by the curve.

soak time A specified time during which some commodity is maintained at a stress outside specified operating conditions. *Note:* When the stress is inside that specified, it is *conditioning time.*

software   A set of programs, procedures, rules, and associated documentation and materials concerned with the use operation, and maintenance of an information or message processing system.

software component   A software item that is subject to configuration management.

software item   A functionally or logically distinct part of the software program. *Note:* Items include documentation, listings, and storage media.

software program   A series of instructions, ultimately translated into machine-readable form, designed to achieve a certain result.

software validation   The formal process by which the developer obtains confirmation that software components are consistent with customer requirements, functional requirements, and specifications.

source of error   The part of a total measuring system which contributes a particular form of uncertainty, e.g., reading error, parallax error, interpolation error, random error, and error of method.

specification [ISO]   The document that describes in detail the requirements with which the product, process, or service has to conform.

specified mean time between failures (SMTBF)   The MTBF value specified in a contract or the equipment specification.

sport   *See* **outlier.**

spot calibration   A method for extracting greater accuracy from a certain piece of measuring instrumentation than would otherwise be possible. It depends on the accurate determination of the indicated value at, usually, one particular indication on the instrument's scale. *Note:* When used, this method should be supported by frequent recalibrations because of the greater tendency for change in a single small region of indication.

spot check   The examination, inspection, or assessment of a single part or a highly localized portion of a larger system, batch, or process.

spread   Not a preferred term; see **scatter.**

stability   The tendency of a measuring instrument or gauge to be free of change, i.e., to retain its accuracy for a long time.

standard   Any reference document, item, or quantity of material against which unknown characteristics are assigned value.

standardization   The reduction of the number of characteristics or features of a system or the reduction of the number of ways these may vary or interact.

standby redundancy   Redundancy such that the alternative means of performing a given function are inoperative until needed.

standby time   The period of time during which an item is needed to be in a condition to perform its required function(s).

state-of-the-art measurement   A measurement which involves the use of principles, methods, or instrumentation that individually or collectively require techniques and/or accuracies beyond those previously accomplished in a routine manner.

statistic [ASQC] A quantity calculated from a sample of observations, most often to form an estimate of some population parameter.

statistical measure [ASQC] A statistic, or mathematical function of a statistic.

statistical quality control The part of quality control in which statistical techniques are used.

statistical sampling Not a preferred term; see **random sampling**.

statistical significance *See* **chi-squared test**.

statistical tolerance limits A set of limits calculated from the results of sample observations and between which, under given assumptions, a stated fraction of the population will lie with a given probability.

step stress test A test, usually of the environmental kind, consisting of stresses of more than one level. The stresses are applied to the sample sequentially for specified periods of time.

storage effects A measurable change in one or more of the characteristics of an item or quantity of material during a period of storage.

storage life The length of time an item can be stored under specified conditions and still meet the specified requirements.

stores test certificate A certificate issued by an inspection body following the inspection of some commodity taken from storage.

stratification The physical or conceptual division of a population into separate parts called strata.

stratified sample (inspection) A sample in the selection of which planned action is taken to ensure that specified proportions of the sample are taken from different strata of the population. The sample inside each stratum is random.

stratified sampling [ASQC] The process of selecting units deliberately from various locations within a lot or batch or from various phases or periods of a process to obtain a sample.

stress analysis The study of the distribution of stresses and their effects on an item, a quantity of material, or a process.

stress cycle The period during which a specified type of stress is carried through one complete cycle of application to an item, a quantity of material, or a process.

stress-strength relation The relative magnitudes of given stresses when compared with the relative magnitudes of measured strengths of some item, quantity of material, or process.

stress tolerance A measure of the capability of an item to endure a given stress with no more than an acceptable degree of change.

subcontractor A supplier who contracts with the prime contractor in support of the supply of some product or service by the prime contractor to the end customer.

subcontractor calibration   A requirement placed on a subcontractor through a requirement on the prime contractor in a contract.

subgroup   A section of a set of elements, individuals, or observations having one or more characteristics in common.

subpopulation   A section of a population having one or more characteristics in common.

subunit   In bulk sampling, the practical or hypothetical subdivision of a unit in connection with the assessment of variability.

subjective characteristic   A characteristic of a feature of an item, a quantity of material, or a process which can only be, or has been, assessed for its value by human estimation largely without the aid of measuring instrumentation. *Note:* Some subjective assessments of certain types of characteristics can be more accurate than objective measurements with instruments of poor accuracy.

successful bidder on tenderer   The person who or company that is successful in forming a contract with the customer.

sudden failure   A failure that could not be anticipated by prior examination.

superseded document   A document in respect to which there has been a change that has made the issue concerned obsolete for some further work.

supplementary document   A document which serves to support some more fundamental or comprehensive document in a system.

supplier   A person or company who supplies or provides some commodity to a customer, usually under a contract.

surveillance   Monitoring or observation to verify whether an item or activity conforms to specified requirements. *Note:* Surveillance may involve time considerations such as deterioration or degradation associated with shelf life.

survival function   A connection between relative survivals and time.

survival probability distribution   The connection between probability of survival and time. *Note:* For the basic population the survival probability distribution represents the lives of the entities making up the population.

survivals   The number of items from the initials that have not failed at an instant of time.

switch   In sampling terminology, a change from one inspection level or severity to another.

switching rules [ASQC]   Guidelines within a sampling scheme for shifting from one sampling plan to another based on demonstrated quality history.

system   A group of items or quantity of material having dependent and independent elements which act in concert to achieve a group function or group functions.

system of quantities   A group that comprises a particular set of base quantities and correspondingly derived quantities and covers one or more fields of science.

system of units of measurement   A set of base and derived units corresponding to a particular group of quantities.

systematic sample   The sample of n items drawn from a population, arranged in order (e.g., the order of production), and numbered 1 to N by taking items numbered $h, h + k, h + 2k,\ldots,h + (n - 1)k$, where h and k are whole numbers satisfying the relation $h < k, nk < N < (n + 1)k$, and h is generally taken at random from the first k whole numbers.

systematic sampling   Sampling by using systematic samples.

systematic variation   The appearance in an otherwise stable process of a cause of nonuniformity in a systematic way, e.g., at regular intervals.

tally   A mark or score as in recording results by the conventional five-barred gate method, i.e., by marking every fifth score across the preceding four scores.

target (sampling sense)   A score set in sequential and multiple sampling which qualifies a batch or a lot for acceptance.

target (in cusum charts)   The value which is subtracted from each observed value before the score is accumulated.

technical determination   A documented interpretation of a technical matter, usually by the design authority, which may alter the requirements of a specification.

technical variation (concession sense)   A documented variation to a specification applying to one contractor, and usually on a temporary basis, that allows acceptance of one lot or a small quantity of material.

temperature cycling   The elevating and lowering of the test environment temperature of some item in a repetitive manner.

temperature-time profile   The graphical representation, usually taken from a recorder, of the time-related changes in temperature during a test.

temporary failure frequency   One minus the value obtained by dividing the survivals at the end by the survivals at the beginning of the specified period of time, divided by the time interval.

tensile test   A test in which the material is subjected to a pull- or extension-type force, usually along some specified axis, to determine the load required for failure.

termination of test   The cessation of inspection, usually because of the degradation of quality in material submitted for acceptance.

test   A critical trial or examination of one or more properties or characteristics of a material, product, service, process, set of observations, etc.

test chamber   A closed chamber in which some atmospheric or other variable is controlled.

test data   Data obtained from observations made during tests and recorded.

test equipment calibration *See* **measuring equipment calibration.**

test level *See* **inspection level.**

test piece A part taken or fabricated from a sample or manufactured from other material for test purposes, usually in a laboratory.

test procedure A measurement instruction describing the method by which one or more quality characteristics is to be assessed and/or determined. Usually it involves one class of characteristics.

test sample Not a preferred term; see **sample** or **unit.**

test specification A specification defining the methods, conditions, and sequence of tests to be carried out on some item or quantity of material and sometimes including the instrumentation and environmental equipment to be used as well as the test limits.

test time The estimted time required to complete a test from start to finish.

test unit *See* **test piece.**

testability The designed aspects which provide an item with the capability to be easily and economically tested.

testing A means of determining the capability of an item to meet specified requirements by subjecting the item to a set of physical, chemical, environmental, or operating actions and conditions.

testing without replacement *See* **sampling without replacement.**

tightened inspection Inspection severity at a level higher than that of normal inspection severity and to which the supplier is required to switch when quality degradation dictates.

time to failure The elapsed time from the beginning of functional stress, or overload stress, to the instant of failure.

tolerance (specification sense) [ASQC] The total allowable variation around a level or state (upper limit minus lower limit), or the maximum acceptable excursion of a characteristic.

tolerance limits [ASQC] Limits that define the conformance boundaries for an individual unit of a manufacturing or service operation.

tolerance zone The zone of values for which a measurable characteristic is in conformance with the specification.

tolerated stress The stress under which the reliability characteristics of an item reaches the set limit.

tool-made sample An item of product or a quantity of material made with all the tools and procedures and by the operators who will be used to produce the manufactured product. *See* **first-piece production sample.**

total quality control A concept wherein *all* organizations, managers, and employees throughout a company, including those who make no direct contribution to the products or services sold, practice planned quality control in all that they do.

traceability (calibration sense) The concept of establishing a valid calibration of a measuring instrument, material measure, or measurement standard by step-by-step comparison with better standards to the level of a national standard.

traceability (data sense) The ability to trace the operational, computational, and recording steps of measurement or evaluation of an item, process, or service.

traceability (distribution sense) The ability to trace the history, application, or location of an item and like items or activities by means of recorded identification.

traceability [ISO] The ability to trace the history, application or location of an item or activity, or similar items or activities, by means of recorded identification. *Note:* Traceability requirements should be specified for some stated period of history or to some point of origin.

transfer standard A physical standard used to transfer accuracy from a secondary reference standard to a working instrument or gauge.

true failure rate The conditional probability at the instant of time t_1 that an item will fail within a given period of time t_1 to t_2.

true mean life The true mean life $m_L(0,\infty)$ is the expected value $f(x)$ of the life of an item:

$$m_L(0,\infty) = f(x) \tag{1.8}$$

true process average The actual mean percent defective or defects per 100 units of the population of original production material from a process for the given characteristic.

true reliability $R(t)$ The probability P that an item will survive for time t, i.e., that the item life x will exceed the time t.

truncated sampling Sampling by which the drawing of samples is restricted to the first or last part of a batch.

type approval Approval given to a design that has been shown by testing to meet all the requirements of the product specification and to be suitable for a specific application.

type tests Tests carried out against a specification for the purpose of collecting data to assist in giving or receiving type approval.

ultrasonic inspection A form of nondestructive testing by which ultrasonic waves at prescribed frequencies are caused to penetrate the test piece and the reflected or transmitted waves are then analyzed for the information they contain.

unacceptable quality level (UQL) [ASQC] *See* **limiting quality level (LQL).**

unbiased estimate An estimate of a parameter such that the expectation equals the true value of the parameter.

uncertainty The degree of error contained in measurement results.

uncertainty of measurement   The part of the expression of the corrected result of a measurement which defines the range of values within which the true value or, if appropriate, the accepted true value is estimated to be. *Note:* The uncertainty is a statement of the extreme error value from all sources summed to give a single error statement.

uncorrectable cause   A cause of nonconforming material which cannot be totally eliminated. Examples are chance variations, energy surges, random tool malfunctions, and peripheral influences.

undetected failure time   The period of time between the instant of failure and the recognition of the failure mode.

unique lot [ASQC]   A lot produced under conditions unique to that lot and not part of a routine production sequence.

unit [ASQC]   An object on which a measurement or observation may be made.

unit of product   An object or a defined quantity of product or service on which an observation is made. *Note:* An item or unit may contain more than one unit of product. There is considerable use of the term "item" to mean unit of product, but it should be realized that there can be a difference.

up time   The period of time during which an item is in condition to perform its required function(s).

upper control limit   An upper limit to a range of values, usually on a control chart, such that values above the limit indicate a likely need for corrective action.

upper tolerance limit (UTL) [ASQC]   A tolerance limit that defines the upper conformance boundary for an individual unit of a manufacturing or service operation.

usage factor   The percent of the total time, or some defined time period, during which a measuring device or physical standard is in actual use.

useful life   The period from a stated time during which, under stated conditions, an item has an acceptable failure rate or until an unrepairable failure occurs.

value of quality   The level of quality in a product or service characteristic required by the customer as compared with the level of quality in the design.

variable   A quantity that may take any one of a specified set or range of values.

variables, method of [ASQC]   Measurement of quality by the method of variables consists of measuring and recording the numerical magnitude of a quality characteristic for each of the units in the group under consideration.

variability (statistics)   The variation in the numerical magnitude of quantities.

variance (population)   A measure of dispersion of a finite population: the arithmetic mean of the squares of the deviations from the arithmetic mean of the population.

variance (sample) The sum of the squares of the deviations from the sample mean divided by the degrees of freedom. The number of degrees of freedom of a random sample of the size n is $n - 1$.

variant [ASQC] An item or event that is classified differently from others of its kind or type.

variant unit [ASQC] A unit of product or service containing at least one variant characteristic or attribute.

variate A quantity that may take any of the values of a specified set with a specified relative frequency or probability. It is defined, not merely by a set of permissible values as a variable is, but also by an associated frequency (probability) function expressing how often the values appear. The variate is also known as a **random variable**.

vendor *See* **supplier**.

vendor appraisal The assessment of a supplier, usually for the purpose of determining that person's or company's ability to satisfy some standard or set of requirements.

vendor control The activities undertaken and carried out for the purpose of ensuring that supplies from the vendor will meet specified requirements.

vendor inspection Inspection of supplies by the supplier, as opposed to supplies inspection by the customer. *Note:* Vendor inspection is normally carried out at the vendor's premises.

vendor rating The measure of an overall assessment of a vendor.

verification [ASQC] The act of reviewing, inspecting, testing, checking, auditing, or otherwise establishing and documenting whether items, processes, services, or documents conform to specified requirements.

verification sampling Sampling of a product or service for the purpose of verifying the validity of the contractor's inspection system.

vibration cycling The cyclical variation of vibration frequency and/or acceleration magnitude through one or more cycles over specified ranges of frequency and G (acceleration).

vibration test A test by which the material is subjected to a range of vibrations at specified frequencies and accelerations, i.e., excursions and then assessed for damage.

view room inspection Inspection by means of suitable qualified inspectors, located in a view room, to which items for inspection are sent. Compare with **patrol inspection**.

voltage cycling The stressing of some item by the application of voltage at one or more magnitudes for stated periods of time in a cyclical manner.

waiver [ASQC] Written authorization to use or release a quantity of material, components, or stores already manufactured but not conforming to the specified requirements.

warning limit A limit that is set "inside" a control limit and is used in process control to indicate the variance of the characteristic value concerned and also when it is desirable to apply corrective action to maintain the process in control.

warranty Assurance given by a supplier of some product or service that the item will satisfy some need or stated requirement.

wear-out The process of attrition which results in increase of the failure rate with increasing age. It is expressed in units of time or distance or in cycles, events, etc., as applicable to the item.

wear-out failure A failure that has a probability of occurrence which increases with time and is a result of processes that are characteristic of the population.

wear-out failure period The possible period during which the failure rate is increasing rapidly in comparison with the preceding period.

weighted average The sum of a set of quantities each of which is multiplied by a numerical coefficient called the weight before summing. The sum is then divided by the sum of the weights.

white noise testing A form of vibration test in which the test piece is subjected to all vibration frequencies, called white noise, during the same time period.

working standard *See* **transfer standard**.

workmanship The degree to which some item of product, or one or more characteristics thereof, conforms to a defined standard of good production or supply.

workmanship assessment The comparison of workmanship characteristics of a product or service against a corresponding workmanship standard, usually for the purpose of acceptance inspection.

workmanship standard A document containing graphic, pictorial, or written expressions of the desired quality of work, or a physical item containing an example of the desired quality of work, against which workpieces are compared for workmanship assessment.

$\bar{x}$ (X-bar) chart A control chart for evaluating the process or subgroup differences in terms of the subgroup average $\bar{x}$.

x-ray inspection The use of x-rays of an appropriate wavelength, in either the reflected or transmitted mode, to interact with material and provide information about the composition and or structure of the material.

Index

About the Author

James R. Taylor, PE, CQE, is currently a consultant in quality systems development and management. Born in the United States, he graduated in engineering in Australia, where he attended the Royal Melbourne Institute of Technology and the Melbourne University. He worked in test instrument design, staff quality engineering, and quality and engineering management for Western Electric, General Electric, and TRW in the United States and in quality systems development and management for the Australian Telecommunications Commission. In addition, he served for twelve years as an active member of the Quality and Reliability Committee of the Standards Association of Australia, where he was instrumental in preparing the national standards for quality and reliability. He is the author of two books, in addition to *Quality Control Systems*, and a number of technical articles.